THE LOEB CLASSICAL LIBRARY

FOUNDED BY JAMES LOEB 1911

EDITED BY

JEFFREY HENDERSON

EDITOR EMERITUS

G. P. GOOLD

CICERO

XXVIII

LCL 462

CICERO

LETTERS TO QUINTUS AND BRUTUS
LETTER FRAGMENTS
LETTER TO OCTAVIAN · INVECTIVES
HANDBOOK OF ELECTIONEERING

EDITED AND TRANSLATED BY

D. R. SHACKLETON BAILEY

HARVARD UNIVERSITY PRESS
CAMBRIDGE, MASSACHUSETTS
LONDON, ENGLAND
2002

Library of Congress catalog card number 2001039432
CIP data available from the Library of Congress

ISBN 0-674-99599-6

CONTENTS

BIBLIOGRAPHICAL NOTE

Editions

Jean Beaujeu, *Cicéron: Correspondance* (Paris: Collection Budé), vol. XI, 1996.

D. R. Shackleton Bailey, *M. Tullius Cicero: Epistulae ad Quintum Fratrem et M. Brutum*, et al. (Stuttgart: Bibliotheca Teubneriana), 1988.

D. R. Shackleton Bailey, *Cicero: Epistulae ad Quintum Fratrem et M. Brutum* (Cambridge Texts and Commentaries), 1980.

W. S. Watt, *M. Tulli Ciceronis epistulae*, vol. III (Oxford Classical Texts), 1958.

Biographies

M. Gelzer, *Cicero: ein biographischer Versuch*, Wiesbaden, 1969.

Elizabeth Rawson, *Cicero*, London, 1975.

D. R. Shackleton Bailey, *Cicero*, London, 1975.

D. Stockton, *Cicero: A Political Biography*, Oxford, 1971.

Study

G. O. Hutchinson, *Cicero's Correspondence: A Literary*

Study, Oxford University Press, 1998. Contains an extensive bibliography.

See also Introductions to individual sections.

Abbreviations in Critical Notes

Corr. = *Corradus*
Crat. = *Cratander*
Ern. = *Ernesti*
Gron. = *Gronovius*
Gul. = *Gulielmius*
Lamb. = *Lambinus*
Man. = *Manutius*
Or. = *Orelli*
SB = *Shackleton Bailey*
T.-P. = *Tyrrell-Purser*
Turn. = *Turnebus*
Vict. = *Victorius*
Wes. = *Wesenberg*

Throughout, all dates are B.C. unless otherwise specified.

CICERO'S LETTERS TO HIS BROTHER QUINTUS

INTRODUCTION

Marcus Cicero's only brother, Quintus, was about two years his junior. They grew up together, and when Marcus went on his eastern travels in 79 Quintus accompanied him. Some ten years later he married the sister of Marcus' closest friend, T. Pomponius Atticus. The marriage, which M. Cicero is said on good authority to have engineered, was a failure, although it lasted nearly a quarter of a century and produced a son. Pomponia was somewhat older than her husband and they made a cantankerous pair from the first.

Following in his elder brother's wake, Quintus embarked on a political career, although he had no taste for public speaking, and stood successfully for Quaestor, Aedile, and Praetor (the last during Marcus' Consulship in 63). In 61 he went out to the province of Asia as Proconsul, a post which he held for the exceptional period of three years. It says much for his integrity as a governor that he was genuinely annoyed when the Senate extended his term a second time. His return from Asia in 58 coincided with his brother's journey into exile. Back in Rome, Quintus was for some time anxious about a threatened prosecution for maladministration in his province, perhaps to be conducted by a nephew of P. Clodius. When nothing came of it, he was able to devote himself wholeheartedly to the

campaign for Marcus' restoration. On one occasion his efforts nearly cost him his life, when he was left for dead on the scene of a riot.

After Marcus' return in 57, Quintus remained for nearly two more years in Italy, with a brief interval of overseas employment in 56, when Pompey stationed him in Sardinia to supervise grain supplies. In the spring of 54 he joined Caesar's staff in Gaul as Legate, where he distinguished himself by a heroic defence of his camp against a rebel tribe. Caesar congratulated him publicly and gives the episode handsome recognition in his *Commentaries*, qualified however by criticism of a subsequent piece of negligence on Quintus' part, which nearly led to a disaster. With his later career down to his death in the Proscriptions of 43 we are not here concerned.

Quintus shared his brother's and brother-in-law's interest in Hellenic culture and was himself a prolific versifier, whiling away inactive spells in Gaul by translating Sophocles' plays into Latin. Twenty uninspired hexameters about the signs of the zodiac, taken from an unknown poem, are attributed to him. We also have four short letters from him in the collection *Letters to Friends* (44, 147, 351, 352) and the tract on electioneering, couched in the form of a letter of advice to his brother on his consular candidature in 64, generally known as *Commentariolum Petitionis (A Short Memorandum on Standing for Office)*. But the authenticity of this last is in serious doubt.

Down to the closing years of their lives the relationship between the brothers remained on the whole close and affectionate, though indications of friction and latent resentments on Quintus' part are not lacking. For details I must refer to my biography, from which I quote the following

summary: 'The deplorable marriage, which Marcus Cicero had made and striven to keep in being for his own reasons, friction over Statius, disappointments in Gaul, untoward incidents in Cilicia, Quintus' strange passivity in the early months of the Civil War—all this and much more of which we are not informed may have gone to nourish an ulcer in Quintus' mind: the mind of a small man, irritable, querulous, and weak; a severe magistrate, who spoiled his son and let himself be run by a slave; a good man in a battle or a riot, but a rabbit in front of his wife; ambitious, but inhibited by a distrust of his talents, which were not of the first order, and handicapped by the unlucky accident of birth, which had made him a bigger man's younger brother.' The outcome was a prolonged and bitter quarrel during the Civil War, which was never more than superficially patched up.[1]

The three Books of Cicero's letters to Quintus may well have been published by his secretary Tiro, like the *Letters to Friends*. The first in the series is no ordinary letter but a tract, presumably meant for at least private circulation, which might have been entitled *Advice to a Governor* and could be regarded as a *quid pro quo* for the *Commentariolum*, if the latter were certainly authentic. A second, genuinely private letter belongs to this period. Then come two letters from exile, followed by the remaining nineteen, which date from the end of 57 to the end of 54.

[1] The conventional view, at least until 1971, that the reconciliation following the return of both brothers to Rome late in 47 was genuine and complete cannot be entertained by anyone who has read the contemporary letters to Atticus with attention and without sentimental prejudice.

The manuscript tradition for the *Letters to Quintus* is the same as for those to Atticus, omitting the (lost) Tornesianus. As in previous volumes in this series (*Letters to Atticus* and *Letters to Friends*) and throughout this volume, my critical notes do not particularize the manuscript sources, but rather aim to give warning where the reading in the text has little or no manuscript support (excluding some as too obvious and generally accepted to need mention). The notes in such cases give the manuscript reading generally followed by the name of the corrector in parenthesis; where no name follows, the siglum ς is to be understood, indicating inferior manuscripts or early editions.

The fullest apparatus criticus is in H. Sjögren's edition (Uppsala 1911), but for most purposes W. S. Watt's Oxford Text of 1958 (the beginning of a new era in the textual criticism and interpretation of Cicero's correspondence) or my Teubner (Stuttgart) edition of 1988 will suffice. Occasional departures from the latter text are again indicated in the critical notes by an asterisk.

My Commentary on the letters to Quintus and to M. Brutus is in the last volume (1980) of my Cambridge edition of the correspondence.

1 (I.1)

Scr. Romae (?) ex. an. 60 aut in. an. 59

MARCUS QUINTO FRATRI SALUTEM

1 Etsi non dubitabam quin hanc epistulam multi nuntii, Fama denique esset ipsa sua celeritate superatura tuque ante ab aliis auditurus esses annum tertium accessisse desiderio nostro et labori tuo, tamen existimavi a me quoque tibi huius molestiae nuntium perferri oportere. nam superioribus litteris non unis sed pluribus, cum iam ab aliis desperata res esset, tamen tibi ego spem maturae decessionis adferebam, non solum ut quam diutissime te iucunda opinione oblectarem sed etiam quia tanta adhibebatur et a nobis et a praetoribus contentio ut rem posse confici non diffiderem.

2 Nunc, quoniam ita accidit ut neque praetores suis opibus neque nos nostro studio quicquam proficere possemus, est omnino difficile non graviter id ferre, sed tamen nostros animos maximis in rebus et gerendis et sustinendis exercitatos frangi et debilitari molestia non oportet. ‹et›[1] quoniam ea molestissime ferre homines debent quae ipsorum culpa contracta sunt, est quiddam in hac re mihi molestius ferendum quam tibi. factum est enim mea culpa, contra quam tu mecum et proficiscens et per litteras egeras, ut priore anno non succederetur. quod ego, dum socio-

1 (*Man.*)

1 (I.1)

Rome, end of 60 or beginning of 59

From Marcus to his brother Quintus greetings.

I don't doubt that this letter will be outpaced by many messengers, indeed by Rumour herself with her well-known speed, and that you will hear from others beforehand that our loss and your labour[1] have been extended for a third year. Still, I thought it proper that this tiresome news should reach you from me as well as others. For in writing to you previously, not once but a number of times, I used to hold out to you the hope of an early homecoming even after others had already despaired of it. That was not just to amuse you as long as possible with a pleasant notion but because the Praetors and I were both working so hard for it that I felt sure the thing could be done.

Well, unfortunately, neither the Praetors' influence nor my own zeal has had any success. It is hard not to feel irked. However, we have had too long a training in the conduct of great affairs and the bearing of great responsibilities to lose heart and strength in our vexation. And in one respect I should be taking it harder than you, since it is the misfortunes for which they are ourselves to blame that ought to distress people the most. It *was* my fault that, against your urgings before you set out and later by letter, you were not relieved the previous year. Thinking of the

[1] As Proconsul in Asia.

rum saluti consulo, dum impudentiae non nullorum negotiatorum resisto, dum nostram gloriam tua virtute augeri expeto, feci non sapienter, praesertim cum id commiserim ut ille alter annus etiam tertium posset adducere.

3 Quod quoniam peccatum meum esse confiteor, est sapientiae atque humanitatis tuae curare et perficere ut hoc minus sapienter a me provisum diligentia tua corrigatur. ac si te ipse vehementius ad omnis partis bene audiendi excitaris, non ut cum aliis sed ut tecum iam ipse certes, si omnem tuam mentem, curam, cogitationem ad excellendi[2] in omnibus <gene>ribus[3] laudis cupiditatem incitaris, mihi crede, unus annus additus labori tuo multorum annorum laetitiam nobis, gloriam vero etiam posteris nostris adferet.

4 Quapropter hoc te primum rogo, ne contrahas ac demittas animum neve te obrui tamquam fluctu sic magnitudine negoti sinas contraque erigas ac resistas sive etiam ultro occurras negotiis; neque enim eius modi partem rei publicae geris in qua Fortuna dominetur, sed in qua plurimum ratio possit et diligentia. quod si tibi bellum aliquod magnum et periculosum administranti prorogatum imperium viderem, tremerem animo quod eodem tempore esse intellegerem etiam Fortunae potestatem in nos prorogatam.
5 nunc vero ea pars tibi rei publicae commissa est in qua aut nullam aut perexiguam partem Fortuna tenet et quae mihi tota in tua virtute ac moderatione animi posita esse videatur. nullas, ut opinor, insidias hostium, nullam proeli dimicationem, nullam defectionem sociorum, nullam inopiam stipendi aut rei frumentariae, nullam seditionem exercitus pertimescimus; quae persaepe sapientissi-

[2] excellentem (*coni. Watt**: -ntis *Ern.*) [3] (*coni. Watt*)*

welfare of the provincials, opposing the effrontery of certain businessmen, and seeking to add to our prestige by your abilities, I acted unwisely, all the more so as I ran the risk of that second year entailing a third.

I acknowledge that the error was mine. Now it is for you, with your great good sense and your kind heart, to take good care to correct my lack of foresight by your pains. If you gird up your loins to the business of gaining approval all round and try to excel, not others, but yourself; if you urge your whole mind and concern and thought into one ambition—to do yourself the utmost credit in all respects: then take my word for it, a single added year of work will bring us happiness for many years ahead and glory to those who come after us as well.

Well then, this is the first thing I ask of you: let there be no inner withdrawal or discouragement. Don't allow yourself to be submerged beneath the flood of a great responsibility. Stand up and face it, contend with business as it comes or even go out to meet it. Success in your sphere of public service is not in the hands of chance, it mainly depends on thought and application. If you were conducting some big, dangerous war and I saw your command extended, I should be alarmed, because I should realize that it also meant an extension of Fortune's power over ourselves. But as matters stand, Fortune has no part, or only a very small part, in the public responsibility which has been entrusted to you. It seems to me to lie wholly in your own ability and discretion. We do not, I think, have to fear a hostile ambuscade or a pitched battle or the desertion of allies or want of means to pay and feed our troops or a mutiny. Such things have happened time and time again to

mis viris acciderunt, ut, quem ad modum gubernatores optimi vim tempestatis, sic illi impetum Fortunae superare non possent. tibi data est summa pax, summa tranquillitas, ita tamen ut ea dormientem gubernatorem vel obruere, vigilantem etiam delectare possit.

6 Constat enim ea provincia primum ex eo genere sociorum quod est ex hominum omni genere humanissimum, deinde ex eo genere civium qui aut quod publicani sunt nos summa necessitudine attingunt aut quod ita negotiantur ut locupletes sint nostri consulatus beneficio se inco-
7 lumis fortunas habere arbitrantur. at enim inter hos ipsos exsistunt graves controversiae, multae nascuntur iniuriae, magnae contentiones consequuntur. quasi vero ego id putem, non te aliquantum negoti sustinere! intellego permagnum esse negotium et maximi consili, sed memento consili me hoc esse negotium magis aliquanto quam Fortunae putare. quid est enim negoti continere eos quibus praesis, si te ipse contineas? id autem sit magnum et difficile ceteris, sicut est difficillimum: tibi et fuit hoc semper facillimum et vero esse debuit, cuius natura talis est ut etiam sine doctrina videatur moderata esse potuisse, ea autem adhibita doctrina est quae vel vitiosissimam naturam excolere[4] possit. tu cum pecuniae, cum voluptati, cum omnium rerum cupiditati resistes, ut facis, erit, credo, periculum ne improbum negotiatorem, paulo cupidiorem publicanum comprimere non possis! nam Graeci quidem sic te ita viventem intuebuntur ut quendam ex annalium memoria aut etiam de caelo divinum hominem esse in provinciam delapsum putent.

[4] accol- *vel* attoll-

very wise men; they could not overcome Fortune's onset any more than the best of seamen can master a violent storm. *Your* portion is perfect peace and calm; and yet if the helmsman falls asleep he could go to the bottom in such weather, while if he keeps wide awake he may actually enjoy it.

Your province consists of a native population the most highly civilized in the world and of Romans who are either tax farmers, and thus very closely connected with us, or wealthy businessmen who think they owe the safety of their money to my Consulship. Ah, but they get into serious disputes among themselves, often do each other harm leading to mighty contentions. Well, I am not under the impression that you have no responsibilities at all! I do realize that you have a very great responsibility, calling for the highest qualities of judgement. But remember that in my opinion it is a good deal more a matter of judgement than of luck. After all, it is not too difficult to control the people under you if you control yourself. Self-control may be a great and difficult achievement for others, is so indeed, most difficult; but for you it has always been quite easy, and why not? You have a nature which would surely have tended to gentleness even without instruction; and instruction such as yours might lend some grace even to the most faulty of natures. In the future, as now, you will resist the temptations of money, pleasure, and every sort of appetite. Small fear then of your finding yourself unable to restrain a crooked businessman or an over-acquisitive tax farmer! As for the Greeks, when they look at you leading the life you do, they will think you are a character from history or a divine being come down from heaven into the province.

8 Atque haec nunc non ut facias sed ut te facere et fecisse gaudeas scribo. praeclarum est enim summo cum imperio fuisse in Asia biennium[5] sic ut nullum te signum, nulla pictura, nullum vas, nulla vestis, nullum mancipium, nulla forma cuiusquam, nulla condicio pecuniae, quibus rebus abundat ista provincia, ab summa integritate continen-
9 tiaque deduxerit. quid autem reperiri tam eximium aut tam expetendum potest quam istam virtutem, moderationem animi, temperantiam non latere in tenebris neque esse abditam, sed in luce Asiae, in oculis clarissimae provinciae atque in auribus omnium gentium ac nationum esse positam? non itineribus tuis perterreri homines, non sumptu exhauriri, non adventu commoveri? esse, quocumque veneris, et publice et privatim maximam laetitiam, cum urbs custodem, non tyrannum, domus hospitem, non expilatorem recepisse videatur?

10 His autem in rebus iam te usus ipse profecto erudivit nequaquam satis esse ipsum has te habere virtutes, sed esse circumspiciendum diligenter ut in hac custodia provinciae non te unum sed omnis ministros imperi tui sociis et civibus et rei publicae praestare videare. quamquam legatos habes eos qui ipsi per se habituri sint rationem dignitatis tuae.[6] de quibus honore et dignitate et aetate praestat Tubero, quem ego arbitror, praesertim cum scribat historiam, multos ex suis annalibus posse deligere quos velit et possit imitari. Al<l>ienus autem noster est cum animo et benevolentia tum vero etiam imitatione vivendi. nam quid ego de Gratidio dicam? quem certo scio ita laborare de

[5] triennium (*Ursinus*) [6] suae

---

[2] M. Gratidius, a relative of the Ciceros.

I do not write all this to tell you how to behave, but to make you glad of your behaviour, past and present. It is a fine thing to have spent two years in Asia in supreme authority without letting any of the commodities in which your province abounds draw you away from the strictest uprightness and integrity—neither statue nor painting nor cup nor fabric nor slave, neither beauty of person nor financial arrangement. And it is a rare and enviable piece of good fortune that your ability, discretion, and self-restraint are not hidden away in some dark corner but placed in the full light of Asia, for the most brilliant of provinces to see and for all peoples and nations to hear tell of: how no man is afraid of your progresses or put to crushing expense or disturbed by your arrival; how there is hearty rejoicing in public and private wherever you go, for you enter a city as a protector, not a tyrant, and a house as a guest, not a looter.

However, your own experience has doubtless taught you that in these matters it is not enough for you to have such virtues yourself; you must look carefully around you, so that as guardian of your province you are seen to take responsibility to the provincials, the Romans, and the commonwealth not only for your individual self but for all your subordinate officials. To be sure you have Legates who of their own volition will pay regard to your good name. Tubero is first among them in official rank, personal consequence, and age. I imagine that as a historian he can choose many a figure from his own chronicles whom he is wishful and able to imitate. Allienus is ours in spirit and good will, and in the way he takes our lives as models for his own. As for Gratidius,[2] what shall I say? I am sure that his

existimatione sua ut propter amorem in nos fraternum
11 etiam de nostra[7] laboret. quaestorem habes non tuo iudicio delectum sed eum quem sors dedit. hunc oportet et sua
sponte esse moderatum et tuis institutis ac praeceptis
obtemperare. quorum si quis forte esset sordidior, ferres
eatenus quoad per se neglegeret eas leges quibus esset
adstrictus, non ut ea potestate quam tu ad dignitatem
permisisses ad quaestum uteretur. neque enim mihi sane
placet, praesertim cum hi mores tantum iam ad nimiam
lenitatem et ad ambitionem incubuerint, scrutari te omnis
sordis, excutere unum quemque eorum, sed, quanta sit in
quoque fides, tantum cuique committere.

Atque [inter nos][8] eos quos tibi comites et adiutores negotiorum publicorum dedit ipsa res publica dumtaxat fini-
12 bus iis praestabis quos ante praescripsi. quos vero aut ex
domesticis convictionibus[9] aut ex[10] necessariis apparitioni-
bus tecum esse voluisti, qui quasi ex cohorte praetoris
appellari solent, horum non modo facta sed etiam dicta
omnia praestanda nobis sunt. sed habes eos tecum quos
possis recte facientis facile diligere, minus consulentis
existimationi tuae facillime coercere. a quibus, rudis cum
esses, videtur potuisse tua liberalitas decipi (nam ut quisque est vir optimus, ita difficillime esse alios improbos sus-
picatur); nunc vero tertius hic annus habeat integritatem
13 eandem quam superiores, cautiorem autem[11] ac diligen-

[7] demonstrare (*Crat. marg.*)
[8] (*SB*)
[9] convinc- *vel* coniunc- (*Vict.*)
[10] in *coni. SB*
[11] etiam (*Lamb.*)

---

[3] Identity unknown.

brotherly affection for us will prompt concern for our reputation along with the concern he feels for his own. You have a Quaestor[3] whom you did not choose of your own judgement but acquired by the luck of the draw. It behoves him to exercise discretion of his own accord and to defer to your rules and advice. If it were by any chance the case that the moral standards of one or other of these gentlemen left something to be desired, you would put up with his disregard of regulations which apply to him as an individual, but not allow him to use for profit the authority which you confer upon him as conducive to his standing. Now that our modern ways have leaned so far in the direction of excessive lenity and popularity-mongering, I would not really have you examine every dark patch and search their pockets man by man; better to assign to each one an amount of responsibility commensurate with the trust he inspires.

Very well, you will answer for the officers whom the commonwealth itself gives you as your companions and assistants in public business within the limits I have just laid down, and no further. What of those whom you have chosen to be with you from your household entourage or necessary staff—members of the Governor's Cohort, as they are usually called? In their case we have to answer not only for everything they do but for everything they say. However, the people with you are people of whom you can easily be fond if they behave well and whom you can even more easily check if they don't pay enough regard to your reputation. When you were new to the job, they could perhaps have taken advantage of your generous instincts—the better a man is, the harder he finds it to suspect rascality in others. Now a third year is opening; let it show the same integrity as the two that preceded it with a greater measure

tiorem. sint aures tuae quae id quod audiunt existimentur
audire, non in quas ficte et simulate quaestus causa insu-
surretur. sit anulus tuus non ut vas aliquod sed tamquam
ipse tu, non minister alienae voluntatis sed testis tuae. accensus sit eo numero quo eum maiores nostri esse voluerunt, qui hoc non in benefici loco sed in laboris ac muneris
non temere nisi libertis suis deferebant, quibus illi quidem
non multo secus ac servis imperabant. sit lictor non suae
sed tuae lenitatis apparitor, maioraque praeferant fasces
illi ac secures dignitatis insignia quam potestatis. toti denique sit provinciae cognitum tibi omnium quibus praesis
salutem, liberos, famam, fortunas esse carissimas. denique
haec opinio sit, non modo iis qui aliquid acceperint sed iis
etiam qui dederint te inimicum, si id cognoveris, futurum;
neque vero quisquam dabit cum erit hoc perspectum, nihil
per eos qui simulant se apud te multum posse abs te solere
14 impetrari. nec tamen haec oratio mea est eius modi ut te in
tuos aut durum esse nimium aut suspiciosum velim. nam si
quis est eorum qui tibi bienni spatio numquam in suspicionem avaritiae venerit, ut ego Caesium et Chaerippum et
Labeonem et audio et quia cognovi existimo, nihil est quod
non et iis et si quis est alius eiusdem modi et committi et
credi rectissime putem. sed si quis est in quo iam offende-
ris, de quo aliquid senseris, huic nihil credideris, nullam
partem existimationis tuae commiseris.

15 In provincia vero ipsa si quem es nactus qui in tuam familiaritatem penitus intrarit, qui nobis ante fuerit ignotus,

of watchfulness and care. Let men think of your ears as hearing what they hear, not as receptacles for false, deceitful, profit-seeking whispers. Let your seal ring be no mere instrument but like your own person, not the tool of other men's wills but the witness of your own. Let your orderly be what our forbears meant him to be. Except for some good reason they gave this function to none but their own freedmen, and that not as a favour but as a task and duty; and their authority over their freedmen differed little from their authority over their slaves. Let your lictor be the servant of *your* clemency, not of his own; let the rods and axes bear before you insignia of rank rather than power. In a word let the whole province know that the lives, children, reputations, and property of all over whom you rule are most precious to you. Finally let it be believed that, if you get to know of a bribe, you will be the enemy of the giver as well as of the taker. Nor will anybody give a bribe once it becomes clear that as a rule nothing is obtained from you through the agency of people who pretend to have much influence with you. Not that what I have been saying means that I want you to be over-austere or suspicious towards your entourage. If any of them in the course of two years has never given you cause to suspect him of money-grubbing, as I hear to be true of Caesius and Chaerippus and Labeo and so judge from my own knowledge of them, I should think it entirely proper to place unlimited trust and confidence in them and in anyone else of the same stamp. But if you have found something wrong with a man or smelt a rat, don't trust him an inch or put any part of your good name in his keeping.

If, however, you have met someone in the province itself, not previously acquainted with us, who has found his

huic quantum credendum sit vide: non quin possint multi esse provinciales viri boni, sed hoc sperare licet, iudicare periculosum est. multis enim simulationum involucris tegitur et quasi velis quibusdam obtenditur unius cuiusque natura; frons, oculi, vultus persaepe mentiuntur, oratio vero saepissime. quam ob rem qui potes reperire ex eo genere hominum qui pecuniae cupiditate adducti careant iis rebus omnibus a quibus nos divulsi esse non possumus, te autem, alienum hominem, ament ex animo ac non sui commodi causa simulent? mihi quidem permagnum videtur, praesertim si idem homines privatum non fere quemquam, praetores semper omnis amant. quo ex genere si quem forte tui cognosti amantiorem (fieri enim potuit) quam temporis, hunc vero ad tuum numerum libenter adscribito; sin autem id non perspicies, nullum genus erit in familiaritate cavendum magis, propterea quod et omnis vias pecuniae norunt et omnia pecuniae causa faciunt et, quicum victuri non sunt, eius existimationi consulere non curant.

16 Atque etiam e Graecis ipsis diligenter cavendae sunt quaedam familiaritates praeter hominum perpaucorum si qui sunt vetere Graecia digni; nunc[12] vero fallaces sunt permulti et leves et diuturna servitute ad nimiam adsentationem eruditi. quos ego universos adhiberi liberaliter, optimum quemque hospitio amicitiaque coniungi dico oportere: nimiae familiaritates eorum neque ‹honestae neque›[13] iam[14] fideles sunt. non enim audent adversari

[12] sic (*Ern.*) [13] (*coni. Watt*) [14] tam (*Ern.*)

[4] The amenities of life in Italy.

way into your closer intimacy, take care how far you should trust him. I don't say that many residents in the provinces are not honest men; but this is something which it is allowable to hope but dangerous to decide. Each man's nature lies hidden under a mass of enveloping pretence, like veils stretched to cover it from sight. Countenance, eyes, expression very often lie, speech yet oftener. These people out of desire for money go without all those amenities from which we cannot bear to be parted.[4] Are you likely to find any man among them to love you, a stranger, sincerely, not just pretending it for his own advantage? That would be most extraordinary in my opinion, especially if these same persons love hardly anybody in a private station but are always fond of every governor. If you have come to know someone in this category as caring more for you than for your temporary position (it is not impossible), by all means write him down as your friend. But unless you see this clearly, there is no class of men with whom as intimates you should be more on your guard. They know all the paths that lead to lucre, everything they do is for lucre's sake, and they are not concerned to guard the reputation of someone who will not be with them indefinitely.

Furthermore, much caution is called for with respect to friendships which may arise with certain among the Greeks themselves, apart from the very few who may be worthy of the Greece of old. Nowadays a great many of these people are false, unreliable, and schooled in over-complaisance by long servitude. My advice is to admit them freely to your company in general and to form ties of hospitality and friendship with the most distinguished; but too close intimacies with them are neither respectable nor trustworthy. They do not dare to oppose our wishes and

nostris voluntatibus et [non] invident non nostris solum verum etiam suis.

17 Iam qui in eius modi rebus in quibus vereor etiam ne durior sim cautus esse velim ac diligens, quo me animo in servis esse censes? quos quidem cum omnibus in locis tum praecipue in provinciis regere debemus. quo de genere multa praecipi possunt, sed hoc et brevissimum est et facillime teneri potest, ut ita se gerant in istis Asiaticis itineribus ut si iter Appia via faceres, neve interesse quicquam putent utrum Trallis an Formias venerint. ac si quis est ex servis egregie fidelis, sit in domesticis rebus et privatis: quae res ad officium imperi tui atque ad aliquam partem rei publicae pertinebunt, de iis rebus ne quid attingat. multa enim quae recte committi servis fidelibus possunt tamen sermonis et vituperationis vitandae causa committenda non sunt.

18 Sed nescio quo pacto ad praecipiendi rationem delapsa est oratio mea, cum id mihi propositum initio non fuisset; quid enim ei praecipiam quem ego in hoc praesertim genere intellegam prudentia non esse inferiorem quam me, usu vero etiam superiorem? sed tamen si ad ea quae faceres auctoritas accederet mea, tibi ipsi illa putavi fore iucundiora. qua re sint haec fundamenta dignitatis tuae: tua primum integritas et continentia, deinde omnium qui tecum sunt pudor, delectus in familiaritatibus et provincialium hominum et Graecorum percautus et diligens, fa-
19 miliae gravis et constans disciplina. quae cum honesta sint in his privatis nostris cottidianisque rationibus, in tanto im-

they are jealous not only of Romans but of their fellow countrymen.

If I am for watchfulness and care in relationships as to which I fear I may actually be taking too austere a view, how do you think I feel about slaves? We ought to keep them firmly in hand wherever we are, but most especially in the provinces. A great deal can be said by way of advice upon this subject, but the shortest rule and the easiest to follow is this: let them conduct themselves on your journeyings in Asia as though you were travelling down the Appian Way, let them not suppose it makes any difference whether they have arrived in Tralles or in Formiae. If you have an outstandingly faithful slave, employ him in household and private concerns, but don't let him touch any that have to do with the duties of your office or with state business in any shape or form. For much that can safely be entrusted to faithful slaves ought not to be entrusted to them even so, in order to avoid talk and criticism.

Somehow or other as I write I have slipped into the role of mentor, which was not my original intention. Why should I give advice to one whom I recognize as not inferior to myself in worldly wisdom, especially in this area, and my superior in experience? And yet I had the feeling that you yourself would find more pleasure in doing what you did if it were done on my authority. Well then, here are the foundations of your prestige: first, your own integrity and self-restraint, next a sense of propriety in all your companions, a very cautious and careful selectivity as regards close friendships with Roman residents and with Greeks, and the maintenance of strict household discipline. Such conduct would be creditable enough in our private, everyday lives, but with so wide an authority, amid such a

perio, tam depravatis moribus, tam corruptrice provincia divina videantur necesse est.

Haec institutio atque haec disciplina potest sustinere in rebus statuendis et decernendis eam severitatem qua tu in iis rebus usus es ex quibus non nullas simultates cum magna mea laetitia susceptas habemus; nisi forte me Paconi nescio cuius, hominis ne Graeci quidem ac Mysi aut Phrygis potius, querelis moveri putas aut Tusceni, hominis furiosi ac sordidi, vocibus, cuius tu ex impurissimis faucibus inhonestissimam cupiditatem eripuisti summa cum
20 aequitate. haec[15] et cetera plena severitatis quae statuisti in ista provincia non facile sine summa integritate sustineremus. qua re sit summa in iure dicendo severitas, dum modo ea ne varietur gratia sed conservetur aequabilis. sed tamen parvi refert abs te ipso ius dici aequaliter et diligenter nisi idem ab iis fiet quibus tu eius muneris aliquam partem concesseris. ac mihi quidem videtur non sane magna varietas esse negotiorum in administranda Asia, sed ea tota iuris dictione maxime sustineri. in qua scientiae, praesertim provincialis, ratio ipsa expedita est: constantia est adhibenda et gravitas, quae resistat non solum gratiae verum etiam suspicioni.

21 Adiungenda etiam est facilitas in audiendo, lenitas in decernendo, in satis faciendo ac disputando diligentia. his rebus nuper C. Octavius iucundissimus fuit, apud quem pr<ox>imus[16] lictor quievit,[17] tacuit accensus, quotiens

15 <sed> h- *coni. SB*
16 (*Or.*)
17 qui fuit (*Pantagathus*)

---

5 As Praetor in 61.

falling-off in moral standards and in a province so rich in temptations, it must surely appear superhuman.

With these principles and this discipline you can safely practise in your decisions and judgements the severity which you have shown in certain matters, by which we have made ourselves some enemies—and very glad I am of it. For you are not to suppose that I pay attention to the grumblings of a fellow called Paconius (not a Greek even, but a Mysian, or rather Phrygian) or the talk of a crazy money-grubber like Tuscenius, whose unsavoury plums you most justly plucked from his disgusting jaws. These and other markedly strict decisions in your province could not easily be sustained against criticism without the highest integrity. So let your judicial rulings be of the strictest, provided that strictness be consistently maintained and never modified by partiality. And yet it is of no great importance that you yourself dispense justice consistently and conscientiously if those to whom you grant some share in this function do not do the like. As it seems to me, the administration of Asia presents no great variety of business; it all rests in the main on the dispensation of justice. The actual knowledge involved in that, especially in a province, is no problem, but there is need of consistency and firmness to resist even the suspicion of partiality.

Other requisites are readiness to listen, mildness of manner in delivering judgement, conscientiousness in arguing with suitors and answering their complaints. C. Octavius recently gained much public regard by these means.[5] The First[6] Lictor in his court had nothing to do,

[6] Lit. 'closest.' He walked immediately in front of the magistrate, hence the title; see my Commentary.

quisque voluit dixit et quam voluit diu; quibus ille rebus fortasse nimis lenis videretur, nisi haec lenitas illam severitatem tueretur. cogebantur Sullani homines quae per vim et metum abstulerant reddere; qui in magistratibus iniuriose decreverant, eodem ipsis privatis erat iure parendum. haec illius severitas acerba videretur, nisi multis condimentis humanitatis mitigaretur.

22 Quod si haec lenitas grata Romae est, ubi tanta adrogantia est, tam immoderata libertas, tam infinita hominum licentia, denique tot magistratus, tot auxilia, tanta vis <populi>,[18] tanta senatus auctoritas, quam iucunda tandem praetoris comitas in Asia potest esse! in qua tanta multitudo civium, tanta sociorum, tot urbes, tot civitates unius hominis nutum intuentur, ubi nullum auxilium est, nulla conquestio, nullus senatus, nulla contio. qua re permagni hominis est et cum ipsa natura moderati tum vero etiam doctrina atque optimarum artium studiis eruditi sic se adhibere in tanta potestate ut nulla alia potestas ab iis quibus
23 is praesit desideretur, <ut est>[19] Cyrus ille a Xenophonte non ad historiae fidem scriptus sed ad effigiem iusti imperi, cuius summa gravitas ab illo philosopho cum singulari comitate coniungitur. quos quidem libros non sine causa noster ille Africanus de manibus ponere non solebat. nullum est enim praetermissum in iis officium diligentis et moderati imperi; eaque si sic coluit ille qui privatus futurus numquam fuit, quonam modo retinenda sunt iis quibus imperium ita datum est ut redderent et ab iis legibus

[18] (*Ern.*) [19] (*SB*)

---

[7] In his *Education of Cyrus*.
[8] The younger Scipio Africanus.

the orderly held his tongue, every man spoke as often as he pleased and as long. Perhaps he might have seemed too indulgent, were it not that his indulgence supported his rigour. Sulla's men were obliged to restore what they had stolen by violence and terror. Magistrates who had given wrongful rulings were obliged as private persons to yield obedience in conformance with the same rules they had made themselves. His rigour would have seemed harsh, had it not been qualified by a generous seasoning of kindliness.

If such mildness is appreciated in Rome, where people have so much arrogance, such unlimited freedom, such unbridled licence, where moreover there are so many magistrates, so many courts of appeal, where the people have so much power and the Senate so much authority, how popular can a governor's courtesy be in Asia, with all that multitude of Roman citizens and provincials, all those cities and communes, watching the nod of one man—no appeal, no protest, no Senate, no popular assembly? Only a really great man, gentle by nature and cultivated by instruction and devotion to the highest pursuits, can so behave himself in a position of such power that those under his rule desire no other power than his. Such a one was Cyrus as described by Xenophon,[7] not according to historical truth but as the pattern of a just ruler; in him that philosopher created a matchless blend of firmness and courtesy. With good reason our Roman Africanus[8] used to keep that book always in his hands. It overlooks no aspect of a conscientious and gentle ruler's duty. And if a monarch, who would never be in a private station, so practised these principles, how sedulously ought they to be observed by those to whom official power is granted only for a

datum est ad quas revertendum est?

24 Ac mihi quidem videntur huc omnia esse referenda iis
qui praesunt aliis, ut ii qui erunt in eorum imperio sint
quam beatissimi. quod tibi et esse antiquissimum et ab initio fuisse, ut primum Asiam attigisti, constanti fama atque
omnium sermone celebratum est. est autem non modo
eius qui sociis et civibus sed etiam eius qui servis, qui mutis
pecudibus praesit eorum quibus praesit commodis utilita-
25 tique servire. cuius quidem generis constare inter omnis
video abs te summam adhiberi diligentiam: nullum aes
alienum novum contrahi civitatibus, vetere autem magno
et gravi multas abs te esse liberatas; urbis compluris diru-
tas ac paene desertas, in quibus unam Ioniae nobilissi-
mam, alteram Cariae, Samum et Halicarnassum, per te
esse recreatas; nullas esse in oppidis seditiones, nullas dis-
cordias; provideri abs te ut civitates optimatium consiliis
administrentur; sublata Mysiae latrocinia, caedis multis
locis repressas, pacem tota provincia constitutam, neque
solum illa itinerum atque agrorum sed multo etiam plura
et maiora oppidorum et fanorum[20] latrocinia esse depulsa;
remotam a fama et a fortunis et ab otio locupletum illam
acerbissimam ministram praetorum avaritiae, calumniam;
sumptus et tributa civitatum ab omnibus qui earum civitatum fines incolant tolerari aequaliter; facillimos esse aditus
ad te, patere auris tuas querelis omnium, nullius inopiam
ac solitudinem non modo illo populari accessu ac tribunali
sed ne domo quidem et cubiculo esse exclusam tuo; toto
denique imperio nihil acerbum esse, nihil crudele, atque

[20] furtorum (*Vict.*)

period, and granted by the laws to which they must eventually return!

I conceive that those who rule over others are bound to take the happiness of their subjects as their universal standard. That this *is* your leading consideration, and has been from the first moment you set foot in Asia, is notorious from consistent report and the talk of all and sundry. Attentiveness to the welfare and needs of those under him is the duty of any ruler, not only over provincials and Roman citizens but even over slaves and dumb animals. I find a universal consensus that you take all possible pains in that regard. The communes, we are told, are contracting no new debts, and many have been relieved by you of a massive load of old obligations; you have restored a number of ruined and almost deserted cities, including Samos and Halicarnassus, one the most famous city of Ionia, the other of Caria; the towns are free of rioting and faction; you take good care that the government of the communes is in the hands of their leading citizens; brigandage has been abolished in Mysia, homicides reduced in many areas, peace established throughout the province, banditry quelled not only on the highways and in the countryside but in greater quantity and on a larger scale in the towns and temples; calumny, that cruellest instrument of governors' greed, has been banished, no longer to threaten the reputations, property, and tranquillity of the rich; communal expenses and taxes are equitably borne by all who live within the communal boundaries. You yourself are very easy of access, ready to lend an ear to every grievance, and no man is so poor and forlorn but he is admitted to your house and bedchamber, to say nothing of the tribunal where you receive the public; your entire conduct as governor is free of

omnia plena clementiae, mansuetudinis, humanitatis.

26 Quantum vero illud est beneficium tuum quod iniquo et gravi vectigali aedilicio cum[21] magnis nostris simultatibus Asiam liberasti! etenim si unus homo nobilis queritur palam te, quod edixeris ne ad ludos pecuniae decernerentur, HS $\overline{\text{CC}}$ sibi eripuisse, quanta tandem pecunia penderetur si omnium nomine quicumque Romae ludos facerent (quod erat iam institutum) erogaretur? quamquam has querelas hominum nostrorum illo consilio oppressimus (quod in Asia nescio quonam modo, Romae quidem non mediocri cum admiratione laudatur), quod, cum ad templum monumentumque nostrum civitates pecunias decrevissent, cumque id et pro meis magnis meritis et pro tuis maximis beneficiis summa sua voluntate fecissent, nominatimque lex exciperet ut ad templum et monumentum capere liceret, cumque id quod dabatur non esset interiturum sed in ornamentis templi futurum, ut non mihi potius quam populo Romano ac dis immortalibus datum videretur, tamen id in quo erat dignitas, erat lex, erat eorum qui faciebant voluntas accipiendum non putavi cum aliis de causis tum etiam ut animo aequiore ferrent ii quibus nec deberetur nec liceret.

27 Quapropter incumbe toto animo et studio omni in eam rationem qua adhuc usus es, ut eos quos tuae fidei potestatique senatus populusque Romanus commisit et credidit

[21] -liciorum (*Hotomanus et Lünemann*)

all trace of harshness and cruelty, entirely pervaded by mercy, gentleness, and humanity.

And then what a boon you conferred on Asia in relieving her from the iniquitous, oppressive Aediles' Tax, thereby making us some powerful enemies. One noble personage is openly complaining that your edict forbidding the voting of public money for shows has picked his pocket of HS 200,000. That gives an idea of the sum that would be involved if money were paid out for the benefit of everybody who gave shows in Rome, as had become the practice. However, I found a means of stifling our fellow countrymen's grumblings on this point—I don't know about Asia, but in Rome my action has been greeted with no little surprise and commendation. I have declined money voted by the communes for a temple and memorial to myself. They had voted it enthusiastically in recognition of their great indebtedness to me and the signal benefits of your government; and the taking of money for a temple and memorial is specifically permitted by law. Moreover, the sum contributed would not have vanished into thin air, but would have remained in the form of temple ornaments, presented, as might well be thought, to the Roman People and the Immortal Gods quite as much as to me. This gift—honourable to myself, legally sanctioned, and made with the good will of the givers—I thought proper to decline, in order, among other reasons, to mitigate the annoyance of those who had lost what nobody owed them and what they had no right to take.

Accordingly, let me urge you to put your whole mind and heart into continuing upon the lines you have followed hitherto; love those whom the Senate and People of Rome have committed to your charge and authority, protect

diligas et omni ratione tueare et[22] esse quam beatissimos velis. quod si te sors Afris aut Hispanis aut Gallis praefecisset, immanibus ac barbaris nationibus, tamen esset humanitatis tuae consulere eorum commodis et utilitati salutique servire; cum vero ei generi hominum praesimus non modo in quo ipsa sit sed etiam a quo ad alios pervenisse putetur humanitas, certe iis eam potissimum tri-
28 buere debemus a quibus accepimus. non enim me hoc iam dicere pudebit, praesertim in ea vita atque iis rebus gestis in quibus non potest residere inertiae aut levitatis ulla suspicio, nos ea quae consecuti simus[23] iis studiis et artibus esse adeptos quae sint nobis Graeciae monumentis disciplinisque tradita. qua re praeter communem fidem quae omnibus debetur, praeterea nos isti hominum generi praecipue debere videmur ut, quorum praeceptis sumus eruditi, apud eos ipsos quod ab iis didicerimus velimus expromere.

29 Atque ille quidem princeps ingeni et doctrinae Plato tum denique fore beatas res publicas putavit si aut docti ac sapientes homines eas regere coepissent aut ii qui regerent omne suum studium in doctrina et sapientia collocarent.[24] hanc coniunctionem videlicet potestatis et sapientiae saluti censuit civitatibus esse posse. quod fortasse aliquando universae rei publicae nostrae, nunc quidem profecto isti provinciae contigit, ut is in ea summam potestatem haberet cui in doctrina, cui in virtute atque humanitate percipienda plurimum ‹positum›[25] a pueritia studi fuisset et

22 ut (*Facciolati*)
23 Sumus (*SB*)
24 -cassent (*Ern.*: -care *coni. SB*)
25 (*Lamb., sed post* temporis)

them in every way, desire their fullest happiness. If the luck of the draw had sent you to govern savage, barbarous tribes in Africa or Spain or Gaul, you would still as a civilized man be bound to think of their interests and devote yourself to their needs and welfare. But we are governing a civilized race, in fact the race from which civilization is believed to have passed to others, and assuredly we ought to give its benefits above all to those from whom we have received it. Yes, I say it without shame, especially as my life and record leaves no opening for any suspicion of indolence or frivolity: everything that I have attained I owe to those pursuits and disciplines which have been handed down to us in the literature and teachings of Greece. Therefore, we may well be thought to owe a special duty to this people, over and above our common obligation to mankind; schooled by their precepts, we must wish to exhibit what we have learned before the eyes of our instructors.

The great Plato, a prince among thinkers and scholars, believed that polities would only be happy either when wise and learned men came to rule them or when rulers devoted all their energies to acquiring virtue and wisdom.[9] That is to say, he laid down that this combination of wisdom and power can bring welfare to communities. Perhaps there was a point in time when our state as a whole had such good fortune;[10] at any rate your province surely has it today, with supreme power vested in one who from boyhood has given the greater part of his time and energy to the acquisition of virtue and culture. So see that this

[9] This famous thought comes from Plato's *Republic*, 473d.
[10] When Cicero was Consul!

30 temporis. qua re cura ut hic annus qui ad laborem tuum
accessit idem ad salutem Asiae prorogatus esse videatur.
quoniam in te retinendo fuit Asia felicior quam nos in
deducendo, perfice ut laetitia provinciae desiderium nostrum leniatur. etenim si in promerendo ut tibi tanti honores haberentur quanti haud scio an nemini fuisti omnium
diligentissimus, multo maiorem in his honoribus tuendis
31 adhibere diligentiam debes. equidem de isto genere honorum quid sentirem scripsi ad te ante. semper eos putavi, si
vulgares essent, vilis, si temporis causa constituerentur, levis; si vero, id quod ita factum est, meritis tuis tribuerentur,
existimabam multam tibi in his honoribus tuendis operam
esse ponendam. qua re quoniam in istis urbibus cum summo imperio et potestate versaris in quibus tuas virtutes
consecratas et in deorum numero collocatas vides, in omnibus rebus quas statues, quas decernes, quas ages, quid
tantis hominum opinionibus, tantis de te iudiciis, tantis
honoribus debeas cogitabis. id autem erit eius modi ut
consulas omnibus, ut medeare incommodis hominum,
provideas saluti, ut te parentem Asiae et dici et haberi
velis.

32 Atque huic tuae voluntati ac diligentiae difficultatem
magnam adferunt publicani. quibus si adversamur, ordinem de nobis optime meritum et per nos cum re publica
coniunctum et a nobis et a re publica diiungemus; sin autem omnibus in rebus obsequemur, funditus eos perire
patiemur quorum non modo saluti sed etiam commodis
consulere debemus. haec est una, si vere cogitare volumus,
in toto imperio tuo difficultas. nam esse abstinentem,
continere omnis cupiditates, suos coercere, iuris aequabi-

[11] By the provincials.

year added to your toil may appear in the light of an extension granted for the welfare of Asia. She has been more fortunate in keeping you than we in bringing you home; then make the happiness of the province console our heartache. Nobody could have taken greater pains to deserve the distinctions which have been conferred upon you[11] in perhaps unprecedented measure, and you should take far greater pains to live up to them. I have already written to you what I feel about honours of this kind. I have always considered them worthless if showered indiscriminately, and trivial if conferred from interested motives. But if they were offered as a tribute to your deserts, as is indeed the case, I thought you should make a point of acting up to them. Since you are living with supreme authority and power in cities where you see your virtues consecrated and deified, you will remember in your every decision, ruling, and act what you owe to such honourable tokens of popular sentiment and esteem. That means you will take thought for all, find remedies for men's misfortunes, make provision for their welfare, aiming to be spoken of and thought of as the father of Asia.

Now there is one great obstacle to this your will and endeavour: the tax farmers. If we oppose them, we shall alienate from ourselves and from the commonwealth a class to which we owe a great deal and which we have brought into alliance with the public interest. On the other hand, if we defer to them all along the line, we shall have to close our eyes to the utter undoing of the people for whose interests, as well as survival, it is our duty to care. If we look facts in the face, this is your only really difficult administrative problem. To have clean hands, to restrain all appetites, to keep your subordinates in order, to maintain an even

lem tenere rationem, diligentem[26] te[27] in rebus cognoscendis, <facilem>[28] in hominibus audiendis admittendisque praebere praeclarum magis est quam difficile. non est enim positum in labore aliquo sed in quadam inductione
33 animi et voluntate. illa causa publicanorum quantam acerbitatem adferat sociis intelleximus ex civibus qui nuper in portoriis Italiae tollendis non tam de portorio quam de non nullis iniuriis portitorum querebantur. qua re non ignoro quid sociis accidat in ultimis terris, cum audierim in Italia querelas civium. hic te ita versari ut et publicanis satis facias, praesertim publicis male redemptis, et socios perire non sinas divinae cuiusdam virtutis esse videtur, id est tuae.

Ac primum Graecis id quod acerbissimum est, quod sunt vectigales, non ita acerbum videri debet, propterea quod sine imperio populi Romani suis institutis per se ipsi ita fuerunt. nomen autem publicani aspernari non possunt, qui pendere ipsi vectigal sine publicano non potuerint quod iis aequaliter Sulla discripserat.[29] non esse autem leniores in exigendis vectigalibus Graecos quam nostros publicanos hinc intellegi potest quod Caunii nuper omnibusque[30] ex insulis quae erant a Sulla Rhodiis attributae confugerunt ad senatum, nobis ut potius vectigal quam Rhodiis penderent. qua re nomen publicani neque ii debent horrere qui semper vectigales fuerunt, neque ii aspernari qui per se pendere vectigal non potuerunt, neque

26 facilem (*SB*) 27 se *Petreius* 28 (*SB*)
29 descr- (*Buecheler*) 30 omnes qui (*SB*)

---

12 As had actually happened; cf. *Letters to Atticus* 17 (1.17).9.

dispensation of justice, to be diligent in looking into people's problems and ready to listen to them and see them—all that is admirable rather than difficult. It is not a matter of work but of a certain set of mind and purpose. How much bitterness the tax farmer question creates in the provinces has been illustrated for us by the attitude of some of our countrymen over the abolition of Italian customs. It was not the duty they complained of so much as certain maltreatments at the hands of customs officers. Having heard the complaints of Roman citizens in Italy I do not need to be told what happens to provincials at the ends of the earth. So to manage that you satisfy the tax farmers, especially when they have made a poor bargain with the Treasury,[12] without letting the provincials go to ruin seems to call for capacity more than human—which is to say, it calls for yours.

Now to begin with, the most painful point to the Greeks is that they have to pay taxes at all. And yet they ought not to feel it so very painfully, since without any Roman empire they were in just the same case under their own institutions, making their own arrangements. They ought not to turn away in disgust at the word 'tax farmer,' seeing that they proved unable to pay their taxes, as fairly allocated by Sulla, on their own without the tax farmer's intervention. That Greeks in this capacity make no more easygoing collectors than Romans is well seen from the recent appeal to the Senate by the Caunians and all the islands assigned to Rhodes by Sulla, that they should in future pay their taxes to Rome instead of to Rhodes. And so I say that people who have always had to pay taxes ought not to shudder at the word 'tax farmer,' that such disgust comes ill from people who were unable to pay their tax by themselves, and that

34 ii recusare qui postulaverunt. simul et illud Asia cogitet,
nullam ab se neque belli externi neque domesticarum dis-
cordiarum calamitatem afuturam fuisse, si hoc imperio
non teneretur; id autem imperium cum retineri sine vectigalibus nullo modo possit, aequo animo parte aliqua suorum fructuum pacem sibi sempiternam redimat atque
35 otium. quod si genus ipsum et nomen publicani non iniquo
animo sustinebunt, poterunt iis consilio et prudentia tua
reliqua videri mitiora. possunt in pactionibus faciendis
non legem spectare censoriam sed potius commoditatem
conficiendi negoti et liberationem molestiae. potes etiam
tu id facere, quod et fecisti egregie et facis, ut commemo-
res quanta sit in publicanis dignitas, quantum nos illi ordini
debeamus, ut remoto imperio ac vi potestatis et fascium
publicanos cum Graecis gratia atque auctoritate coniungas
[sed][31] et ab iis de quibus optime tu meritus es et qui tibi
omnia debent hoc petas, ut facilitate sua nos eam necessitudinem quae est nobis cum publicanis obtinere et conser-
vare patiantur.

36 Sed quid ego te haec hortor quae tu non modo facere potes tua sponte sine cuiusquam praeceptis sed etiam magna iam ex parte perfecisti? non enim desistunt nobis agere cottidie gratias honestissimae et maximae societates, quod quidem mihi idcirco iucundius est quod idem faciunt Graeci. difficile est autem ea quae commodis <et>[32] utilitate et prope natura diversa sunt voluntate coniungere. at ea quidem quae supra scripta sunt non ut te instituerem

31 (*Kahnt*)

32 (*Watt*: utilitate<que> *iam SB*)

those who have what they asked for should not raise objections. Asia must also remember that if she were not in our empire she would have suffered every calamity that foreign war and strife at home can inflict. Since the empire cannot possibly be maintained without taxation, let her not grudge a part of her revenues in exchange for permanent peace and quiet. Now if they will only tolerate the actual existence and name of the tax farmer with some degree of equanimity, your policy and wisdom will make all else seem easier to bear. In making their compacts they need not worry about the censorial contract, but rather look to the convenience of settling the business and freeing themselves of its annoyance. You yourself can help, as you have admirably done and are doing, by dwelling on the high status of the tax farmers as a class and how much we[13] owe them, using your influence and moral authority to bring the two sides together without any show of magisterial power and constraint. You may ask it as a favour from people for whom you have done so much and who ought to refuse you nothing, that they be willing to stretch a point or two in order to let us preserve our friendly relations with the tax farmers unimpaired.

No doubt these exhortations are superfluous. You can do all this yourself without advice from anybody, in fact to a great extent you have done it already. The most important and respectable companies are constantly expressing their gratitude to me, which I find the more agreeable because the Greeks do the same. It is no easy matter to create harmony where there is an opposition of material interest and almost of nature. However, I have not written the forego-

[13] Cicero and his brother.

scripsi (neque enim prudentia tua cuiusquam praecepta desiderat), sed me in scribendo commemoratio tuae virtutis delectavit. quamquam in his litteris longior fui quam aut vellem aut quam me putavi fore.

37 Unum est quod tibi ego praecipere non desinam neque te patiar, quantum erit in me, cum exceptione laudari. omnes enim qui istinc veniunt ita de tua virtute, integritate, humanitate commemorant ut in tuis summis laudibus excipiant unam iracundiam. quod vitium cum in hac privata cottidianaque vita levis esse animi atque infirmi videtur, tum vero nihil est tam deforme quam ad summum imperium etiam acerbitatem naturae adiungere. qua re illud non suscipiam ut quae de iracundia dici solent a doctissimis hominibus ea nunc tibi exponam, cum et nimis longus esse nolim et ex multorum scriptis ea facile possis cognoscere: illud, quod est epistulae proprium, ut is ad quem scribitur de iis rebus quas ignorat certior fiat, praetermittendum esse non puto.

38 Sic ad nos omnes fere deferunt: nihil, cum absit iracundia, dicere solent te fieri posse iucundius; sed cum te alicuius improbitas perversitasque commoverit, sic te animo incitari ut ab omnibus tua desideretur humanitas. qua re quoniam in eam rationem vitae nos non tam cupiditas quaedam gloriae quam res ipsa ac Fortuna deduxit ut sempiternus sermo hominum de nobis futurus sit, caveamus, quantum efficere et consequi possumus, ut ne quod in nobis insigne vitium fuisse dicatur. neque ego nunc hoc contendo, quod fortasse cum in omni natura tum iam in nostra aetate difficile est, mutare animum et, si quid est penitus insitum moribus, id subito evellere, sed te illud ad-

ing to instruct you (you know the world too well to require anyone's advice), but the writing gave me pleasure, the pleasure of dwelling upon your fine qualities. But I must admit that this letter has turned out more lengthy than I expected or should have wished.

There is one point on which I shall continue to offer you advice. I shall never, so far as in me lies, let you be praised with a qualification. All who come from out there are loud in praise of your ability, integrity, and courtesy, but they make one reservation: your tendency to lose your temper. In everyday private life this is regarded as the fault of a weak, unstable mind; but nothing looks so ill as the combination of natural acerbity and supreme power. I won't take it upon myself here to expound to you what philosophers are apt to say on the subject of irascibility, for I don't want to take too long, and you can easily find it in many books. It is the proper function of a letter to inform one's correspondent of what he does not know, and that I think I ought not to leave undone.

Pretty well everyone tells us the same tale. They say that no man could be more agreeable than you when you are not out of temper, but that once irritated by some piece of rascality or perverseness you become so worked up that everybody wonders what has become of your gentlemanly self. Not so much by any appetite for glory as by accident of circumstance we have been led into a way of life which will make us a theme of talk for all time to come. So let us take care that, if we can possibly help it, they don't say 'he had one glaring fault.' I am not urging you to change your disposition and eradicate at one pull a deep-rooted habit. That is perhaps difficult to achieve in every nature and particularly at our time of life. I would only suggest, if you can-

moneo ut, si hoc plane[33] vitare non potes, quod ante occupatur animus ab iracundia quam providere ratio potuit ne occuparetur, ut te ante compares cottidieque meditere resistendum esse iracundiae, cumque ea maxime animum moveat tum tibi esse diligentissime linguam continendam; quae quidem mihi virtus interdum non[34] minor videtur quam omnino non irasci. nam illud est non solum gravitatis sed non numquam etiam lentitudinis; moderari vero et animo et orationi cum sis iratus, aut etiam tacere et tenere in sua potestate motum animi et dolorem, etsi non est perfectae sapientae, tamen est non mediocris ingeni.

39 Atque in hoc genere multo te esse iam commodiorem mitioremque nuntiant. nullae tuae vehementiores animi concitationes, nulla maledicta ad nos, nullae contumeliae perferuntur. quae cum abhorrent a litteris, ab humanitate, tum vero contraria sunt imperio ac dignitati. nam si implacabiles iracundiae sunt, summa est acerbitas; sin autem exorabiles, summa levitas, quae tamen ut in malis acerbita-
40 ti anteponenda est. sed quoniam primus annus habuit de hac reprehensione plurimum sermonis, credo propterea quod tibi hominum iniuriae, quod avaritia, quod insolentia praeter opinionem accidebat et intolerabilis videbatur, secundus autem multo levior‹em›,[35] quod et consuetudo et ratio et, ut ego arbitror, meae quoque litterae te patientiorem lenioremque fecerunt, tertius annus ita debet esse emendatus ut ne minimam quidem rem quisquam possit ullam reprehendere.

41 Ac iam hoc loco non hortatione neque praeceptis sed precibus tecum fraternis ago, totum ut animum, curam

[33] plene (*Ern.*?)
[34] non interdum (*R. Klotz*)
[35] (*Madvig*)

not avoid the failing altogether because anger seizes your mind before reason can look ahead to prevent it, that you prepare yourself in advance and make a daily resolve not to lose your temper and in moments of extreme exasperation to be particularly careful to restrain your tongue. To do this, I sometimes think, is as great a moral accomplishment as not to be angry at all. The latter is not exclusively a product of moral strength, it sometimes comes of a phlegmatic humour; whereas to govern one's spirit and speech in anger, or even to hold one's tongue and keep the spiritual disturbance and passion under one's own control, though not the part of the perfect sage, does imply a mind beyond the ordinary.

However, reports are that you have become much milder and more amenable in this respect. We hear of no violent excitement on your part, no abuse or insults—behaviour far removed from literary culture and civilized manners and no less at odds with official authority and dignity. For implacable anger is the extreme of harshness, while appeasable anger is the extreme of levity—which, however, given the choice of evils, is to be preferred to harshness. Well, your first year produced a great deal of criticism in this regard, I imagine because you had not expected to meet with so much injustice, greed, and insolence and found it more than you could tolerate. The second year was a great improvement; habit, reason, and also (as I suppose) my letters having made you more patient and gentle. The third year ought to be so impeccable that nobody will be able to find fault with the smallest detail.

And now I no longer exhort and advise, I beg you as a brother to set your whole mind, your entire thought and

cogitationemque tuam ponas in omnium laude undique
colligenda. quod si [in] mediocris tantum[36] sermonis ac
praedicationis nostrae res essent, nihil abs te eximium,
nihil praeter aliorum consuetudinem postularetur. nunc
vero propter earum rerum in quibus versati sumus splen-
dorem et magnitudinem, nisi summam laudem ex ista provincia adsequimur, vix videmur summam vituperationem
posse vitare. ea nostra ratio est ut omnes boni cum faveant
tum etiam omnem a nobis diligentiam virtutemque et pos-
tulent et exspectent, omnes autem improbi, quod cum iis
bellum sempiternum suscepimus, vel minima re ad repre-
42 hendendum contenti esse videantur. qua re quoniam eius
modi theatrum totius Asiae virtutibus tuis est datum, cele-
britate refertissimum, magnitudine amplissimum, iudicio
eruditissimum, natura autem ita resonans ut usque Romam significationes vocesque referantur, contende, quaeso, atque elabora non modo ut his rebus dignus fuisse sed
43 etiam ut illa omnia tuis artibus superasse videare; et quoniam mihi casus urbanam in magistratibus administratio-
nem rei publicae, tibi provincialem dedit, [et][37] si mea pars
nemini cedit, fac ut tua ceteros vincat. simul et illud cogita,
nos non de reliqua et sperata gloria iam laborare sed de
parta dimicare, quae quidem non tam expetenda nobis fuit
quam tuenda est.

Ac si mihi quicquam esset abs te separatum, nihil amplius desiderarem hoc statu qui mihi iam partus est. nunc vero sic res sese habet ut, nisi omnia tua facta atque dicta

[36] si in mediocri statu (*Sedgwick*)
[37] (*Faërnus*)

concern, on gathering universal praise from every quarter. If the talk and public blazoning of our achievements had not been exceptional, nothing extraordinary, nothing beyond the practice of other governors, would be demanded of you. As it is, the lustre and magnitude of the affairs which have engaged us are such that unless we gain the highest credit from your administration it looks as though we shall hardly be able to avoid bitter censure. Consider our situation: all the honest men wish us well, but also demand and expect of us the utmost in conscientiousness and ability; all the rascals, since we have declared unending war on them, will evidently want only the slightest excuse to censure us. Therefore, since so great a theatre has been given for your virtues to display themselves, the whole of Asia[14] no less, a theatre so crowded, so vast, so expertly critical, and with acoustic properties so powerful that cries and demonstrations echo as far as Rome, pray strive with all your might not only that you may appear worthy of what was achieved here[15] but that men may rate your performance above anything that has been seen out there. As chance has decreed, my public work in office has been done in Rome, yours in a province. If my part stands second to none, make yours surpass the rest. Also reflect that we are no longer working for glory hoped for in the future but fighting for what we have gained, and we are more bound to maintain this than we were to seek it.

If I had anything apart from you, I should want no more than this standing which I have already won. But the case is such that, unless all your acts and words out there match

[14] Of course this refers, as elsewhere, to the Roman province in the west of Asia Minor.

[15] By Cicero as Consul.

nostris rebus istinc respondeant, ego me tantis meis laboribus tantisque periculis, quorum tu omnium particeps fuisti, nihil consecutum putem. quod si ut amplissimum nomen consequeremur unus praeter ceteros adiuvisti, certe idem ut id retineamus praeter ceteros elaborabis. non est tibi his solis utendum existimationibus ac iudiciis qui nunc sunt hominum sed iis etiam qui futuri sunt; quamquam illorum erit verius iudicium, obtrectatione et
44 malevolentia liberatum. denique etiam illud debes cogitare, non te tibi soli gloriam quaerere; quod si esset, tamen non neglegeres, praesertim cum amplissimis monumentis consecrare voluisses memoriam nominis tui. sed ea tibi est communicanda mecum, prodenda liberis nostris. in qua cavendum est ne, si neglegentior fueris, ‹non›[38] tibi parum consuluisse sed etiam tuis invidisse videaris.

45 Atque haec non eo dicuntur ut te oratio mea dormientem excitasse sed potius ut currentem incitasse videatur. facies enim perpetuo quae fecisti, ut omnes aequitatem tuam, temperantiam, severitatem integritatemque laudarent. sed me quaedam tenet propter singularem amorem infinita in te aviditas gloriae. quamquam illud existimo, cum iam tibi Asia sicuti uni cuique sua domus nota esse debeat, cum ad tuam summam prudentiam tantus usus accesserit, nihil esse quod ad laudem attineat quod non tu optime perspicias et tibi non sine cuiusquam hortatione in mentem veniat cottidie. sed ego quia, cum tua lego, te audire, et quia,[39] cum ad te scribo, tecum loqui videor, idcirco et tua longissima quaque epistula maxime delector et ipse in scribendo sum saepe longior.

38 (*SB*: non solum ς)
39 (*Wes.*)

my record, I shall feel I have achieved nothing by those toils and hazards of mine, in all of which you took your part. More than any other you have helped me to gain so great a name; assuredly you will work harder than any other to let me keep it. You should not think only of the esteem and judgement of contemporaries but of posterity too; its judgement, to be sure, will be fairer, freed of detraction and malice. Finally, you ought to reflect that you are not seeking glory only for yourself, though even if you were you would not think lightly of it, especially as you have desired to immortalize your name by your splendid works.[16] But you must share that glory with me and hand it on to our children. If you make too light of it, you will run the risk of seeming to begrudge it to your family as well as of caring too little for yourself.

Now I do not wish it to appear as though my words were meant to wake a sleeper; rather, to spur a runner. As in the past, so to the end you will make all men praise your justice, temperance, strictness, and integrity. But my deep affection inspires me with an almost infinite appetite for your glory. However, after all, you should now know Asia as well as a man knows his own house; you now have a mass of experience to back your excellent judgement. I suppose then that there is nothing tending to credit which you do not best perceive and which does not enter your mind every day without anybody's prompting. But when I read your letters I seem to hear you talk, and when I write to you it is as though I were talking to you. That is why the longer your letters the better I like them, and why I myself often write rather lengthily.

[16] A compliment to Quintus' literary productions.

46 Illud te ad extremum et oro et hortor ut, tamquam poetae boni et actores industrii solent, sic tu in extrema parte et conclusione muneris ac negoti tui diligentissimus sis, ut hic tertius annus imperi tui †tamquam tertius†[40] perfectissimus atque ornatissimus fuisse videatur. id facillime facies si me, cui semper uni magis quam universis placere voluisti, tecum semper esse putabis et omnibus iis rebus quas dices et facies interesse.

Reliquum est ut te orem ut valetudini tuae, si me et tuos omnis valere vis, diligentissime servias.

2 (I.2)

Scr. Romae inter VIII *Kal. Nov. et* IV *Id. Dec. an.* 59

MARCUS QUINTO FRATRI SALUTEM

1 Statius ad me venit a. d. VIII Kal. Nov. eius adventus, quod ita scripsisti, direptum iri te[1] a tuis dum is abesset, molestus mihi fuit; quod autem exspectationem sui[2] concursumque eum qui erat futurus si una tecum decederet neque antea visus esset sustulit, id mihi non incommode visum est accidisse. exhaustus est enim sermo hominum et multae emissae iam eius modi voces, ‘ἀλλ’ *αἰεί τινα φῶτα μέγαν*’; quae te absente confecta esse laetor.

2 Quod autem idcirco a te missus est mihi ut se purgaret, id necesse minime fuit. primum enim numquam ille mihi

40 ta- tertius <actus> ς: ta- ultimus a- *coni. SB*: *del. Constans*
1 erit (*Vict.*) 2 tui (*Schütz*)

1 Q. Cicero's much-prized freedman.

This lastly I beg and urge of you: like good playwrights and hard-working actors, take your greatest pains in the final phase, the rounding off, of your appointed task. Let this third year of your term as governor be like the last (?) act of a play: the most highly finished, best fitted-out of the three. This you will most easily accomplish if you imagine that I, whose single approval has always meant more to you than that of mankind at large, am ever with you, at your side in anything you say or do.

It only remains for me to beg you to pay particular attention to your health, if you value mine and that of all your folk.

2 (I.2)

Rome, between 25 October and 10 December 59

From Marcus to his brother Quintus greetings.

Statius[1] arrived at my house on 25 October. I was sorry to see him come because you wrote that you would be plucked to pieces by your entourage while he was gone. On the other hand, I felt it just as well to have avoided the curiosity and crowding around that there would have been if he came back with you without having made a previous appearance. The talk has exhausted itself. 'Methought to see a mighty man'[2]—such things have now been said a good many times. And I am glad to have got all that over in your absence.

It was not in the least necessary, however, for you to send him to clear himself to me. To begin with, I never sus-

[2] *Odyssey* 9.513.

fuit suspectus, neque ego quae ad te de illo scripsi scripsi meo iudicio; sed cum ratio salusque omnium nostrum qui ad rem publicam accedimus non veritate solum sed etiam fama niteretur, sermones ad te aliorum semper, non mea iudicia perscripsi. qui quidem quam frequentes essent et quam graves adventu suo Statius ipse cognovit. etenim intervenit non nullorum querelis quae apud me de illo ipso habebantur et sentire potuit sermones iniquorum in suum potissimum nomen erumpere.

3 Quod autem me maxime movere solebat, cum audiebam illum plus apud te posse quam gravitas istius[3] aetatis, imperi, prudentiae postularet—quam multos enim mecum egisse putas ut se Statio commendarem, quam multa autem ipsum ἀφελῶς[4] mecum in sermone ita posuisse, 'id mihi non placuit,' 'monui,' 'suasi,' 'deterrui'? quibus in rebus etiam si fidelitas summa est (quod prorsus credo, quoniam tu ita iudicas), tamen species ipsa tam gratiosi liberti aut servi dignitatem habere nullam potest. atque hoc sic habeto (nihil enim[5] nec temere dicere nec astute reticere debeo), materiam omnem sermonum eorum qui de te detrahere velint Statium dedisse; antea tantum intellegi potuisse iratos tuae <se>veritati esse non nullos, hoc manumisso iratis quod loquerentur non defuisse.

4 Nunc respondebo ad eas epistulas quas mihi reddidit L. Caesius, cui,[6] quoniam ita te velle intellego, nullo loco deero; quarum altera est de Blaundeno[7] Zeuxide, quem

[3] illius (*Vict.*)
[4] ἀσφαλῶς (*Vict.*)
[5] tamen (*Brunus*)
[6] qui
[7] blainde(no) *vel sim.* (*Tyrrell*)

pected him. What I wrote to you about him did not represent my own opinion. But the success and security of all of us in public life rests not only on the truth but on common report, and that is why I have all along kept you informed of what others were saying, not what I myself was thinking. How much talk there was, and how strongly critical, Statius himself found out on his arrival here. He was present just when certain parties were complaining about him to me, and could see how unfriendly talk made his name its principal target.

What used to disturb me most when I heard that he had more to say with you than befitted the weight of your age, official authority, and worldly wisdom—how many people, do you suppose, have asked me to recommend them to Statius? How often do you suppose he himself in talking to me has innocently used phrases like 'I didn't approve of that,' 'I suggested . . . ,' 'I advised . . . ,' 'I warned . . .'? Even if his loyalty in these matters is implicit (which I thoroughly believe, since you are persuaded it is so), the look of the thing, a freedman or slave with so much influence, could not but be highly undignified. I should be wrong if I spoke without good grounds, and wrong if I kept diplomatically silent: please realize that all the grist to the mills of your would-be detractors has been furnished by Statius. Previously it could only be thought that some people might have been annoyed by your strictness, but after his manumission that those who were had got something to talk about.

Let me now reply to the letters delivered to me by L. Caesius (I shall do all I can for him since I understand that you so wish). One of them concerns Zeuxis of Blaundus. You say that I have warmly recommended to you an in-

scribis certissimum matricidam tibi a me intime commendari. qua de re et de hoc genere toto, ne forte me in Graecos tam ambitiosum factum esse mirere, pauca cognosce. ego cum Graecorum querelas nimium valere sentirem propter hominum ingenia ad fallendum parata, quoscumque de te queri audivi quacumque potui ratione placavi. primum Dionys<opol>itas, qui erant inimicissimi, lenivi; quorum principem Hermippum non solum sermone meo sed etiam familiaritate devinxi. ego Apamensem Hephaestium,[8] ego levissimum hominem, Megaristum Antandrium, ego Niciam Smyrnaeum, ego nugas maximas omni mea comitate sum complexus, Nymphonem etiam Colophonium. quae feci omnia, non quo me aut hi homines aut tota natio delectaret. pertaesum est levitatis, adsentationis, animorum non officiis sed temporibus servientium.

5 Sed ut ad Zeuxim revertar, cum is de M. Cascelli sermone secum habito, quae tu scribis, ea ipsa loqueretur, obstiti eius sermoni et hominem in familiaritatem recepi. tua autem quae fuerit cupiditas tanta nescio, quod scribis cupisse te, quoniam Smyrnae duos Mysos insuisses in culleum, simile in superiore parte provinciae edere exemplum severitatis tuae et idcirco Zeuxim elicere[9] omni ratione voluisse. quem adductum in iudicium fortasse an dimitti non oportuerit, conquiri vero et elici blanditiis, ut tu scribis, ad iudicium necesse non fuit, eum praesertim

[8] et ephesium *vel sim.* (*Or.*)
[9] eligere (*Brunus*)

---

[3] Or perhaps 'because men's minds are so gullible.'
[4] The traditional punishment of parricides.

dividual who beyond a shadow of doubt murdered his mother. As to that, and to the whole topic, let me tell you one or two things, in case you are surprised that I have become so anxious to curry favour with Greeks. I found that the complaints of these people carried more weight than I liked because of their natural talent for deception;[3] and so I tried in whatever way I could to appease whichever of them I heard complaining about you. First I smoothed down the group from Dionysopolis, who were extremely hostile, and made a friend of their leader, Hermippus, by talking to him and even associating with him on familiar terms. I have showered courtesies on Hephaestius of Apamea, on that little fribble Megaristus of Antandros, on Nicias of Smyrna, on the most arrant good-for-nothings, including Nympho of Colophon. All this I did not do because I have any taste for these specimens or for their whole tribe. On the contrary I am sick and tired of their fribbling, fawning ways and their minds always fixed on present advantage, never on the right thing to do.

But to return to Zeuxis: He was talking about his conversation with M. Cascellius, just the same points as in your letter. So I set myself to stop his gossip and took him into my familiar circle. I don't quite understand this ambition of yours: you write that having sewn up two Mysians in a sack[4] at Smyrna you wanted to show a similar example of your severity in the interior of the province, and for that reason to entice Zeuxis by any means available. Once brought to trial it would not perhaps have been right to let him go, but it was hardly necessary to have him searched for and wheedled into court with soft words, as you put it;

hominem quem ego et ex suis civibus et ex multis aliis cottidie magis cognosco nobiliorem esse prope quam civitatem suam.

6 At enim Graecis solis indulgeo. quid? L. Caecilium nonne omni ratione placavi? quem hominem! qua ira, quo spiritu! quem denique praeter Tuscenium, cuius causa sanari non potest, non mitigavi? ecce supra caput homo levis ac sordidus sed tamen equestri censu,[10] Catienus! etiam is lenietur. cuius tu in patrem quod fuisti asperior non reprehendo. certo enim scio te fecisse cum causa. sed quid opus fuit eius modi litteris quas ad ipsum misisti? illum crucem sibi ipsum constituere, ex qua tu eum ante detraxisses; te curaturum fumo[11] ut combureretur plaudente tota provincia. quid vero ad C. Fabium nescio quem (nam eam quoque epistulam T. Catienus circumgestat), renuntiari tibi Licinium plagiarium cum suo pullo miluino tributa exigere? deinde rogas Fabium ut et patrem et filium vivos comburat, si possit; si minus, ad te mittat uti iudicio comburantur. hae litterae abs te per iocum missae ad C. Fabium, si modo sunt tuae, cum leguntur, invidiosam atrocitatem verborum habent.

7 Ac si omnium mearum litterarum praecepta repetes, intelleges esse nihil a me nisi orationis acerbitatem et iracundiam et, si forte, raro litterarum missarum indiligentiam reprehensam. quibus quidem in rebus si apud te plus auctoritas mea quam tua sive natura paulo acrior sive

[10] incessu (*Vict.*) [11] vivus *Housman ap. Watt*

---

[5] I understand this to mean that Zeuxis was too insignificant to be worth so much trouble. Blaundus was not one of the leading towns.

particularly as his fellow Blaundians and others give me to understand more and more every day that he is almost more distinguished than his town![5]

It is not as though I am nice only to Greeks. Didn't I try all I knew to propitiate L. Caecilius? What a fellow he is! What fire and fury! Is there anyone except Tuscenius, a hopeless case, whom I haven't mollified? And now down comes Catienus, a mercenary rogue to be sure, but with a Knight's qualification. He too shall be appeased. You bore pretty hard on his father, which I do not criticize—I am sure you had your reasons. But where was the need to write a letter such as you sent Catienus himself: that he was building his own gallows, from which you had once before taken him down; you would see to it that he is smoked to death to the applause of the whole province? Why did you have to write to C. Fabius, whoever he may be (that's another letter which T. Catienus is toting around), that it was reported to you that taxes were being collected by 'yon kidnapping villain Licinius and his young sparrowhawk of a son'? You proceed to ask Fabius to burn both father and son alive if he can; if not, he is to send them to you so that they can be burnt up in court. You sent the letter to Fabius as a joke (if you really wrote it), but when folk read it the ferocity of the wording raises a prejudice against you.

If you will recall the advice I have given you in all my letters, you will see that my only criticism has been on the score of harsh language, irritability, and perhaps now and then a lack of care in your official letters. If my counsel had counted more with you in these respects than, shall we say, your somewhat hasty temper, or a certain pleasure you

quaedam dulcedo iracundiae sive dicendi sal facetiaeque valuissent, nihil sane esset quod nos paeniteret. et mediocri me dolore putas adfici cum audiam qua sit existimatione Vergilius, qua tuus vicinus, C. Octavius? nam si te interioribus vicinis tuis, Ciliciensi et Syriaco, anteponis, valde magnum facis! atque is dolor est quod, cum ii quos nominavi te innocentia non vincant, vincunt tamen artificio benevolentiae colligendae, qui neque Cyrum Xenophontis neque Agesilaum noverint, quorum regum summo imperio nemo umquam verbum ullum asperius audivit.

8 Sed haec a principio tibi praecipiens quantum profecerim non ignoro. nunc tamen decedens, id quod mihi iam facere videris, relinque, quaeso, quam iucundissimam memoriam tui. successorem habes perblandum; cetera valde illius adventu tua requirentur. in litteris mittendis (saepe ad te scripsi) nimium te exorabilem[12] praebuisti. tolle omnis, si potes, iniquas, tolle inusitatas, tolle contrarias. Statius mihi narravit scriptas ad te solere adferri, a se legi, et si iniquae sint[13] fieri te certiorem; ante quam vero ipse ad te venisset, nullum delectum litterarum fuisse, ex eo esse volumina selectarum epistularum quae reprehendi
9 solerent. hoc de genere nihil te nunc quidem moneo (sero est enim, ac scire potes multa me varie diligenterque monuisse); illud tamen quod Theopompo mandavi cum

[12] inex- (*Corr.*) [13] essent *Wes.*

---

[6] Governors of Syria and Macedonia respectively.

[7] The governor of Syria was Cn. Cornelius Lentulus Marcellinus, Consul in 56. The governor of Cilicia is unknown.

[8] T. Ampius Balbus.

take in letting fly, or your gift for pungent and witty expression, we should really have had nothing to regret. You must appreciate the pain I feel when I am told how highly people think of Vergilius and of your neighbour C. Octavius[6] (as for your neighbours on the other side in Cilicia and Syria,[7] you are not claiming much if you compare yourself favourably with them!). And the distressing thing is that your hands are just as clean as theirs. They put you into the shade by their technique of gaining good will. And yet they know nothing of Xenophon's Cyrus nor yet his Agesilaus. Nobody ever heard a harsh word from either monarch, autocrats though they were.

Well, I have been telling you all this from the beginning and I am well aware how much good it has done. All the same, in quitting the province, as I understand you are now in process of doing, do leave behind you as pleasant a memory as possible. Your successor[8] is a man of very agreeable manners. Other qualities which you possess will be very much to seek when he arrives. In sending out official letters (I have often written to you about this) you have been too ready to accommodate. Destroy, if you can, any that are inequitable or contrary to usage or contradictory. Statius has told me that they used to be brought to you already drafted, and that he would read them and inform you if they were inequitable, but that before he joined you letters were dispatched indiscriminately. And so, he said, there are collections of selected letters and these are adversely criticized. I am not going to warn you about this now. It is too late for that, and you are in a position to know how many warnings I have given on various occasions and with no lack of particularity. But as I asked Theopompus to

essem admonitus ab ipso, vide per homines amantis tui, quod est facile, ut haec genera tollantur epistularum: primum iniquarum, deinde contrariarum, tum absurde et inusitate scriptarum, postremo in aliquem contumeliosarum. atque ego haec tam esse quam audio non puto; et si sunt occupationibus tuis minus animadversa, nunc perspice et purga. legi epistulam quam ipse scripsisse Sulla nomenclator dictus est, non probandam; legi non nullas iracundas.

10 Sed tempore ipso de epistulis. nam cum hanc paginam tenerem, L. Flavius, praetor designatus, ad me venit, homo mihi valde familiaris. is mihi te ad procuratores suos litteras misisse, quae mihi visae sunt iniquissimae, ne quid de bonis quae L. Octavi Nasonis fuissent, cui L. Flavius heres est, deminuerent ante quam C. Fundanio pecuniam solvissent, itemque misisse ad Apollonidensis ne de bonis quae Octavi fuissent deminui paterentur prius quam Fundanio debitum solutum esset. haec mihi veri similia non videntur. sunt enim a prudentia tua remotissima. ne deminuat heres? quid si infitiatur? quid si omnino non debet? quid? praetor solet iudicare deberi? quid? ego Fundanio non cupio, non amicus sum, non misericordia moveor? nemo magis. sed vis[14] iuris eius modi est quibusdam in rebus ut nihil sit loci gratiae. atque ita mihi dicebat Flavius scriptum in ea epistula quam tuam esse dicebat, te aut quasi amicis tuis gratias acturum aut quasi inimicis incom-
11 modaturum. quid multa? ferebat id[15] graviter, vehementer mecum querebatur orabatque ut ad te quam diligentissime scriberem. quod facio et te prorsus vehementer

[14] via (*Mueller*)

[15] gr- id (*SB*: gr- *Watt*: gr- et *Lamb. marg.*)

tell you at his own suggestion, do see to it through friendly agents (it is easy enough) that the following categories are destroyed: first, inequitable letters; second, contradictory letters; third, letters drafted inappropriately and contrary to accepted usage; and finally, letters insulting to any person. I don't believe all I am told; and if there has been some negligence due to pressure of business, look into it now and set it right. I have read an improper letter which your nomenclator Sulla is said to have written himself and I have read some angry ones.

The subject of letters is apropos. As I was on this page, Praetor-Elect L. Flavius, a close friend of mine, came to see me. He told me that you had written a letter to his agents which appeared to me quite inequitable, directing them not to touch the estate of L. Octavius Naso, who left Flavius as his heir, until they had paid a sum of money to C. Fundanius; also that you had written directions to the town of Apollonis not to allow Octavius' estate to be touched until Fundanius' debt was paid. This all sounds improbable to me; it is so completely foreign to your usual good judgement. Must the heir not touch the estate? Suppose he denies the debt? Suppose there *is* no debt? Is it usual for a governor to rule that a debt exists? And am *I* not Fundanius' friend and well-wisher, am I not sorry for him? Nobody more. But in some matters the path of justice is not wide enough for favour. Flavius further told me that the letter which he alleged came from you contained a promise 'either to thank them as friends or to make things uncomfortable for them as enemies.' In short, he was much put out and expostulated with me strongly, asking me to write to you most particularly. That I am doing, and I ask you again most earnestly to countermand your order to

etiam atque etiam rogo ut et procuratoribus Flavi remittas de deminuendo et Apollonidensibus ne quid praescribas, quod contra Flavium sit, amplius. et Flavi causa et scilicet Pompei facies omnia. nolo me dius fidius ex tua iniuria in illum tibi liberalem me videri; sed et te oro ut tu ipse auctoritatem et monumentum aliquod decreti aut litterarum tuarum relinquas quod sit ad Flavi rem et ad causam accommodatum. fert enim graviter homo et mei observantissimus et sui iuris dignitatisque retinens se apud te neque amicitia nec iure valuisse. et, ut opinor, Flavi aliquando rem et Pompeius et Caesar tibi commendarunt et ipse ad te scripserat Flavius et ego certe. qua re si ulla res est quam tibi me petente faciendam putes, haec ea sit. si me amas, cura, elabora, perfice ut Flavius et tibi et mihi quam maximas gratias agat. hoc te ita rogo ut maiore studio rogare non possim.

12 Quod ad me de Hermia scribis mihi mehercule valde molestum fuit. litteras ad te parum fraterne scripseram, quas oratione Diodoti, Luculli liberti, commotus, de pactione statim quod audieram, iracundius scripseram et revocare cupiebam. huic tu epistulae non fraterne scriptae fraterne debes ignoscere.

13 De Censorino, Antonio, Cassiis, Scaevola, te ab iis diligi, ut scribis, vehementer gaudeo, cetera fuerunt in eadem epistula graviora quam vellem, *'ὀρθὰν τὰν ναῦν'* et *'ἅπαξ*

---

[9] The circumstances are unknown.

[10] These young noblemen were not Legates and cannot credibly be regarded as belonging to the 'cohort of friends.' How or why they had shown their friendly feelings is quite uncertain, but possibly they had promised support in the event of a prosecution.

Flavius' agents about touching the estate, and not to give any further directions to Apollonis against Flavius' interests. I am sure you will do all you can both for Flavius' sake and, no doubt, for Pompey's. Upon my word, I don't wish to appear as obliging Flavius in consequence of your unfairness. On the contrary, I beg you yourself to leave behind you an official declaration in writing in the form of a ruling or a letter which will help Flavius' interests and case. Being most attentive to me and careful of his own rights and dignity, he is greatly put out to find that neither friendship nor justice have counted with you in his favour. I believe that both Pompey and Caesar at one time or other recommended Flavius' interests to you; Flavius himself had written to you, and certainly I did so. So if there is anything you would think proper to do at my request, let this be it. If you love me, spare no pains to ensure that Flavius thanks both you and me as heartily as may be. I could not ask anything of you more urgently.

What you write about Hermia has really vexed me a lot. I had written you a not very brotherly letter—I was annoyed by what Lucullus' freedman Diodotus said, and wrote in some irritation immediately after hearing about the agreement.[9] I wanted to recall it. This unbrotherly letter you must like a good brother forgive.

As for Censorinus, Antonius, the Cassii, and Scaevola, I am very pleased to hear that they are so friendly to you.[10] The remainder of your letter took a graver tone than I could have wished: 'I'll go down with my flag flying,'[11]

[11] The Greek saying partially quoted means: Know, Poseidon, that the ship when I sink her will be on an even keel.

θανεῖν.' maiora ista erant.[16] meae obiurgationes fuerunt amoris plenissimae. †quae† sunt[17] non nulla, sed tamen mediocria et parva potius. ego te numquam ulla in re dignum minima reprehensione putassem, cum te sanctissime gereres, nisi inimicos multos haberemus. quae ad te aliqua ‹cum[18] ad›monitione[19] aut obiurgatione scripsi, scripsi propter diligentiam cautionis meae, in qua et maneo et manebo et idem ut facias non desistam rogare.

14 Attalus Hypaepenus[20] mecum egit ut se ne impedires quo minus quod ad Q. Publici statuam[21] decretum est erogaretur. quod ego te et rogo et admoneo, ne talis viri tamque nostri necessari honorem minui per te aut impediri velis. praeterea Aesopi, nostri [tragoedi][22] familiaris, Licinus[23] servus tibi notus aufugit. is Athenis apud Patronem Epicureum pro libero fuit, inde in Asiam venit. postea Plato quidam Sardianus, Epicureus, qui Athenis solet esse multum et qui tum Athenis fuerat cum Licinus eo venisset [et],[24] cum eum fugitivum esse postea ex Aesopi litteris cognosset, hominem comprehendit et in custodiam Ephesi tradidit; sed in publicamne[25] an in pistrinum, non satis ex litteris eius intellegere potuimus. tu, quoquo modo est, quoniam Ephesi est, hominem investiges velim summaque diligentia vel ‹Romam mittas vel›[26] tecum deducas. noli spectare quanti homo sit. parvi enim preti est qui

16 erunt (*Tunstall*: *del. Wes.*)
17 questus sum *Wes.*: quae ‹questus sum,› sunt *coni. SB*
18 (*Or.*: *post* te *Lamb.*) 19 (ς)
20 hyphemenus *vel sim.* (*Or.*)
21 publiceni st- *vel* publice inst- (*Schütz*) 22 (*Or.*)
23 licinius *et item infra* (*Torrentius*) 24 (*Man.*)
25 publicam vel (*Lamb.*) 26 (*Wes.*)

and 'better die once.'[12] That was surely overdoing it. My scoldings were full of affection. There *are* some things that I complained of, but of no vast consequence, quite small in fact. Behaving as uprightly as you do, I should never have thought you deserving of the slightest criticism if we did not have many enemies. What I wrote to you in a somewhat warning or reproving strain was written out of the care I take to be always on guard. That I maintain and shall continue to do so and to ask you to do the same.

Attalus of Hypaepa has been talking to me. He wants you not to stand in the way of his arranging payment of the money decreed for a statue of Q. Publicius. I request accordingly, and would advise you not to wish to be responsible for whittling down or obstructing an honour to so worthy a man and so good a friend of ours. Furthermore, a slave called Licinus (you know him) belonging to our friend Aesopus has run away. He was in Athens with Patro the Epicurean posing as a free man, and passed from there to Asia. Later, one Plato of Sardis, an Epicurean, who is a good deal in Athens and was there when Licinus arrived, having later learned from a letter of Aesopus' that he is a runaway, arrested him and gave him into custody in Ephesus; but from his letter we are not sure whether the fellow was put into gaol or into the mill. However that may be, he is in Ephesus, so will you please search for him and take good care either to send him to Rome or to bring him with you? Don't consider what he's worth—such a good-

12 From Aeschylus (?), *Prometheus Bound* 750: 'Better die once for all than be miserable all one's days.'

tam nihil‹i›[27] sit. sed tanto dolore Aesopus est adfectus propter servi scelus et audaciam ut nihil ei gratius facere possis quam si illum per te reciperarit.

15 Nunc ea cognosce quae maxime exoptas. rem publicam funditus amisimus, adeo ut ‹C.›[28] Cato, adulescens nullius consili sed tamen civis Romanus et Cato, vix vivus effugerit quod, cum Gabinium de ambitu vellet postulare neque praetores diebus aliquot adiri possent vel potestatem sui facerent, in contionem ascendit et Pompeium 'privatum dictatorem' appellavit. propius nihil est factum quam ut occideretur. ex hoc qui sit status totius rei publicae videre potes.

16 Nostrae tamen causae non videntur homines defuturi. mirandum in modum profitentur, offerunt se, pollicentur. equidem cum spe sum maxima tum maiore etiam animo: spe, ut[29] superiores fore nos confidam;[30] animo, ut in hac re publica ne casum quidem ullum pertimescam.[31] sed tamen se res sic habet: si diem nobis dixerit, tota Italia concurret, ut multiplicata gloria discedamus; sin autem vi agere conabitur, spero fore studiis non solum amicorum sed etiam alienorum ut vi resistamus. omnes et se et suos amicos, clientis, libertos, servos, pecunias denique suas pollicentur. nostra antiqua manus bonorum ardet [et][32] studio nostri atque amore. si qui antea aut alieniores fuerant aut languidiores, nunc horum regum odio se cum bonis coniungunt. Pompeius omnia pollicetur et Caesar; quibus ego ita credo ut nihil de mea comparatione deminuam. tribuni pl. designati sunt nobis amici, consules se

[27] iam nihil (*Man.*) [28] (*Or.*)
[29] sperent (*A. Klotz*) [30] confidant (*R. Klotz*)
[31] -escant [32] (*Man.*)

for-nothing can't be worth much. But Aesopus is so distressed by the slave's criminal audacity that you can do him no greater favour than by getting him back his property.

Now let me tell you what you are most eager to know. Our free constitution is a total loss, so much so that C. Cato, a young harum-scarum but a Roman citizen and a Cato, had a narrow escape with his life when he addressed a public meeting and called Pompey 'our unofficial Dictator.' He wanted to charge Gabinius with bribery and for several days the Praetors would not let themselves be approached or give him a hearing. It was really touch and go with him. You can see from this what the state of the whole commonwealth is like.

As for my own prospects, however, I do not think I shall lack general support. It is amazing how people are coming forward with declarations and offers and promises. For my own part, I am in good hope and even better courage: hope, because I am confident I shall win; courage, because in the present state of the commonwealth I am not afraid of anything, even an accident. Anyway, this is how things stand: if Clodius takes me to court, all Italy will rally and I shall come out of it with much additional kudos; if he tries force, I trust to oppose him with force, supported not only by my friends but by outsiders as well. Everyone is pledging himself and his friends, dependents, freedmen, slaves, even money. My old band of honest men is passionately enthusiastic and loyal. Those who were formerly not so well disposed or not so energetic are now joining the honest men out of disgust with our present tyrants. Pompey is lavish with promises, and so is Caesar. If I take their word, I do not on that account relax my preparations in the slightest. The Tribunes-Elect are my good friends. The

optime ostendunt, praetores habemus amicissimos et acerrimos[33] civis, Domitium, Nigidium, Memmium, Lentulum; bonos etiam alios, sed hos singularis. qua re magnum animum fac habeas et spem bonam. de singulis tamen rebus quae cottidie gerentur[34] faciam te crebro certiorem.

3 (I.3)

Scr. Thessalonica Id. Iun. an. 58

MARCUS QUINTO FRATRI SALUTEM

1 Mi frater, mi frater, mi frater, tune id veritus es ne ego iracundia aliqua adductus pueros ad te sine litteris miserim aut etiam ne te videre noluerim? ego tibi irascerer? tibi ego possem irasci? scilicet; tu enim me adflixisti, tui me inimici, tua me invidia ac non ego te misere perdidi. meus ille laudatus consulatus mihi te, liberos, patriam, fortunas, tibi velim ne quid eripuerit praeter unum me. sed certe a te mihi omnia semper honesta et iucunda ceciderunt, a me tibi luctus meae calamitatis, metus tuae, desiderium, maeror, solitudo. ego te videre noluerim? immo vero me a te videri nolui. non enim vidisses fratrem tuum, non eum quem reliqueras, non eum quem noras, non eum quem flens flentem, prosequentem proficiscens dimiseras, ne vestigium quidem eius nec simulacrum sed quandam effigiem spirantis mortui.

[33] acerbissimos [34] gerantur (*SB*)

---

[13] I.e. Consuls-Elect, L. Calpurnius Piso and A. Gabinius. The signs turned out to be delusive.

Consuls[13] show every sign of good will. Among the Praetors I can count on Domitius, Nigidius, Memmius, and Lentulus[14] as warm friends and vigorous patriots—others too are good enough, but these are outstanding. Courage then and good cheer! On particulars, I shall send you frequent news of what goes on from day to day.

3 (I.3)

Thessalonica, 13 June 58

From Marcus to his brother Quintus greetings.

My brother, my brother, my brother! Were you really afraid that I was angry with you for some reason and on that account sent boys to you without a letter, or even did not want to see you?[1] *I* angry with *you*? How could I be? As though it was *you* who struck me down, *your* enemies, *your* unpopularity, and not *I* who have lamentably caused *your* downfall! That much-lauded Consulship of mine has robbed me of you, and my children, and my country, and my possessions; I only hope it has robbed you of nothing but myself. Sure it is that you have never given me cause for anything but pride and pleasure, whereas I have brought you sorrow for my calamity, fear of your own, loss, grief, loneliness. *I* not want to see *you*? No, it was rather that I did not want to be seen by you! You would not have seen your brother, the man you left in Rome, the man you knew, the man who saw you off and said good-bye with mutual tears—you would not have seen any trace or shadow of *him*; only the likeness of a breathing corpse.

14 L. Cornelius Lentulus Crus. Praetors = Praetors-Elect.

1 Cf. *Letters to Atticus* 54 (III.9).1.

Atque utinam me mortuum prius vidisses aut audisses,
utinam te non solum vitae sed etiam dignitatis meae super-
2 stitem reliquissem! sed testor omnis deos me hac una voce
a morte esse revocatum, quod omnes in mea vita partem
aliquam tuae vitae repositam esse dicebant. qua in re pec-
cavi scelerateque feci. nam si occidissem, mors ipsa meam
pietatem amoremque in te facile defenderet: nunc com-
misi ut vivo me careres, vivo me aliis indigeres, mea vox in
domesticis periculis potissimum occideret, quae saepe
alienissimis praesidio fuisset.

Nam quod ad te pueri sine litteris venerunt, quoniam
vides non fuisse iracundiam[1] in causa,[2] certe pigritia fuit et
3 quaedam infinita vis lacrimarum et dolorum. haec ipsa me
quo fletu putas scripsisse? eodem quo te legere certo scio.
an ego possum aut non cogitare aliquando de te aut umquam sine lacrimis cogitare? cum enim te desidero, fratrem solum desidero? ego vero suavitate [prope] fratrem,
‹aetate›[3] prope aequalem, obsequio filium, consilio parentem. quid mihi sine te umquam aut tibi sine me iucundum fuit? quid quod eodem tempore desidero filiam? qua
pietate, qua modestia, quo ingenio! effigiem oris, sermonis, animi mei. quid ‹quod›[4] filium venustissimum mihique dulcissimum? quem ego ferus ac ferreus e complexu
dimisi meo, sapientiorem puerum quam vellem; sentiebat
enim miser iam quid ageretur. quid vero ‹quod›[5] tuum

1 -diae (*Lamb.**)
2 causam (*Lamb. marg.** (*om.* in))
3 (*Lamb.*)
4 (*Lamb. marg.*)
5 (*coni. Watt*)

Would that you had seen me or heard of me dead before this happened! Would that I had left you as the survivor not of my life only but of my standing! But I call all the gods to witness that one saying called me back from death: everyone told me that some part of your life was bound up in mine. I was wrong, criminally wrong. If I had died, my death itself would easily defend my brotherly love for you.[2] Instead, through my fault you have to do without me and stand in need of others while I am alive, and my voice, which has often defended strangers, is silent when my own flesh and blood is in danger.[3]

As for the fact that my boys came to you without a letter, since you see that anger was not the reason, the reason was surely inertia and an endless stream of tears and grieving. You can imagine how I weep as I write these lines, as I am sure you do as you read them. Can I put you out of my mind sometimes, or ever think of you without tears? When I miss you, I do not miss you as a brother only, but as a delightful brother almost of my own age,[4] a son in deference, a father in wisdom. What pleasure did I ever take apart from you or you apart from me? And then at the same time I miss my daughter, the most loving, modest, and clever daughter a man ever had, the image of my face and speech and mind.[5] Likewise my charming, darling little boy, whom I, cruel brute that I am, put away from my arms. Too wise for his years, the poor child already understood what was

[2] A dead Cicero could not be blamed for failing his brother in need. [3] Quintus had reason to fear that a charge might be brought against him relative to his record as governor.

[4] Text doubtful.

[5] Cicero's family had remained in Rome.

filium, [quid][6] imaginem tuam,[7] quem meus Cicero et amabat ut fratrem et iam ut maiorem fratrem verebatur? quid quod mulierem miserrimam, fidelissimam coniugem, me prosequi non sum passus, ut esset quae reliquias communis calamitatis, communis liberos tueretur?

4 Sed tamen, quoquo modo potui, scripsi et dedi litteras ad te Philogono, liberto tuo, quas credo tibi postea redditas esse; in quibus idem te hortor et rogo quod pueri tibi verbis meis nuntiarunt, ut Romam protinus pergas et properes. primum enim te ‹in›[8] praesidio esse volui, si qui essent inimici quorum crudelitas nondum esset nostra calamitate satiata; deinde congressus nostri lamentationem pertimui, digressum vero non tulissem atque etiam id ipsum quod tu scribis metuebam, ne a me distrahi non posses. his de causis hoc maximum malum quod te non vidi, quo nihil amantissimis et coniunctissimis fratribus acerbius ac miserius videtur accidere potuisse, minus acerbum, minus miserum fuit quam fuisset cum congressio tum vero digressio nostra.

5 Nunc, si potes, id quod ego qui tibi semper fortis videbar non possum, erige te et confirma, si qua subeunda dimicatio erit. spero, si quid mea spes habet auctoritatis, tibi et integritatem tuam et amorem in te civitatis et aliquid etiam misericordiam nostri praesidi laturum. sin eris ab isto periculo vacuus, ages scilicet si quid agere posse de nobis putabis. de quo scribunt ad me quidem multi multa et se sperare demonstrant. sed ego quid sperem non dis-

6 (*Schütz*)
7 meam (*Man.*)
8 (*Madvig*)

going on. Likewise your son, your image, whom my boy loved like a brother and had begun to respect like an elder brother. As for my loyalest of wives, poor, unhappy soul, I did not let her come with me so that there should be someone to protect the remnants of our common disaster, the children we have in common.

However, I did write to you as best I could and gave the letter to your freedman Philogonus. I expect it was delivered to you later. In it I urge and ask of you, as in the verbal message brought you by my boys, to go straight on to Rome and make haste. To begin with, I wanted you to stand guard in case there may be enemies whose cruelty is not yet satisfied by our downfall. Secondly, I was afraid of the outburst of grief which our meeting would have brought on. As for parting, I could not have borne it, and I feared the very thing you say in your letter, that you might not endure to be separated from me. For these reasons the heavy affliction of not seeing you, which seems the bitterest, saddest thing that could happen to brothers so affectionate and close as we are, was less bitter and sad than our meeting would have been, and still more our parting.

Now if you can do what I, whom you always thought a strong man, am unable to do, then stand up and brace yourself for the struggle you may have to sustain. I should hope (if any hope of mine counts for anything) that your integrity, the affection in which you are held in the community, and in some degree also the pity felt for myself will bring you protection. If, however, it turns out that you are clear of that danger, you will doubtless do what you think can be done, if anything, about me. I get many letters from many people on the subject and they make themselves out to be hopeful. But for my own part I can't see any grounds

picio, cum inimici plurimum valeant, amici partim deseruerint me, partim etiam prodiderint; qui in meo reditu fortasse reprehensionem sui sceleris pertimescunt. sed ista qualia sint tu velim perspicias mihique declares. ego tamen, quam diu tibi opus erit, si quid periculi subeundum videbis, vivam; diutius in hac vita esse non possum. neque enim tantum virium habet ulla aut prudentia aut doctrina
6 ut tantum dolorem possit sustinere. scio fuisse et honestius moriendi tempus et utilius. sed non hoc solum, multa alia praetermisi; quae si queri velim praeterita, nihil agam nisi ut augeam dolorem tuum, indicem stultitiam meam. illud quidem nec faciendum est nec fieri potest, me diutius quam aut tuum tempus aut firma spes postulabit in tam misera tamque turpi vita commorari, ut, qui modo fratre fuerim, liberis, coniuge, copiis, genere ipso pecuniae beatissimus, dignitate, auctoritate, existimatione, gratia non inferior quam qui umquam fuerunt amplissimi, is nunc in hac tam adflicta perditaque fortuna neque me neque meos lugere diutius possim.

7 Qua re quid ad me scripsisti de permutatione? quasi vero nunc me non tuae facultates sustineant; qua in re ipsa video miser et sentio quid sceleris admiserim, cum de visceribus tuis et fili tui satis facturus sis quibus debes, ego acceptam ex aerario pecuniam tuo nomine frustra dissiparim. sed tamen et M. Antonio quantum tu scripseras ‹et›[9]

[9] (*Lamb.*)

[6] Apart from his inherited fortune this was mainly derived from legacies left by grateful clients.

[7] Quintus will have offered to negotiate a bill in Rome, the money to be paid to his brother in Thessalonica.

for hope, when my enemies are in power and my friends have either deserted or actually betrayed me. Perhaps the idea of my coming home frightens them as involving blame for their own villainy. But please see how things stand in Rome and make them clear to me. In spite of all, I shall go on living as long as you need me, if you have to go through an ordeal. Live any longer in this kind of life I cannot. No worldly wisdom or philosophic instruction is strong enough to endure such anguish. I know I had the opportunity to die a more honourable and useful death, but that is only one of many chances I let slip. If I were to bewail past mistakes, I should only be adding to your sorrow and exposing my own folly. One thing I ought not and cannot do, and that is to linger on in so miserable and dishonourable an existence any longer than your predicament or a well-grounded hope shall demand. Once I was happy indeed, in my brother, children, wife, means, even in the very nature of my wealth,[6] the equal of any man that ever lived in prestige, moral standing, reputation, influence. Now in my abject ruin I cannot bear to mourn myself and mine much longer.

Why then did you write to me about a bill of exchange?[7] As though your resources were not supporting me at present. Ah, how well I see and feel what a wicked thing I did! You are about to pay your creditors with your heart's blood and your son's, while I squandered to no purpose the money that I received from the Treasury on your behalf.[8] However, both M. Antonius and Caepio[9] were paid the

[8] Cf. *Letters to Atticus* 26 (II.6).2, 36 (II.16).4. How the money was squandered is uncertain.

[9] Better known as M. Brutus.

Caepioni tantundem solutum est. mihi ad id quod cogito hoc quod habeo satis est. sive enim restituimur sive desperamur, nihil amplius opus est.

Tu, si forte quid erit molestiae, te ad Crassum et ad Ca-
8 lidium conferas censeo. quantum Hortensio credendum sit nescio. me summa simulatione amoris summaque adsiduitate cottidiana sceleratissime insidiosissimeque tractavit adiuncto Q.[10] Arrio. quorum ego consiliis, promissis, praeceptis destitutus in hanc calamitatem incidi. sed haec
9 occultabis, ne quid obsint; illud caveto (et eo puto per Pomponium fovendum tibi esse ipsum Hortensium), ne ille versus, qui in te erat collatus cum aedilitatem petebas, de lege Aurelia, falso testimonio confirmetur. nihil enim tam timeo quam ne, cum intellegent[11] homines quantum misericordiae nobis tuae preces et tua salus adlatura sit, oppugnent te vehementius. Messallam tui studiosum esse arbitror. Pompeium etiam simulatorem puto. sed haec utinam ⟨ne⟩[12] experiare! quod precarer deos nisi meas preces audire desissent. verum tamen precor ut his infinitis nostris malis contenti sint, in quibus non modo tamen nullius inest peccati infamia sed omnis dolor est quod optime factis poena maxima est constituta.

10 quoque (*Lamb. marg.*)
11 -gant (*coni. SB**)
12 (*Baiter*)

---

10 In 66.

11 It can be supposed that the epigram was offensive to Pompey and Crassus, since the lex Aurelia of 70, revising the Roman jury system, was passed in their Consulship with their support. Cicero seems to have been afraid that Hortensius might con-

sums you had mentioned. As for me, what I have is enough for my present purposes. Whether I am restored or given up for lost, no more is needed.

If you have any trouble, I advise you to go to Crassus and Calidius. How much faith you should put in Hortensius I don't know. He behaved to *me* most villainously and treacherously, while pretending the warmest affection and sedulously keeping up our daily intercourse. Q. Arrius joined him in this. Through their policies and promises and advice I was left in the lurch and fell into my present plight. But you will keep all this under cover, lest it tell against you. Be careful of one thing (and for that reason I think you should conciliate Hortensius himself through Pomponius): that epigram about the lex Aurelia which was attributed to you when you were standing for the Aedileship,[10] mind it doesn't get established by false evidence.[11] My principal fear is that when people realize how much pity your entreaties and your escape from a prosecution is going to arouse for us, they will attack you the more vigorously. I think Messalla[12] is on your side. Pompey, I think, is still pretending. If only you don't have to put all this to the test! I should pray to the gods for that if they had not given up listening to my prayers. None the less, I do pray that they may be content with these boundless afflictions of ours, which, however, are free from any stigma of wrongdoing. The whole tragedy is that fine actions have been cruelly penalized.

firm Quintus' authorship out of spite. As an opponent of the law he would be a credible witness.

[12] The Consul of 61, as generally supposed. Perhaps more probably, Hortensius' nephew, Messalla Rufus, Consul in 53.

10 Filiam meam et tuam Ciceronemque nostrum quid ego, mi frater, tibi commendem? quin illud maereo quod tibi non minorem dolorem illorum orbitas adferet quam mihi. sed te incolumi orbi non erunt. reliqua ita mihi salus aliqua detur potestasque in patria moriendi ut me lacrimae non sinunt scribere! etiam Terentiam velim tueare mihique de omnibus rebus rescribas, sis fortis quoad rei natura patiatur.

Id. Iun. Thessalonicae.

4 (I.4)

Scr. Thessalonicae c. Non. Sext. an. 58

MARCUS QUINTO FRATRI SALUTEM

1 Amabo te, mi frater, ne,[1] si uno meo facto et tu et omnes mei corruistis, improbitati et sceleri meo potius quam imprudentiae miseriaeque adsignes. nullum est meum peccatum nisi quod iis credidi a quibus nefas putarem esse me decipi aut etiam quibus ne id expedire quidem arbitrabar. intimus, proximus, familiarissimus quisque aut sibi pertimuit aut mihi invidit. ita mihi nihil misero praeter fidem amicorum, cautum meum consilium, <de>fuit.[2]

2 Quod si te satis innocentia tua et misericordia hominum vindicat hoc tempore a molestia, perspicis profecto ecquaenam nobis spes salutis relinquatur. nam me Pomponius et Sestius et Piso noster adhuc Thessalonicae retinuerunt, cum longius discedere propter nescio quos motus

[1] nisi (*Brunus*)
[2] (*Malaespina*)

My brother, I need not commend my daughter (and yours) and our Marcus to your care. On the contrary, I grieve to think that their orphaned state will bring you no less sorrow than me. But while you are safe, they will not be orphans. I swear that tears forbid me to write of other things—so may I be granted some salvation and the power to die in my country! Please look after Terentia too, and write back to me on all matters. Be as brave as the nature of the case permits.

Ides of June, Thessalonica.

4 (I.4)

Thessalonica, ca. 5 August 58

From Marcus to his brother Quintus greetings.

Dear brother, if a single act of mine has brought you and all my family low, I beg you not to attribute this to wickedness and evildoing on my part but rather to imprudence and ill fortune. My only fault lay in trusting men in whom I thought it would be an abomination to deceive me or even imagined that it was not in their interest to do so. My closest, most intimate, most familiar friends were either afraid for themselves or jealous of me. So I lacked nothing, unfortunate that I was, except good faith on my friends' part and good judgement on my own.

If your own innocence and public compassion prove sufficient to protect you from annoyance at this time, you doubtless perceive whether any hope of deliverance is left for me. Pomponius, Sestius, and our Piso have kept me in Thessalonica so far, telling me not to move further away on account of certain developments. But it is because of their

vetarent. verum[3] ego magis exitum illorum litteris quam spe certa exspectabam. nam quid sperem potentissimo inimico, dominatione obtrectatorum, infidelibus amicis, plu-
3 rimis invidis? de novis autem tribunis pl. est ille quidem in me officiosissimus Sestius et (spero) Curtius, Milo, Fadius, Atilius,[4] sed valde adversante Clodio, qui etiam privatus eadem manu poterit contiones concitare. deinde etiam intercessor parabitur.

4 Haec mihi proficiscenti non proponebantur, sed saepe triduo summa cum gloria dicebar esse rediturus. 'quid tu igitur?' inquies. quid? multa convenerunt quae mentem exturbarent meam: subita defectio Pompei, alienatio consulum, etiam praetorum, timor publicanorum, ‹servorum›[5] arma. lacrimae meorum me ad mortem ire prohibuerunt, quod certe et ad honestatem ‹tuendam›[6] et ad effugiendos intolerabilis dolores fuit aptissimum. sed de hoc scripsi ad te in ea epistula quam Phaëthonti dedi.

5 Nunc tu, quoniam in tantum luctum ‹et› laborem detrusus es quantum nemo umquam [a], si levare potest communem causam misericordia hominum, scilicet incredibile quiddam adsequeris; sin plane occidimus, me miserum! ego omnibus meis exitio fuero, quibus ante dedecori non eram.

Sed tu, ut ante ad te scripsi, perspice rem et pertempta

[3] quorum *coni. Watt*
[4] gratidius (*SB*)
[5] (*SB*) [6] (*SB*)

---

[1] Clodius.

[2] I.e Sex. Atilius Serranus Gavianus, originally friendly to Cicero, though in office he joined Clodius. Hence I read *Atilius*

letters rather than from any definite hope that I am waiting for the outcome. What am I to hope for, with my enemy[1] wielding great power, my detractors ruling the state, my friends unfaithful, so many jealous of me? As for the new Tribunes, certainly Sestius is most anxious to help me and so, I hope, are Curtius, Milo, Fadius, and Atilius.[2] But Clodius is in strong opposition, and even after he goes out of office he will be able to stir up public meetings with the same gang. And someone will be found to cast a veto.

That is not the prospect that was painted to me when I left Rome. I was often told that I could expect a glorious return within three days. You will ask what I thought myself. Well, a combination of factors upset the balance of my mind: Pompey's sudden desertion, the unfriendly attitude of the Consuls, and even the Praetors, the timidity of the tax farmers, the weapons of slaves (?). The tears of my family and friends forbade me to go to my death, which would certainly have been the most honourable course and the best way of protecting my good name and escaping intolerable distresses. But I wrote to you on the subject in the letter I gave to Phaëtho.

As matters stand, if public compassion can alleviate our common plight, yours will doubtless be an incredible achievement, thrust down as you are into an abyss of mourning and trouble the like of which no man has ever known. But if we are really lost, oh, the misery of it! I shall have been the ruin of all my family, to whom in time gone by I was no discredit.

But, as I wrote to you earlier, view the situation thor-

for *Gratidius* (there was no Tribune of that name in 57). Some editors read *Fabricius*.

et ad me, ut tempora nostra non ut amor tuus fert, vere perscribe. ego vitam, quoad aut putabo tua interesse aut ad spem servandam esse, retinebo. tu nobis amicissimum Sestium cognosces. credo tua causa velle Lentulum, qui erit consul, quamquam sunt facta verbis difficiliora. tu et quid opus sit[7] et quid sit videbis.

Omnino si tuam solitudinem communemque calamitatem nemo despexerit, aut per te aliquid confici aut nullo modo poterit; sin te quoque inimici vexare coeperint, ne cessaris. non enim gladiis tecum[8] sed litibus agetur. verum haec absint velim. te oro ut ad me de omnibus ‹rebus›[9] rescribas et in me animi aut potius[10] consili minus putes esse quam antea, amoris vero et offici non minus.

5 (II.1)

Scr. Romae paulo ante XVI *Kal. Ian. an. 57*

MARCUS QUINTO FRATRI SALUTEM

1 Epistulam quam legisti mane dederam; sed fecit humaniter Licinius[1] quod ad me misso senatu vesperi venit, ut si quid esset actum ad te, si mihi videretur, perscriberem.

Senatus fuit frequentior quam putabamus esse posse mense Decembri sub dies festos. consulares nos fuimus et duo consules designati, P. Servilius, M. Lucullus, Lepidus, Volcacius, Glabrio; praetorii sane frequentes. fuimus om-

[7] quid possit *coni. Watt* [8] mecum (*Man.*)
[9] (*Or.*) [10] potius aut (*Gul.*)
[1] Licinus *coni. SB*

---

[1] Perhaps Licinus, a letter-carrying slave or freedman.

oughly, take your soundings, and write me the truth; that is what our situation, though not your affection, requires. I shall hold on to life as long as I think that it is in your interest for me to do so or that it should be preserved in hope of better things. You will find Sestius very friendly to us. I think Lentulus, who will be Consul, wishes you well. But actions are not so easy as words. You will see what is needed and how things are.

If nobody scorns your loneliness and our common calamity, something will be achievable through you or not at all. But if our enemies start persecuting you too, don't take it lying down. In your case the weapons will be lawsuits, not swords. But I hope there will be none of that. I beg you to write back to me on all matters and to believe that, however much I may have lost in spirit, or rather in judgement, my affection and family feeling remain the same.

5 (II.1)

Rome, shortly before 15 December 57

From Marcus to his brother Quintus greetings.

I dispatched a letter this morning which you will have already read. But Licinius[1] was kind enough to call on me this evening after the Senate had risen to give me the opportunity of writing to you an account of the day's proceedings.

The House met in larger numbers than I thought possible in December just before the holiday. Of the Consulars, there were, besides myself and the two Consuls-Elect, P. Servilius, M. Lucullus, Lepidus, Volcacius, Glabrio. The ex-Praetors were in good force. In all we were about 200.

nino ad CC. commorat exspectationem Lupus; egit causam agri Campani sane accurate, auditus est magno silentio. materiam rei non ignoras. nihil ex nostris actionibus praetermisit; fuerunt non nulli aculei in Caesarem, contumeliae in Gellium, expostulationes cum absente Pompeio. causa sero perorata sententias se rogaturum negavit, ne quod onus simultatis nobis imponeret; ex superiorum temporum conviciis et ex praesenti silentio quid senatus sentiret se intellegere dixit. senatum[2] || coepit dimittere. tum Marcellinus 'noli' inquit 'ex taciturnitate nostra, Lupe, quid aut probemus hoc tempore aut improbemus iudicare. ego, quod ad me attinet, itemque arbitror ceteros, idcirco taceo quod non existimo, cum Pompeius absit, causam agri Campani agi convenire.' tum ille se senatum negavit tenere.

2 Racilius surrexit et de iudiciis referre coepit; Marcellinum quidem primum rogavit. is cum graviter de Clodianis incendiis, trucidationibus, lapidationibus questus esset, sententiam dixit ut ipse iudices [per] praetor urbanus[3] sortiretur, iudicum sortitione facta comitia haberentur; qui iudicia impedisset, eum contra rem publicam esse facturum. approbata valde sententia C. Cato contra dixit et Cassius[4] maxima acclamatione senatus, cum comitia iudiciis

[2] senatus (*Watt, quem de foliorum in archetypo permutatione vide*) [3] per praetorem urbanum (*Man.*)
[4] Caninius *coni. SB*

---

[2] Lupus, who had just come into office as Tribune, later figures as an adherent of Pompey. Hence probably the interest in his speech.

Lupus'[2] speech was awaited with interest. He dealt with the Campanian Land question very fully, to an extremely attentive House. You know the material. He covered all my own contributions. There were some barbs to Caesar's address, some insults to Gellius', some complaints to Pompey's—who was not present. It was getting late when he wound up, and he said he would not ask for a debate since he did not wish to put any pressure on us to make ourselves enemies. The high words of days gone by and the present silence told him the feeling of the House. He began to dismiss the meeting. Marcellinus observed: 'I must ask you, sir, not to draw any conclusions as to what we now approve or disapprove of from the fact that we have nothing to say. So far as I myself am concerned, and I imagine the same applies to the rest of the House, I am holding my peace because I do not think the question of the Campanian Land can properly be handled in Pompey's absence.' Lupus then said that he would not detain the House.

Racilius then rose and laid the question of the trials before the House, calling on Marcellinus to open the debate. After a powerful indictment of Clodius' arsons, killings, and stonings he proposed that the City Praetor should personally appoint a jury by lot, and that when this process was complete elections should be held; any person obstructing the trials to be regarded as acting contrary to public order. This proposal was warmly approved. C. Cato spoke against it, as did Cassius,[3] amid loud cries of protest

[3] Unknown. Possibly read *Caninius*. As Tribunes the two will have spoken later in the debate. See critical notes.

3 anteferre<n>t.[5] Philippus adsensit Lentulo. postea Racilius de privatis me primum sententiam rogavit. multa feci verba de toto furore latrocinioque P. Clodi. tamquam reum accusavi multis et secundis admurmurationibus cuncti senatus. orationem meam collaudavit satis multis verbis non mehercule indiserte Vetus[6] Antistius, isque iudiciorum causam suscepit antiquissimamque se habiturum dixit. ibatur in eam sententiam. tum Clodius rogatus diem dicendo eximere coepit. furebat a Racilio se contumaciter urbaneque vexatum. deinde eius operae repente a Graecostasi et gradibus clamorem satis magnum sustulerunt, opinor, in Q. Sextilium[7] et amicos Milonis incitatae. eo metu iniecto repente magna querimonia omnium discessimus.

Habes acta unius diei; reliqua, ut arbitror, in mensem Ianuarium reicientur. de tribunis pl. longe optimum Racilium habemus; videtur etiam Antistius amicus nobis fore. nam Plancius totus noster est.

Fac, si me amas, ut considerate diligenterque naviges de mense Decembri.

[5] (*Or.*). C. Cato . . . anteferrent *melius puto infra fort. post* dixit *ponenda*

[6] severus (*Anton. Augustinus*)

[7] Sestullium *coni. SB* (*cf. comm.*)

when they put the elections before the trials. Philippus concurred with Lentulus. Then Racilius called upon me first of the private members. I spoke at length on the whole issue of P. Clodius' sedition and banditry, arraigning him like a man in the dock with frequent murmurs of approval from the whole House. Vetus Antistius[4] praised my speech at some length—his was not at all a bad performance. He also took up the question of the trials and said that he would regard it as of primary importance. A vote to that effect was about to take place, when Clodius was called and proceeded to talk out the motion. Racilius' insulting and witty attack had infuriated him. Then his roughs suddenly set up quite a formidable shouting from Ambassadors' Lodge[5] and the steps. I believe they had been stirred up against Q. Sextilius and Milo's friends. On that alarm we broke up in haste, amid loud and general protest.

There you have one day's proceedings. The sequel, I suppose, will be deferred till January. Racilius is much the best of the Tribunes, but I think Antistius too will be friendly to us. Plancius, of course, is completely devoted.

If you love me, be sure to be cautious and careful about putting to sea in December.[6]

[4] Another Tribune, L. Antistius Vetus, to be distinguished from C. Antistius Vetus of *Letters to Atticus* 363 (XIV.9).3, as established by E. Badian.

[5] Graecostasis, a platform from which envoys listened to senatorial debates.

[6] Quintus was going to Sardinia as Legate to Pompey, now in supreme charge of grain supplies.

6 (II.2)

Scr. Romae XIV *Kal. Febr. an. 56*

MARCUS QUINTO FRATRI SALUTEM

1 Non occupatione, qua eram sane impeditus, sed parvula lippitudine adductus sum ut dictarem hanc epistulam et non, ut ad te soleo, ipse scriberem.

Et primum me tibi excuso in eo ipso in quo te accuso. me enim nemo adhuc rogavit num quid in Sardiniam velim, te puto saepe habere qui num quid Romam velis quaerant.

Quod ad me <de>[1] Lentuli et Sesti nomine scripsisti, locutus sum cum Cincio. quo modo res se habet, non est facillima. sed habet profecto quiddam Sardinia appositum ad recordationem praeteritae memoriae. nam ut ille Gracchus augur, postea quam in istam provinciam venit, recordatus est quid sibi in campo Martio comitia consulum habenti[2] contra auspicia accidisset, sic tu mihi videris in Sardinia de forma Numisiana et de nominibus Pomponianis in otio recogitasse. sed ego adhuc emi nihil. Culleonis auctio facta est; Tusculano emptor nemo fuit. si condicio
2 valde bona fuerit, fortassis non amittam. de aedificatione tua Cyrum urgere non cesso. spero eum in officio fore. sed omnia sunt tardiora propter furiosae aedilitatis exspecta-

[1] (*Man.*) [2] consulibus habentibus (*Vict.*)

---

[1] Which Lentulus is uncertain, and we have no further information about the matter in reference. Cincius was Atticus' agent.

[2] Father of the Gracchi. Cicero tells the story in his treatise *On the Nature of the Gods* (2.10f.).

6 (II.2)

Rome, 17 January 56

From Marcus to his brother Quintus greetings.

Contrary to my habit when writing to you I am dictating this letter instead of writing it myself, not because of pressure of business (though busy I certainly am) but because I have a touch of ophthalmia.

And first I want to excuse myself and accuse you on one and the same count. Nobody has so far asked me whether I have a message for Sardinia, while I think you often have people who ask you whether you have a message for Rome.

As regards what you write to me about Lentulus'[1] and Sestius' debt, I have talked with Cincius. As the matter stands, it's not any too easy. But there must be something about Sardinia which arouses dormant memories. Just as Gracchus the Augur[2] after arriving in that province remembered what had happened to him when he held the consular elections in the Campus Martius contrary to the auspices, so you in your Sardinian leisure seem to have brought Numisius'[3] ground plan and the transactions with Pomponius back to your recollection. But so far I have bought nothing. Culleo's auction has taken place, and the property at Tusculum[4] did not find a buyer. If I can get really good terms, perhaps I shall not let it slip. I keep on urging Cyrus about your building[5] and hope he will do a good job. But everything goes slowly because of the prospect of

[3] Presumably an architect, in connection with the rebuilding of Quintus' house on the Palatine.

[4] Culleo's, not Cicero's.

[5] Cf. Letter 8 (II.4).2.

tionem. nam comitia sine mora futura videntur; edicta sunt ‹in›[3] a.d. XI Kal. Febr. te tamen sollicitum esse nolo. omne genus a nobis cautionis adhibebitur.

3 De rege Alexandrino factum est senatus consultum cum multitudine eum reduci periculosum rei publicae videri. reliqua cum esset in senatu contentio Lentulusne an Pompeius reduceret, obtinere causam Lentulus videbatur. in ea re nos et officio erga Lentulum mirifice et voluntati Pompei praeclare satis fecimus; sed per obtrectatores Lentuli calumnia extracta est. consecuti sunt dies comitiales, per quos senatus haberi non poterat. quid futurum sit latrocinio tribunorum non divino, sed tamen suspicor per vim rogationem Caninium perlaturum. in ea re Pompeius quid velit non dispicio; familiares eius quid cupiant, || omnes vident. creditores vero regis aperte pecunias suppeditant contra Lentulum. sine dubio res a Lentulo remota videtur esse cum magno meo dolore, quamquam multa fecit qua re, si fas esset, iure ei suscensere possemus.

4 Tu, si ista expedieris,[4] velim quam primum bona et certa tempestate conscendas ad meque venias. innumerabiles enim res sunt in quibus te cottidie in omni genere desiderem. tui nostrique valent.

XIIII Kal. Febr.

3 (*Wes.*) 4 *varia velut* -diri tibi (*Constans*)

6 Clodius. 7 Ptolemy XII ('the Piper'), king of Egypt.

8 Cf. *Letters to Friends* 12 (I.1).2.

9 I.e. as to how I should speak. Or perhaps 'Pompey's friendly attitude (towards me'); cf. e.g. *Letters to Brutus* 20.1 *nihil ego possum in sororis meae liberis facere quo possit expleri voluntas mea aut officium.* Not 'wishes regarding the Egyptian assignment,' since these were uncertain.

a madman[6] as Aedile. For it looks as though elections will be held without delay—they have been announced for 20 January. However, I don't want you to be anxious. I shall take all manner of precautions.

As for his Alexandrian majesty,[7] the Senate has passed a decree pronouncing it dangerous to the commonwealth for him to be restored 'with a host.'[8] That left a tussle in the Senate as to whether Lentulus or Pompey should restore him, and Lentulus appeared to be winning his point. In that affair I performed my duty to Lentulus to a marvel, at the same time meeting Pompey's wishes[9] in fine style, but the matter was dragged out by the maneuvring of Lentulus' ill-wishers. Then followed the comitial days during which the House could not meet. What will come of the Tribunes' freebooting I can't prophesy, but I suspect that Caninius will carry his bill by violence. I can't fathom Pompey's wishes in the matter; but everyone sees what his friends want, and the king's creditors are openly putting up money against Lentulus. He certainly seems to have lost the assignment, which I am very sorry for, though he has given me many good reasons to feel annoyed with him[10] if that were not against my conscience.

When you have sorted matters out over there, I hope you will board ship at the first spell of fair, settled weather and join me. There are numberless things in which I miss you, every day and in every way. Your folk and mine are well.

17 January.

10 Cicero was dissatisfied with Lentulus Spinther in respect to his indemnities; cf. *Letters to Atticus* 74 (IV.2.5).5.

7 (II.3)

Scr. Romae prid. Id. Febr. (d. xv Kal. Mart.) an. 56

MARCUS QUINTO FRATRI SALUTEM

1 Scripsi ad te antea superiora. nunc cognosce postea quae sint acta. [a][1] Kal. Febr. legationes in Id. Febr. reiciebantur; eo die res confecta non est. a. d. IIII Non. Febr. Milo adfuit. ei Pompeius advocatus venit. dixit M. Marcellus a me rogatus. honeste discessimus. prodicta[2] dies est in VII Id. Febr. interim reiectis legationibus in Idus referebatur de provinciis quaestorum et de ornandis praetoribus; sed res multis querelis de re publica interponendis nulla transacta est. C. Cato legem promulgavit de imperio Lentuli abrogando. vestitum filius mutavit.

2 A. d. VII Id. Febr. Milo adfuit. dixit Pompeius, sive voluit. nam ut surrexit, operae Clodianae clamorem sustulerunt, idque ei perpetua oratione contigit, non modo ut acclamatione sed ut convicio et maledictis impediretur. qui ut peroravit (nam in eo sane fortis fuit, non est deterritus, dixit omnia atque interdum etiam silentio, cum auctoritate pervicerat[3])—sed ut peroravit, surrexit Clodius. ei tantus clamor a nostris (placuerat enim referre gratiam) ut neque mente nec lingua neque ore consisteret. ea res acta est, cum hora sexta vix Pompeius perorasset, usque ad horam octavam, cum omnia maledicta, versus denique obscenissimi in Clodium et Clodiam dicerentur. ille furens et exsanguis interrogabat suos in clamore ipso quis esset

[1] (*Sternkopf*)
[2] producta (*Drakenborch*)
[3] peregerat (*Watt*)

7 (II.3)

Rome, 12–15 February 56

From Marcus to his brother Quintus greetings.

I gave you the earlier news in my last. Now for the sequel: On the Kalends of February there was a move to postpone the embassies to the Ides. No conclusion reached that day. On 2 February Milo appeared to stand trial with Pompey as supporting counsellor. M. Marcellus spoke (I had asked him) and we came off creditably. Case adjourned to 7 February. Meanwhile the embassies were postponed to the Ides and the House was asked to consider the Quaestors' provinces and the Praetors' establishments. But business was interrupted by numerous complaints about the state of the commonwealth and nothing done. C. Cato gave notice of a bill to relieve Lentulus of his command, and Lentulus' son put on mourning.

Milo appeared on 7 February. Pompey spoke—or rather tried to speak, for no sooner was he on his feet than Clodius' gang raised a clamour, and all through the speech he was interrupted not merely by shouting but by booing and abuse. When he wound up (and I will say he showed courage; he was not put off, delivered all he had to say, sometimes even managing to get silence by his personal authority)—well, when he wound up, Clodius rose. Wishing to repay the compliment, our side gave him such an uproarious reception that he lost command of thoughts, tongue, and countenance. That lasted till half past one, Pompey having finished just after midday—all manner of insults, ending up with some highly scabrous verse to the address of Clodius and Clodia. Pale with fury, he started a game of question and answer in the middle of the shouting:

qui plebem fame necaret: respondebant operae 'Pompeius.' quis Alexandriam ire cuperet: respondebant 'Pompeius.' quem ire vellent: respondebant 'Crassum' (is aderat tum Miloni,[4] animo non amico). hora fere nona quasi signo dato Clodiani nostros consputare coeperunt. exarsit dolor. urgere illi ut loco nos moverent. factus est a nostris impetus. fuga operarum, eiectus de rostris Clodius. ac nos quoque tum fugimus, ne quid in turba. senatus vocatus in curiam. Pompeius domum; neque ego tamen in senatum, ne aut de tantis rebus tacerem aut in Pompeio defendendo (nam is carpebatur a Bibulo, Curione, Favonio, Servilio filio) animos bonorum virorum offenderem. res in posterum dilata est. Clodius in Quirinalia prodixit diem.

3 A. d. VI Id. Febr. senatus ad Apollinis fuit, ut Pompeius adesset. acta res est graviter a Pompeio. eo die nihil perfectum est. a. d. V[5] Id. Febr. senatus ad Apollinis. senatus consultum factum est ea quae facta essent a. d. VII[6] Id. Febr. contra rem publicam esse facta. eo die Cato vehementer est in Pompeium invectus et eum oratione perpetua tamquam reum accusavit; de me multa me invito cum mea summa laude dixit, cum illius in me perfidiam increparet. auditus est magno silentio malevolorum. respondit ei vehementer Pompeius Crassumque descripsit dixitque aperte se munitiorem ad custodiendam vitam suam fore quam Africanus fuisset, quem C. Carbo interemisset.

[4] *post* tum *dist. vulg.* (*SB*)
[5] VI vel III (*Tunstall*)
[6] VI vel III (*Sjögren*)

---

[1] Outside the ancient city boundary. As holding *imperium* Pompey could come inside only by special dispensation.

'Who's starving the people to death?' 'Pompey,' answered the gang. 'Who wants to go to Alexandria?' Answer: 'Pompey.' 'Whom do you want to go?' Answer: 'Crassus' (who was present as a supporter of Milo, wishing him no good). About 2:15 the Clodians started spitting at us, as though on a signal. Sharp rise in temperature! They made a push to dislodge us, our side countercharged. Flight of gang. Clodius was hurled from the Rostra, at which point I too made off for fear of what might happen in the free-for-all. The Senate was convened in its House, and Pompey went home. I did not attend, however, not wishing to keep mum about so remarkable an incident nor yet to offend honest men by standing up for Pompey, who was under fire from Bibulus, Curio, Favonius, and Servilius junior. The debate was adjourned to the following day. Clodius had the trial postponed to Quirinus' Day.

On 8 February the Senate met in the temple of Apollo[1] in order that Pompey could be present. Pompey spoke strongly—nothing concluded that day. 9 February, Senate in temple of Apollo. A decree was passed pronouncing the doings of 7 February contrary to public interest. That day C. Cato delivered a broadside against Pompey—a set speech like a prosecuting counsel's with Pompey in the dock. He said many highly laudatory things about me, which I could have done without, denouncing Pompey's treachery towards me. He was heard in rapt silence. Pompey replied warmly, making oblique allusion to Crassus and saying plainly that he intended to take better care of his life than Africanus had done, whom C. Carbo murdered.[2]

[2] In 129. But it was never proved.

4 Itaque magnae mihi res iam moveri videbantur. nam Pompeius haec intellegit nobiscumque communicat, insidias vitae suae fieri, C. Catonem a Crasso sustentari, Clodio pecuniam suppeditari, utrumque et ab eo et a Curione, Bibulo, ceterisque suis obtrectatoribus confirmari; vehementer esse providendum ne opprimatur, contionario illo populo a se prope alienato, nobilitate inimica, non aequo senatu, iuventute improba. itaque se comparat; homines ex agris accersit. operas autem suas Clodius confirmat; manus ad Quirinalia paratur. in ea multo sumus superiores ipsius Milo<nis>[7] || copiis, sed magna manus ex Piceno et Gallia exspectatur, ut etiam Catonis rogationibus de Milone et Lentulo resistamus.

5 A. d. IIII Id. Febr. Sestius ab indice Cn. Nerio Pupinia de ambitu est postulatus et eodem die a quodam M. Tullio de vi. is erat aeger. domum, ut debuimus, ad eum statim venimus eique nos totos tradidimus idque fecimus praeter hominum opinionem, qui nos ei iure suscensere putabant, ut humanissimi gratissimique et ipsi et omnibus videremur; itaque faciemus. sed idem Nerius index edidit [ad][8] adligatos Cn. Lentulum Vatiam et C. Cornelium Stel.[9] eodem die senatus consultum factum est ut sodalitates decuriatique discederent lexque de iis ferretur, ut qui non discessissent ea poena quae est de vi tenerentur.

[7] milo (*Sternkopf*)
[8] (*Turn.*)
[9] *varia velut* staei (*SB, auct. Constans*)

---

[3] The reason is unknown; cf. Letter 8.1.
[4] Pledged to stick to their stories.

So I think big things are on the way. Pompey has information (and talks about it to me) that a plot against his life is on foot, that Crassus is backing C. Cato and supplying Clodius with funds, and that both are getting support both from Crassus and from Curio, Bibulus, and his other detractors. He says he must take very good care not to be caught napping, with the meeting-going public pretty well alienated, the nobility hostile, the Senate ill-disposed, and the younger generation ill-conditioned. So he is getting ready and bringing up men from the country. Clodius on his side is reinforcing his gang in readiness for Quirinus' Day. With the same date in view we have much the advantage even with Milo's own forces, but a large contingent is expected from Picenum and Gaul, which should further enable us to make a stand against Cato's bills concerning Milo and Lentulus.

On 10 February Sestius was charged with bribery by an informer, Cn. Nerius of the tribe Pupinia, and on the same day with breach of the peace by a certain M. Tullius. He was unwell, so, as was only proper, I called on him immediately and promised him my services without reservation. And I did this contrary to what people were expecting in the belief that I was justifiably annoyed with him.[3] So I figure in his eyes and everyone else's as an eminently forgiving and grateful character. And I shall so continue. The same informer Nerius has produced as tied witnesses[4] Cn. Lentulus Vatia and C. Cornelius of the tribe Stellatina. The same day the Senate passed a decree to the effect that the political clubs and caucuses should be dissolved and a bill put through providing that persons not complying with this ordinance be liable to the same penalty as those guilty of breach of peace.

6 A. d. iii[i][10] Id. Febr. dixi pro Bestia de ambitu apud praetorem Cn. Domitium in foro medio maximo conventu incidique in eum locum in dicendo cum Sestius multis in templo Castoris vulneribus acceptis subsidio Bestiae servatus esset. hic *προῳκοδομησάμην* quid‹d›am[11] *εὐκαίρως* de iis quae in Sestium apparabantur crimina et eum ornavi veris laudibus magno adsensu omnium. res homini fuit vehementer grata. quae tibi eo scribo quod me de retinenda Sesti gratia litteris saepe monuisti.

7 Prid. Id. Febr. haec scripsi ante lucem. eo die apud Pomponium in eius nuptiis eram cenaturus.

Cetera sunt in rebus nostris cuius[12] modi tu mihi fere diffidenti praedicabas, plena dignitatis et gratiae; quae quidem tua, mi frater, patientia, virtute, pietate, suavitate etiam tibi mihique sunt restituta.

Domus tibi ad lacum[13] Pisonis †Luciniana† conducta est; sed, ut spero, paucis mensibus post Kal. Quint. in tuam commigrabis. tuam in Carinis mundi habitatores Lamiae[14] conduxerunt.

A te post illam Ulbiensem epistulam nullas litteras accepi. quid agas et ut te oblectes scire cupio maximeque te ipsum videre quam primum.

Cura, mi frater, ut valeas et, quamquam est hiems, tamen Sardiniam istam esse cogites.

xv Kal. Mart.

10 (*Aldus*) 11 (*Vict.*) 12 huius (*Man.*)
13 lucum (*Jordan*) 14 cami(a)e (*Man.*)

---

5 To Pilia. 6 Generally read, but only one of several paleographically plausible possibilities. Piso's Pond is also unknown. 7 The climate of Sardinia was notoriously unhealthy, more so, naturally, in summer than in winter.

On 11 February I defended Bestia on a bribery charge before Praetor Cn. Domitius in mid Forum: There was a large crowd in court. In the course of my speech I came to the occasion on which Bestia saved Sestius' life when he was lying covered with wounds in the temple of Castor. I took the favourable opportunity to lay down a foundation for my defence of Sestius against the charges which are being got up against him and pronounced a well-deserved eulogy, which was received with great approval by all. Sestius was highly pleased. I tell you all this because you have often referred in your letters to the desirability of preserving good relations with him.

I am writing this before dawn on 12 February. This evening I shall be dining with Pomponius at his wedding.[5]

In the rest of my affairs it is as you foretold when I was far from hopeful—my prestige and influence flourishes. This restitution, in which we both share, is due, my dear brother, to your patience, courage, devotion, and, let me add, your personal charm.

A house (the Liciniana[6]) at Piso's Pond has been rented for you, but I hope you will be moving into your own in a few months' time, after the Kalends of July. The Lamiae have taken your house in Carinae—nice, clean tenants.

Since your letter from Olbia I have heard nothing, from you. I am anxious to know how you are and how you amuse yourself, and above all to see you as soon as possible.

Take care of your health, my dear brother, and don't forget that it's Sardinia where you are, winter time though it be.[7]

15 February.

8 (II.4)

Scr. Romae medio m. Mart. an. 56

MARCUS QUINTO FRATRI SALUTEM

1 Sestius noster absolutus est a. d. II Id. Mart. et, quod vehementer interfuit rei publicae, nullam videri in eius modi causa dissensionem esse, omnibus sententiis absolutus est. illud quod tibi curae saepe esse intellexeram, ne cui iniquo relinqueremus vituperandi locum, qui nos ingratos esse diceret nisi illius perversitatem quibusdam in rebus quam humanissime ferremus, scito hoc nos in eo iudicio consecutos esse ut omnium gratissimi iudicaremur. nam defendendo moroso homini cumulatissime satis fecimus et, id quod ille maxime cupiebat, Vatinium, a quo palam oppugnabatur, arbitratu nostro concidimus dis hominibusque plaudentibus. quin etiam Paullus noster, cum testis productus esset in Sestium, confirmavit se nomen Vatini delaturum si Macer Licinius cunctaretur, et Macer ab Sesti subselliis surrexit ac se illi non defuturum adfirmavit. quid quaeris? homo petulans et audax [Vatinius][1] valde perturbatus debilitatusque discessit.

2 Quintus, filius tuus, puer optimus, eruditur egregie. hoc nunc magis animum adverto quod Tyrannio docet apud me. domus utriusque nostrum aedificatur strenue. redemptori tuo dimidium pecuniae curavi. spero nos ante hiemem contubernalis fore. de nostra Tullia tui mehercule amantissima spero cum Crassipede nos confecisse. ‹sed›[2]

[1] (*Baiter*)
[2] (*Sternkopf*)

---

[1] In the speech *In Vatinium*.

8 (II.4)

Rome, mid March 56

From Marcus to his brother Quintus greetings.

Our friend Sestius was acquitted on 14 March, and by a unanimous vote, which was politically of great importance as showing that no difference of opinion exists in a case like this. I have often noticed your anxiety lest I gave a handle to a hostile critic who might accuse me of ingratitude if I did not put up with his cussedness in certain respects with the best of grace. Well, you may rest assured that my conduct in that trial has made me pass for a model of gratitude. By my defence I have more than discharged what was due to this peevish personage, and I cut up his overt adversary Vatinius just as I pleased to the applause of gods and men,[1] which was what he wanted more than anything. What is more, our friend Paullus, who was produced as a witness against Sestius, undertook to prosecute Vatinius if Macer Licinius[2] did not get on with the job; on which Macer rose from Sestius' benches and promised not to fail him. In short, that bullying ruffian left the court much disconcerted and unnerved.

Your son Quintus, who is a fine boy, is getting on famously with his lessons. I notice this more now because Tyrannio is teaching at my house. Building of both our houses goes briskly forward. I have paid your contractor half his money. I hope we shall be under the same roof[3] before winter. I hope we have settled matters with Crassipes about our Tullia, who loves you very much indeed. But it is

[2] The poet and orator C. Licinius Macer Calvus.

[3] The houses were adjoining.

dies erant duo qui post Latinas habentur religiosi (ceterum confectum erat Latiar), ‹et›[3] erat exiturus. ||

9 (II.5)

Scr. Romae ex. m. Mart. an. 56

‹MARCUS QUINTO FRATRI SALUTEM›

1 * * * *ἀμφιλαφίαν* autem illam quam tu soles dicere bono modo desidero, sic prorsus ut advenientem excipiam libenter, latentem etiam nunc non excitem. tribus locis aedifico, reliqua reconcinno. vivo paulo liberalius quam solebam; opus erat. si te haberem, paulisper fabris locum dares.[1] sed et haec, ut spero, brevi inter nos communicabimus.

2 Res autem Romanae sese sic habent. consul est egregius Lentulus non impediente collega, sic, inquam, bonus ut meliorem non viderim. dies comitialis exemit omnis; nam etiam Latinae instaurantur, nec tamen deerant sup-
3 plicationes. sic legibus perniciosissimis obsistitur, maxime Catonis; cui tamen egregie[2] imposuit Milo noster. nam ille vindex gladiatorum et bestiariorum emerat de Cosconio et Pomponio bestiarios nec sine iis armatis umquam in publico fuerat. hos alere non poterat, itaque vix tenebat. sensit Milo. dedit cuidam non familiari negotium qui sine suspi-

[3] (*Sternkopf*)

[1] darem (*SB*)

[2] egregiam (ς: -iam ‹plagam› *Goodyear*: -iam (*sc. plagam*) *coniecerat SB*)

the two days after the Latin Festival (now ended), which are holy days, and he is just leaving town.

9 (II.5)

Rome, end of March 56

CICERO TO HIS BROTHER

* * * As for the *abondance* you often talk about, I want it moderately; that is to say, if the animal comes my way I shall be glad to snap it up, but if it stays in hiding I don't intend to flush it out. I am building in three places and refurbishing the rest. I live on a rather more handsome scale nowadays than I used—it was called for. If I had you with me, you would take second place to the builders for a spell! But all this too I hope we shall soon be talking over between us.

The situation in Rome is as follows: Lentulus makes an excellent Consul, and his colleague does not stand in his way—yes, really good, I have never seen a better. He has blocked all the comitial days—even the Latin Festival is being repeated, and no lack of Supplications either. So pernicious bills are blocked, especially Cato's.[1] Our friend Milo has played that patron of gladiators and beast fighters a fine trick. Cato had bought some beast fighters from Cosconius and Pomponius and never appeared in public without their armed escort. He could not feed them and was having difficulty in keeping them. Milo got to know, and employed an agent to buy the troupe from Cato, a man

[1] Cf. *Letters to Friends* 15 (I.5a).2. Cato is the Tribune, C. Cato.

cione emeret eam familiam a Catone. quae simul atque abducta est, Racilius, qui unus est hoc tempore tribunus pl., rem patefecit eosque homines sibi emptos esse dixit (sic enim placuerat) et tabula[3] proscripsit se familiam Catonianam venditurum. in eam tabulam magni risus consequebantur.

Hunc igitur Catonem Lentulus a legibus removit et eos qui de Caesare monstra promulgarunt, quibus intercederet nemo. nam quod de Pompeio Caninius agit sane quam refrixit. neque enim res probatur et Pompeius noster in amicitia P. Lentuli vituperatur. et hercule non est idem; nam apud perditissimam illam atque infimam faecem populi propter Milonem suboffendit et boni multa ab eo desiderant, multa reprehendunt. Marcellinus autem hoc uno mihi quidem non satis facit quod eum nimis aspere tractat, quamquam id senatu non invito facit; quo ego me libentius a curia et ab omni parte rei publicae subtraho.

4 In iudiciis ii sumus qui fuimus. domus celebratur ita ut cum maxime. unum accidit ‹im›prudentia Milonis incommodum de Sex. C‹l›oelio,[4] quem neque hoc tempore

[3] tabulam (*Pareus**)

[4] coelio *vel* caelio *vel* caecilio (*SB praeeunte Gruter*: Clodio *Man.*, *vulg.*)

---

[2] I.e. for acting disloyally by intriguing to get the Egyptian assignment for himself. In September 57 the Senate had commissioned Lentulus, as proximate governor of Cilicia, to restore the exiled king of Egypt, Ptolemy XII, to his throne. But in January the custodians of the Sibylline prophecies produced an oracle forbidding the employment of a host. This was no doubt also a move against Pompey, who came more and more to be suspected of

who was not a crony of his own and so could do it without arousing suspicion. No sooner had they been led off than Racilius (the only Tribune worth the name at present) gave the show away, announcing by prearrangement with Milo that these men had been bought for himself and putting out an advertisement that he was going to sell 'Cato's troupe' by auction. There was great amusement over that advertisement.

Well, Lentulus has kept this fellow Cato away from legislation, as also some others who have given notice of bills about Caesar—monstrous things, and nobody to veto them. As for Caninius' campaign regarding Pompey, it has fallen quite flat. The proposal finds little favour in itself, Pompey is criticized because of his friendship with P. Lentulus,[2] and frankly his position is not what it was. He has incurred some unpopularity with the vicious elements, the dregs of the mob, because of Milo, while the honest men find him lacking in many respects and blameworthy in many others. The only fault *I* have to find with Marcellinus is his excessive asperity towards Pompey. But the Senate does not disapprove, which makes me all the more glad to withdraw from the Senate House and public affairs altogether.

In the courts I stand where I stood. My house is as full of callers as in my heyday. One unfortunate incident happened through Milo's imprudence, about Sex. Cloelius—I was against a prosecution at the present time and with

wanting to handle the restoration himself. The business dragged on for a while, but in the end Lentulus did nothing, and Ptolemy was reinstated by the enterprising governor of Syria, A. Gabinius, in 55.

neque ab imbecillis accusatoribus mihi placuit accusari. ei tres sententiae deterrimo in consilio defuerunt. itaque hominem populus revocat et retrahatur necesse est. non enim ferunt homines et, quia cum apud suos diceret paene damnatus est, vident damnatum. ea ipsa in re Pompei offensio nobis obstitit. senatorum enim urna copiose absolvit, equitum adaequavit, tribuni aerarii condemnarunt. sed hoc incommodum consolantur cottidianae damnationes inimicorum, in quibus me perlibente Sevius adlisus est, ceteri conciduntur. C. Cato contionatus est comitia haberi non siturum si sibi cum populo dies agendi essent exempti. Appius a Caesare nondum redierat.

5 Tuas mirifice litteras exspecto; atque adhuc clausum mare fuisse scio, sed quosdam venisse tamen Ostiam dicebant qui te unice laudarent plurimique in provincia fieri dicerent. eosdem aiebant nuntiare te prima navigatione transmissurum. id cupio et, quamquam te ipsum scilicet maxime, tamen etiam litteras tuas ante exspecto.

Mi frater, vale.

10. (II.6)

Scr. Romae et in itinere in Anagninum v Id. Apr. an. 56

MARCUS QUINTO FRATRI SALUTEM

1 Dederam ad te litteras antea quibus erat scriptum Tul-

---

[3] To explain the distinction I have suggested that Sevius (an unknown: *Servius* used to be read before Watt, mistakenly identified with Servius Pola) had been condemned for some nonpolitical offence. His fate, then, was a kind of accident, whereas the other Clodians had been prosecuted by their political enemies on charges arising out of their public activities.

weak prosecutors. It only needed three more votes in a deplorable jury. The people are demanding another trial and he will have to be brought back; they won't tolerate it, and look upon him as already convicted since he was almost found guilty by a jury of his own men. In this affair too Pompey's unpopularity stood in our way. The Senators acquitted him by a large margin, the Knights were tied, the Paymaster Tribunes voted guilty. But to make up for this misadventure, my enemies are being convicted every day. Sevius ran on the rocks to my great satisfaction, and the rest are being broken up.[3] C. Cato has told a public meeting that he won't allow elections to be held if his days for moving legislation in the Assembly are blocked. Appius has not yet got back from Caesar.

I am waiting for a letter from you with the greatest impatience. I know that the sea has been closed to shipping up till now, but they say that certain persons arrived in Ostia bringing glowing accounts of you and your great reputation in the province. They also say you are giving out that you will cross at the first sailing. I hope so, and although naturally it is yourself I most want, I am none the less expecting a letter in advance.

Good-bye, dear brother.

10 (II.6)

Rome and en route to Anagnia, 9 April 56

From Marcus to his brother Quintus greetings.

I sent you a letter[1] the other day telling you that our

[1] Lost.

liam nostram Crassipedi prid. <Non.> Apr. esse desponsam, ceteraque de re publica privataque perscripseram. postea sunt haec acta: Non. Apr. senatus consulto Pompeio pecunia decreta in rem frumentariam ad HS ⌈CCCC⌉ sed eodem die vehementer actum de agro Campano clamore
2 senatus prope contionali. acriorem causam inopia pecuniae faciebat et annonae caritas. non praetermittam ne illud quidem: M. Furium Flaccum, equitem Romanum, hominem nequam, Capitolini et Mercuriales de collegio eiecerunt praesentem ad pedes unius cuiusque iacentem. ||

A. d. VIII Id. Apr. sponsalia Crassipedi praebui. huic convivio puer optimus, Quintus tuus meusque, quod perleviter commotus fuerat, defuit. a. d. VI Id. Apr. veni ad Quintum eumque vidi plane integrum, multumque is mecum sermonem habuit et perhumanum de discordiis mulierum nostrarum. quid quaeris? nihil festivius. Pomponia autem etiam de te questa est. sed haec coram agemus.

3 A puero ut discessi, in aream tuam veni. res agebatur multis structoribus. Longidium[1] redemptorem cohortatus sum; <f>idem[2] mihi faciebat se velle nobis placere. domus erit egregia (magis enim cerni iam poterat quam quantum ex forma iudicabamus); itemque nostra celeriter aedificabatur.

Eo die cenavi apud Crassipedem. cenatus in hortos ad

[1] longilium (*Harvey*)
[2] (*Vict.*)

---

[2] Probably a descendant of M. Furius Flaccus, Tribune in 270, in Valerius Maximus 2.7.15f., where he has masqueraded as M. Fulvius Flaccus. See my Loeb edition (2000) I, p. 196, n. 22.

Tullia was betrothed to Crassipes on 4 April, along with the rest of the news, public and private. Subsequent items are as follows: On the Nones of April the Senate decreed HS 40,000,000 to Pompey as Grain Commissioner. The same day there was a warm debate on the Campanian Land—the shouting in the House was like at a public meeting. The shortage of funds and the high price of grain made the question more acute. I must not fail to mention that M. Furius Flaccus,[2] a Roman Knight and a scoundrel, was expelled from the Capitoline College and the Guild of Mercury,[3] he being present and throwing himself at the feet of every member in turn.

On 6 April I gave a dinner for Crassipes to celebrate the engagement. Your and my boy Quintus (a very good boy) could not come because of a very slight indisposition. On the 8th I went to see him and found him quite recovered. He talked to me at length and in the nicest way about the disagreements between our ladies. It was really most entertaining. Pomponia has been grumbling about you too, but we will talk of this when we meet.

On leaving the boy I went over to your site. Work was going ahead with a crowd of builders. I said a few animating words to Longidius the contractor, and he convinced me that he wants to give us satisfaction. Your house will be splendid. One can see more now than we could judge from the plan. Mine too is going ahead rapidly.

I dined that evening at Crassipes' and after dinner had

[3] The *Capitolini* were in charge of the Capitoline Games held every Ides of October. The *Mercuriales* were a corporation of merchants (Mercury being the god of gain).

Pompeium lectica latus sum. luci eum convenire non potueram quod afuerat; videre autem volebam quod eram postridie Roma exiturus et quod ille in Sardiniam iter habebat. hominem conveni et ab eo petivi ut quam primum te nobis redderet; statim dixit. erat autem iturus, ut aiebat, a. d. III Id. Apr. ut aut ‹Sa›lebrone[3] aut Pisis conscenderet. tu, mi frater, simul et ille venerit, primam navigationem, dum modo idonea tempestas sit, ne omiseris.

4 A.d. V Id. Apr. ante lucem hanc epistulam dictaveram conscripseramque in itinere, ut eo die apud T. Titium in Anagnino manerem. postridie autem in Laterio cogitabam, inde, cum in Arpinati quinque dies fuissem, ire in Pompeianum, rediens aspicere Cumanum, ut, quoniam in Non. Mai. Miloni dies prodic‹t›a est, prid. Non. Romae essem teque, mi carissime et suavissime frater, ad eam diem, ut sperabam, viderem. aedificationem Arcani ad tuum adventum sustentari placebat.

Fac, mi frater, ut valeas quam primumque venias.

11 (II.7)

Scr. Romae paulo post Id. Mai. an. 56

MARCUS QUINTO FRATRI SALUTEM

1 O litteras mihi tuas iucundissimas exspectatas, ac primo

[3] labrone (*Wesseling**)

---

[4] His villa in the Campus Martius. Such properties, outside the old city boundary, were called *horti*, usually and misleadingly rendered 'gardens.'

myself carried to Pompey's,[4] not having been able to meet him during the day because he had been away—I wanted to see him because I was leaving Rome next day and he had a trip to Sardinia in view. So I met him and asked him to send you back to us as soon as possible. 'Straight away,' said he. He would be leaving, he said, on 11 April and taking ship from Salebro[5] or Pisae. Now as soon as he arrives, my dear fellow, be sure to take the next boat, provided the weather is suitable.

On 9 April I dictated this letter before daylight and am writing the rest on the road, expecting to stay the night with T. Titius near Anagnia. Tomorrow I intend to stay at Laterium, and then, after five days in the Arpinum area, go on to Pompeii. I shall have a look at my Cumae place on the way back, and so to Rome (since Milo's trial has been scheduled for the Nones of May) on the 6th, then, as I hope, to see you, my dearest and sweetest of brothers. I thought it best to hold up the building at Arcanum pending your arrival.

Be sure to keep well, my dear fellow, and come as soon as you can.

11 (II.7)

Rome, shortly after 15 May 56

From Marcus to his brother Quintus greetings.

At last, your delightful letter! I have been waiting for it

[5] On the coast of Etruria, north of Populonia. Elsewhere the name occurs only in ancient Itineraries, where it takes various forms (see my Commentary).

quidem cum desiderio, nunc vero etiam cum timore! atque has scito litteras me solas accepisse post illas quas tuus nauta attulit Ulbia datas.

Sed cetera, ut scribis, praesenti sermoni reserventur; hoc tamen non queo differre: Id. Mai. senatus frequens divinus fuit in supplicatione Gabinio deneganda. adiurat Procilius hoc nemini accidisse. foris valde plauditur. mihi cum sua sponte iucundum tum iucundius quod me absente. est enim εἰλικρινὲς iudicium, sine oppugnatione,
2 sine gratia nostra. ‹ab›eram autem[1] quod Idibus et postridie fuerat dictum de agro Campano actum iri, ut est actum. in hac causa mihi aqua haeret. sed plura quam constitueram. coram enim.

Vale, mi optime et optatissime frater, et advola. idem te pueri nostri rogant.

Illud scilicet: cenabis cum veneris.

12 (II.9)

Scr. in Tusculano c. m. Iun. an. 56, ut vid.

MARCUS QUINTO FRATRI SALUTEM

1 Tu metuis ne me interpelles? primum, si in isto essem,[1] tu scis quid sit interpellare otiantem. sed[2] mehercule mihi

[1] eram ante (*Sternkopf*)

[1] essent

[2] antea (*vel* ante a) te is (*SB*)

---

[1] In fact there may have been only one precedent, that of T. Albucius, governor of Sardinia ca. 104.

so impatiently, and of late apprehensively too. I must tell you that this is the only letter I have had from you since the one dispatched from Olbia which your skipper brought.

Let all else be kept for talk in person, as you say, but one thing I cannot let wait: on the Ides of May the Senate refused Gabinius a Supplication—a magnificent performance! Procilius takes his oath that this has never happened to anyone before.[1] Outside the House it is heartily applauded. To me it is agreeable in itself, and the more so because it was done in my absence—an unbiased judgement, without any aggressive action or influence on my part. I did not attend because it had been reported that the Campanian Land would be debated on the Ides and the day following, as indeed it was. On this question I am up against a brick wall.[2] But I am writing more than I intended—we shall talk.

Good-bye, my best and most longed-for of brothers, and hurry you home. Our boys make the same plea of you.

Oh, and of course you will come to dinner when you arrive.

12 (II.9)

Tusculum, June 56

From Marcus to his brother Quintus greetings.

What, *you* afraid of interrupting me? To start with, even if I were occupied in the way you think, you know

[2] Cf. *Letters to Friends*, 20 (I.9).8. *Aqua haeret*, lit. 'the water sticks,' has been variously explained; see my Commentary.

docere videris istius generis humanitatem, qua quidem ego nihil utor abs te. tu vero ut me et appelles et interpelles et obloquare et colloquare velim. quid enim mihi suavius? non mehercule quisquam *μουσοπάτακτος* libentius sua
2 recentia poemata legit quam ego te audio quacumque de re, publica privata, rustica urbana. sed mea factum est insulsa[3] verecundia ut te proficiscens non tollerem. opposuisti semel *ἀν<αν>τί<λ>εκτον*[4] causam, Ciceronis nostri valetudinem: conticui. iterum Cicerones:[5] quievi. nunc mihi iucunditatis plena epistula hoc adspersit molestiae, quod videris ne mihi molestus esses veritus esse atque etiam nunc vereri. litigarem tecum, si fas esset; sed mehercule, istuc si umquam suspicatus ero—nihil dicam aliud nisi verebor ne quando ego tibi, cum sum una, molestus sim. video te ingemuisse. sic fit: '*εἰ δεὶν' ἔφησας*'[6]—numquam enim dicam '*ἔδρασας*.'[7]

Marium autem nostrum in lecticam mehercule coniecissem—non illam regis Ptolomaei Asicianam; memini enim, cum hominem portarem ad Baias Neapoli octaphoro Asiciano machaerophoris centum sequentibus, miros

3 infusa 4 *ἀντίεκτον* (*Vict.*)
5 ceteri omnes (*Man.*) 6 *εἰ δ' ἐν αἴᾳ ἔζησας vel sim.* (*Watt, praeeuntibus fere Sternkopf et Rothstein*)
7 *ἔα πάσας vel sim.* (*Gurlitt*)

---

1 See critical note. Cicero may be supposed to allude to a saying that to interrupt an idle man was to do him a service. Private study or literary work came under the heading of *otium* (leisure, idleness).

2 The Greek verse part of which Cicero quotes is from a lost play of Sophocles: 'If what you did was terrible, so must what you suffer be terrible also.'

what 'interrupting an idler' is![1] But upon my word it looks as though you are giving me a lesson in this kind of thoughtfulness, for which I have no use when it comes from you. No, no, I hope you will interpose and interrupt and talk me down and talk me out! Nothing would please me better. No moonstruck poet is so willing to recite his latest effusions as I to listen to you talking on any topic, public or private, country or town. It was my stupid diffidence that stopped me from taking you along when I left Rome. You put up an unanswerable excuse the first time, the ill health of our little boy; so I held my tongue. Then again it was the boys, and I said nothing. And now your most agreeable letter bothers me a little, because it looks as though you were afraid, and still are, of being a bother! I should quarrel with you if brotherly love permitted. But mark my words; if ever I suspect anything of the kind again—well, I'll say only this: I shall be afraid when we are together of bothering *you*. That touches you on the raw, doesn't it? Well, that's the way it goes: 'whoso evil speaketh . . .'[2] (I'll never say 'evil doeth').

As for our friend Marius, I assure you I should have thrown him into the litter—not the one Asicius[3] had from King Ptolemy (I remember that occasion when I was transporting him from Naples to Baiae in Asicius' eight-bearer palanquin with a hundred swordsmen following; Marius

[3] Charged with the murder of the chief of a delegation from Ptolemy the Piper's revolted subjects, he was successfully defended by Cicero.

risus nos edere cum ille ignarus sui comitatus repente aperuit lecticam et paene ille timore, ego risu corrui. hunc,[8] ut dico, certe sustulissem, ut aliquando subtilitatem veteris urbanitatis et humanissimi sermonis attingerem. sed hominem infirmum in villam apertam ac ne rudem quidem
3 etiam nunc invitare nolui. hoc vero mihi peculiare fuerit, hic etiam isto frui; nam illorum praediorum scito mihi vicinum Marium lumen esse. apud Anicium vide<bi>mus ut paratum sit. nos enim ita philologi sumus ut vel cum fabris habitare possimus. habemus hanc philosophiam non ab Hymetto sed ab Arce nostra.[9] Marius et valetudine est et natura imbecillior. de interpellatione, tantum sumam a vobis temporis ad scribendum quantum dabitis. utinam nihil detis, ut potius vestra iniuria quam ignavia mea cessem!

De re publica nimium te laborare doleo et meliorem civem esse quam Philoctetam, qui accepta iniuria ea spectacula quaerebat quae tibi acerba esse video. amabo te, advola; consolabor te et omnem abstergebo dolorem. et adduc, si me amas, Marium. sed approperate.

Hortus domi est.

[8] tunc (*Man.*)
[9] araxira *vel sim.* (*SB*: arce Ψυρίᾳ *Tunstall*)

---

[4] Lit. 'from our Arx,' with *arce nostra* (written *arce nra*) for the meaningless *araxira* in the manuscripts. There was a place called Arx (citadel) in the neighbourhood of Arpinum. Cicero means that he did not need Greek philosophy to teach him to put up with inconvenience; early training in his native hill country had done that.

knew nothing about this escort and I laughed till I cried when he suddenly opened the curtains and we both almost collapsed—he with fright and I with laughter). Well, as I say, I should certainly have taken him along to sample after so long the subtlety of his old-time wit and civilized conversation, but I did not like to invite an invalid to a drafty house, still not even roughly finished. It will be a special treat for me to enjoy his company here too—I can tell you that Marius as my neighbour is the pride and glory of my property at Pompeii. I shall take care that Anicius' place is ready for him. As for me, bookworm though I be, I can live with the carpenters, a philosophy which I get, not from Mt Hymettus, but from our native Peak.[4] Marius is not so tough, either in health or nature. As for interruptions, I shall borrow from you people just so much time for writing as you allow, and I hope you don't allow any; that way, if I do nothing, you will be to blame instead of my own laziness.

I am sorry you take the political situation overmuch to heart and that you are a better citizen than Philoctetes, who being wronged wanted to see such sights as are evidently painful to you.[5] Be a good fellow, and hurry over. I shall comfort you and wipe away all sorrows. And bring Marius, if you love me. But make haste, both of you.

The kitchen garden is in good shape.[6]

[5] Evidently an allusion to a lost play. Sophocles' *Philoctetes* contains nothing relevant.

[6] Perhaps in response to something in Quintus' letter. For this interpretation of *domi est* see *Letters to Atticus* 377 (XV.1).2, *Dolabellam spero domi esse* (can be counted on). The kitchen garden (*hortus*) at Cicero's villa also produced flowers; *Letters to Friends* 219 (XVI.18).2.

13 (II.8)

Scr. Romae paulo post III Id. Febr. an. 55

MARCUS QUINTO FRATRI SALUTEM

1 Placiturum tibi esse librum II suspicabar, tam valde placuisse quam scribis valde gaudeo. quod me admones de †non curantia†[1] suadesque ut meminerim Iovis orationem quae est in extremo illo libro, ego vero memini et illa omnia mihi magis scripsi quam ceteris.

2 Sed tamen postridie quam tu es profectus multa nocte cum Vibullio veni ad Pompeium; cumque ego egissem de istis operibus atque inscriptionibus, per mihi benigne respondit, magnam spem attulit, cum Crasso se dixit loqui velle mihique ut idem facerem suasit. Crassum consulem ex senatu domum reduxi. suscepit rem dixitque esse quod Clodius hoc tempore cuperet per se et per Pompeium consequi; putare se, si ego eum non impedirem, posse me adipisci sine contentione quod vellem. totum ei negotium permisi meque in eius potestate dixi fore. interfuit huic sermoni P. Crassus adulescens, nostri, ut scis, studiosissimus. illud autem quod cupit Clodius est legatio aliqua (si minus per senatum, per populum) libera aut Byzantium aut ‹ad›[2] Brogitarum aut utrumque, plena res nummo-

[1] *ἀδιαφορίᾳ Sternkopf* [2] (*Man.*)

---

[1] Of the poem *On My Vicissitudes*; cf. *Letters to Friends* 20 (I.9).23. [2] I translate a Greek word taken from Stoic terminology and conjectured here by W. Sternkopf in place of *non curantia* in the manuscripts, which seems to be an attempt to render it in Latin. Cicero uses the word in *Letters to Atticus* 37 (II.17).2 and in *Academica* 2.130. [3] Jupiter will have ad-

13 (II.8)

Rome, shortly after 11 February 55

From Marcus to his brother Quintus greetings.

I thought you would like Canto II,[1] but I'm very glad you liked it so very much as you say in your letter. You remind me of Indifference[2] and advise me to remember Jupiter's speech at the end of the Canto.[3] Yes, I remember. I wrote it all for myself more than for the rest of the world.

However, the day after you left I paid Pompey a late-night visit in company with Vibullius and spoke to him about those buildings and inscriptions.[4] He answered very kindly and held out high hopes, saying that he would like to discuss it with Crassus and advising me to do the same. I accompanied Consul Crassus from the Senate to his house. He undertook to do his best and said there was something Clodius wanted to get just now through Pompey and himself; if I did not put a spoke in his wheel, he thought I could gain my point without a fight. I put the whole business in his hands and said I would do just as he thought fit. Young P. Crassus, who is devoted to me as you know, was present during our talk. As for what Clodius wants, it's a Free Commissionership (if not through the Senate, then through the Assembly) either to Byzantium or to Brogitarus or both.[5] There's plenty of money in it, but

vised the poet to leave politics and devote himself to letters; cf. end of next paragraph. [4] The reference is obscure, but cf. Letter 21.14. [5] As Tribune Clodius had brought about the recall of some Byzantine exiles and had got Brogitarus appointed High Priest of Cybele at Pessinus. He now proposed to go and collect. Though his business was essentially private, the Free Commissionership would give him official status.

rum. quod ego non nimium laboro, etiam si minus adsequor quod volo. Pompeius tamen cum Crasso locutus est. videntur negotium suscepisse. si perficiunt, optime; si minus, ad nostrum Iovem revertamur.

3 A. d. III Id. Febr. senatus consultum est factum de ambitu in Afrani sententiam, quam ego dixeram cum tu adesses. sed magno cum gemitu senatus consules non sunt persecuti eorum sententias qui, Afranio cum essent adsensi, addiderunt ut praetores ita crearentur ut dies sexaginta privati essent. eo die Catonem plane repudiarunt. quid multa? tenent omnia idque ita omnis intellegere volunt.

14 (II.10)

Scr. in. m. Febr. an. 54

MARCUS QUINTO FRATRI SALUTEM

1 Epistulam hanc convicio efflagitarunt codicilli tui. nam res quidem ipsa et is dies quo tu es profectus nihil mihi ad scribendum argumenti sane dabat. sed quem ad modum coram cum sumus sermo nobis deesse non solet, sic epistulae nostrae debent interdum alucinari.

2 Tenediorum igitur libertas securi Tenedia praecisa est,

---

[6] Since the Praetors for 55 had not been elected until February of that year, they would, failing special provision, take office immediately after election and so become immune from prosecution for electoral malpractice for the duration of their term. M. Cato had been a candidate in opposition to the Consuls, Pompey and Crassus, who secured his defeat. He was, however, elected for 54.

that doesn't trouble me too much—even if I don't get what I'm after. However, Pompey has talked to Crassus, and they seem to have taken the thing on. If they do it, fine! If not, let us return to our Jupiter.

On 11 February the Senate passed a decree about bribery on Afranius' motion, which was the one I proposed myself when you were here. But to the loudly voiced disappointment of the House the Consuls did not pursue the proposal of certain members who, after concurring with Afranius, added that the Praetors should remain private citizens for two months after election. That day they flatly repudiated Cato.[6] The fact is, they are all-powerful and want everybody to know it.

14 (II.10)

Rome, early February 54

From Marcus to his brother Quintus greetings.

Your tablets[1] clamorously demanded[2] this letter. Otherwise, in actual material the day of your departure really offers no subject for my pen. But when we are together we are seldom at a loss for talk, and in the same way our letters must sometimes just ramble on.

Well then, the liberties of the good folk of Tenedos have

1 See Glossary.

2 'A humourous reference to *flagitatio*, the popular method of extra-legal redress . . . The characteristic feature of this procedure was aggressive demand backed by strongly worded insult' (A. J. Marshall). See my Commentary.

cum eos praeter me et Bibulum et Calidium et Favonium nemo defenderet. de te a Mag‹net›i‹bu›s[1] ab Sipylo mentio est honorifica facta, cum te unum dicerent postulationi L. Sesti Pansae restitisse. reliquis diebus si quid erit quod te scire opus sit, aut etiam si nihil erit, tamen scribam cottidie aliquid. prid. Id. neque tibi neque Pomponio deero.

3 Lucreti poemata ut scribis ita sunt, multis luminibus ingeni, multae tamen artis. sed cum veneris. virum te putabo si Sallusti Empedoclea legeris; hominem non putabo.

15 (II.11)

Scr. Romae c. Id. Febr. an. 54

MARCUS QUINTO FRATRI SALUTEM

1 Gaudeo tibi iucundas esse meas litteras, nec tamen habuissem scribendi nunc quidem ullum argumentum nisi tuas accepissem.

Nam prid. Id., cum Appius senatum infrequentem coegisset, tantum fuit frigus ut pipulo[1] [convicio][2] coactus sit
2 nos dimittere. de Commageno, quod rem totam discusse-

[1] magis (*Vict.*)   [1] populi (*Tyrrell*)   [2] (*Housman*)

[3] The people of Tenedos seem to have petitioned the Senate for the status of a 'free community' and to have been summarily refused. The origin of the expression 'axe of Tenedos' has been variously explained, but has to do with the eponymous hero of the island, Ten(n)es, who was supposed to have introduced a peculiarly drastic legal code. [4] Nothing is known of this Pansa or his demand. He may have been a tax farmer.

[5] According to St Jerome, Cicero edited Lucretius' poem *On the Nature of the Universe* after the poet's death.

been chopped by their own axe;[3] nobody came to their defence except myself, Bibulus, Calidius, and Favonius. You got an honourable mention from the men of Magnesia by Mt Sipylus; they said you were the only one to stand up to L. Sestius Pansa's demand.[4] If there is anything you ought to know on the remaining days, or for that matter if there is nothing, I shall still write you a daily line. On the 12th I shall not fail you, nor Pomponius either.

Lucretius' poetry is as you say—sparkling with natural genius, but plenty of technical skill.[5] But of that more when you come. If you read Sallustius' *From Empedocles*,[6] I'll rate you both more and less than ordinary humanity.[7]

15 (II.11)

Rome, ca. 13 February 54

From Marcus to his brother Quintus greetings.

I am glad my letters give you pleasure, though just now I should not have had any subject to write about if I had not had a letter from you.

Appius called a thinly attended meeting of the Senate on the 12th, but it was so chilly that the outcry forced him to dismiss us. As for him of Commagene,[1] I quite settled

6 Presumably a Latin translation of the fifth-century Sicilian philosopher-poet Empedocles. The translator is likely to have been Cicero's friend Cn. Sallustius.

7 Lit. 'I shall think you a *man* (*virum*), but not a human being.'

1 Antiochus. He had received his kingdom, formerly part of Syria, when Pompey set up the Roman province at the end of the war against Mithridates.

ram, mirifice mihi et per se et per Pomponium blanditur Appius. videt enim, hoc genere dicendi si utar in ceteris,
3 Februarium sterilem futurum; eumque lusi iocose satis, neque solum illud extorsi oppidulum quod ‹eius›[3] erat, positum in Euphrati Zeugmate, sed praeterea togam sum eius praetextam, quam erat adeptus Caesare consule, magno hominum risu cavillatus. 'quod vult' inquam 'renovari[4] honores eosdem, quo minus togam praetextam quotannis interpolet decernendum nihil censeo. vos autem homines nobiles, qui Burrenum[5] praetextatum non ferebatis, Commagenum feretis?' genus vides et locum iocandi. multa dixi in ignobilem regem, quibus totus est explosus. quo genere commotus, ut dixi, Appius totum me amplexatur. nihil est enim facilius quam reliqua discutere. sed non faciam ut illum offendam,

3 (*Wes.*)

4 renovare (*Or.*)

5 quibus r(h)enum (*cod. Palatinus, Wiseman*: qui Burrhinum *iam SB*)

---

2 The Senate dealt with foreign delegations in February. As Consul Appius was in a position to help them, for which Cicero implies that he would expect to be paid.

3 Zeugma; see my Commentary. The little town cannot be identified.

4 It seems that in 59 the king had been accorded the right to wear the purple-bordered gown (*toga praetexta*) worn by Roman curule magistrates, perhaps on a particular annual occasion, and that the Senate had been asked to confirm it. The conjecture *qui*

his hash and so Appius is paying me extravagant court both in person and through Pomponius. He sees that if I take the same tone in other matters he will have a lean February.[2] I poked fun at the king comically enough, not merely twisting that little town of his in the Bridge of Euphrates[3] out of his grip but raising a storm of laughter by my jibes at the purple-bordered gown he got during Caesar's Consulship: 'Now as for his request for the renewal of the honours accorded to him, far be it from me to suggest that this House should gainsay his right to give the purple-bordered gown an annual touching up. But I appeal to members of the nobility here present: you gentlemen drew the line at Oxnose; are you going to accept Commagene ointment?'[4] You perceive the genre and the theme. I cut so many jokes at this inglorious monarch's expense that he was totally exploded. Appius, as I say, was alarmed by this procedure and is smothering me in courtesies. It would be the easiest thing in the world to spoke the other wheels. But no, I shall not offend him,

Burrhinum for *quibus (r(h)enum* assumes a characteristic double pun. There was a medicament *commagenum* made from a herb *commagene*; and there was a herb *burrhinon* (*burrhinum*, 'oxnose,' also called *bucranion*, 'oxskull'). The missing link will be a lowborn person named or nicknamed Burrhinus, whose election to a magistracy was resented or ridiculed by the nobility—or rather, as suggested by T. P. Wiseman and as I think likely, to one Burrienus (or Burrenus), City Praetor in 83. But the chasing of phantoms has continued; cf. G. W. Bowersock, *Roman Arabia*, 36f.

ne imploret fidem
Iovis Hospitalis, Graios omnis convocet,

per quos mecum in gratiam rediit.

4 Theopompo satis faciemus. de Caesare, fugerat me ad te scribere. video enim quas tu litteras exspectaris. sed ille scripsit ad Balbum fasciculum illum epistularum in quo fuerat mea et Balbi totum sibi aqua madidum redditum esse, ut ne illud quidem sciat, meam fuisse aliquam epistulam. sed ex Balbi epistula pauca verba intellexerat, ad quae rescripsit his verbis: 'de Cicerone te video quiddam scripsisse quod ego non intellexi. quantum autem coniectura consequebar, id erat eius modi ut magis optandum quam sperandum putarem.' itaque postea misi ad Caesarem eodem illo exemplo litteras. iocum autem illius de sua egestate ne sis aspernatus; ad quem ego rescripsi nihil esse quod posthac arcae nostrae fiducia conturbaret lusique in eo genere et familiariter et cum dignitate. amor autem eius erga nos perfertur omnium nuntiis singularis. litterae quidem ad id quod exspectas fere cum tuo reditu iungentur.

Reliqua singulorum dierum scribemus ad te, si modo tabellarios tu praebebis. quamquam eius modi frigus im-

[5] A quotation from an unknown Latin play. Jove, guardian of (hospitable) troth (Jupiter Hospitalis) = Zeus Xenios, defender of the laws of hospitality. Cicero may be thought to have in mind the feasts which doubtless celebrated his and Appius' reconciliation. As for the Greeks, they are not, as some commentators naively suppose, actual Greeks; rather, as Cicero expressly says, they stand for the intermediaries who had recently brought about the

lest upon Jove he cry,
Guardian of Troth, and all the Greeks convoke[5]

—that is, the intermediaries in our reconciliation.

I shall do my best for Theopompus. As for Caesar, I forgot to tell you—yes, I understand what kind of a letter you have been waiting for. But he wrote to Balbus that the parcel containing Balbus' letter and mine was delivered to him completely waterlogged so that he doesn't even know that a letter from me was inside. But he had made out a few words in Balbus' letter, to which he replies as follows: 'I see you have written something about Cicero which I cannot make out. But so far as I could follow it by guesswork, it looked like something I should have wished rather than hoped for.'[6] So I proceeded to send Caesar a copy of my letter. And don't be put off by his joke about being hard up. I replied that he had better not spend his last penny depending on *my* strongbox, and some more banter on the same lines—familiar but not undignified. All reports speak of his special regard for me. The letter replying to the point you have in mind should just about coincide with your return to Rome.

I shall write you day-by-day newsletters always provided you supply the couriers. But there's a hard frost

reconciliation, principally Pompey; cf. *Letters to Atticus* 124 (VII.1).4, where, likewise in quotations, the 'Trojan men and dames' stand for public opinion and 'Polydamas' for Atticus.

6 This no doubt refers to Q. Cicero's desire for a command in Caesar's army.

pendebat ut summo in periculo[6] esset [ne][7] Appius ne aedes urerentur.

16 (II.12)

Scr. Romae XVI *Kal. Mart. an. 54*

MARCUS QUINTO FRATRI SALUTEM

1 Risi nivem atram teque hilari animo esse et prompto ad iocandum valde me iuvat. de Pompeio adsentior tibi, vel tu potius mihi. nam, ut scis, iam pridem istum canto Caesarem. mihi crede, in sinu est neque ego discingor.

2 Cognosce nunc Idus: decimus erat Caelio dies. Domitius ad numerum iudices non habuit. vereor ne homo taeter et ferus, Pola Servius, ad accusationem veniat. nam noster Caelius valde oppugnatur a gente Clodia. certi nihil est adhuc, sed veremur.

Eodem igitur die Tyriis est senatus datus frequens. frequentes contra Syriaci publicani. vehementer vexatus Gabinius. exagitati tamen[1] a Domitio publicani quod eum

[6] summum periculum (*SB*) [7] (*SB*)

[1] etiam *Madvig*

---

[7] There is an untranslatable joke here in the word *urerentur*, which can mean 'may be burned' or 'may be frostbitten.' The meaning is that Appius' unpopularity was such that a mob might set his house on fire.

[1] The point of Quintus' joke is obscure.

[2] An interval of at least ten days by inclusive reckoning was required between arraignment and trial. Nothing further is known of this trial.

ahead. In fact Appius stands in grave danger of seeing his house become a bonfire.[7]

16 (II.12)

Rome, 14 February 54

From Marcus to his brother Quintus greetings.

Your 'black snow' made me laugh,[1] and I am very glad to find you so cheerful and ready for a joke. I agree with you about Pompey, or rather you agree with me, for, as you know, I have been chanting your Caesar's praises this long while past. Believe me, he is grappled to my heart and I have no intention of disengaging.

Well, now for the Ides. It was the tenth day for Caelius.[2] Domitius[3] didn't have a complement of jurors. I'm afraid that horrible savage Pola Servius may join the prosecution, for our friend Caelius is vigorously assailed by the Clodian clan.[4] There's nothing for certain so far, but we are apprehensive.

That same day a well-attended Senate gave audience to the delegation from Tyre. Numerous Syrian tax farmers appeared in opposition. Gabinius was hauled over the coals in lively style, but the tax farmers were harried by

3 Probably a Cn. Domitius (not Calvinus) who had presided at Caelius' first trial (*Pro Caelio* 32). See next note.

4 Already in 56 Caelius Rufus had been successfully defended by Cicero in the speech *Pro Caelio*. The charge was instigated by Clodia, half-sister to P. Clodius.

essent cum equis prosecuti. <a>t[2] noster Lamia paulo ferocius, cum Domitius dixisset 'vestra culpa haec acciderunt, equites Romani. dissolute enim iudicatis,' 'nos iudicamus, vos laudatis' inquit. actum est eo die nihil. nox diremit.

3 Comitialibus diebus qui Quirinalia sequuntur Appius interpretatur non impediri se lege Pupia quo minus habeat senatum et, quod Gabinia sanctum sit, etiam cogi ex Kal. Febr. usque ad Kal. Mart. legatis senatum cottidie dare.[3] ita putantur detrudi comitia in mensem Martium. sed tamen his comitialibus tribuni pl. de Gabinio se acturos esse dicunt.

Omnia colligo ut novi scribam aliquid ad te, sed, ut vi-
4 des, res me ipsa deficit. itaque ad Callisthenem et ad Philistum redeo, in quibus te video volutatum. Callisthenes quidem vulgare et not<h>um[4] negotium, quem ad modum aliquot Graeci locuti sunt. Siculus[5] ille capitalis; creber, acutus, brevis, paene pusillus Thucydides. sed utros eius habueris libros (duo enim sunt corpora) an utrosque nescio. me magis *De Dionysio* delectat. ipse est enim vetera-

[2] C(aius) (*SB*) [3] dari (*Faërnus*) [4] (*SB*)
[5] secutus (*Vict.*)

---

[5] Ptolemy the Piper had finally been restored to his throne by Gabinius, now governor of Syria. This Domitius is L. Domitius Ahenobarbus, Consul of the year.

[6] Such testimonials to defendants' character (*laudationes*) were given in court either orally or in writing; cf. *Letters to Friends* 20 (I.9).7, 19. [7] See Letter 15, n. 2.

[8] Of magistrates for the current year, 54, whether Praetors or Aediles is uncertain, as is the reason why they had not been held in 55.

Domitius for having escorted him on horseback.[5] Our friend Lamia went a little far. When Domitius said: 'All this is the fault of you Roman Knights. You give lax verdicts,' Lamia retorted: 'We give verdicts, and you give testimonials!'[6] Nothing was concluded that day before nightfall ended the session.

According to Appius' interpretation, he is not debarred by the lex Pupia from holding meetings of the Senate on the comitial days following the Feast of Quirinus, and is actually obliged, as laid down in the lex Gabinia, to hold a meeting every day from the Kalends of February to the Kalends of March for the hearing of embassies.[7] So it's thought that the elections[8] are pushed away into March. All the same, the Tribunes say they intend to bring Gabinius' action before the Assembly on these coming comitial days.

I rake together all I can find to put some news in my letter, but, as you see, I am simply out of matter. So I come back to Callisthenes and Philistus—I can see you have been wallowing in them. Callisthenes is a common, bastard[9] piece of work, as certain of his fellow countrymen have put it. But the Sicilian is capital—full of matter, penetrating, concise, almost a miniature Thucydides. But which of his books you have had (there are two works), or whether you have had them both, I don't know. I prefer his *Dionysius*. Dionysius is a grand old fox and on very familiar

9 'Callisthenes did not write genuine, honest history but a meretricious and counterfeit mixture of history, adulterated by flattery . . . and excessive rhetoric' (from the note in my Commentary, which see).

tor magnus et perfamiliaris Philisto Dionysius. sed quod adscribis, adgrederisne ad historiam, me auctore potes. et quoniam tabellarios subministras, hodierni diei res gestas Lupercalibus habebis.

Oblecta te cum Cicerone nostro quam bellissime.

17 (II.13)

Scr. in Cumano vel Pompeiano m. Mai. an. 54

‹MARCUS QUINTO FRATRI SALUTEM›

1 Duas adhuc a te accepi epistulas, [quarum][1] alteram in ipso discessu nostro, alteram Arimino datam. pluris quas scribis te dedisse non acceperam.

Ego me in Cumano et Pompeiano, praeter quam quod sine te, ceterum satis commode oblectabam,[2] et eram in isdem locis usque ad Kal. Iun. futurus. scribebam illa quae dixeram πολιτικά, spissum sane opus et operosum. sed si ex sententia successerit, bene erit opera posita; sin minus, in illud ipsum mare deiciemus quod spectantes scribimus, adgrediemur alia, quoniam quiescere non possumus.

2 Tua mandata persequar diligenter et in adiungendis hominibus et in quibusdam non alienandis. maximae vero mihi curae erit ut Ciceronem tuum nostrumque videam scilicet cottidie sed inspiciam quid discat quam saepissime; et nisi ille contemnet, etiam magistrum me ei profitebor, cuius rei non nullam consuetudinem nactus

[1] (*Ern.*)
[2] oblectabar (*Man.*)

terms with Philistus. You add a question—shall you embark on history? You have my full encouragement. And since you are furnishing couriers, you shall have today's activities on the Lupercalia.

Have a perfectly delightful time with our young man.

17 (II.13)

Cumae or Pompeii, May 54

From Marcus to his brother Quintus greetings.

Up to date I have received two letters from you, one dispatched just as we said good-bye,[1] the other from Ariminum; the further letters which you say you sent I have not received.

Except that I lack your company I am in other respects quite enjoying myself at Cumae and Pompeii and shall be staying in those places till the Kalends of June. I am writing the political book[2] I mentioned earlier, and a pretty sticky, laborious job it is. However, if it turns out satisfactory, the time will have been well spent. If not, I'll toss it into the sea that is before my eyes as I write, and attack something else, since I can't do nothing.

I shall carefully attend to your charges, both in conciliating people and in not estranging certain persons. But my greatest concern will be to see your boy (*our* boy) every day, which goes without saying, and to look into what he is learning as often as possible. If he is willing to accept it, I shall even offer my services as his teacher, having gained

[1] Quintus had left to join Caesar for service in Gaul.

[2] *On the Republic*.

sum in hoc horum dierum otio Cicerone nostro minore producendo.

3 Tu, quem ad modum scribis (quod etiam si non scriberes facere te diligentissime tamen sciebam), facies scilicet ut mea mandata digeras, persequare, conficias. ego, cum Romam venero, nullum praetermittam Caesaris tabellarium cui litteras ad te non dem. his diebus ignosces; cui darem fuit nemo ante hunc M. Orfium, equitem Romanum, nostrum et per <se>[3] necessarium et quod est ex municipio Atellano, quod scis esse in fide nostra. itaque eum tibi commendo in maiorem modum, hominem domi splendidum, gratiosum etiam extra domum. quem fac ut tua liberalitate tibi obliges. est tribunus militum in exercitu vestro. gratum hominem observantemque cognosces.

Trebatium ut valde ames vehementer te rogo.

18 (II.14)

Scr. Romae in. m. Iun. an. 54

MARCUS QUINTO FRATRI SALUTEM

1 A. d. IIII Non. Iun., quo die Romam veni, accepi tuas litteras datas Placentia, deinde alteras postridie datas Blandenone cum Caesaris litteris refertis omni officio, diligentia, suavitate. sunt ista quidem magna, vel potius maxima; habent enim vim magnam ad gloriam et ad summam dignitatem. sed, mihi crede quem nosti, quod in istis rebus

[3] (*Baiter*)

---

[3] Marcus junior. [1] Has been identified with Biandrenno on Lago di Varese. See my Commentary.

some practice in this employment in bringing our younger boy[3] forward during this holiday season.

On your side, as you say in your letter (though even if you did not say so I know you are doing it most conscientiously), you will of course take care to sort out my commissions and follow them up and polish them off. When I get back to Rome I shall not let a single courier of Caesar's leave without a letter for you. As for these present days you will forgive me; there was nobody to take a letter until this M. Orfius, a Roman Knight who is connected with me both on personal grounds and because he comes from the town of Atella, which you know to be under my patronage. So I recommend him to you warmly. He is a man of distinction in his own community and of influence even outside it. Be sure to treat him handsomely and so attach him to yourself. He is a Military Tribune in your army. You will find him grateful and attentive.

Let me earnestly beg you to be very fond of Trebatius.

18 (II.14)

Rome, beginning of June 54

From Marcus to his brother Quintus greetings.

On 2 June, the day I got back to Rome, I received your letter dispatched from Placentia, and then another dispatched the following day from Blandeno,[1] together with a letter of Caesar's full of all manner of friendly attention, thoughtfulness, and charm. The things you speak of are indeed important, or rather *most* important, tending powerfully, as they do, to great kudos and the highest prestige. But take the word of one you know: what I value most in

ego plurimi aestimo, id iam habeo, te scilicet primum tam inservientem communi dignitati, deinde Caesaris tantum in me amorem, quem omnibus iis honoribus quos me a se exspectare vult antepono. litterae vero eius una datae cum tuis, quarum initium est quam suavis ei tuus adventus fuerit et recordatio veteris amoris, deinde se effecturum ut ego in medio dolore ac desiderio tui te, cum a me abesses, potissimum secum esse laetarer, incredibiliter delectarunt.

2 Qua re facis tu quidem fraterne quod me hortaris, sed mehercule currentem nunc quidem, ut omnia mea studia in istum unum conferam. ego vero ardenti quidem studio, ac fortasse efficiam quod saepe viatoribus cum properant evenit, ut, si serius quam voluerint forte surrexerint, properando etiam citius quam si de nocte vigilassent perveniant quo velint; sic ego, quoniam in isto homine colendo tam indormivi diu te mehercule saepe excitante, cursu corrigam tarditatem cum equis tum vero,[1] quoniam tu[2] scribis poema ab eo nostrum probari, quadrigis poeticis. modo mihi date Britanniam quam pingam coloribus tuis, penicillo meo. sed quid ago? quod mihi tempus, Romae praesertim, ut iste me rogat, manenti, vacuum ostenditur? sed videro. fortasse enim, ut fit, vincet unus amor omnis difficultates.

3 Trebatium quod ad se miserim persalse et humaniter etiam gratias mihi agit. negat enim in tanta multitudine eorum qui una essent quemquam fuisse qui vadimonium

[1] viris (*Brunus*) [2] ut (*Or.*)

---

[2] An epic poem addressed to Caesar which Cicero had begun and eventually finished (Letter 27.6).

these matters I already have, and that is, first, yourself so dedicated to the support of our common standing, and second, such affection for me on Caesar's part. That means more to me than all the distinctions he wants me to expect at his hands. The letter he sent along with yours pleased me beyond words. He begins by saying how delighted he was at your arrival and the memory of old affection, then goes on to promise that, knowing how sorely I shall miss you, he will make me glad that in your absence from me you are with him rather than anywhere else.

It is good brotherly advice you give me to make Caesar the one man I exert myself to please, but *now* upon my word the horse is willing. Yes, that I shall do enthusiastically. It often happens to travellers in a hurry that after getting up rather later than they intended they put on speed and thus arrive at their destinations faster even than if they had been astir in the middle of the night. So perhaps with me. In cultivating this man's friendship I have been asleep a long while, though I must admit that you often tried to wake me up. Now I shall compensate my slowness by putting my horse to a gallop—and not just my horse but my poetic chariot, since you say my poem[2] meets with his approval. All you have to do is to give me Britain to paint. I'll use your colours with my brush. But what am I about? Where can I spy the spare time, especially if I stay in Rome, as he asks me to do? Well, I'll see. Perhaps love alone will conquer all obstacles. It often does.

He actually thanks me for sending him Trebatius, very wittily and kindly, saying that in all his multitudinous entourage there wasn't a man who could draw up a bail bond.

concipere posset. M. Curtio tribunatum ab eo petivi (nam Domitius se derideri putasset, si esset a me rogatus; hoc enim est eius cottidianum, se ne tribunum militum quidem facere. etiam in senatu lusit Appium collegam propterea isse ad Caesarem ut aliquem tribunatum auferret), sed in alterum annum. id enim[3] Curtius ita volebat.

4 Tu quem ad modum me censes oportere esse et in re publica et in nostris inimicitiis, ita et esse et fore, oricula
5 infima, scito, molliorem. res Romanae se sic habebant: erat non nulla spes comitiorum sed incerta, erat aliqua suspicio dictaturae, ne ea quidem certa, summum otium forense sed senescentis magis civitatis quam acquiescentis, sententia autem nostra in senatu eius modi magis ut alii nobis adsentiantur quam nosmet ipsi. *‘τοιαῦθ’ ὁ τλήμων πόλεμος ἐξεργάζεται.’*

19 (II.15)

Scr. Romae ex. m. Quint. an. 54

‹MARCUS QUINTO FRATRI SALUTEM›

1 Calamo ‹bono›[1] et atramento temperato, charta etiam dentata res agetur. scribis enim te meas litteras superiores vix legere potuisse. in quo nihil eorum, mi frater, fuit quae putas. neque enim occupatus eram neque perturbatus nec iratus alicui. sed hoc facio semper ut, quicumque calamus in manus meas venerit, eo sic utar tamquam bono.

2 Verum attende nunc, mi optime et suavissime frater, ad

[3] et (*Mueller**)
[1] (*Wes.**)

I asked him for a Tribunate for M. Curtius (if I had asked Domitius he would have thought I was making game of him; it's his daily grumble that he can't even appoint a Military Tribune; he even made a joke in the Senate to the effect that his colleague Appius had gone to Caesar for the gift of a Tribune's commission), but for next year. That is how Curtius himself wanted it.[3]

Rest assured that in public life and in my personal feuds I am and shall be just what you recommend, softer than the lobe of your ear. Public affairs stand as follows: there is some hope of elections, but doubtful; some suspicion of a Dictatorship, but that too not definite; peace reigns in the Forum, but it's the peace of a senile community rather than a contented one. In the Senate my speeches are of a nature to win agreement from others rather than from myself. 'Such are the sorry works of woeful war.'[4]

19 (II.15)

Rome, end of July 54

From Marcus to his brother Quintus greetings.

This time it will be quality pen and well-mixed ink and ivory-finished paper, since you say you could hardly read my last letter. No, my dear fellow, it was for none of the reasons you suppose. I was neither busy nor upset nor annoyed with anybody. It's just that I always take the first pen that comes to hand as though it was a good one.

But now, my best and sweetest of brothers, pay careful

[3] Cf. Letter 21.10 and *Letters to Friends* 26 (VII.5).2.

[4] From Euripides' *Suppliant Women* 119.

ea dum rescribo quae tu in hac eadem brevi epistula πραγματικῶς valde scripsisti. de quo petis ut ad te nihil occultans, nihil dissimulans, nihil tibi indulgens ingenue[2] fraterneque rescribam, id est, utrum ‹ad›voles,[3] ut dixeramus, ‹an›[4] ad expediendum te, si causa sit, commorere: si, mi Quinte, parva aliqua res esset in qua sciscitarere quid vellem, tamen, cum tibi permissurus essem ut faceres quod velles, ego ipse quid vellem ostenderem. in hac vero re * * *[5] hoc profecto quaeris, cuius modi illum annum qui sequitur exspectem: plane aut tranquillum nobis aut certe munitissimum; quod cottidie domus, quod forum, quod theatri significationes declarant. nec labor, ut quondam,[6] conscientia copiarum nostrarum. quod Caesaris, quod Pompei gratiam tenemus, haec me ut confidam faciunt. sin aliquis erumpet amentis hominis furor, omnia sunt ad eum frangendum expedita.

3 Haec ita sentio, iudico, ad te explorate scribo; dubitare te non adsentatorie sed fraterne veto. qua re [si] suavitatis equidem nostrae fruendae causa cuperem te ad id tempus venire quod dixeras, sed illud malo tamen quod putas magis[7] e ‹re› tua.[8] illa etiam magni aestimo [me],[9] ἀμφιλαφίαν illam tuam et explicationem[10] debitorum tuorum. illud quidem sic habeto, nihil nobis expeditis, si valebimus, fore fortunatius. parva sunt quae desunt pro[11] nostris qui-

[2] genuine *vel* gemine (*Boot*) [3] (*Schütz*)
[4] (*Man.*) [5] *lac. statuit SB*
[6] laborant quod mea (*SB*)
[7] magis ‹esse› *Lamb.*
[8] etiam (*Lamb.*) [9] (*Lamb.*)
[10] exspectat- (*Schütz*)
[11] quo (*Or.*)

attention while I answer that very mundane passage in this same short letter. You ask me to reply in brotherly candour, without concealment or dissimulation or attempt to spare your feelings, to tell you, that is, whether you should hurry back as we had agreed or stay on (given sufficient reason) with a view to disembarrassing yourself. My dear Quintus, if you were enquiring about my wishes on some small matter, I should leave it to you to do as you chose, but at the same time make my own wishes clear. In this matter, however, * * * I take it that you are really asking how I expect next year to turn out: well, definitely a peaceful year for me, or at any rate a very well-protected one. My house, the Forum, and the demonstrations in the theatre declare as much every day. And I am not making the mistake I made once before in my consciousness of the forces behind me.[1] What gives me confidence is that I am in Pompey's and Caesar's good graces. But if the madman breaks out in some wild attempt, everything is ready to crush him.

This is my true feeling and judgement, written after a careful survey. You must have no misgivings; I forbid it as a brother, not because that is what you want to be told. To enjoy the pleasure we take in each other's society I should wish you to come home at the time you stated originally, but above that I put what you think to be in your own interest. I also attach great importance to your *abondance* and the liquidation of your debts. Be sure of one thing: once free of embarrassments, we shall be the most fortunate folk in the world, given health. Our habits being what they

[1] But perhaps *confidentia* (Wesenberg), 'confidence in,' is right.

dem moribus et ea sunt ad explicandum expeditissima, modo valeamus.

4 Ambitus redit immanis. numquam fuit par. Id. Quint. faenus[12] fuit bessibus ex triente coitione Memmi et consulum[13] cum Domitio. hanc Scaurus unus ‹vix potest›[14] vincere. Messalla flaccet. non dico ὑπερβολάς; vel HS centies constituunt in praerogativa pronuntiare. res ardet invidia. tribunicii candidati compromiserunt HS quingenis[15] in singulos apud M. Catonem depositis petere eius arbitratu, ut qui contra fecisset ab eo condemnaretur. quae quidem comitia si gratuita fuerint, ut putantur, plus unus Cato potuerit[16] quam omnes leges omnesque iudices.

20 (II.16)

Scr. Romae ex. m. Sext. an. 54

‹MARCUS QUINTO FRATRI SALUTEM›

1 Cum a me litteras librari manu acceperis, ne paulum ‹quidem›[1] me oti habuisse iudicato, cum autem mea, paulum. sic enim habeto, numquam me a causis et iudiciis districtiorem fuisse, atque id anni tempore gravissimo et caloribus maximis. sed haec, quoniam tu ita praescribis, ferenda sunt, neque committendum ut aut spei aut cogita-

[12] quin(c)tanus *vel* qui ne tantus (*Vict.*)
[13] est quo (*Purser*) [14] (*coni. Watt*)
[15] D *vel* qu(a)e (*Budaeus*) [16] fuerit (*Faërnus*)
[1] (*Crat.*)

---

[2] Lit. from 1/3% to 2/3% (monthly).
[3] There were four candidates for the Consulship of 53: M.

are, the gaps are small, and if health holds, filling them is no problem.

Bribery is rampant again, dreadful, worse than ever before. On the Ides the rate of interest rose from 4 to 8%[2] because of a coalition between Memmius and the Consuls with Domitius. Scaurus on his own can hardly defeat this. Messalla is a tired horse.[3] I do not speak in hyperbole: they are settling to distribute ten million sesterces among the first Century. It is a flaming scandal. The candidates for the Tribunate have agreed among themselves to deposit HS 500,000 each with M. Cato and make him referee of the elections, anyone contravening his rulings to be condemned by him. If these elections go through without corruption, as is thought likely, Cato will have achieved more on his own than all the laws and all the juries.

20 (II.16)

Rome, late August 54

From Marcus to his brother Quintus greetings.

When you get a letter from me in the hand of one of my secretaries you are to infer that I did not have a minute to spare; when in my own, that I had—a minute! For let me tell you that I have never in my life been more inundated with briefs and trials, and in a heat wave at that, in the most oppressive time of the year. But I must put up with it, since you so advise. I shall not let it appear that *I* have disap-

Aemilius Scaurus, Cn. Domitius Calvinus, C. Memmius, and M. Valerius Messalla Rufus. On the coalition cf. *Letters to Atticus* 91 (IV.17).2.

tioni vestrae ego videar defuisse, praesertim cum, si id difficilius fuerit, tamen ex hoc labore magnam gratiam magnamque dignitatem sim collecturus. itaque, ut tibi placet, damus operam ne cuius animum offendamus atque ut etiam ab iis ipsis qui nos cum Caesare tam coniunctos dolent diligamur, ab aequis vero aut etiam a propensis in
2 hanc partem vehementer et colamur et amemur. de ambitu cum atrocissime ageretur in senatu multos dies, quod ita erant progressi candidati consulares ut non esset ferendum, in senatu non fui. statui ad nullam medicinam rei publicae sine magno praesidio accedere.

3 Quo die haec scripsi Drusus erat de praevaricatione a tribunis aerariis absolutus in summa quattuor sententiis, cum senatores et equites damnassent. ego eodem die post meridiem Vatinium eram[2] defensurus; ea res facilis est. comitia in mensem Septembrem reiecta sunt. Scauri iudicium statim exercebitur, cui nos non deerimus.

‘Συνδείπνους’ Σοφοκλέους, quamquam a te ‹f›actam[3] fabellam video esse festive, nullo[4] modo probavi.

4 Venio nunc ad id quod nescio an primum esse debuerit. o iucundas mihi tuas de Britannia litteras! timebam Oceanum, timebam litus insulae; reliqua non equidem contemno, sed plus habent tamen spei quam timoris magisque

[2] aderam (*Lamb.*) [3] (*Buecheler*)
[4] bono *coni. SB*

---

[1] Quintus' and Caesar's. Cf. Letter 18.1 and 25.3. The honours there in view are probably an Augurate (actually realized in 53 or 52) and perhaps the Censorship.

[2] For extortion in Sardinia; cf. *Letters to Atticus* 89 (IV.16).6, 90 (IV.15).9, 91 (IV.17).3.

pointed your[1] joint hope or plan, especially as, if that prove difficult, at any rate I shall reap a rich harvest of influence and prestige from my labour. So I follow your wishes. I take care to offend nobody, to be highly regarded even by those who deplore my having become so closely involved with Caesar, and an object of much attention and friendly feeling from nonpartisans or from those whose sympathies actually lie this way. There has been a debate in the Senate lasting a number of days on the bribery question. The most drastic action was called for, the candidates for the Consulship having gone to intolerable lengths. I did not attend. I have decided not to come forward to cure the ills of the body politic without powerful backing.

The day I write this letter Drusus has been acquitted of collusive prosecution by the Paymaster Tribunes. The overall majority was four, the Senators and Knights having found him guilty. This afternoon I shall be defending Vatinius—an easy matter. The elections have been put off to September. Scaurus' trial[2] will proceed straight away, and I shall not let him down.

I don't at all approve of Sophocles' *Banqueters*,[3] though I see you have made an amusing little play.

Now I come to what ought perhaps to have been put first. How pleased I was to get your letter from Britain! I dreaded the Ocean and the island coast. Not that I make light of what is to come, but there is more to hope than to

[3] Sophocles wrote a satyr play so entitled. On the manuscript reading *actam* see my Commentary. Such plays were apt to contain indecencies, which might account for Cicero's negative reaction, if *nullo modo* is sound; but that seems very doubtful. *Bono modo* would mean 'moderately.'

sum sollicitus exspectatione ea quam metu. te vero *ὑπόθεσιν* scribendi egregiam habere video. quos tu situs, quas naturas rerum et locorum, quos mores, quas gentis, quas pugnas, quem vero ipsum imperatorem habes! ego te libenter, ut rogas, quibus rebus vis, adiuvabo et tibi versus quos rogas, hoc est Athenas noctuam, mittam.

5 Sed heus tu! celari videor a te. quo modo nam, mi frater, de nostris versibus Caesar? nam primum librum se legisse scripsit ad me ante, et prima sic ut neget se ne Graeca quidem meliora legisse; reliqua ad quendam locum *ῥᾳθυμότερα* (hoc enim utitur verbo). dic mihi verum: num aut res eum aut *χαρακτὴρ* non delectat? nihil est quod vereare. ego enim ne pilo quidem minus me amabo. hac de re *φιλαλήθως* et, ut[5] soles [scribere],[6] fraterne.

21 (III.1)

Scr. partim in Arpinati partim Romae m. Sept. an. 54

MARCUS QUINTO FRATRI SALUTEM

1 Ego ex magnis caloribus (non enim meminimus maiores) in Arpinati summa cum amoenitate ‹tum salubritate›[1] fluminis me refeci ludorum diebus, Philotimo tribulibus commendatis.

In Arcano a. d. IIII Id. Sept. fui. ibi Mescidium cum Philoxeno aquamque, quam ii ducebant non longe a villa, belle sane fluentem vidi, praesertim maxima siccitate,

[5] tu (*Crat.*) [6] (*SB*) [1] (*Ern.**, *coll. Leg.* 2.3)

---

[4] The equivalent of a coal to Newcastle.

[5] A poem, 'On My Vicissitudes' (*De Temporibus suis*).

fear, and my suspense is more a matter of anticipation than of anxiety. You evidently have some splendid literary material: the places, the natural phenomena and scenes, the customs, the peoples, the fight, and, last but not least, the Commander-in-Chief! I shall be glad to help you, as you ask, in any way you wish, and I shall send you the verses you ask for (an owl to Athens!).[4]

But see here, you seem to be keeping me in the dark. Tell me, my dear fellow, how does Caesar react to my verses?[5] He wrote to me before that he read the first Canto and has never read anything better than the earlier part, even in Greek, but finds the rest, down to a certain point a trifle 'languid.' The truth, please! Is it the material or the style he doesn't like? No need for you to be nervous: my self-esteem won't drop a hair's-breadth. Just write to me *en ami de la vérité* and in your usual fraternal way.

21 (III.1)

Arpinum and Rome, September 54

From Marcus to his brother Quintus greetings.

Escaped from the great heat wave (I don't remember a greater), I have refreshed myself on the banks of our delightful and salubrious river at Arpinum during the Games period, after putting our fellow tribesmen in the hands of Philotimus.

I was at Arcanum on 10 September. There I saw Mescidius and Philoxenus and the stream which they are bringing over not far from the house. It was flowing merrily enough, particularly in view of the severe drought, and

uberioremque aliquanto sese collecturos esse dicebant. apud Her<i>um[2] recte erat.

In Maniliano offendi Diphilum Diphilo tardiorem. sed tamen nihil ei restabat praeter balnearia et ambulationem et aviarium. villa mihi valde placuit propterea quod summam dignitatem pavimentata porticus habebat, quod mihi nunc denique apparuit postea quam et ipsa tota patet et columnae politae sunt. totum in eo est, quod mihi erit curae, tectorium ut concinnum sit. pavimenta recte fieri videbantur; cameras quasdam non probavi mutarique iussi.

2 Quo loco in porticu te scribere aiunt ut atriolum fiat, mihi ut est magis placebat. neque enim satis loci videbatur esse atriolo <neque> fere solet nisi in iis aedificiis fieri in quibus est atrium maius nec habere poterat adiuncta cubicula et eius modi membra. nunc hoc vel honestae testudinis vel valde boni aestivi[3] locum obtinebit. tu tamen si aliter sentis, rescribe quam primum.

In balneariis assa in alterum apodyteri angulum promovi propterea quod ita erant posita ut eorum vaporarium [ex quo ignis erumpit][4] esset subiectum cubiculi<s>.[5] subgrande cubiculum autem et hibernum alt<er>um[6] valde probavi quod et ampla erant et loco posita ambulationis uno latere, eo quod est proximum balneariis. columnas neque rectas neque e regione Diphilus collocarat; eas scili-

[2] herum (*SB*)
[3] aestivum (*Turn.*: -vi <cenaculi> *coni. SB*)
[4] (*Scaliger*)
[5] (*Man.*: cubiculi subgrundae *Goodyear*)
[6] (*Lehmann*)

they said they would be collecting a considerably larger volume of water. All was well at Herius'.[1]

On the Manilius property[2] I found Diphilus, slower than—Diphilus. However, he had nothing left to do except for the baths, promenade, and aviary. I was very pleased with the house, because the paved colonnade is a most imposing feature; it struck me only this visit, now that its whole range is open to view and the columns have been smoothed. All depends on the elegance of the stucco, and that I shall attend to. The paving seemed to be going nicely. I did not care for some of the ceilings and gave orders to alter them.

They say you have written instructions for a small court in a certain area of the colonnade. I like that area better as it is. I don't think there is enough space for a small court, and it is not very usual to have one except in buildings which contain a larger court. Nor could it have adjoining bedrooms and suchlike appurtenances. As it is, it will make a handsome vault or a very good summer room. But if you feel otherwise, please write back as soon as possible.

In the baths I moved the sweat bath into the other corner of the dressing room because in the original position its steampipe lay immediately underneath the bedrooms. I was very pleased with a largish bedroom and another bedroom for winter; they are a good size and well situated on the side of the promenade next to the baths. The columns placed by Diphilus are neither straight nor properly aligned. He will pull them down, of course. One day he

[1] Probably the bailiff, therefore a slave or possibly freedman. On his name see my Commentary with addendum.

[2] Seemingly near Arpinum and recently acquired by Quintus.

cet demolietur. aliquando perpendiculo et linea discet uti. omnino spero paucis mensibus opus Diphili perfectum fore. curat enim diligentissime Caesius, qui tum mecum fuit.

3 Ex eo loco recta Vitularia via profecti sumus in Fufidianum fundum, quem tibi proximis nundinis[7] Arpini de Fufidio HS CCCIↃↃↃCIↃ emeramus. ego locum aestate umbrosiorem vidi numquam, permultis locis aquam profluentem[8] et eam uberem. quid quaeris? iugera L prati Caesius irrigaturum facile te arbitrabatur; equidem hoc quod melius intellego adfirmo, mirifica suavitate te villam habiturum piscina et salientibus additis, palaestra et silva †virdicata†. fundum audio te nunc[9] †Bobilianum† velle retinere. de eo quid videatur ipse constitues. Caesius[10] aiebat aqua dempta et eius aquae iure constituto et servitute fundo illi imposita tamen nos pretium servare posse si vendere vellemus. Mescidium mecum habui. is sese ternis nummis in pedem tecum transegisse dicebat, sese autem mensum pedibus aiebat passuum IIICIↃ. mihi plus visum est; sed praestabo sumptum nusquam melius posse poni. Cillonem arcessieram Venafro, sed eo ipso die quattuor eius conservos et discipulos Venafri cuniculus oppresserat.

4 Id. Sept. in Laterio fui. viam perspexi; quae mihi ita placuit ut opus publicum videretur esse, praeter CL passuum (sum enim ipse mensus) ab eo ponticulo qui est ad

[7] nuntiis (*Schütz*)
[8] profluentem <habentem> *coni. SB*
[9] hunc
[10] calibus (*Man.*)

may learn how to use a rule and plumb line. To be sure, I hope Diphilus' job will be finished in a few months. Caesius, who was with me at the time, is keeping a very watchful eye on it.

From there I set off straight down Steer Street to the Fufidius farm which I bought for you from Fufidius in Arpinum last market day for HS 101,000. I never saw a shadier place in summer. There is running water all over and plenty of it. In fact Caesius thinks you will irrigate thirty-five acres of meadow with ease. For my part I'll promise what I better understand, that you will have an exceptionally charming country house when certain extras have been put in: a fish pond, fountains, a palaestra, a * wood. I hear you now want to keep the Bobilius[3] place. You will decide for yourself what you think best about that. Caesius says that with the water taken off, and the right to the water legally certified, and a servitude placed on the property, we can still keep our price if we wanted to sell. I had Mescidius with me. He says he agreed with you on three sesterces per foot,[4] and that he has measured the distance by walking as 3,000 paces. It looked more to me, but I will guarantee that the money could not be better invested. I had sent for Cillo from Venafrum, but that very day at Venafrum a tunnel had fallen in, crushing four of his fellow slaves and pupils.

On the Ides of September I was at Laterium. I examined the road, which I thought good enough to be a public highway, except for 150 paces (I measured it myself) from

[3] Another property, called after its owner. But the name may be corrupt, perhaps Babullius or Babuleius.

[4] For the construction of an aquaduct.

Fur<r>inae,[11] Satricum versus. eo loco pulvis non glarea iniecta est (id[12] mutabitur) et ea viae pars valde acclivis est; sed intellexi aliter duci non potuisse, praesertim cum tu neque per Lucustae neque Varronis velles ducere. ille viam[13] ante suum fundum probe munierat; Lucusta non attigerat. quem ego Romae adgrediar, et, ut arbitror, commovebo, et simul M. Taurum, quem tibi audio promisisse, qui nunc Romae erat, de aqua per fundum eius ducenda rogabo.

5 Nicephorum, vilicum tuum, sane probavi quaesivique ex eo ecquid ei de illa aedificatiuncula Lateri de qua mecum locutus es mandavisses. tum is mihi respondit se ipsum eius operis HS $\overline{\text{XVI}}$ conductorem fuisse, sed te postea multa addidisse ad opus, nihil ad pretium; itaque id se omisisse. mihi mehercule valde placet te illa ut constitueras addere; quamquam ea villa quae nunc est tamquam philosopha videtur esse quae obiurget ceterarum villarum insaniam. verum tamen illud additum delectabit. topiarium laudavi. ita omnia convestivit hedera, qua basim villae, qua intercolumnia ambulationis, ut denique illi palliati topiariam facere videantur et hederam vendere. iam *ἀποδυτηρίῳ* nihil alsius, nihil muscosius.

6 Habes fere de rebus rusticis. urbanam expolitionem urget ille quidem [et][14] Philotimus et Cincius, sed etiam ipse crebro interviso, quod est facile factu. quam ob rem ea te cura liberatum volo.

11 (*SB*) 12 et (*Or.*)
13 vel vinum (*SB*) 14 (*Watt*)

5 An ancient Roman goddess of whom little is known.

the little bridge at Furrina's[5] chapel leading to Satricum. In that stretch powdered earth has been used instead of gravel (that will be altered), and that part of the road has a steep uphill gradient. But I saw that no other direction was possible, especially as you did not want to take it through either Lucusta's land or Varro's. Varro had made the road in front of his property in good style, whereas Lucusta has not touched his section. I shall tackle him in Rome and think I shall get him moving. At the same time I shall ask M. Taurus, who is now in Rome, about taking a conduit through his farm—I hear he has made you a promise.

Your bailiff Nicephorus impressed me very favourably. I asked him whether you had given him any instructions about that little bit of building at Laterium of which you had spoken to me. He answered that he had contracted to do the job himself for HS 16,000, but that you had later made considerable additions to the work and none to the price, so he had done nothing about it. For my part, I am really strongly in favour of making the additions you proposed. True, the house at present has an air of high thinking which rebukes the wild extravagance of other country houses; but still that addition will be pleasant. I commended the gardener. He has covered everything with ivy, the foundation wall of the house and the intervals between the columns in the promenade, so that the statues in their Greek cloaks look as though they were doing ornamental gardening and advertising their ivy. Then there is the little undressing room which is cool and mossy to a degree.

That's about all from the country. Philotimus and Cincius are pushing on with the finishing touches to your house, but I often put in an appearance myself, which is easy to do. So please set your mind at rest on that score.

7 De Cicerone quod me semper rogas, ignosco equidem tibi sed tu quoque mihi velim ignoscas; non enim concedo tibi plus ut illum ames quam ipse amo. atque utinam his diebus in Arpinati, quod et ipse cupierat et ego non minus, mecum fuisset! quod ad Pomponiam, si tibi videtur, scribas velim, cum aliquo exibimus eat nobiscum puerumque <e>ducat.[15] clamores efficiam si eum mecum habuero otiosus;[16] nam Romae respirandi non est locus. id me scis antea gratis tibi esse pollicitum. quid nunc putas, tanta mihi abs te mercede proposita?

8 Venio nunc ad tuas litteras, quas pluribus epistulis accepi dum sum in Arpinati; nam mihi uno die tres sunt redditae et quidem, ut videbantur, eodem abs te datae tempore, una pluribus verbis. in qua primum erat quod antiquior dies in tuis fuisset adscripta litteris quam in Caesaris: id facit Oppius non numquam necessario ut, cum tabellarios constituerit mittere litterasque a nobis acceperit, aliqua re nova impediatur et necessario serius quam constituerat mittat, neque nos datis iam epistulis diem commutari curamus.

9 Scribis de Caesaris summo in nos amore: hunc et tu fovebis et nos quibuscumque poterimus rebus augebimus. de Pompeio et facio diligenter et faciam quod mones. quod tibi mea permissio mansionis tuae grata est, id ego summo meo dolore et desiderio tamen ex parte gaudeo. in Hippodamo et non nullis aliis arcessendis quid cogites non intellego. nemo istorum est quin abs te munus fundi sub-

[15] (*Or.*) [16] otiosum (*Lamb.*)

[6] Mentioned again in Letter 23.4, but its nature is not disclosed.

I pardon your continual enquiries about young Quintus, but I hope you on your side will pardon me if I refuse to admit that you love him any more than I do myself. I only wish he could have been with me these days at Arpinum, which he wanted and I no less. So I'd like you to write to Pomponia, if you see fit, and ask her to come with me when I make an excursion and bring the boy. I shall do wonders if I have him by me on vacation—in Rome there isn't a moment to get one's breath. You know I gave you my word earlier gratis, so you can imagine what will happen now that you have offered me such a splendid fee.[6]

I come now to the letter which I received at Arpinum in several instalments—three letters were delivered to me in one day, apparently dispatched by you simultaneously. One, which was rather long, began by noting that my letter to you bore an earlier date than the one to Caesar. It sometimes happens unavoidably that when Oppius has arranged to send couriers and been given a letter from me, he is held up by something unexpected and dispatches it unavoidably later than he had arranged; and once the letters are handed in, I don't trouble about getting the date changed.

You write about Caesar's warm affection for us. You will cherish that, and I shall do everything in my power to increase it. As regards Pompey, I am and shall be careful to do what you advise. You say you are grateful for my licence to stay on; I miss you very sorely indeed, but still I am partially glad of it. I don't understand your purpose in sending for Hippodamus and certain others. Every one of these gentry expects a present from you to the value of a prop-

urbani instar exspectet. Trebatium vero meum quod isto admisceas nihil est. ego illum ad Caesarem misi, qui mihi iam satis fecit; si ipsi minus, praestare nihil debeo teque item ab eo vindico et libero. quod scribis te a Caesare cottidie plus diligi, immortaliter gaudeo. Balbum vero, qui est istius rei, quem ad modum scribis, adiutor, in oculis fero. Trebonium meum a te amari teque ab illo pergaudeo.

10 De tribunatu quod scribis, ego vero nominatim petivi Curtio et mihi ipse Caesar nominatim Curtio paratum esse rescripsit[17] meamque in rogando verecundiam obiurgavit. si cui praeterea petiero, id quod etiam Oppio dixi ut ad illum scriberet, facile patiar mihi negari, quoniam illi qui mihi molesti sunt sibi negari a me non facile patiuntur. ego Curtium, id quod ipsi dixi, non modo rogatione sed etiam testimonio tuo diligo, quod litteris tuis studium illius in salutem nostram facile perspexi.

De Britannicis rebus cognovi ex tuis litteris nihil esse nec quod metuamus nec quod gaudeamus. de publicis negotiis, quae vis ad te Tironem scribere, neglegentius ad te ante scribebam quod omnia minima maxima ad Caesarem mitti sciebam.

11 Rescripsi epistulae maximae, audi nunc de minuscula. in qua primum est de Clodi ad Caesarem litteris; in quo Caesaris consilium probo, quod tibi amantissime petenti veniam non dedit uti ullum ad illam furiam verbum rescri-

[17] perscripsit (*cod. Ambrosianus**)

erty in the suburbs. But you don't have to mix up my friend Trebatius in that category. I sent him to Caesar, who has already done all I expected of him. If he has not done all that Trebatius expected, I am not obliged to answer for anything and I likewise absolve and acquit you of all responsibility for him. I am tremendously pleased that you say you are rising in Caesar's good graces every day. Balbus, who you say is your helper in this, is the apple of my eye. I am glad that you and my friend Trebonius are such good friends.

As for what you write about the Tribunate, I did request one for Curtius[7] and Caesar himself wrote back to me personally that one was waiting for Curtius, mentioning his name; and he took me to task for my backwardness in making such requests. If I make one for anybody else (and I have told Oppius to write to Caesar accordingly), I shall not mind a refusal, seeing that the people who pester me *do* mind *my* refusing them. I have a regard for Curtius, as I told him, not only because you ask me but because of your testimonial, for your letter made it clear to me how zealous he was for my restoration.

As to British matters, I see from your letter that we have no cause for alarm nor for rejoicing either. On public affairs, which you want Tiro to write up for you, I have hitherto written rather perfunctorily because I know that everything, from greatest to least, is reported to Caesar.

I have answered the big letter, now for the little one: First you tell me about Clodius' letter to Caesar. I think Caesar was right to say no to the request you so affectionately made of him and not to write a single word to that

[7] Cf. Letter 18.3.

beret. alterum est de Calventi Mari oratione: quod scribis tibi placere me ad eam rescribere, miror,[18] praesertim cum illam nemo lecturus sit si ego nihil rescripsero, meam in illum pueri omnes tamquam dictata perdiscant. libros meos [omnis] quos exspectas incohavi, sed conficere non possum his diebus. orationes efflagitatas pro Scauro et pro Plancio absolvi. poema ad Caesarem quod instituerам incidi. tibi quod rogas, quoniam ipsi fontes iam sitiunt, si quid habebo spati, scribam.

12 Venio ad tertiam. Balbum quod ais mature Romam bene comitatum esse venturum mecumque adsidue usque ad Id. Mai. futurum, id mihi pergratum perque iucundum. quod me in eadem epistula, sicut saepe antea, cohortaris ad ambitionem et ad laborem, faciam equidem; sed quando vivemus?

13 Quarta epistula mihi reddita est Id. Sept., quam a. d. IIII Id. Sext. ex Britannia dederas. in ea nihil sane erat novi praeter Erigonam (quam si ab Oppio accepero, scribam ad te quid sentiam, nec dubito quin mihi placitura sit) et, quod ‹paene›[19] praeterii, de eo quem scripsisti de Milonis

[18] miror *post* scribis (*SB*)
[19] (*Wes.*)

[8] Quintus in brotherly solicitude had urged Caesar to rebuke or restrain Clodius, but Caesar had thought it best not to reply at all, a decision which M. Cicero approves.

[9] L. Calpurnius Piso, Consul in 57, whose maternal grandfather was an Insubrian Gaul named Calventius. Cicero's speech against him, delivered and edited for circulation in 55, compares him (naturally to his disadvantage) with Marius, who was responsible for Metellus Numidicus' exile in 100; cf. *In Pisonem* 20. Piso had evidently published a rejoinder.

embodiment of mischief.[8] Next, as to Calventius Marius' speech,[9] I am surprised that you think I should write a rejoinder to that, especially as nobody will read it if I don't reply, whereas all the schoolchildren learn mine against him by heart as though it was part of their lessons. I have begun the work which you are waiting for,[10] but I can't finish it this trip. I have completed the speeches for Scaurus and for Plancius[11] according to demand. I have broken off the poem addressed to Caesar which I had begun, but for you I shall write what you ask[12] (since the very springs are now athirst),[13] if I get any time.

Now I come to the third letter. You say that Balbus will be coming to Rome in good time with a goodly company and that he will be with me constantly until the Ides of May; much obliged, and much pleased to hear it. And then in the same letter, as often in the past, you urge me to go on winning friends and working. I shall. But when are we going to start living?

A fourth letter was delivered to me on the Ides of September, which you dispatched from Britain on 10 August. There was really nothing new in it except about *Erigona*[14] (and when I get her from Oppius I shall send you my opinion, though I don't doubt I shall like her) and (this I almost forgot) about the person who you say wrote to Caesar

[10] The treatise *On the Republic*.

[11] Part of the former and the whole of the latter are extant.

[12] Cf. Letter 24.4.

[13] Cicero affects to consider Quintus a better poet than himself.

[14] A tragedy of Sophocles latinized by Quintus.

plausu scripsisse ad Caesarem. ego vero facile patior ita Caesarem existimare, illum quam maximum fuisse plausum, et prorsus ita fuit; et tamen ille plausus qui illi datur quodam modo nobis videtur dari.

14 Reddita etiam mihi est pervetus epistula sed sero adlata, in qua de aede Telluris et de porticu Catuli me admones. fit utrumque diligenter. ad Telluris quidem etiam tuam statuam locavi. item de hortis me quod admones, nec fui umquam valde cupidus et nunc domus suppeditat mihi hortorum amoenitatem.

Romam cum venissem a. d. XIII Kal. Oct., absolutum offendi in aedibus tuis tectum. quod supra conclavia non placuerat tibi esse multorum fastigiorum, id nunc honeste vergit in tectum inferioris porticus.

Cicero noster dum ego absum[20] non cessavit apud rhetorem. de eius eruditione quod labores nihil est, quoniam ingenium eius nosti, studium ego video. cetera eius suscipio, ut me putem praestare debere.

15 Gabinium tres adhuc factiones postulant: L. Lentulus, flaminis filius, qui iam de maiestate postulavit; Ti. Nero cum bonis subscriptoribus; C. Memmius tribunus pl. cum L. Capitone. ad urbem accessit a. d. XII Kal. Oct.; nihil turpius nec desertius. sed his iudiciis nihil audeo confidere. quod Cato non valebat, adhuc de pecuniis repetundis non

[20] adsum (*Vict.*)

---

[15] Quintus may have written something to the effect that Caesar's correspondent might better have dwelt upon applause for Cicero. [16] The latter, adjoining Cicero's house on the Palatine, had been demolished by Clodius. Cicero seems to have been in charge of restoring both.

about the applause for Milo. Well, I am quite happy that Caesar should think the applause was tremendous. In point of fact, it was; though applause for him seems in a way like applause for me.[15]

Also, a very old letter was delivered to me, a late arrival, in which you remind me about the temple of Tellus and Catulus' portico.[16] Work is going busily forward on both. I have even put up your statue in the former. You also remind me about a place in the suburbs, but I was never very eager for one and my house now affords me that amenity.

When I returned to Rome on 18 September I found the roof on your house finished. You had not wished it to have many gables above the living rooms. It now slopes handsomely down to the roof of the lower portico.

Our boy has not been idle with his tutor in rhetoric during my absence. You need have no anxiety about his progress, for you know his abilities and I see his keenness. All else that concerns him I take upon myself and regard as my responsibility.

So far there are three groups out to prosecute Gabinius: L. Lentulus, the Flamen's son, who has already brought a charge of lese majesty; Ti. Nero, with some good assistant prosecutors; and Tribune C. Memmius,[17] with L. Capito. Gabinius arrived in the neighbourhood of Rome on 19 September. It was an ignominious homecoming with hardly a soul to welcome him. But the courts being what they are nowadays, I dare not feel confident about anything. He has not yet been charged with extortion because

[17] To be distinguished from his namesake, the consular candidate.

erat postulatus. Pompeius a me valde contendit de reditu
in gratiam, sed adhuc nihil profecit nec, si ullam partem
16 libertatis tenebo, proficiet. tuas litteras vehementer exspecto. quod scribis te audisse in candidatorum consularium coitione me interfuisse, id falsum est. eius modi enim
pactiones in ea coitione factae sunt, quas postea Memmius
patefecit, ut nemo bonus interesse debuerit, et simul mihi
committendum non fuit ut iis coitionibus interessem quibus Messalla excluderetur. cui quidem vehementer satis
facio rebus omnibus; ut arbitror, etiam Memmio. Domitio
ipsi multa iam feci quae voluit quaeque a me petivit. Scaurum beneficio defensionis valde obligavi. adhuc erat valde
incertum et quando comitia et qui consules futuri essent.

17 Cum hanc iam epistulam complicarem, tabellarii a vobis venerunt a. d. XI Kal., septimo vicesimo die. o me sollicitum! quantum ego dolui in Caesaris suavissimis litteris!
sed quo erant suaviores, eo maiorem[21] dolorem illius ille
casus adferebat. sed ad tuas venio litteras. primum tuam
remansionem etiam atque etiam probo, praesertim cum,
18 ut scribis, cum Caesare communicaris. Oppium miror
quicquam cum Publio; mihi enim non placuerat. quod
inferiore[22] epistula scribis me Id. Sept. Pompeio legatum
iri, id ego non audivi scripsique ad Caesarem ‹neque›[23]
Vibullium [Caesaris][24] mandata de mea mansione ad Pom-

[21] maiorem ‹mihi› *coni. SB*
[22] interiore (*Pluygers*)
[23] (*Madvig*) [24] (*SB*)

---

[18] His daughter's death.
[19] Clodius.
[20] In 55 Pompey received a five-year command in Spain and in

Cato is ill. Pompey is putting a lot of pressure on me for a reconciliation, but so far he has got nowhere, nor ever will if I keep a scrap of personal independence. I am waiting impatiently for a letter from you. It is untrue that I had anything to do with the coalition between the consular candidates, as you say you have heard. In view of the nature of the bargains struck in that coalition, which were subsequently made public by Memmius, no honest man could decently have had a hand in it. Besides, it would not have been right for me to take part in coalitions from which Messalla was excluded. He is very pleased with the support I am giving him in all ways. I think Memmius is pleased too. Even Domitius has had many favours from me, things he wanted or asked of me. Scaurus is under a great obligation to me for defending him. So far both the date of the elections and the result are highly uncertain.

Just as I was folding up this letter, couriers arrived from you—on the 20th, twenty-seven days' journey. How anxious I was! And how distressed to read Caesar's charming letter—the more charming the letter, the more distress I feel at the blow which has befallen him.[18] But to come to your letter: First, once again I approve of your staying on, especially as you have discussed it, as you say, with Caesar. I am surprised that Oppius has had any dealings with Publius[19]—I did not want it. Further on in your letter you say that I am to be appointed Pompey's Legate on the Ides of September.[20] That is news to me. I have written to Caesar to say that neither Vibullius nor Oppius has brought any message from Caesar to Pompey about my

the autumn of 54 he appointed Cicero as his Legate. But neither he nor Cicero went there. Cf. *Letters to Friends* 26 (VII.5).1.

peium pertulisse nec [ad][25] Oppium. quo consilio? quamquam Oppium ego tenui, quod priores partes Vibulli erant; cum eo enim coram Caesar[26] egerat, ad Oppium scripserat. ego vero nullas δευτέρας φροντίδας habere possum in Caesaris rebus. ille mihi secundum te et liberos nostros ita est ut sit paene par. videor id iudicio facere (iam enim debeo), sed tamen amore sum incensus.

19 Cum scripsissem haec infima quae sunt mea manu, venit ad nos Cicero tuus ad cenam, cum Pomponia foris cenaret. dedit mihi epistulam legendam tuam quam paulo ante acceperat, Aristophaneo[27] modo valde mehercule et suavem et gravem, qua sum admodum delectatus. dedit etiam alteram illam mihi, qua iubes eum mihi esse adfixum tamquam magistro. quam illum epistulae illae delectarunt, quam me! nihil puero illo suavius, nihil nostri amantius. hoc inter cenam Tironi dictavi, ne mirere alia manu esse.

20 Annali pergratae litterae tuae fuerunt, quod et curares de se diligenter et tamen consilio se verissimo iuvares. P. Servilius pater, ex litteris quas sibi a Caesare missas esse dicebat, significat valde te sibi gratum fecisse quod de sua voluntate erga Caesarem humanissime diligentissimeque locutus esses.

21 Cum Romam ex Arpinati revertissem, dictum mihi est Hippodamum ad te profectum esse. non possum scribere me miratum esse illum tam inhumaniter fecisse ut sine meis litteris ad te proficisceretur; illud scribo, mihi molestum fuisse. iam enim diu cogitaveram ex eo quod tu ad me

25 (*Madvig*) 26 Caesare (*Man.**)
27 Aristoteleo *coni. SB*

21 Or Aristotle? See my Commentary.

staying in Rome. What was the reason? Well, it's true that I held Oppius back, because the leading role belonged to Vibullius; Caesar had talked to him in person on the subject, only written to Oppius. No, I cannot have any second thoughts where Caesar is concerned. He comes next with me after you and our children, and only just after. I think I am wise in this (after all, it is time for some wisdom), but my affection is truly kindled.

After I had written these last lines which are in my own hand, your son came over to us for dinner, as Pomponia was dining out. He gave me your letter to read, which he had received shortly before—a charming, serious letter upon my word, in the manner of Aristophanes.[21] I was quite delighted with it. He also gave me the other letter, in which you tell him to stick close to me and regard me as his teacher. How pleased these letters made him, and me likewise! He is the most charming boy, and no one could be fonder of me. I dictated the above to Tiro at dinner, in case the different handwriting may surprise you.

Annalis was very grateful for your letter, grateful to you for taking trouble on his behalf and at the same time for honestly advising him for his own good. P. Servilius senior, speaking of a letter which he says he has had from Caesar, intimates that he is very much obliged to you for having spoken so kindly and with such particularity about his friendly feelings towards Caesar.

When I got back to Rome from Arpinum I was told that Hippodamus had set out to join you. I cannot say that I was surprised by his lack of consideration in leaving to join you without a letter from me. I say only that it vexed me. You see, it had been in my mind for a long time, from what you had written to me, that if there was anything that I wanted

scripseras ut, si quid esset quod ad te diligentius perferri vellem, illi darem, quod mehercule hisce litteris quas vulgo ad te mitto nihil fere scribo quod, si in alicuius manus inciderit, moleste ferendum sit. <nunc>[28] Minucio me et Salvio et Labeoni reservabam. Labeo aut tarde proficiscetur aut hic manebit. Hippodamus ne num quid vellem quidem rogavit.

22 T. Pinarius amabilis ad me de te litteras mittit, se maxime litteris, sermonibus, cenis denique tuis delectari. is homo semper me delectavit fraterque eius mecum est multum. qua re, uti instituisti, complectere adulescentem.

23 Quod multos dies epistulam in manibus habui propter commorationem tabellariorum, ideo <eo>[29] multa coniecta sunt, aliud alio tempore, velut hoc: T. Anicius mihi saepe iam dixit sese tibi suburbanum si quod invenisset non dubitaturum esse emere. in eius sermone ego utrumque soleo admirari, et te de suburbano emendo cum ad illum scribas non modo ad me non scribere sed etiam aliam in sententiam [de suburbano][30] scribere, et cum ad illum scribas nihil te recordari [de se][31] de ep<ist>ulis illis quas in Tusculano eius tu mihi ostendisti, nihil de praeceptis Epicharmi, *γνῶθι πῶς ἄλλῳ κέχρηται*, totum denique vultum, sermonem, animum eius, quem ad modum con-
24 icio, quasi *.[32] sed haec tu videris. de suburbano cura ut sciam quid velis et simul ne quid ille turbet vide.

Quid praeterea? quid? etiam. Gabinius a.d. IIII Kal. Oct. noctu in urbem introierat[33] et hodie hora VIII, cum

[28] (*SB*) [29] (*Goodyear*)
[30] (*Man.*) [31] (*Hervagius*)
[32] *excidit aliquid velut ἀπομεμαθηκέναι* (*T–P*)
[33] introierit (*Wes.*)

conveyed to you with extra care I should give it to him; for in these letters which I send you in the ordinary way the fact is that I write practically nothing which would be awkward if it fell into the wrong hands. Now I am reserving myself for Minucius and Salvius and Labeo. Labeo will either leave late or stay here. Hippodamus did not even bid me good-bye.

T. Pinarius sends me an amiable letter about you, saying that he takes great pleasure in your writings, your conversation, and, not least, your dinners. I always liked him, and his brother is much in my company. So go on being nice to the young man.

I have had this letter in my hands for many days past because of the courier's tarrying, and so collected many items at different times. For instance: T. Anicius has often told me that he would not hesitate to buy a suburban property for you if he found one. This talk of his surprises me in two ways. I think it strange that you should write to him about buying a suburban property, whereas not only do you not write to *me* but you write in a different sense. I also think it odd that when you write to him you don't remember anything about those letters of his which you showed me at his place at Tusculum or the precept of Epicharmus ('find how he behaves to others'), that in fact you have as it were obliterated (?), so I suppose, his whole face and talk and mind. But it's your affair. As to a suburban property, make sure that I know your wishes, and mind he doesn't do something idiotic.

What else? Oh yes, Gabinius entered Rome after dark on 27 September and today at two o'clock, when he had to

edicto C. Alfi de maiestate eum adesse oporteret, concursu magno et odio universi populi paene adflictus est. nihil illo turpius; proximus est tamen Piso. itaque mirificum embolium cogito in secundum librum meorum temporum[34] includere, dicentem Apollinem in concilio deorum qualis reditus duorum imperatorum futurus esset, quorum alter exercitum perdidisset, alter vendidisset.

Ex Britannia Caesar ad me Kal. Sept. dedit litteras, quas ego accepi a. d. IIII Kal. Oct., satis commodas de Britannicis rebus, quibus, ne admirer quod a te nullas acceperim; scribit se sine te fuisse cum ad mare accesserit. ad eas ego ei litteras nihil rescripsi, ne gratulandi quidem causa, propter eius luctum.

Te oro etiam atque etiam, mi frater, ut valeas.

22 (III.2)

Scr. Romae V *Id. Oct. an. 54*

‹MARCUS QUINTO FRATRI SALUTEM›

1 A. d. VI Id. Oct. Salvius Ostiam[1] vesperi navi profectus erat cum iis rebus quas tibi domo mitti volueras. eodem die Gabinium ad populum luculente calefecerat Memmius, sic ut Calidio verbum facere pro eo non licuerit. postridie autem eius diei qui erat tum futurus cum haec scribebam ante lucem, apud Catonem erat divinatio in Gabinium futura inter Memmium et Ti. Neronem et C. L. Antonios M. f. putabamus fore ut Memmio daretur, etsi erat Neronis

[34] librorum (*Mueller*)
[1] *anne* Ostia ?

---

[1] The Tribune.

appear to answer a charge of lese majesty on C. Alfius' order, he was almost crushed by a huge, hostile assembly of the whole people. He cuts the sorriest of figures, but Piso runs him close. I am thinking of putting a marvellous episode into Canto II of my Vicissitudes: Apollo in the assembly of the gods foretelling the return of the two generals, one of them after losing his army, the other after selling it.

Caesar dispatched a letter to me from Britain on the Kalends of September which I received on 27 September, giving a good enough account of the British campaign. He says that, in case I might wonder why I got no letter from you, you were not with him when he got to the coast. I have not replied, not even to congratulate him, because of his bereavement.

Once again, my dear fellow, I beg you take care of your health.

22 (III.2)

Rome, 11 October 54

From Marcus to his brother Quintus greetings.

On the evening of 10 October Salvius left for Ostia by boat with the articles you wanted sent to you from Rome. That same day Memmius[1] gave Gabinius a rare warming-up at a public meeting; Calidius was not allowed to say a word in his defence. The day following the day that is about to break as I write, Memmius, Ti. Nero, and the Antonius brothers (Gaius and Lucius, sons of Marcus) will plead before Cato for the right to prosecute Gabinius. We think it will go to Memmius, though Nero is remarkably

mira contentio. quid quaeris? probe premitur, nisi noster Pompeius dis hominibusque invitis negotium everterit.

2 Cognosce nunc hominis audaciam et aliquid in re publica perdita delectare. cum Gabinius quacumque veniebat triumphum se postulare dixisset subitoque bonus imperator noctu in urbem hostium plenam[2] invasisset, in senatum se non committebat. †interim†[3] ipso decimo die, quo eum oportebat hostiarum numerum et militum renuntiare, irrepsit summa infrequentia. cum vellet exire, a consulibus retentus est. introducti publicani. homo undique †atius[4]† [et],[5] cum a me maxime vulneraretur, non tulit et me trementi voce exsulem appellavit. hic (o di! nihil umquam honorificentius nobis accidit) consurrexit senatus cum clamore ad unum, sic ut ad corpus eius accederet; pari clamore atque impetu publicani. quid quaeris? omnes tamquam tu esses ita fuerunt. nihil hominum sermone foris clarius. ego tamen ‹me› teneo ab accusando, vix mehercule, sed tamen teneo, vel quod nolo cum Pompeio pugnare (satis est quod instat de Milone) vel quod iudices

[2] plane (*Koch*) [3] inde primum *coni. SB*
[4] *multa coniecta, velut* saucius (*Tyrrell*) [5] (*Man.*)

---

[2] *In urbem* can also mean 'into Rome.' Under a recent law a Triumphator had to swear before the City Quaestors within ten days (inclusive reckoning) of his triumphal entry to the truth of his report to the Senate of enemy and and Roman casualties (Valerius Maximus 2.8.1). As here appears (if the text is sound; see my Commentary), he was also required to report the number of immolated victims and of soldiers taking part. Gabinius, says Cicero, had talked of claiming a Triumph, but actually had entered Rome

keen. In a word, he is properly under pressure—unless our friend Pompey spoils the sport to the disgust of gods and men.

Now let me tell you about the fellow's insolence—something to give you a little pleasure in this twilight of the commonwealth. After giving out wherever he went that he was claiming a Triumph and then (good general that he is) suddenly bursting into the enemy capital[2] at night, he didn't trust himself inside the Senate. Not until[3] the statutory tenth day, on which he was required to report the number of sacrificial victims and soldiers, did he creep into a very thin House.[4] As he was about to leave, he was detained by the Consuls and the tax farmers brought in. Harassed from all sides as he was, I hit him hardest. Unable to stand it, he called out 'exile' in a quavering voice. Thereupon (gods above, it was the most flattering thing that ever happened to me) the Senate rose like one man, shouting and physically bearing down on him. The tax farmers shouted as loud and moved as smartly. To put it in a nutshell, every man of them behaved as though he was you. Outside the House nothing has ever been more talked of. However, I refrain from prosecuting him myself—with difficulty I can assure you, but I refrain. I don't want a fight with Pompey (what's coming over Milo is enough) and

by stealth and slunk into the Senate ten days later, the very day by which had he triumphed he would have had to take the oath.

3 Translating *inde primum* for *interim*.

4 By entering Rome Gabinius had forfeited his claim to a Triumph, which in any case could not be taken seriously after the Senate's refusal of a Supplication. Cicero's remarks are therefore sarcastic.

nullos habemus. ἀπότευγμα formido, addo etiam malevolentiam hominum et timeo ne illi me accusante aliquid accedat;[6] nec despero rem et sine me et non nihil per me confici posse.

3 De ambitu postulati sunt omnes qui consulatum petunt: a Memmio Domitius, a Q. Acutio, bono et erudito adulescente, Memmius, a Q. Pompeio Messalla, a Triario Scaurus. magna res in motu est, propterea quod aut hominum aut legum interitus ostenditur. opera datur ut iudicia ne fiant. res videtur spectare ad interregnum. consules comitia habere cupiunt; rei nolunt, et maxime Memmius, quod Caesaris adventu se sperat futurum consulem; sed mirum in modum iacet.[7] Domitius cum Messalla certus esse videbatur. Scaurus refrixerat. Appius sine lege curiata confirmat se Lentulo nostro successurum. qui quidem mirificus illo die, quod paene praeterii, fuit in Gabinium. accusavit maiestatis. nomina data, cum ille verbum nullum.

Habes forensia. domi recte est.[8] ipsa domus a redemptoribus tractatur non indiligenter.

23 (III.3)

Scr. Romae XII *Kal. Nov. an. 54*

‹MARCUS QUINTO FRATRI SALUTEM›

1 Occupationum mearum tibi signum sit librari manus.

[6] accidat (*Schütz*) [7] tacet (*Vict.*) [8] et (*Wes.*)

---

[5] Probably the candidate. [6] As governor of Cilicia.
[7] Lit. 'names were given,' but the meaning is uncertain.

there are no juries any more. I'm afraid of a fiasco. And then people are so malicious—I'm nervous that he might gain some advantage with myself as prosecutor. And I don't despair of seeing the thing go through without me, and in some degree with my assistance.

All the candidates for the Consulship have been charged with bribery: Domitius by Memmius,[5] Memmius by Q. Acutius (a good, well-instructed young man), Messalla by Q. Pompeius, Scaurus by Triarius. Something big is on the way, for it looks like the end of either the men or the laws. Efforts are being made to prevent the trials, and there's the prospect of an Interregnum. The Consuls are eager to hold elections, but the defendants don't want them, especially Memmius, because he hopes that when Caesar arrives he will be elected. But he is in remarkably low water. It seems a certainty for Domitius and Messalla. Scaurus has gone flat. Appius says definitely that he will take over from our friend Lentulus[6] without a curiate law. I almost forgot to say that he was magnificent that day against Gabinius—charged him with lese majesty. Members volunteered (?),[7] while Gabinius never said a word.

So much for public affairs. At home all is well. As to the home itself, the contractors are making reasonably good progress.

23 (III.3)

Rome, 21 October 54

From Marcus to his brother Quintus greetings.

You may take my clerk's handwriting as a sign of how

diem scito esse nullum quo die non dicam pro reo. ita, quicquid conficio aut cogito, in ambulationis tempus fere confero.

Negotia se nostra sic habent, domestica vero ut volumus. valent pueri, studiose discunt, diligenter docentur, et nos et inter se amant. expolitiones utriusque nostrum sunt in manibus, sed tua ad perfectum iam res rustica Arcani et Lateri. praeterea de aqua,[1] de via nihil praetermisi quadam epistula quin enucleate ad te perscriberem. sed me illa cura sollicitat angitque vehementer quod dierum iam amplius quadraginta intervallo nihil a te, nihil a Caesare, nihil ex istis locis non modo litterarum sed ne rumoris quidem adfluxit. me autem iam et mare istuc et terra sollicitat neque desino, ut fit in amore, ea quae minime volo cogitare. qua re non equidem iam te rogo ut ad me de te, de rebis istis scribas (numquam enim, cum potes, praetermittis), sed hoc te scire volo, nihil fere umquam me sic exspectasse ut, cum haec scribebam, tuas litteras.

2 Nunc cognosce ea quae sunt in re publica. comitiorum cottidie singuli dies tolluntur obnuntiationibus magna voluntate bonorum omnium; tanta invidia sunt consules propter suspicionem pactorum a candidatis praemiorum. candidati consulares quattuor omnes rei. causae sunt difficiles, sed enitemur ut Messalla noster salvus sit, quod est etiam cum reliquorum salute coniunctum. Gabinium de ambitu reum fecit P. Sulla subscribente privigno Mem-

[1] ad ea qua

busy I am. I tell you, there is not a day on which I don't make a speech for the defence. So practically everything I do or think about I put into my walking time.

Our affairs stand as follows: domestically they are as we wish them. The boys are well, keen at their lessons and conscientiously taught. They love us and each other. The finishing touches to both our houses are in train, but your country residences at Arcanum and Laterium are already all but complete. Furthermore, I wrote to you in full detail about the water and the road in one of my letters,[1] omitting nothing. But I am very anxious and worried by the fact that for more than six weeks now I have heard nothing either from you or from Caesar. Not a letter, not even a rumour has trickled in from that part of the world. Sea and land out there both make me anxious now, and, as usual when people one is fond of are concerned, I am continually imagining the worst. I won't ask you to write to me about yourself and about what is going on, for you never lose an opportunity; but I do want you to know that I have never been so impatient for anything in my life as I am for a letter from you as I write these lines.

Now let me tell you about politics. Day by day election days are cancelled by declarations of contrary omens, to the great satisfaction of all honest men. That is because the Consuls are in very bad odour owing to the suspicion that they have sold themselves to the candidates. All four consular candidates have been charged. The cases are difficult to defend, but I shall work hard to save Messalla, and that involves the survival of the others. P. Sulla has charged Gabinius with bribery, with his stepson Memmius, his

[1] Letter 21.

mio, fratre Caecilio, Sulla filio. contra dixit L. Torquatus
3 omnibusque libentibus non obtinuit. quaeris quid fiat de Gabinio: sciemus de maiestate triduo; quo quidem in iudicio odio premitur omnium generum, maxime testibus laeditur,[2] accusatoribus frigidissimis utitur. consilium varium, quaesitor gravis et firmus Alfius, Pompeius vehemens in iudicibus rogandis. quid futurum sit nescio, locum tamen illi[3] in civitate non video. animum praebeo ad illius perniciem moderatum, ad rerum eventum lenissimum.

4 Habes fere de omnibus rebus. unum illud addam: Cicero tuus nosterque summo studio est Paeoni sui rhetoris, hominis, opinor, valde exercitati et boni. sed nostrum instituendi genus esse paulo eruditius et *θετικώτερον* non ignoras. qua re neque ego impediri Ciceronis iter atque illam disciplinam volo et ipse puer magis illo declamatorio genere duci et delectari videtur. in quo quoniam ipsi quoque fuimus, patiamur illum ire nostris itineribus, eodem enim perventurum esse confidimus; sed tamen, si nobiscum eum rus aliquo eduxerimus, in hanc nostram rationem consuetudinemque inducemus. magna enim nobis a te proposita merces est, quam certe nostra culpa numquam minus adsequemur.

Quibus in locis et qua spe hiematurus sis ad me quam diligentissime scribas velim.

[2] caeditur (*Pluygers*)
[3] illum (*Vict.*)

brother Caecilius,[2] and his son Sulla as assistant prosecutors. L. Torquatus put in a rival claim to prosecute and everyone was glad it failed. You will want to know what is happening about Gabinius. We shall know about the lese majesty in three days' time. In that trial he is weighed down by his unpopularity with all classes, and the witnesses are most damaging; the prosecutors are extremely ineffective, the jury is a mixed bag, the President, Alfius, is responsible and firm, Pompey is urgently trying to influence the jurors. I don't know what will happen, but I don't see any place for him in the community. I take a moderate attitude as to his ruin, and a very easy one as to the outcome of events.

That is about all my news. I will add one thing: your (our) boy Quintus is greatly devoted to his tutor in rhetoric, Paeonius, a very good experienced man, I think; but, as you are aware, my method of instruction is a little more scholarly and abstract. Accordingly, I don't want Quintus' progress and the teaching he is getting held up; and the boy himself seems to find the declamatory mode more attractive and agreeable. We have been through it ourselves, so let us allow him to follow in our footsteps. I am confident he will reach the same goal. All the same, when I take him away with me somewhere in the country, I shall introduce him to my method and practice. You have offered me a big fee, and it won't be my fault if I don't earn it.

Do write to me in full detail where you will be spending the winter and with what prospects.

[2] L. Caecilius Rufus, Praetor in 57.

24 (III.4)

Scr. Romae IX *Kal. Nov. an. 54*

MARCUS QUINTO FRATRI SALUTEM

1 Gabinius absolutus est. omnino nihil accusatore Lentulo subscriptoribusque eius infantius, nihil illo consilio sordidius; sed tamen nisi incredibilis contentio preces Pompei, dictaturae etiam rumor plenus timoris fuisset, ipsi Lentulo non respondisset, qui tamen illo accusatore illoque consilio sententiis condemnatus sit ‹x›xxii[1] cum LXX tulissent. est omnino tam gravi fama hoc iudicium ut videatur reliquis iudiciis periturus et maxime de pecuniis repetundis. sed vides nullam esse rem publicam, nullum senatum, nulla iudicia, nullam in ullo nostrum dignitatem. quid plura?[2] de iudicibus duo praetorii sederunt, Domitius Calvinus (is aperte absolvit ut omnes viderent) et Cato (is diribitis[3] tabellis de circulo se subduxit et Pompeio primus nuntiavit).

2 Aiunt non nulli, ut Sallustius, me oportuisse accusare. his ego iudicibus committerem? quid essem, si me agente esset elapsus? sed me alia moverunt: non putasset sibi Pompeius de illius salute sed de sua dignitate mecum esse

1 (*Man.*)
2 *post* iudicibus *dist. vulg.* (*SB*)
3 diruptis (*Ferrarius*)

---

1 C. Cato, who used to be eliminated because he was Tribune in 56 and so on the face of it could not be an ex-Praetor in 54 (as for M. Cato, he *was* Praetor in 54). J. Linderski, however, has removed the block: since no elections were held in 56, he could have been elected Praetor early in 55 and entered office straight away,

24 (III.4)

Rome, 24 October 54

From Marcus to his brother Quintus greetings.

Gabinius has been acquitted. To be sure, the prosecutor Lentulus and his assistants were stutterers and the jury was a disgrace. None the less, but for Pompey's incredible lobbying and importunity, also the formidable rumour of a Dictatorship, he would not have answered, not even to Lentulus. Even with such a prosecutor and such a jury he was found guilty by 32 votes out of 70 cast. To be sure, this trial has caused so much scandal that he looks likely to go under in the forthcoming trials, especially for extortion. But you see that we have neither commonwealth nor Senate nor courts of justice, and that none of us has any standing. Further as to the jury, two ex-Praetors sat on it, Domitius Calvinus (who openly voted for acquittal for all to see) and Cato[1] (when the votes had been counted he slipped off and was the first to bring the good news to Pompey).

Some, like Sallustius, say I ought to have prosecuted. Was I to trust myself with such a jury as this? How should I have looked if he had got away with me conducting the business? But I had other reasons. Pompey would have felt that it was a fight between him and me, and that the stake was not Gabinius' survival but his own prestige. He would

so becoming an ex-Praetor the following year. As Tribune this Cato had been bitterly hostile to Pompey, but shortly before the date of this letter had changed his tune and reconciled with Cicero and Milo (*Letters to Atticus* 89 (IV.16).5). Courting Pompey would fit the pattern. This is the last we hear of him.

certamen, in urbem introisset, ad inimicitias res venisset; cum Aesernino Samnite Pacideianus comparatus viderer, auriculam fortasse mordicus abstulisset, cum Clodio quidem certe redisset in gratiam. ego vero meum consilium, si praesertim tu non improbas, vehementer approbo. ille cum a me [in] singularibus meis studiis ornatus esset cumque ego illi nihil deberem, ille mihi omnia, tamen in re publica me a se dissentientem non tulit (nihil dicam gravius) et minus potens eo tempore quid in me florentem posset ostendit; nunc, cum ego ne curem quidem multum posse, res quidem publica certe nihil possit, unus ille omnia possit, cum illo ipso contenderem? sic enim faciendum fuisset. non existimo te putare id mihi suscipiendum
3 fuisse. 'alterutrum' inquit idem Sallustius. 'defendisses idque Pompeio contendenti dedisses' (etenim vehementer orabat). lepidum amicum Sallustium, qui mihi aut inimicitias putet periculosas subeundas fuisse aut infamiam sempiternam! ego vero hac mediocritate delector, ac mihi illud iucundum est quod, cum testimonium secundum fidem et religionem gravissime dixissem, reus [se][4] dixit, si in civitate licuisset sibi esse, mihi se satis facturum, neque me quicquam interrogavit.

4 De versibus quos tibi a me scribi vis, deest mihi quidem opera sed abest[5] etiam *ἐνθουσιασμός*,[6] qui[7] non modo tempus sed etiam animum vacuum ab omni cura deside-

[4] (*Brunus*) [5] habes (*Brunus*)
[6] sed . . . *ἐνθ- post* desiderat (*SB*) [7] quae (*SB*)

[2] Some fragments of Lucilius recount a match between these two gladiators. Pacideianus won, but as here appears, his ear was bitten off by his opponent. See my Commentary.

have entered Rome, it would have come to a feud. I should have looked like Pacideianus matched against Aeserninus the Samnite.[2] He might have bitten off my ear, and he would certainly have made it up with Clodius. No, I strongly approve of my decision, especially if you don't disapprove of it. Think of what Pompey did. I had shown extraordinary zeal for his advancement, I was under no obligation to him, whereas his to me were unlimited; and yet he couldn't tolerate (I will use no harsher phrase) my political disagreement with himself, and though less powerful then than now he showed what he could do to me at the height of my career. *Now*, when I don't even trouble about having power and the commonwealth certainly has none and Pompey alone is all-powerful, was I to lock horns with Pompey himself? For that is what I should have had to do. I don't believe you would have had me take that upon myself. 'One thing or the other,' says that same Sallustius. 'You ought to have defended him and yielded to Pompey's insistence' (he certainly begged me earnestly to do that). What a charming friend Sallustius is! He thinks I ought to have chosen between a dangerous feud and eternal disgrace. For my part, I like this middle way. And I am glad to remember that after I had given my evidence very gravely in accordance with my honour and conscience the defendant said that if he was allowed to remain in the community he would make me amends. Nor did he ask me a single question.

As for the verses you want me to write for you, I lack the leisure, but I also lack divine *afflatus*, which calls not only for time but for a mind free of all anxiety. For I am not al-

rat. non enim sumus omnino sine cura venientis anni, etsi sumus sine timore. simul et illud (sine ulla mehercule ironia loquor): tibi istius generis in scribendo priores partis tribuo quam mihi.

5 De bibliotheca tua Graeca supplenda, libris commutandis, Latinis comparandis, valde velim ista confici, praesertim cum ad meum quoque usum spectent. sed ego mihi ipsi ista per quem agam non habeo. neque enim venalia sunt, quae quidem placeant, et confici nisi per hominem et peritum et diligentem non possunt. Chrysippo tamen imperabo et cum Tyrannione loquar. de fisco quid egerit Scipio quaeram; quod videbitur rectum esse curabo. de Ascanione tu vero quod voles facies; me nihil interpono. de suburbano quod non properas laudo, ut habeas hortor.

6 Haec scripsi a. d. VIIII Kal. Nov., quo die ludi committebantur, in Tusculanum proficiscens ducensque mecum Ciceronem meum in ludum discendi, non lusionis, ea re non longius, quod[8] vellem, quod Pomptino ad triumphum a. d. IIII Non. Nov. volebam adesse. etenim erit nescio quid negotioli. nam Cato et Servilius praetores prohibituros se minantur, nec quid possint scio; ille enim et Appium consulem secum habebit et praetores et tribunos pl. sed minantur tamen in primisque Ἄρη πνέων Q. Scaevola.

Cura, mi suavissime et carissime frater, ut valeas.

[8] quam (*Lallemand*)

---

[3] Nothing is known about this business, but cf. Letter 25.6, last sentence.

together without anxiety about next year, though I have no fear. And furthermore, truly without false modesty, I recognize you as my superior in that line of authorship.

As regards filling the gaps in your Greek library and exchanging books and acquiring Latin ones, I should very much like all this done, especially as I too stand to benefit. But I have nobody I can employ on such business, not even for myself. Books, at least such as one would like to have, are not on the market and they can't be obtained except through an expert who is willing to take trouble. However, I'll give an order to Chrysippus and talk to Tyrannio. I shall enquire what Scipio has done about the Treasury,[3] and shall pay what appears proper. As to Ascanio, you will do what you wish—I don't interfere. You are wise to be in no hurry about a suburban property, though I do encourage you to get one.

I am writing this on 24 October, the opening day of the Games, as I leave for Tusculum. I am taking my son with me, to work, not to play. The reason I go no further away, as I should have liked to do, is that I want to put in an appearance for Pomptinus, whose Triumph is on 2 November. And there will be some little trouble, for Praetors Cato and Servilius are threatening to forbid it. I don't know what they can do (he will have Consul Appius with him and most of the Praetors and Tribunes), but threaten they do, especially Q. Scaevola, 'breathing war.'[4]

Take care of your health, my sweetest and dearest of brothers.

4 Cf. Aeschylus, *Agamemnon* 375, Quintus of Smyrna I.343. The Latin equivalent is in *Letters to Atticus* 389 (XV.11).1.

25 (III.5)

Scr. in Tusculano ex. m. Oct. aut in. m. Nov. an. 54

MARCUS QUINTO FRATRI SALUTEM

1 Quod quaeris quid de illis libris egerim quos cum essem in Cumano scribere institui, non cessavi neque cesso, sed saepe iam scribendi totum consilium rationemque mutavi. nam iam duobus factis libris, in quibus novendialibus feriis quae fuerunt Tuditano et Aquillio consulibus sermo est a me[1] institutus Africani paulo ante mortem et Laeli, Phili, Man<i>li,[2] <P. Rutili>,[3] Q. Tuberonis, et Laeli generorum, Fanni et Scaevolae, sermo autem in novem et dies et libros distributus de optimo statu civitatis et de optimo cive. sane texebatur opus luculente hominumque dignitas aliquantum orationi ponderis adferebat. ii libri cum in Tusculano mihi legerentur audiente Sallustio, admonitus sum ab illo multo maiore auctoritate illis de rebus dici posse si ipse loquerer de re publica, praesertim cum essem non Heraclides Ponticus sed consularis et is qui in maximis versatus in re publica rebus essem; quae tam antiquis hominibus attribuerem, ea visum iri ficta[4] esse; oratorum sermonem in illis nostris libris qui essent[5] de ratione dicendi, belle a me removisse, ad eos tamen rettulisse quos ipse vidissem; Aristotelem denique quae de re publica et praestanti viro scribat ipsum loqui.

2 Commovi<t> me, et eo magis quod maximos motus nostrae civitatis attingere non poteram, quod erant infe-

1 tamen 2 (*Man.*) 3 (*Wes.*)
4 visu(m) mirifica (*Brunus*) 5 quod esset (*Wes.**)

1 *On the Republic.* 2 129.

25 (III.5)

Tusculum, end of October or beginning of November 54

From Marcus to his brother Quintus greetings.

You ask what has become of the work[1] which I started to write when I was at Cumae. Well, I have not been and am not idle, but several times already I have changed the whole plan and framework. I had two Books in which I presented a conversation held during the nine-day holiday in the Consulship of Tuditanus and Aquillius,[2] the speakers being Africanus (shortly before his death), Laelius, Philus, Manilius, P. Rutilius, Q. Tubero, and Laelius' sons-in-law, Fannius and Scaevola. The conversation, distributed over nine days and nine Books, concerned the ideal constitution and the ideal citizen. The composition of the work was going forward very nicely and the high rank of the participants lent weight to their words. But when these two Books were read to me at Tusculum in Sallustius' hearing, he pointed out that these matters could be treated with much more authority if I spoke of the commonwealth in my own person. After all, he said, I was no Heraclides of Pontus but a Consular, one who had been involved in most important state affairs. Speeches attributed to persons so remote in time would appear fictitious. In my earlier work on the theory of oratory, he said, I had tactfully separated the conversation of the orators from myself, but I had put it into the mouths of men whom I had personally seen. Finally, Aristotle's writings on the state and the preeminent individual are in his own person.

This shook me, all the more so as I was debarred from touching upon the greatest upheavals in our community because they took place after the lifetimes of the interlocu-

riores quam illorum aetas qui loquebantur. ego autem id ipsum tum eram secutus, ne in nostra tempora incurrens offenderem quempiam. nunc et id vitabo et loquar ipse[6] tecum et tamen illa quae institueram ad te, si Romam venero, mittam. puto enim te existimaturum a me illos libros non sine aliquo meo stomacho esse relictos.

3 Caesaris amore quem ad me perscripsit unice delector; promissis iis quae ostendit non valde pendeo. nec sitio honores nec desidero gloriam magisque eius voluntatis perpetuitatem quam promissorum exitum exspecto. vivo tamen in ea ambitione et labore quasi[7] id quod non postulo exspectem.

4 Quod me de versibus faciendis rogas, incredibile est, mi frater, quam egeam tempore, nec sane satis commoveor animo ad ea quae vis canenda. *ἀμπώτεις* vero et ea quae ipse ego ne cogitando quidem consequor tu, qui omnis isto eloquendi et exprimendi genere superasti, a me petis? facerem tamen ut possem, sed, quod te minime fugit, opus est ad poema quadam animi alacritate, quam plane mihi tempora eripiunt. abduco equidem me ab omni rei publicae cura dedoque litteris, sed tamen indicabo tibi quod mehercule in primis te celatum volebam. angor, mi suavissime frater, angor nullam esse rem publicam, nulla iudicia, nostrumque hoc tempus aetatis, quod in illa auctoritate senatoria florere debe‹ba›t,[8] aut forensi labore iactari aut domesticis litteris sustentari, illud vero quod a puero adamaram, '*πολλὸν ἀριστεύειν καὶ ὑπείροχος ἔμμεναι*

[6] et ipse [7] quam (*Ursinus*) [8] (*Man.*)

[3] Quintus had solicited descriptions of British natural phenomena in verse (Letter 20.4), including the ocean tides.

tors. In point of fact that was my object at the time, to avoid giving offence in any quarter if I came into contact with our own period. Now, while avoiding this, I shall speak myself in conversation with you; none the less I shall send you what I had begun when I return to Rome. I think you will appreciate that it cost me some heartburning to give up those two Books.

Caesar's affection as expressed in his letter pleases me beyond anything, but I set no great store by the promises he holds out. I am not thirsty for honours nor do I hanker after glory. I look forward to his lasting good will more than to the outcome of his promises. And yet I live constantly toiling to win friends as though I *were* looking forward to what I do not ask.

As for your request about writing verses, my dear fellow, you cannot believe how short I am of time; and frankly I am not sufficiently stimulated by the theme on which you want me to poetize. Do you ask me for tides[3] and things which I myself cannot even imagine—you, who have excelled everyone in this kind of descriptive eloquence? Even so I should make a job of it, but, as you are very well aware, poetry calls for a certain mental *élan* of which the times we live in quite deprive me. To be sure, I am withdrawing from all political concerns and giving myself up to literary work; all the same, I will tell you something which I assure you I used to want to hide from you of all people. My sweetest brother, it wrings my heart to think that we have no commonwealth, no courts of justice, and that these years of my life which ought to be passing in the plenitude of senatorial dignity are spent in the hurly-burly of forensic practice or rendered tolerable by my studies at home. As for my childhood dream, 'Far to excel, outtop-

ἄλλων,' totum occidisse, inimicos a me partim non oppugnatos, partim etiam esse defensos, meum non modo animum sed ne odium quidem esse liberum, unumque ex omnibus Caesarem esse inventum qui me tantum quantum ego vellem amaret, aut etiam, sicut alii putant, hunc unum esse qui ‹a me amari›[9] vellet. quorum tamen nihil est eius modi ut ego me non multa[10] consolatione cottidie leniam: sed illa erit consolatio maxima, si una erimus. nunc ad illa vel gravissimum accedit desiderium tui.

5 Gabinium si, ut Pansa putat oportuisse, defendissem, concidissem. qui illum oderunt (ii sunt toti ordines), propter quem oderunt, me ipsum odisse coepissent. tenui me, ut puto, egregie, tantum ut facerem quantum ‹faciendum›[11] omnes viderent; et in omni summa, ut mones, valde me ad otium pacemque converto.

6 De libris Tyrannio est cessator; Chrysippo dicam. sed res operosa est et hominis perdiligentis. sentio ipse, qui in summo studio nihil adsequor. de Latinis vero quo me vertam nescio; ita mendose[12] et scribuntur et veneunt. sed tamen, quod fieri poterit, non neglegam. †Crebrius†,[13] ut ante ad te scripsi, Romae est et, quod valde iuvat, omnia debere tibi[14] renuntiat. ab aerario puto confectum esse dum absum.

7 Quattuor tragoedias sedecim diebus absolvisse cum

[9] (*SB*) [10] multa non (*Crat.*) [11] (*coni. Watt*)
[12] mendosi *coni. SB* [13] C. Rebilus *Or.*
[14] qui omnia adnuat debere tibi valde (*SB*)

---

[4] Cf. *Letters to Friends* 317 (XIII.15).2. πολλὸν (far) is here substituted for αἴεν (always) and ὑπείροχος for ὑπείροχον, accidentally no doubt. [5] As to blame for Cicero's exile.

ping all the rest,'[4] it has perished utterly. Some of my enemies I have refrained from attacking, others I have actually defended. My mind, even my animosities, are in chains. And in all the world Caesar is the only man who cares for me as much as I could wish, or even (as others would have it) who wants *me* to care for *him*. And yet nothing of all this is so painful but that I find many consolations to make life easier day by day. But the greatest consolation will be for us to be together. As it is, I have to bear the heavy burden of your absence on top of the rest.

If I had defended Gabinius, as Pansa thought I ought to have done, it would have been my undoing. Those who hate him (and this includes all categories of society) would have begun to hate me—the very person on whose account they hate *him*.[5] I held my horses to admiration, I think, doing just so much as everyone saw I had to do. And in the sum total I am resolutely facing in the direction of tranquillity and peace, as you advise.

As for the books, Tyrannio is a dawdler. I shall speak to Chrysippus. But it is a laborious business and needs somebody who will take a lot of trouble. I know that from my own experience of trying very hard and making no headway. As for the Latin ones, I don't know where to turn, the copies are made and sold so full of errors. None the less, I shall not neglect to do what can be done. *,[6] as I wrote to you earlier, is in Rome and reports himself as infinitely obliged to you, which is very gratifying. I think our business has been settled by the Treasury during my absence.

You write that you have finished off four tragedies in

[6] 'Crebrius' in the manuscripts, probably corrupt.

scribas, tu quicquam ab alio mutuaris? et †πλεος†[15] quaeris, cum Electram et †Troadam†[16] scripseris? cessator esse noli et illud '*γνῶθι σεαυτόν*' noli putare ad adrogantiam minuendam solum esse dictum verum etiam ut bona nostra norimus. sed et istas et Erigonam mihi velim mittas. habes ⟨ad⟩[17] duas epistulas proximas.

8 Romae et maxime in[18] Appia ad Martis mira proluvies. Crassipedis ambulatio ablata, horti, tabernae plurimae. magna vis aquae usque ad piscinam publicam. viget illud Homeri:

> *ἤματ᾽ ὀπωρινῷ, ὅτε λαβρότατον χέει ὕδωρ*
> *Ζεύς, ὅτε δή ῥ᾽ ἄνδρεσσι κοτεσσάμενος*
> *χαλεπήνῃ.*

cadit enim in absolutionem Gabini:

> *οἳ βίῃ εἰν ἀγορῇ σκολιὰς κρίνωσι θέμιστας,*
> *ἐκ δὲ δίκην ἐλάσωσι, θεῶν ὄπιν οὐκ ἀλέγοντες.*

9 sed haec non curare decrevi. Romam cum venero, quae perspexero scribam ad te et maxime de dictatura, et ad Labienum et ad Ligurium litteras dabo.

Hanc scripsi ante ⟨lucem⟩ ad lychnuchum ligneolum, qui mihi erat periucundus quod eum te aiebant, cum esses Sami, curasse faciendum.

Vale, mi suavissime et optime frater.

15 Πλέοντας *coni. SB*
16 Troadas *Wes.*
17 (*Vict.*) 18 et *vel om.* (*Wes.*)

---

7 See my Commentary. The play represented by *trodam* in the manuscripts may be *Troilus* or *Procris*, lost plays by Sophocles,

sixteen days; and are *you* trying to borrow anything from someone else? And are you asking for *Sailors* (?) when you have written an *Electra* and a *?[7] Don't be so lazy. And don't suppose that the old maxim 'know thyself' was made only to reduce conceit; it also tells us to know our strong points. But please send me these new ones and *Erigona*. There are your two last letters answered.

In Rome and especially on the Appian Way near the temple of Mars we are having extraordinarily heavy floods. Crassipes' promenade has been swept away along with a great number of residences and shops. The vast expanse of water stretches as far as the public fish pond. Homer's lines are much quoted:

> An autumn day, when Zeus most mightily
> Doth rain, in ire against unrighteous men,

pat as they are to Gabinius' acquittal:

> Who, rendering crooked judgements openly,
> Drive justice out nor reck of wrath divine.[8]

But I am resolved not to trouble myself about such matters. When I get back to Rome I shall write to you what I observe, especially about the Dictatorship, and shall send letters to Labienus and Ligurius.

I am writing this before dawn by the light of a little lamp with a wooden stand, which delights me because they say you had it made when you were in Samos.

Good-bye, my sweetest and best of brothers.

who is not known to have written a *Troades* (*Women of Troy*). But Quintus may not have restricted himself to Sophocles.

[8] *Iliad* 16.385–88.

26 (III.6)

Scr. Romae ex. m. Nov. an. 54

‹MARCUS QUINTO FRATRI SALUTEM›

1 Superiori epistulae quod respondeam nihil est, quae plena stomachi et querelarum est, quo in genere alteram quoque te scribis pridie Labeoni[1] dedisse, qui adhuc non venerat. delevit enim mihi omnem molestiam recentior epistula. tantum te et moneo et rogo ut in istis molestiis et laboribus et desideriis recordere consilium nostrum quod fuerit profectionis tuae. non enim commoda quaedam sequebamur parva ac[2] mediocria. quid enim erat quod discessu nostro emendum putaremus? praesidium firmissimum petebamus ex optimi et potentissimi viri benevolentia ad omnem statum nostrae dignitatis. plura ponuntur in spe quam in pecuniis; ‹qua relicta›[3] reliqua ad iacturam struentur.[4] qua re, si crebro referes animum tuum ad rationem et veteris consili nostri et spei, facilius istos militiae labores ceteraque quae te offendunt feres, et tamen cum voles depones. sed eius rei maturitas nequedum venit et tamen iam appropinquat.

2 Etiam illud te admoneo, ne quid ullis litteris committas quod, si prolatum sit, moleste feramus. multa sunt quae ego nescire malo quam cum aliquo periculo fieri certior. plura ad te vacuo animo scribam cum, ut spero, se Cicero meus belle habebit. tu velim cures ut sciam quibus nos dare oporteat eas quas ad te deinde litteras mittemus, Caesarisne tabellariis, ut is ad te protinus mittat, an Labieni.

[1] labieno (*Ziehen*)
[2] aut *coni. SB* [3] (*SB*)
[4] reserventur *vel* serv-

26 (III.6)

Rome, end of November 54

From Marcus to his brother Quintus greetings.

I have no answer to make to your earlier letter, which is full of spleen and grumblings (you say you gave another in similar vein to Labeo the previous day, but that has not yet arrived); for the letter which followed it obliterated all my vexation. I only warn and beg you amid these annoyances and labours and privations to be mindful of our purpose when you went to Gaul. They were no trifling or ordinary advantages that we had in view. What would have seemed worth the price of our separation? Our object was to gain reliable, comprehensive support for our public position and status from the good will of a very fine and very powerful personage. Our capital is invested in hope rather than in money; if that hope be abandoned, all else will be amassed only to be lost later on. Accordingly, if you will frequently carry your mind back to our old reasoned purpose and hope, you will find it easier to put up with your military labours and the other irritants—which, however, you will lay aside when you so desire; but the time is not yet ripe for that, though it is already drawing near.

I would also advise you not to trust anything to a letter which might embarrass us if it became public property. There are many things of which I had sooner be ignorant than informed, if the information carries risk. I shall write to you at greater length when, as I hope, my boy is himself again and my mind is easy. On your part please see to it that I know to whom I ought to give the letter which I shall then be sending you—should it be Caesar's couriers, so that he forwards it to you straight away, or Labienus'? For where

ubi enim isti sint Nervii et quam longe absint nescio.

3 De virtute et gravitate Caesaris, quam in summo dolore adhibuisset, magnam ex epistula tua cepi voluptatem. quod me institutum ad illum poema iubes perficere, etsi distentus cum opera tum animo sum multo magis, tamen quoniam ex epistula quam ad te miseram cognovit Caesar me aliquid esse exorsum, revertar ad institutum idque perficiam his supplicationum otiosis diebus, quibus Messallam iam nostrum reliquosque molestia levatos vehementer gaudeo; eumque quod certum consulem cum Domitio numeratis nihil a nostra opinione dissentitis. ego Messallam Caesari praestabo. sed Memmius in adventu Caesaris habet spem, in quo illum puto errare; hic quidem friget. Scaurum autem iam pridem Pompeius abiecit.

4 Res prolatae, ad interregnum comitia adducta. rumor dictatoris[5] iniucundus bonis, mihi etiam magis quae loquuntur. sed tota res et timetur et refrigescit. Pompeius plane se negat velle; antea mihi ipse non negabat. Hirrus auctor fore videtur (o di, quam ineptus, quam se ipse amans sine rivali!). Crassum Iunianum, hominem mihi deditum, per me deterruit. velit nolit scire difficile est; Hirro tamen agente nolle se non probabit. aliud hoc tempore de re publica nihil loquebantur; agebatur quidem certe nihil.

[5] delatoris (*Brunus*)

---

[1] Julia's death.

[2] A Tribune in 53, identified with Licinius Crassus Damasippus of Caesar, *Civil War* 2.44.3. See my *Select Classical Papers*, 304f.

those Nervii of yours live and how far they are away from us I don't know.

It gave me much pleasure to learn from your letter of the courage and dignity of Caesar's bearing in his great sorrow.[1] As for your command that I finish that poem addressed to him which I had begun, my time is much distracted and my mind far more so, but since Caesar knows from my letter to you that I have started on something, I shall go back to what I began and finish it during these leisure days of Supplications. I am very glad that thanks to them our friend Messalla and the others have been relieved of annoyance, and when you folk reckon him as certain of election along with Domitius you don't at all run counter to our opinion. I make myself responsible to Caesar for Messalla's behaviour. But Memmius pins hopes on Caesar's return to Italy, wherein I fancy he is making a mistake. Here at any rate he is in the cold. Scaurus was thrown over by Pompey some time ago.

Business has been adjourned and the elections brought to an Interregnum. There is talk of a Dictator, disagreeable to the honest men; what they are saying is to me still less agreeable. But the whole idea is viewed with alarm, and at the same time it's falling flat. Pompey categorically denies any desire for it. Talking to me himself earlier on he did not use to deny it. It looks as though Hirrus will make the proposal. (Gods, what an ass he is! How he loves himself—in which regard he has no competitor!) He got me to frighten off Crassus Junianus,[2] who is at my service. Does he want it or doesn't he? Hard to tell, but if Hirrus is the mover, he will never persuade the world that he doesn't. At present they are talking of nothing else in the way of politics; certainly nothing is a-doing.

5 Serrani, Domiti[6] fili, funus perluctuosum fuit a. d. VIII Kal. Dec. laudavit pater scripto meo.

6 Nunc de Milone: Pompeius ei nihil tribuit et omnia Guttae dicitque se perfecturum ut in illum[7] Caesar incumbat. hoc horret Milo nec iniuria; et si ille dictator factus sit, paene diffidit. intercessorem dictaturae si iuverit manu et praesidio suo, Pompeium metuit inimicum; si non iuverit, timet ne per vim perferatur. ludos apparat magnificentissimos, sic, inquam, ut nemo sumptuosiores, stulte bis terque, ‹vel quia›[8] non postulatos vel quia munus magnificum dederat vel quia facultates non erant; vel magis quam ter,[9] quia potuerat magistrum se, non aedilem, putare.

Omnia fere scripsi. cura, mi carissime frater, ut valeas.

27 (III.7)

Scr. Romae m. Dec. an. 54

MARCUS QUINTO FRATRI SALUTEM

1 De Gabinio nihil fuit faciendum istorum quae ‹a te

[6] domestici *vel* -stitii (*Münzer*)
[7] in illo (*Lamb.*: illo *Ern.*) [8] (*SB*)
[9] vel quia magister vel (*SB**)

[3] I.e. a son of L. Domitius Ahenobarbus adopted by an Atilius Serranus, probably the adoptive father of Sex. Atilius Serranus Gavianus, the Tribune of 57 (at this point deceased?).

[4] Surely not an unknown candidate, but a nickname for one of two known ones, P. Plautius Hypsaeus or (much more likely)

The funeral of Serranus, Domitius' son,[3] took place on 23 November, a very sad occasion. His father spoke a eulogy of my composition.

Now about Milo: Pompey does nothing to help him and everything to help Gutta.[4] He says that he will see to it that Caesar throws his weight that way. This appalls Milo, as well it may, and he is almost in despair should Pompey become Dictator. If he assists anyone vetoing the Dictatorship with his organized band he fears Pompey's hostility, whereas if he doesn't give such assistance he's afraid it will be carried through by force. He is preparing some most magnificent Games, in fact they will cost as much as any that ever were—which is double and triple folly, for (a) nobody, asked him, (b) he had previously given a splendid show, (c) he can't afford it; or rather more than triple because (d) he could have seen himself as a President,[5] not an Aedile.

That's about all. Take care of your health, my dearest brother.

27 (III.7)

Rome, December 54

From Marcus to his brother Quintus greetings.

It would not have been right for me to take any of the

Pompey's future father-in-law and consular colleague Metellus Scipio.

[5] The meaning of *magistrum* is uncertain. Perhaps Milo had become chairman of a *collegium*, 'probably one of the more respectable kind, like the Capitolini or Mercuriales' (A. W. Lintott).

sa>ne[1] amantissime cogitata sunt; ‘τότε μοι χάνοι’! feci summa cum gravitate, ut omnes sentiunt,[2] et summa cum lenitate quae feci. illum neque ursi neque levavi, testis vehemens fui, praeterea quievi. exitum iudici foedum et perniciosum lenissime tuli; quod quidem bonum mihi nunc denique redundat, ut his malis rei publicae licentiaque au-
2 dacium, qua ante rumpebar, nunc ne movear quidem. nihil est enim perditius his hominibus, his temporibus. itaque ex re publica quoniam nihil iam voluptatis capi potest, cur stomacher nescio. litterae me[3] et studia nostra et otium villaeque delectant maximeque pueri nostri. angit unus Milo; sed velim finem adferat consulatus. in quo enitar non minus quam sum enisus in nostro, tuque istinc, quod facis, adiuvabis. de quo cetera, nisi plane vis eripuerit, recte sunt; de re familiari timeo. ‘ὁ δὲ μαίνεται οὐκέτ’ ἀνεκτῶς,’ qui ludos †CCCↃ† comparet. cuius in hoc uno <in>considerantiam[4] et ego sustinebo ut potero et tu ut possis est tuorum nervorum.

3 De motu temporum venientis anni, nihil te intellegere volueram domestici timoris sed de communi rei publicae statu, in quo etiam si nihil procuro, tamen nihil curare vix

1 (*A. Klotz*)
2 sentiant (*Man.*)
3 me(a)e
4 considerant iam (*Man.*)

---

1 *Iliad* 4.182 = 8.150.
2 *Iliad* 8.355.
3 I am not convinced by the conjecture *Nerviorum*, adopted in Watt's text for *nervorum*, though the choice is virtually open. It would mean that Quintus, whose winter headquarters were

courses with regard to Gabinius which you, in the warmth of your affection to be sure, have been considering. 'Then let the earth yawn wide for me.'[1] What I did I did, as everybody feels, with the utmost responsibility and moderation. I have neither borne hard on him nor lent a helping hand. I spoke forcibly on the witness stand but otherwise held my peace. As for the outcome of the trial, shocking and detrimental as it was, I took it with complete composure. Now at long last I have gained this much: the evils in our public life and the licence of bold, bad men, which used to make me boil with rage, now leave me quite unmoved. For the men and the times could not be worse than they are; so, since public affairs can no longer yield any pleasure, I don't know why I should get my temper up. I have sources of joy in my writings and studies, my leisure, my country houses, and above all else in our children. Milo is my only worry, but I hope his Consulship will put an end to that. I shall make as big an effort in that as I made for my own, and you will help from over there, as you are doing. In this matter, unless sheer violence breaks loose, everything is in good shape with one exception—his pocket. That alarms me. 'Mad he is, past all bearing'[2]—planning a show to cost HS *. His unwisdom in this one particular I shall restrain as best I can, and your force of character[3] should enable you to do the like with effect.

As for the changes in the coming year, I did not mean you to understand anything in the nature of private alarm, I was referring to the general state of the commonwealth. Even though I have no responsibility, I can hardly be indif-

among the Nervii, could get rich at their expense and so come to Milo's assistance. *Sustinebo* then = I shall support.

possum. quam autem te velim cautum esse in scribendo ex hoc conicito quod ego ad te ne haec quidem scribo quae palam in re publica turbantur, ne cuiusquam animum meae litterae interceptae offendant. qua re domestica cura te levatum volo; in re publica scio quam sollicitus esse soleas.

Video Messallam nostrum consulem, si per interregem, sine iudicio; si per dictatorem, tamen sine periculo. odi nihil habet, Hortensi calor multum valebit, Gabini absolutio lex impunitatis putatur. *ἐν παρέργῳ*: de dictatore tamen actum adhuc nihil est. Pompeius abest, Appius miscet, Hirrus parat, multi intercessores numerantur, populus non curat, principes nolunt, ego quiesco.

4 De mancipiis quod mihi polliceris, valde te amo et sum equidem, uti scribis, et Romae et <in> praediis infrequens. sed cave, amabo, quicquam quod ad meum commodum attineat, nisi maximo tuo commodo et maxima tua facultate, mi frater, cogitaris.

5 De epistula Vatini risi. sed me ab eo ita observari sci<t>o[5] ut eius ista odia non sorbeam solum sed etiam concoquam.

6 Quod me hortaris ut absolvam, habeo absolutum suave, mihi quidem uti videtur, *ἔπος* ad Caesarem; sed quaero locupletem tabellarium, ne accidat[6] quod Erigonae tuae,

[5] scio (*SB*) [6] accipiat (*Vict.*)

---

[4] If the elections were held by an Interrex in 53 (as ultimately happened), Messalla would take office immediately the result was declared and so become immune from prosecution until the end of his term. But even if they were held before the year end, Cicero thought he was not likely to be convicted.

ferent. How cautious I want you to be in what you write you may infer from the fact that in writing to you I don't mention even overt political disorders, for fear of the letters getting intercepted and giving offence in any quarter. So I want you to ease your mind of private concern. I know how anxious you are apt to be about public affairs.

I expect to see our friend Messalla Consul; if by an Interrex he will not be on trial, if by a Dictator he will still be in no danger.[4] Nobody hates him, Hortensius' ardour[5] will have a powerful effect, and Gabinius' acquittal is regarded as a statute of impunity. *En passant*, nothing has so far been done about a Dictator after all. Pompey is away, Appius is stirring the pot, Hirrus making ready, many veto casters are being counted, the public is indifferent, the leaders are opposed, I lie low.

Thank you very much for your promise of slaves.[6] As you say, I am indeed understaffed, both in Rome and on my estates. But, my dear fellow, please don't consider anything to do with my convenience unless it is absolutely convenient and easy for you.

I was amused to hear about Vatinius' letter,[7] but I may tell you that he is so attentive to me that I not only swallow those nastinesses of his but digest them too.

The epic to Caesar which you urge me to finish, finished I have, a delectable piece, so it seems to *me*. But I am looking for a trustworthy courier for fear it share the fate of your *Erigona*, the only traveller from Gaul under Caesar's

5 Hortensius was Messalla's uncle.

6 From Gaul or Britain.

7 Probably a letter to Caesar which had been shown to Quintus.

cui[7] soli Caesare imperatore iter ex Gallia tutum non fuit.
7 quid si[8] canem tam bonam[9] non haberet?[10]

‹Quid?›[11] deturbem aedificium? quod quidem mihi cottidie magis placet, in primisque inferior porticus et eius conclavia fiunt recte. de Arcano, Caesaris opus est ‹elegantia›[12] vel mehercule etiam elegantioris alicuius. imagines enim istae et palaestra et piscina et nilus multorum Philotimorum est, non Diphilorum. sed et ipsi ea adibimus[13] et mittemus et mandabimus.

8 De Felicis testamento tum magis querare, si scias. quas enim tabulas se putavit obsignare, in quibus in uncia[14] firmissimum ‹locum›[15] tenes, vero (lapsus est per errorem et suum et Scurrae[16] servi) non obsignavit; quas noluit, eas obsignavit. *ἀλλ᾽ οἰμωζέτω*, nos modo valeamus.

9 Ciceronem et ut rogas amo et ut meretur et debeo. dimitto autem a me et ut a magistris ne abducam et quod mater †porcia non†[17] discedit, sine qua edacitatem pueri pertimesco. sed sumus una tamen valde multum.

Rescripsi ad omnia. mi suavissime et optime frater, vale.

[7] quod (*Vict.*) [8] quid ? si *vulg.* (*SB*)
[9] bonum (*Goodyear*) [10] haberem (*SB*) [11] (*SB*)
[12] (*Watt*) [13] adhibemus (*Man.*)
[14] unciis (*SB*) [15] (*Tyrrell*) [16] sicurae (*SB*)
[17] pr(idie) Non. *Gurlitt*: propriam in ‹domum› *coni. SB*

[8] Lit. 'what would have happened to her if she didn't have such a good dog?' The messenger who brought Quintus' *Erigona* to Italy seems to have been attacked on the road. The mythical Erigone's dog Maera was proverbially faithful, an Athenian Gelert.

government who found the road unsafe. And she at least had an excellent dog to protect her![8]

What, demolish the building?[9] I like it better every day. The lower portico and its rooms are coming on particularly well. As for Arcanum, we need Caesar's good taste, or even better taste than his upon my word! Those busts of yours, the palaestra, the fish pool, the canal, call for a multitude of Philotimi—not Diphili![10] However, I shall visit them myself, and send people over, and give instructions.

You would be more indignant about Felix' will than you are if you knew. The document which he thought he signed, in which you were firmly down for a twelfth share, he did not in fact sign, being misled by an error of his own and of his slave Scurra's;[11] the one he signed was contrary to his wishes. But to the devil with him! So long as we stay healthy!

I love your son as you ask and as he deserves and as I ought, but I am letting him go because I don't want to take him away from his teachers and because his mother is leaving for her own house (?). Without her I am terrified of the young fellow's appetite! But we are a great deal together all the same.

I have answered all your points. My best and most delectable of brothers, good-bye.

[9] Apparently on the Manilius property; see Letter 21.1.

[10] Cicero had a low opinion of Diphilus' competence; cf. Letter 21.2. Philotimus was concerned in work on Quintus' house in Rome (Letter 20.6).

[11] Epigraphically attested as a slave name (= buffoon, wag).

CICERO'S LETTERS TO MARCUS BRUTUS

INTRODUCTION

Born in 85, M. Junius Brutus was adopted in early life by a maternal uncle, so that his name became for official purposes Q. (Servilius) Caepio Brutus. But the original style remained in general use among his contemporaries and posterity. His natural father was a nobleman supposedly descended from Rome's first Consul, who held office under the Marians and was killed by Pompey in 78 for his part in an insurrection against the post-Sullan regime. His mother, Servilia, not only belonged to a patrician family with wide aristocratic connections but was half-sister to M. Cato and, according to general report, Julius Caesar's mistress. A second marriage and the marriages of three resulting daughters linked her and her son to yet other leading families and individuals. Brutus himself married a daughter of Appius Claudius Pulcher, whose other daughter was the wife of Pompey's elder son (Brutus later divorced her to marry Cato's daughter, the 'Portia' of Shakespeare's *Julius Caesar*). The great account in which he was held by his contemporaries is partly attributable to the extent and brilliance of these family connections.

But Brutus' personal qualities and attainments were far out of the ordinary. An austere intellectual with a deep interest in Greek philosophy, he became as a young man one of the foremost public speakers of the day in the so-called

'Atticist' manner, which aimed at simple elegance in opposition to Ciceronian orotundity. Moreover, he did nothing by halves. 'When he wants something,' said Julius Caesar of Brutus, 'he wants it badly.'

In 58 he accompanied his uncle Cato on a special mission to supervise the annexation of Cyprus to the Roman empire. In 53 he served as Quaestor under his father-in-law, Appius Claudius, the governor of Cilicia, and in 49 as Legate to Cicero's successor in the same province, P. Sestius. The Civil War had now broken out and Brutus passed from Cilicia to Pompey's camp in Greece, where Cicero wrote of him to Atticus as 'zealous in the cause.' But after Pharsalia he was not only pardoned by Caesar but taken into favour, made governor of Cisalpine Gaul in 46 and City Praetor in 44. Early that year a plot was hatched to assassinate the Dictator, which took effect on 15 March. Brutus was its leader, along with his brother-in-law, C. Cassius Longinus, and a distant kinsman, Decimus Brutus.

The conspirators seem to have planned no further than the act. Mark Antony, the surviving Consul, soon showed a disposition to step into Caesar's shoes. His ascendancy was challenged by Caesar's heir, the eighteen-year-old Octavian, while Brutus and Cassius, the 'Liberators' as they were called, remained helpless spectators until the autumn, when they left for the East. There it was a very different story. The Caesarian commanders in Syria and Egypt, whether from republican sympathies or lack of personal ambition, handed over to Cassius, while Brutus took possession of Greece, defeating and capturing Antony's brother Gaius. By the spring of 43 the Liberators were in control from the Euphrates to the Adriatic. Despite all appeals, they made no effort to come to the rescue of the re-

publican cause in Italy, preferring to wait to be attacked by the new coalition of Antony and Octavian. The end came at Philippi in October 42. Brutus and Cassius perished and the Roman Republic perished with them.

Atticus, who was on friendly terms with Cato and his circle, found himself much drawn to Cato's gifted nephew, and through Atticus an intimacy arose between Brutus and Cicero. It may have ripened when they were together in Pompey's army, and after Cicero's return to Rome in the autumn of 47 we find it fully established. It was publicly signalized among other things by Cicero's dialogue on the history of Roman oratory, to which he gave Brutus' name, and by the dedication of the *Orator*, a work of which Cicero was particularly proud. All this despite angularities on one side and hypersensitivity on the other.

Apart from four (or, as I believe, five) letters of recommendation in *Letters to Friends* the extant correspondence between Cicero and Marcus Brutus consists of one 'Book' and a portion of another, twenty-six letters in all, including two apocrypha. They date from March or April to July 43. The first five (= Book II) are known only from Cratander's edition printed in 1528, the manuscript which contained them being no longer extant.

The genuineness of the collection was impugned in the eighteenth century and long remained in doubt. It is now generally recognized, with the exception of Letters 25 (I.16) and 26 (I.17), on which see the introduction to my Cambridge edition of 1980 (pp. 10–14). For Brutus' sake one is glad to have relieved him of responsibility for these two repetitious and unjust diatribes, coming purportedly from the security of Macedonia against the man who was upholding the Republic in Italy by the only means open to

him at the ultimate cost of his life. Historians need not regret these 'rhetorical blow-ups' of the sentiments expressed by the supposed author in Letters 11 and 12.

Manuscript sources for the correspondence with Brutus are the same as for the letters to Quintus.

1 (II.1)

Scr. Romae c. Kal. Apr. an. 43

CICERO BRUTO SALUTEM

1 Cum haec scribebam, res existimabatur in extremum adducta discrimen. tristes enim de Bruto nostro litterae nuntiique adferebantur. me quidem non maxime conturbabant. his enim exercitibus ducibusque quos habemus nullo modo poteram diffidere, neque adsentiebar maiori parti hominum; fidem enim consulum non condemnabam, quae suspecta vehementer erat, desiderabam non nullis in rebus prudentiam et celeritatem. qua si essent usi, iam pridem rem <publicam>[1] reciperassemus. non enim ignoras quanta momenta sint in re publica temporum et quid intersit idem illud utrum ante an post decernatur, suscipiatur, agatur. omnia quae severe decreta sunt hoc tumultu, si aut quo die dixi sententiam perfecta essent et non in diem ex die dilata aut quo ex tempore suscepta sunt ut agerentur non tardata et procrastinata, bellum iam nullum haberemus.

2 Omnia, Brute, praestiti rei publicae quae praestare debuit is qui esset <in>[2] eo quo ego sum gradu senatus populique iudicio collocatus, nec illa modo quae nimirum sola ab homine <tenui>[3] sunt postulanda, fidem, vigilantiam,

[1] (*Patricius*)
[2] (*Lamb.*)
[3] (*SB*)

1 (II.1)

Rome, ca. 1 April 43

From Cicero to Brutus greetings.

As I write, the ultimate crisis is thought to be upon us. Gloomy letters and messengers are coming in about our friend Brutus.[1] They do not disturb *me* overmuch, for I cannot possibly lack confidence in our armies and generals, nor do I subscribe to the majority opinion—I do not judge unfavourably of the loyalty of the Consuls, which is under strong suspicion; though in certain matters I could have wished for more wisdom and promptitude. Had that been forthcoming, we should have had public order restored a while ago. You are well aware of the importance of the right moment in political affairs, and what a vast difference it makes whether the same decree or enterprise or action be adopted before or after. If only all the strong measures decreed during this turmoil had been carried through the day I proposed them, or not put off from one day to the next or dragged out and procrastinated *after* action upon them had been taken in hand, we should now have no war.

My dear Brutus, I have done for our country all that lies with one who stands where I, by judgement of Senate and People, stand today. I have not only given all that I suppose can fairly be demanded of an ordinary man: good faith,

[1] Decimus Brutus.

patriae caritatem; ea sunt enim quae nemo est qui non praestare debeat. ego autem ei qui sententiam dicat in principibus de re publica puto etiam prudentiam esse praestandam, nec me, cum mihi tantum sumpserim ut gubernacula rei publicae prehenderem, minus putarim reprehendendum si inutiliter aliquid senatui suaserim quam si infideliter.

3 Acta quae sint quaeque agantur scio perscribi ad te diligenter. ex me autem illud est quod te velim habere cognitum, meum quidem animum in acie[4] esse neque respectum ullum quaerere nisi me utilitas civitatis forte converterit. maioris autem partis animi te Cassiumque respiciunt. quam ob rem ita te para, Brute, ut intellegas aut, si hoc tempore bene res gesta sit, tibi meliorem rem publicam esse faciendam aut, si quid offensum sit, per te esse eandem reciperandam.

2 (II.3)

Scr. Dyrrachii Kal. Apr. an. 43

BRUTUS CICERONI SALUTEM

1 Litteras tuas valde exspecto, quas scripsisti post nuntios nostrarum rerum et de morte Treboni. non enim dubito quin mihi consilium tuum explices. indigno scelere et civem optimum amisimus et provinciae possessione pulsi sumus, quam ‹neque›[1] reciperare[2] facile est neque minus turpe aut flagitiosum erit ‹si›[3] potest reciperari.

[4] aciem (*Lamb.*)
[1] (*hic SB, post* recip- *Or.*)
[2] reciperari (*Lamb. marg.*)
[3] (*SB*)

vigilance, patriotism; for these are what it is everybody's duty to render. But I conceive that something more is required of one whose voice is heard among leading statesmen, namely wisdom. And having presumed to take the helm of state, I should hold myself no less to blame if any counsel I gave the Senate were inexpedient than I should if it were dishonest.

I know you receive full and accurate reports of events both past and current. As coming from myself, I should like you to be well aware that *my* mind is in the fighting line. I am not looking over my shoulder, unless it so happen that the interests of the community make me turn my head; but the minds of the majority are looking back, to you and Cassius. So, Brutus, I would have you adjust yourself to the realization that it will be your duty either to improve our body politic, should the present conflict go well, or to restore it, should we meet with a reverse.

2 (II.3)

Dyrrachium, 1 April 43

From Brutus to Cicero greetings.

I am eagerly waiting for a letter from you written after the news of my doings and of Trebonius' death, not doubting that you will set out your views for me. By a dastardly crime we have lost a fine Roman and have been ousted from a province, which is neither easy to regain nor will the thing be the less shameful and outrageous if it *can* be regained.

2 Antonius adhuc est nobiscum, sed me dius fidius et moveor hominis precibus et timeo ne illum aliquorum furor excipiat. plane aestuo. quod si scirem quid tibi placeret, sine sollicitudine essem; id enim optimum esse persuasum esset mihi. qua re quam primum fac me certiorem quid tibi placeat.

3 Cassius noster Syriam, legiones Syriacas habet, ultro quidem a Murco et a Marcio et ab exercitu ipso accersitus. ego scripsi ad Tertiam sororem et matrem ne prius ederent hoc quod optime ac felicissime gessit Cassius quam tuum consilium cognovissent tibique visum esset.

4 Legi orationes duas tuas, quarum altera Kal. Ian. usus es, altera de litteris meis, quae[4] habita est abs te contra Calenum. non[5] scilicet hoc exspectas, dum eas laudem. nescio animi an ingeni tui maior in his libellis laus contineatur. iam concedo ut vel Philippici vocentur, quod tu quadam epistula iocans scripsisti.

5 Duabus rebus egemus, Cicero, pecunia et supplemento. quarum altera potest abs te expediri, ut aliqua pars militum istinc mittatur nobis vel secreto consilio adversus Pansam vel actione in senatu; altera quo[6] magis est necessaria, neque meo exercitui magis quam reliquorum, hoc magis doleo Asiam ||[7] nos amisisse; quam sic vexari a Dolabella audio ut iam non videatur crudelissimum eius facinus

[4] usus es *et* quae *del. coni. SB* [5] nunc (*SB*)
[6] quae (*Streng*) [7] *vide Watt app. crit.*

---

[1] Mark Antony's brother Gaius. Appointed governor of Macedonia, he had been defeated and taken prisoner by Brutus.

[2] Wife of Cassius.

[3] The Fifth and Seventh Philippics.

Antonius[1] is still with me, but upon my word I am moved by his pleas and I am afraid that the fanaticism of certain people may pick him off. I am really troubled. If I knew what course you favoured I should not be worried, for I should be satisfied that it was best. So please let me know your opinion as soon as possible.

Our friend Cassius holds Syria and the Syrian legions. He was called in by Murcus and Marcius and the army itself. I have written to my sister Tertia[2] and my mother to tell them not to make this splendid success of Cassius' public before consulting with you and before you think proper.

I have read your two speeches,[3] the one you made on the Kalends of January and the one concerning my dispatch which you delivered against Calenus. You won't be waiting for me to praise them.[4] I don't know whether these pieces say more for your spirit or for your genius. I am now willing to let them be called by the proud name of 'Philippics,'[5] as you jestingly suggested in one of your letters.

My dear Cicero, I have now two needs: money and reinforcements. The latter you can provide by arranging for a contingent of troops to be sent to me from Italy either by way of a secret understanding with Pansa or through action in the Senate. The former is a necessity, as much for the other armies as for mine, which makes me all the sorrier that we have lost Asia. I hear that Dolabella's oppression of the province makes Trebonius' murder no longer appear

4 Reading *non* for *nunc,* which would mean 'Now, no doubt, you expect me to praise them.' Despite *Letters to Atticus* 115 (VI.1).7, Brutus cannot have written anything so churlish or else so ambiguous (see my Commentary).

5 After Demosthenes' speeches against Philip of Macedon.

interfectio Treboni. Vetus Antistius me tamen pecunia sublevavit.

6 Cicero, filius tuus, sic mihi se probat industria, patientia, labore, animi magnitudine, omni denique officio ut prorsus numquam dimittere videatur cogitationem cuius sit filius. qua re, quoniam efficere non possum ut pluris facias eum qui tibi est carissimus, illud tribue iudicio meo ut tibi persuadeas non fore illi abutendum gloria tua ut adipiscatur honores paternos.

Kal. Apr. Dyrrachio.

3 (II.2)

Scr. Romae III *Id. Apr. an. 43*

CICERO BRUTO SALUTEM

1 Planci animum in rem publicam egregium, legiones, auxilia, copias ex litteris eius quarum exemplum tibi missum arbitror perspicere potuisti. Lepidi, tui necessari, qui secundum fratrem adfinis habet quos oderit proximos, levitatem et inconstantiam animumque semper inimicum rei publicae iam credo tibi ex tuorum litteris esse perspectum.

2 Nos exspectatio sollicitat * * *,[1] quae est omnis iam in extremum adducta discrimen. est enim spes omnis in Bruto expediendo, de quo vehementer timebamus.

[1] de re Mutinensi *vel sim. excidisse coni. Watt*

---

[6] C. Antistius Vetus had been in charge of Syria until succeeded by Staius Murcus. Probably late in 44 he entered into Brutus' service, handing over the tribute money which he was taking back to Rome. Cf. Letter 16.

the worst of his savageries. However, Vetus Antistius[6] has given me financial help.

Your son Cicero earns my approval by his energy, endurance, hard work, and unselfish spirit, in fact by every kind of service. Indeed he seems never to forget whose son he is. I cannot make you think more of one whom you so deeply love than you already do, but trust my judgement in assuring yourself that he will have no need to exploit your renown in order to attain his father's honours.

Kalends of April, Dyrrachium.

3 (II.2)

Rome, 11 April 43

From Cicero to Brutus greetings.

From Plancus' dispatch,[1] of which I think you have been sent a copy, you will have been able to perceive his fine spirit of patriotism as well as the legions, auxiliaries, and resources at his disposal. On the other hand I suppose that letters from your own circle will already have made evident to you the irresponsibility, fickleness, and consistently unpatriotic attitude of your connection Lepidus, who hates his relatives by marriage only one degree less than his brother.[2]

We are anxiously waiting for news ‹from Mutina›, where the whole situation is at ultimate crisis point. All hope lies in relieving Brutus.[3] We are in grave fear for him.

[1] *Letters to Friends* 371 (X.8).
[2] L. Aemilius Paullus, Consul in 50.
[3] Decimus Brutus.

3 Ego hic cum homine furioso satis habeo negoti, Servilio; quem tuli diutius quam dignitas mea patiebatur, sed tuli rei publicae causa, ne darem perditis civibus hominem parum sanum illum quidem sed tamen nobilem quo concurrerent; quod faciunt nihilo minus. sed eum alienandum a re publica non putabam. finem feci eius ferendi; coeperat enim esse tanta insolentia ut neminem liberum duceret. in Planci vero causa exarsit incredibili dolore mecumque per biduum ita contendit et a me ita fractus est ut eum in perpetuum modestiorem sperem fore. atque in hac contentione ipsa, cum maxime res ageretur, a. d. V Id. Apr. litterae mihi in senatu redditae sunt a Lentulo nostro de Cassio, de legionibus, de Syria. quas statim cum recitavissem, cecidit Servilius, complures praeterea; sunt enim insignes aliquot qui improbissime sentiunt. sed acerbissime tulit Servilius adsensum esse mihi de Planco. magnum illud monstrum in re publica est, sed diu,[2] || mihi crede, non erit.

‹III› Id.Apr.

4 (II.4)

Scr. Romae prid. Id. Apr. an. 43

CICERO BRUTO SALUTEM

1 Datis mane a. d. III[1] Id. Apr. Scaptio litteris eodem die tuas accepi Kal. Apr. Dyrrachio datas vesperi. itaque mane prid. Id. Apr., cum a Scaptio certior factus essem non esse eos profectos quibus pridie dederam et statim ire, hoc pau-

[2] quo (*SB*)
[1] VI (*Sigonius*)

Here I have trouble enough on my hands with that madman Servilius. I put up with him longer than suited my dignity, but I did that for the public sake, not wishing to give traitors a rallying point—a semi-lunatic, to be sure, but a nobleman; though rally to him they do none the less. Still I thought he had better not be estranged from the national cause. Well, my patience with him is at an end. His insolence reached the point that he treated everybody else like slaves. He flared up in an incredible passion over Plancus' matter and battled with me for two days. I quashed him so effectively that I hope he will mend his manners once and for all. Just when this combat was at its height, on 9 April, a letter was delivered to me in the Senate from our friend Lentulus[4] about Cassius and the legions and Syria. I read it out at once and Servilius, along with several more (there are a number of prominent persons who are thoroughly disloyal), collapsed. But Servilius bitterly resented my gaining my point about Plancus. He is a political monstrosity, but will not last long, take my word.

11 April.

4 (II.4)

Rome, 12 April 43

From Cicero to Brutus greetings.

After giving a letter to Scaptius on the morning of 11 April I received that same evening yours dispatched from Dyrrachium on the Kalends of April. So on the morning of the 12th, having been informed by Scaptius that the persons to whom I gave my letter yesterday have not yet left

[4] The younger Lentulus Spinther. The letter is not extant.

lulum exaravi ipsa in turba matutinae salutationis.

2 De Cassio laetor et rei publicae gratulor, mihi etiam qui repugnante et irascente Pansa sententiam dixerim ut Dolabellam bello Cassius persequeretur. et quidem audacter dicebam sine nostro senatus consulto iam illud eum bellum gerere. de te etiam dixi tum quae dicenda putavi. haec ad te oratio perferetur, quoniam te video delectari Philippicis nostris.

3 Quod me de Antonio consulis, quoad Bruti exitum cognorimus custodiendum puto. ex his litteris quas mihi misisti, Dolabella Asiam vexare videtur et in ea se gerere taeterrime. compluribus autem scripsisti Dolabellam a Rhodiis esse exclusum; qui si ad Rhodum accessit, videtur mihi Asiam reliquisse. id si ita est, istic tibi censeo commorandum; sin eam semel cepit, || a t‹e›[2] in Asiam censeo persequendum. nihil mihi videris hoc tempore melius acturus.

4 Quod egere te duabus necessariis rebus scribis, supplemento et pecunia, difficile consilium est. non enim mihi occurrunt facultates quibus uti te posse videam praeter illas quas senatus decrevit, ut pecunias a civitatibus mutuas sumeres. de supplemento autem non video quid fieri possit. tantum enim abest ut Pansa de exercitu suo aut dilectu tibi aliquid tribuat ut etiam moleste ferat tam multos ad te ire voluntarios, quo modo equidem credo, quod his rebus quae in Italia decernuntur nullas copias nimis magnas esse arbitretur, quo modo autem multi suspicantur, ‹quod›[3] ne te quidem nimis firmum esse velit; quod ego non suspicor.

[2] at (*SB*) [3] (*Lamb.*)

---

[1] The Eleventh Philippic.

but are leaving directly, I am scribbling these few words in the hubbub of my morning levee.

I am happy about Cassius and congratulate the commonwealth, and myself too in that against Pansa's angry opposition I proposed that Cassius should take military action against Dolabella. Indeed I ventured to maintain that he was already engaged in such action without any decree of ours. I also said what I thought proper about yourself. The speech[1] will be sent to you, since I see you enjoy my Philippics.

With regard to your question about Antonius, I think he should be held in custody until we know what happens to Brutus. From the letter you have sent me it seems that Dolabella is oppressing Asia and behaving there abominably. Now you have written to several people that Dolabella was refused admission by the Rhodians. If he has approached Rhodes, then I suppose he has left Asia. If that is so, I would advise you to remain where you are, but if he has got possession of Asia I would advise you to pursue him there. I do not think you can do better at this time.

You say you are in want of two necessities, reinforcements and money. It is hard to make any suggestion. No financial resources occur to me as available for your use other than those which the Senate has decreed, namely that you should borrow sums from civic bodies. As to reinforcements, I do not see what can be done. So far from Pansa assigning you anything from his own army or levies he is not happy that so many volunteers are joining you, because, as I for my part suppose, he thinks that no forces are too large for the issues which are being determined in Italy—but as many suspect, because he does not want even you to be too strong. *I* have no such suspicion.

5 Quod scribis te ad Tertiam sororem ‹et matrem›[4] scripsisse ut ne prius ederent ea quae gesta a Cassio essent quam mihi visum esset, video te veritum esse id quod verendum fuit, ne animi partium Caesaris, quo modo etiam nunc [partes][5] appellantur, vehementer commoverentur. sed ante quam tuas litteras accepimus, audita res erat et pervulgata. tui etiam tabellarii ad multos familiaris tuos litteras attulerant. qua re neque supprimenda res erat, praesertim cum id fieri non posset, neque, si posset, non divulgandam potius quam occultandam putaremus.

6 De Cicerone meo et, si tantum est in eo quantum scribis, tantum scilicet quantum debeo gaudeo et, si quod amas eum eo maiora facis, id ipsum incredibiliter gaudeo, a te eum diligi.

5 (II.5)

Scr. Romae XVIII *(?) Kal. Mai. an. 43*

CICERO BRUTO SALUTEM

1 Quae litterae tuo nomine recitatae sint[1] Id. Apr. in senatu eodemque tempore Antoni credo ad te scripsisse tuos. quorum ego nemini concedo, sed nihil necesse erat eadem omnis; illud necesse, me ad te scribere quid sentirem tota de constitutione huius belli et quo iudicio essem quaque sententia.

Voluntas mea, Brute, de summa re publica semper eadem fuit quae tua, ratio quibusdam in rebus (non enim

4 (*Wes.*) 5 (*Watt*) 1 sunt (*Lamb.*)

1 C. Antonius.

You say you wrote to your sister Tertia and your mother telling them not to make Cassius' successes public before I thought proper. Evidently you were afraid, and with good reason, that Caesar's party, as it is still called, would be much upset by the news. But the matter was common knowledge before we got your letter. Even your own couriers had brought letters to many of your friends. Accordingly, it was not advisable to suppress it, particularly as that was impossible; and even had it been possible, I should have been in favour of publication rather than concealment.

If my son Marcus has all the qualities with which you credit him, I am naturally no less glad than I ought to be. And if your affection for him makes you exaggerate, the very fact of your caring for him makes me exceedingly happy.

5 (II.5)

Rome, 14 (?) April 43

From Cicero to Brutus greetings.

I expect you have heard from your own people about your dispatch which was read out in the Senate on the Ides of April and Antonius'[1] letter which was read at the same time. None of them thinks more of you than I do, but there is no need for everyone to tell you the same tale. There *is* need for me to tell you my views about the nature of this war, how I judge and what I advise.

My general political aims have always been identical with yours, my dear Brutus; my policy in certain matters

omnibus) paulo fortasse vehementior. scis mihi semper placuisse non rege solum sed regno liberari rem publicam; tu lenius, immortali omnino cum tua laude. sed quid melius fuerit magno dolore sensimus, magno periculo sentimus. recenti illo tempore tu omnia ad pacem, quae oratione confici non poterat, ego omnia ad libertatem, qua sine pax[2] nulla est. pacem ipsam bello atque armis effici posse arbitrabar. studia non deerant arma poscentium, quorum repressimus impetum ardoremque restinximus.
2 itaque res in eum locum venerat ut, nisi Caesari Octaviano deus quidam illam mentem dedisset, in potestatem perditissimi hominis et turpissimi M. Antoni veniendum fu<er>it;[3] quocum vides hoc tempore ipso quod sit quantumque certamen. id profecto nullum esset, nisi tum conservatus esset Antonius.

Sed haec omitto; res enim a te gesta memorabilis et paene caelestis repellit omnis reprehensiones, quippe quae ne laude quidem satis idonea adfici possit. exstitisti nuper vultu severo; exercitum, copias, legiones idoneas per te brevi tempore comparasti. di immortales! qui ille nuntius, quae illae litterae, quae laetitia senatus, quae alacritas civitatis erat! nihil umquam vidi tam omnium consensione laudatum. erat exspectatio reliquiarum Antoni, quem equitatu legionibusque magna ex parte spoliaras; ea quoque habuit exitum optabilem. nam tuae litterae quae recitatae in senatu sunt et imperatoris et militum virtutem

[2] quae sine pace (*Timpanaro*)
[3] (*Sigonius*)

---

[2] Mark Antony should have been killed along with Caesar.

(not in all) has perhaps been a little more forceful. You know I have always held that the commonwealth should be freed from monarchy, not merely from a monarch. You took a milder view, no doubt to your own eternal credit. But we have realized to our bitter distress, and are realizing to our grave peril, what the better course would have been.[2] In the period we have lately been through your supreme object was peace—which could not be accomplished with words; mine was freedom, for without freedom peace is meaningless. I thought that peace itself could be achieved by war and weapons. Men with the zeal to demand them were not lacking, but we checked their enthusiasm and damped down their ardour. And so matters reached the point that, if some higher power had not inspired Caesar Octavian, we should have lain at the mercy of an abandoned villain, Mark Antony. How desperate a struggle with him is going on at this moment you see. Obviously there would have been none, if Antony's life had not then been spared.

But I leave all this aside. That memorable, almost godlike deed of yours is proof against all criticisms; indeed it can never be adequately praised. Latterly you have appeared in a new and sterner guise. In a short time and by your own efforts you have got an army—forces, legions in sufficient strength. Ah, that was news, that was a dispatch! The Senate was in transports, the whole community afire. I have never seen anything so universally applauded. News was still awaited about Antonius' remnants—you had despoiled him of the greater part of his horse and foot. That too came out according to our prayers. Your dispatch, read out in the Senate, declares the valour of the soldiers and their commander, and the zealous efforts of your friends,

et industriam tuorum, in quibus Ciceronis mei, declarant. quod si tuis placuisset de his litteris referri et nisi in tempus turbulentissimum post discessum Pansae consulis incidissent, honos quoque iustus et debitus dis immortalibus decretus esset.

3 Ecce tibi Id. Apr. advolat mane Celer Pil<i>us, qui vir, di boni, quam gravis, quam constans, quam bonarum in re publica partium! hic epistulas adfert duas, unam tuo nomine, alteram Antoni. dat Servilio tribuno pl., ille Cornuto, recitantur in senatu. 'ANTONIUS PRO CONSULE':[4] magna admiratio, ut si esset recitatum 'DOLABELLA IMPERATOR'; a quo quidem venerant tabellarii, sed nemo Pili similis qui proferre litteras auderet aut magistratibus reddere. tuae recitantur, breves illae quidem sed in Antonium admodum lenes. vehementer admiratus senatus. mihi autem non erat explicatum quid agerem. falsas dicerem?
4 quid si tu eas approbasses? confirmarem? non erat dignitatis tuae. itaque ille dies silentio. postridie autem, cum sermo increb<r>uisset Pil<i>usque oculos vehementius hominum offendisset, natum omnino est principium a me. de pro consule Antonio multa. Sestius causae non defuit post me, cum quanto suum filium, quanto meum in periculo futurum diceret, si contra pro consule arma tulissent. nosti hominem; causae[5] non defuit. dixerunt etiam alii.

[4] PROCOS. (*SB, et similiter infra*)
[5] causae <inquam> *coni. SB*

including my son. If your people here had thought fit that a motion be made on this dispatch, and if it had not arrived at a moment of great confusion after Consul Pansa's departure, a thank offering to the immortal gods, just and due, would have been decreed.

And then! On the morning of the Ides of April along runs Celer Pilius. What a personage, in heaven's name! So responsible, so consistent, such a fine political record! Two letters he brings, one in your name, the other from Antonius, and delivers them to Tribune Servilius, who hands them to Cornutus. They are read out in the Senate. 'Antonius, Proconsul'! That produced a sensation, as though it had been 'Dolabella, Imperator'—and couriers *had* arrived from Dolabella, but nobody like Pilius with the courage to produce the letter or deliver it to the magistrates. Your letter was read, brief but distinctly mild in tone as regards Antonius. The House was greatly surprised. As for myself, it was not clear to me what I ought to do. If I called this letter a forgery, it might turn out that you had approved it; whereas to acknowledge it as genuine would be bad for your prestige. So that day passed in silence. On the following, after talk had become rife and the sight of Pilius had given strong and general offence, I must admit that I opened the game, with a good deal to say about 'Antonius, Proconsul.' Sestius followed me and supported the cause, pointing out what a dangerous position his son and mine would be in if they had taken up arms against a Proconsul. You know Sestius. He supported the cause. Others spoke as well. Our friend Labeo remarked that your seal was not on the letter, that it was not dated, and

Labeo vero noster nec signum tuum in epistula nec diem appositum nec te scripsisse ad tuos, ut soleres. hoc cogere volebat, falsas litteras esse, et, si quaeris, probabat.

5 Nunc tuum est consilium, Brute, de toto genere belli. video te lenitate delectari et eum putare[6] fructum esse maximum; praeclare quidem, sed aliis rebus, aliis temporibus locus esse solet debetque clementiae. nunc quid agitur, Brute? templis deorum immortalium imminet hominum egentium et perditorum spes, nec quicquam aliud decernitur hoc bello nisi utrum simus necne. cui parcimus aut quid agimus? his ergo consulimus quibus victoribus vestigium nostrum nullum relinquetur? nam quid interest inter Dolabellam et quemvis Antoniorum trium? quorum si cui parcimus, duri fuimus in Dolabella. haec ut ita sentiret senatus populusque Romanus, etsi res ipsa cogebat, tamen maxima ex parte nostro consilio atque auctoritate perfectum est. tu si hanc rationem non probas, tuam sententiam defendam, non relinquam meam. neque dissolutum a te quicquam homines exspectant nec crudele. huius rei moderatio facilis est, ut in duces vehemens sis, in milites liberalis.

6 Ciceronem meum, mi Brute, velim quam plurimum tecum habeas. virtutis disciplinam meliorem reperiet nullam quam contemplationem atque imitationem tui.

X‹V›III[7] Kal. Mai.

[6] putare ‹victoriae› *coni. SB*
[7] (*Gurlitt*)

that you had not written to your own people as you usually do. He drew the conclusion that the letter was forged, and, if you wish to know, the House agreed with him.

Now, Brutus, it is for you to judge of the whole character of the war. Clearly lenience is to your liking and you think it is the most rewarding policy. Admirable! But the place for clemency is apt to be found, and ought to be found, in other matters and circumstances. In the present situation what is to be done, my friend? The hopes of needy desperados hang over the temples of the immortal gods. What is at issue in this war is our existence; no more, no less. Whom are we sparing? What are we about? Are we concerned for men who, if they win the day, will wipe us out without a trace? For what difference is there between Dolabella and any one of the three Antonii? If we spare any of them, we have been too hard on Dolabella.[3] That this is the sentiment of the Senate and People of Rome comes from the logic of the situation, but also in large measure from my advice and influence. If you do not approve of this attitude, I shall defend your view, but I shall not relinquish my own. Men expect from you neither laxity nor cruelty. It is easy to strike a balance; you need only be strong with the leaders and generous to the rank and file.

I hope you will keep my son at your side as much as possible, my dear Brutus. He will find no better training in manly excellence than by watching and imitating you.

14 (?) April.

[3] Who had been declared a public enemy.

6 (I.2a)[1]

Scr. Romae XII *(?) Kal. Mai. an. 43*

<CICERO BRUTO SALUTEM>

1 * * * te benevolentiam exercitus equitumque expertum vehementer gaudeo. de Dolabella, ut scribis, si quid habes novi, facies me certiorem; in quo delector me ante providisse ut tuum iudicium liberum esset cum Dolabella belli gerendi. id valde pertinuit, ut ego tum intellegebam, ad rem publicam, ut nunc iudico, ad dignitatem tuam.

2 Quod scribis me maximo †otio†[2] egisse ut insectarer Antonios idque laudas, credo ita videri tibi. sed illam distinctionem tuam nullo pacto probo; scribis enim acrius prohibenda bella civilia esse quam in superatos iracundiam exercendam. vehementer a te, Brute, dissentio; nec clementiae tuae concedo, sed salutaris severitas vincit inanem speciem clementiae. quod si clementes esse volumus, numquam deerunt bella civilia. sed de hoc tu videris. de me possum idem quod Plautinus pater in Trinummo: 'mihi
3 quidem aetas acta ferme est: tua istuc refert maxime.' opprimemini, mihi crede, Brute, nisi providetis. neque enim populum semper eundem habebitis neque senatum neque senatus ducem. haec ex oraculo Apollinis Pythi edita tibi puta. nihil potest esse verius.

XII Kal. Mai.

[1] *cum ep. 14 coniungunt codd.* (*Gurlitt*)
[2] animo ς*

6 (I.2a)

Rome, 20 (?) April 43

CICERO TO M. BRUTUS

* * * I am delighted that you find the army and the cavalry so loyally disposed towards you. If you get any news of Dolabella, you will inform me, as you say. I am glad that I had the forethought to leave you free to decide about making war on him. That was important for the commonwealth, as I recognized at the time, and I now consider that it was important for your prestige.

You say that I * * *[1] to attack the Antonii and commend the same. I don't doubt that you think so. But I am far from approving the distinction you draw when you say that we should be keener to prevent civil wars than to wreak vengeance on the defeated. I strongly disagree with you, Brutus. I consider myself as merciful a man as you, but salutary severity is better than the hollow appearance of mercy. If we want to be merciful, we shall never be without a civil war. However, that is your problem. I can say of myself what Plautus' father says in *Song of Sixpence*: 'My time is nearly over. You're the party most concerned.'[2] Believe me, Brutus, you and your friends will be overwhelmed if you do not take care. You will not always have a people and a Senate and a leader of the Senate as they are today. You may take this as a Delphic oracle. Nothing can be more true.

20 (?) April.

[1] The manuscript reading makes no sense and has not been satisfactorily corrected.

[2] *Trinummus* 319.

7 (I.3)

Scr. Romae c. XI Kal. Mai. an. 43

CICERO BRUTO SALUTEM

1 Nostrae res meliore loco videbantur. scripta enim ad te certo scio quae gesta sint. qualis tibi saepe scripsi consules, tales exstiterunt. Caesaris vero pueri mirifica indoles virtutis. utinam tam facile eum florentem et honoribus et gratia regere ac tenere possimus quam facile adhuc tenuimus! est omnino illud difficilius, sed tamen non diffidimus. persuasum est enim adulescenti, et maxime per me, eius opera nos esse salvos; et certe, nisi is Antonium ab urbe avertisset, perissent omnia.

2 Triduo vero aut quadriduo ante hanc rem pulcherrimam timore quodam perculsa civitas tota ad te se cum coniugibus et liberis effundebat. eadem recreata a. d. XII Kal. Mai. te huc venire quam se ad te ire malebat. quo quidem die magnorum meorum laborum multarumque vigiliarum ‹fructum› cepi maximum, si modo est aliquis fructus ex solida veraque gloria. nam tantae multitudinis quantam capit urbs nostra concursus est ad me factus. a qua[1] usque in Capitolium deductus, maximo clamore atque plausu in rostris collocatus sum. nihil est in me inane, neque enim debet; sed tamen omnium ordinum consensus, gratiarum actio gratulatioque me commovet propterea quod popularem esse in populi salute praecla-
3 rum est. sed haec te malo ab aliis.

Me velim de tuis rebus consiliisque facias diligentissime certiorem illudque consideres, ne tua liberalitas dissolutior videatur. sic sentit senatus, sic populus Romanus,

[1] ea cum (*Crat. marg.*)

7 (I.3)

Rome, ca. 21 April 43

From Cicero to Brutus greetings.

Our affairs seem in better shape. I am sure your correspondents have informed you of what has occurred. The Consuls have proved such as I have often described them to you. As for the boy Caesar, his natural worth and manliness is extraordinary. I only pray that I may succeed in guiding and holding him in the fulness of honours and favour as easily as I have done hitherto. That will be more difficult, it is true, but still I do not despair. The young man is persuaded (chiefly through me) that our survival is his work; and certain it is that if he had not turned Antony back from Rome, all would have been lost.

Three or four days before this splendid victory the whole city fell into a panic and poured out with wives and children to join you; but on 20 April they recovered and would now like you to come over here instead. That day I reaped the richest of rewards for my many days of labour and nights of wakefulness—if there is any reward in true, genuine glory. The whole population of Rome thronged to my house and escorted me up to the Capitol, then set me on the Rostra amid tumultuous applause. I am not a vain man, I do not need to be; but the unison of all classes in thanks and congratulations does move me, for to be popular in serving the people's welfare is a fine thing. But I would rather you heard all this from others.

Please keep me very particularly informed about your doings and plans, and take care that your generosity does not look like laxity. It is the feeling of the Senate and of

nullos umquam hostis digniores omni supplicio fuisse quam eos civis qui hoc bello contra patriam arma ceperunt. quos quidem ego omnibus sententiis ulciscor et persequor omnibus bonis approbantibus. tu quid de hac re sentias, tui iudici est. ego sic sentio, trium fratrum unam et eandem esse causam.

8 (I.3a)[1]

Scr. Romae v *(?) Kal. Mai. an. 43*

‹CICERO BRUTO SALUTEM›

Consules duos, bonos quidem sed dumtaxat bonos consules, amisimus. Hirtius quidem in ipsa victoria occidit, cum paucis diebus ante magno proelio vicisset. nam Pansa fugerat vulneribus acceptis quae ferre non potuit. reliquias hostium Brutus persequitur et Caesar. hostes autem omnes iudicati qui M. Antoni sectam secuti sunt. itaque id senatus consultum plerique interpretantur etiam ad tuos sive captivos sive dediticios pertinere. equidem nihil disserui durius cum nominatim de C. Antonio decernerem, quod ita statueram, a te cognoscere causam eius senatum oportere.

v Kal. Mai.

[1] *cum priore coniungunt codd.* (*Ruete*)

the People of Rome that no public enemies ever deserved the harshest penalties more than those Romans who have taken up arms against their country in this war. In all my speeches I punish and harry them with the approval of all honest men. Your view on the matter is for you to determine. Mine is that the three brothers are in one and the same boat.

8 (I.3a)

Rome, 27 (?) April 43

From Cicero to M. Brutus greetings.

We have lost two good Consuls—but 'good' is as much as one can say. Hirtius fell in the moment of victory after winning a great battle a few days earlier. Pansa had fled after receiving wounds which were too much for him. Brutus and Caesar are in pursuit of the remnant of the enemy. And all those who have followed Mark Antony's lead have been pronounced public enemies. Most people interpret that decree of the Senate as applying to those whom you have captured or whose surrender you have accepted. For my part I used no harsh language in making a proposal about C. Antonius by name, having made up my mind that the Senate should learn of his case from yourself.

27 April.

9 (I.5)

Scr. Romae III *Non. Mai. an. 43*

CICERO BRUTO SALUTEM

1 A. d. v Kal. Mai., cum de iis qui hostes iudicati sunt bello persequendis sententiae dicerentur, dixit Servilius et cetera de Ventidio et ut Cassius persequeretur Dolabellam. cui cum essem adsensus, decrevi hoc amplius, ut tu, si arbitrarere utile exque re publica esse, persequerere bello Dolabellam; si minus id commodo rei publicae facere posses sive non existimares ex re publica esse, ut in isdem locis exercitum contineres. nihil honorificentius potuit facere senatus quam ut tuum esset iudicium quid maxime conducere rei publicae tibi videretur. equidem sic sentio, si manum habet, si castra, si ubi consistat uspiam Dolabella,
2 ad fidem et ad dignitatem tuam pertinere eum persequi. de Cassi nostri copiis nihil sciebamus. neque enim ab ipso ullae litterae neque nuntiabatur quicquam quod pro certo haberemus. quanto opere autem intersit opprimi Dolabellam profecto intellegis, cum ut sceleris poenas persolvat tum ne sit quo se latronum duces ex Mutinensi fuga conferant. atque hoc mihi iam ante placuisse potes ex superioribus meis litteris recordari. quamquam tum et fugae portus erat in tuis castris et subsidium salutis in tuo exercitu. quo magis nunc liberati, ut spero, periculis in Dolabella opprimendo occupati esse debemus. sed haec cogitabis diligentius, statues sapienter, facies nos quid constitueris et quid agas, si tibi videbitur, certiores.

9 (I.5)

Rome, 5 May 43

From Cicero to Brutus greetings.

In a debate of 27 April on military operations against those who have been declared public enemies, Servilius made a speech mostly about Ventidius, but he also moved that Cassius should take action against Dolabella. I concurred, and proposed in addition that you should take military action against Dolabella if you thought it expedient and in the public interest; but that, if you could not do so with benefit to the commonwealth or did not think it in the public interest, you should keep your army where it now is. The Senate could not pay you a greater compliment than to let you decide for yourself what course you judge most advantageous to the commonwealth. My personal feeling is that if Dolabella has a following, a camp, anywhere to make a stand, you should move against him as a matter of loyalty and prestige. We know nothing about our friend Cassius' forces. No letters have arrived from him nor have we any report on which we can firmly rely. I am sure you appreciate how important it is that Dolabella should be crushed, so that he pay for his crime and so that the traitor chiefs in flight from Mutina do not have a rallying point. You may remember from my previous letters that I held this view at an earlier stage, although at that time your camp was our harbour of refuge and your army our vital reserve. Now that our dangers are, as I hope, safely over, we ought to be all the more concerned about crushing Dolabella. But you will give careful thought to all this and come to a wise conclusion and if you see fit, please let us know what you have decided and what you are doing.

3 Ciceronem nostrum in vestrum collegium cooptari volo. existimo omnino absentium rationem sacerdotum comitiis posse haberi; nam et factum est antea. Gaius enim Marius, cum in Cappadocia esset, lege Domitia factus est augur nec quo minus id postea liceret ulla lex sanxit. est etiam in lege Iulia, quae lex est de sacerdotiis proxima, his verbis: 'qui petet cuiusve ratio habebitur.' aperte indicat posse rationem haberi etiam non petentis. hac de re scripsi ad eum ut tuo iudicio uteretur sicut in rebus omnibus. tibi autem statuendum est de Domitio, de Catone nostro. sed quamvis liceat absentis rationem haberi, tamen omnia sunt praesentibus faciliora. quod si statueris in Asiam tibi eundum, nulla erit ad comitia nostros accersendi facultas.
4 omnino Pansa vivo celeriora omnia putabamus. statim enim collegam sibi subrogavisset; deinde ante praetoria sacerdotum comitia fuissent. nunc per auspicia longam moram video. dum enim unus erit patricius magistratus, auspicia ad patres redire non possunt. magna sane perturbatio. tu tota de re quid sentias velim me facias certiorem.

III Non. Mai.

---

[1] That of Pontiffs.

I should like our Marcus to be coopted into your College.[1] I think that candidates at elections to priesthoods can be admitted *in absentia*. It has been done before. C. Marius was elected Augur under the lex Domitia when he was in Cappadocia, and no later law has made this any the less permissible in the future. Also the lex Julia, the most recent law on priesthoods, reads as follows: 'Whosoever shall stand or whose candidature shall be admitted.' That clearly implies that the candidature of one not personally standing is admissible. I have written to him on this subject telling him to abide by your judgement, as in all matters. And you must decide about Domitius and our young friend Cato.[2] However, even though candidature *in absentia* is allowable, everything is easier for those on the spot. But if you decide that you ought to go to Asia, there will be no chance of fetching our young men back for the elections. To be sure, I thought everything would go more quickly with Pansa alive. He would have had his new colleague elected at once, and then the elections for the priesthoods would have been held before the praetorian elections. Now I expect a long delay because of the auspices, since so long as we have a single patrician magistrate the auspices cannot revert to the patriciate.[3] It is certainly a very confused situation. I hope you will inform me of your views on the whole matter.

5 May.

[2] Sons of L. Domitius Ahenobarbus and M. Porcius Cato, now serving with Brutus. They too were prospective candidates for a priesthood, probably an Augurate; see on Letter 19.2.

[3] Thus creating an Interregnum and making possible the holding of consular elections.

10 (I.4)

Scr. Dyrrachii c. Non. Mai. an. 43

BRUTUS CICERONI SALUTEM

1 Quanta sim laetitia adfectus cognitis rebus Bruti nostri et consulum facilius est tibi existimare quam mihi scribere. cum alia laudo et gaudeo accidisse tum quod Bruti eruptio non solum ipsi salutaris fuit sed etiam maximo ad victoriam adiumento.

2 Quod scribis mihi trium Antoniorum unam atque eandem causam esse, quid ego sentiam mei iudici esse, statuo nihil nisi hoc, senatus aut populi Romani iudicium esse de iis civibus qui pugnantes non interierint. 'at hoc ipsum' inquies 'inique facis qui hostilis animi in rem publicam homines civis appelles.' immo iustissime. quod enim nondum senatus censuit nec populus Romanus iussit, id adroganter non praeiudico neque revoco ad arbitrium meum. illud quidem non muto quod ei quem me occidere res non coegit neque crudeliter quicquam eripui neque dissolute quicquam remisi habuique in mea potestate quoad bellum fuit.

Multo equidem honestius iudico magisque quod conducere possit rei publicae[1] miserorum fortunam non
insectari quam infinite tribuere potentibus quae cupidita-
3 tem et adrogantiam incendere possint. qua in re, Cicero,
vir optime ac fortissime mihique merito et meo nomine et
rei publicae carissime, nimis credere videris spei tuae, sta-
timque, ut quisque aliquid recte fecerit, omnia dare ac

[1] concedere . . . res publica

---

[1] C. Antonius.

10 (I.4)

Dyrrachium, ca. 7 May 43

From Brutus to Cicero greetings.

How delighted I am to learn of the successes of our friend Brutus and the Consuls it is easier for you to imagine than for me to write. I applaud and rejoice at all of it, but especially the fact that Brutus' breakout not only brought safety to himself but also made a major contribution to the victory.

You tell me that the three Antonii are in one and the same boat, and that my view is for me to determine. My only conclusion is that the Senate or the People of Rome must pass judgement on those citizens who have not died fighting. You will say that my calling men hostile to the state 'citizens' is an impropriety in itself On the contrary, it is quite proper. What the Senate has not yet decreed, nor the Roman People ordered, I do not take it upon myself to prejudge, I do not make myself the arbiter. This much I maintain: in dealing with a person[1] whose life circumstances did not oblige me to take, I have neither despoiled him cruelly nor indulged him laxly, and I have kept him in my power for the duration of the war.

In my judgement it is much more honourable and profitable to the commonwealth to refrain from bearing hard on the unfortunate than to make endless concessions to the powerful which may whet their appetite and arrogance. In which regard, my excellent and gallant friend, whom I love so well and so deservedly both on my own account and on that of the commonwealth, you seem to me to be trusting your hopes too fondly. The moment somebody behaves well you seem to set no bounds to your favours

permittere, quasi non liceat traduci ad mala consilia corruptum largitionibus animum. quae tua est humanitas, aequo animo te moneri patieris, praesertim de communi salute. facies tamen quod tibi visum fuerit. etiam ego, cum me docueris * * *.

11 (I.4a)[1]

Scr. in castris Id. Mai an. 43

<BRUTUS CICERONI SALUTEM>

1 * * * nunc, Cicero, nunc agendum est ne frustra oppres-
sum esse Antonium gavisi simus neu semper primi cuiusque mali excidendi <cura>[2] causa sit ut aliud renascatur
2 illo peius. nihil iam neque opinantibus aut patientibus nobis adversi evenire potest in quo non cum omnium culpa
tum praecipue tua futura sit, cuius tantam auctoritatem
senatus ac populus Romanus non solum esse patitur sed
etiam cupit quanta maxima in libera civitate unius esse
potest. quam tu non solum bene sentiendo sed etiam pru-
denter <agendo>[3] tueri debes; prudentia porro, quae tibi
superest, nulla abs te desideratur nisi modus in tribuendis
honoribus. alia omnia sic adsunt ut cum quolibet antiquo-
rum comparari possint tuae virtutes. unum hoc <a> grato
animo liberalique profectum *, cautiorem ac moderatio-
rem liberalitatem desiderant. nihil enim senatus cuiquam
dare debet quod male cogitantibus exemplo aut praesidio
sit. itaque timeo de consulatu, ne Caesar tuus altius se

[1] *cum priore continuant codd.* (*O. E. Schmidt*)
[2] (*Becher*)
[3] (ς*)

and concessions, as though a mind corrupted by largesse could not possibly be swayed to bad courses. Your heart is too good to take offence at a warning, especially where the common welfare is at stake. But you will do as you think best. I too, when you have informed me * * *.

11 (I.4a)

Camp, 15 May 43

M. BRUTUS TO CICERO

* * * Now, Cicero, now is the time to act so that our joy over Antony's collapse does not turn out an illusion and so that care to excise one evil does not always generate a new and worse one. If anything untoward happens now, to our surprise or with our tolerance, we shall all be to blame, but you more than any; for the Senate and People of Rome not only allows but desires you to exercise an authority as great as can belong to any one man in a free community. You should live up to that not only by thinking legally but by acting wisely. Moreover, the only form of wisdom (of which you have enough and to spare) felt to be lacking on your part is restraint in bestowing honours. All else you have in such ample measure that your qualities can be compared with any of the great men of history. This one thing only, which comes from a grateful and generous heart, people criticize (?): they would like to see your generosity tempered by caution and moderation. The Senate ought not to grant any man a favour which might serve as a precedent or a support to evil-designing persons. Accordingly, I am alarmed about the Consulship. I fear your young friend Caesar may think he has climbed so high through your de-

escendisse putet decretis tuis quam inde, si consul factus sit, escensurum.

3 quod si Antonius ab alio relictum regni instrumentum occasionem regnandi habuit, quonam animo fore putas si quis auctore non tyranno interfecto sed ipso senatu putet se imperia quaelibet concupiscere posse? qua re tum et felicitatem et providentiam laudabo tuam cum exploratum habere coepero Caesarem honoribus quos acceperit extraordinariis fore contentum. 'alienae igitur' inquies 'culpae me reum subicies?' prorsus alienae, si provideri potuit ne exsisteret. quod utinam inspectare posses timorem de illo meum!

4 His litteris scriptis consulem te factum audivimus. tum vero incipiam proponere mihi rem publicam iustam et iam suis nitentem viribus si istuc videro.

Filius valet et in Macedoniam cum equitatu praemissus est.

Id. Mai. ex castris.

12 (I.6)

Scr. in castris ad imam Candaviam XIV *Kal. Iun. an. 43*

BRUTUS CICERONI SALUTEM

1 Noli exspectare dum tibi gratias agam. iam pridem hoc ex nostra necessitudine, quae ad summam benevolentiam pervenit, sublatum esse debet.

2 Filius tuus a me abest. in Macedonia congrediemur. iussus est enim Ambracia ducere equites per Thessaliam. scripsi ad eum ut mihi Heracleam[1] occurreret. cum eum

[1] *anne* ‹ad› Heracleam?

---

[1] I.e. he might think that the further climb to the Consulship would be shorter than the one he had already made.

crees that the ascent from that point, if he is made Consul, will be briefer.[1] Antony made use of the apparatus of monarchy left behind by another to make himself a monarch. What do you suppose will be the mentality of one who thinks himself in a position to covet any office of power with the backing, not of a slaughtered tyrant, but of the Senate itself? So I shall applaud your good fortune and foresight when, and only when, I begin to feel assurance that Caesar is going to be satisfied with the extraordinary honours that have come his way. You may ask whether I am going to make you answerable for somebody else's fault. Indeed I am, if it could have been foreseen and prevented. I only wish you could see into my heart, how I fear that young man.

After I wrote the above, we heard that you have been elected Consul. The day I see that, I shall begin to envisage a true commonwealth, relying on its own strength.

Your son is well and has been sent to Macedonia in advance with a force of cavalry.

Ides of May, from camp.

12 (I.6)

Camp on the border of lower Candavia, 19 May 43

From Brutus to Cicero greetings.

Don't wait for me to thank you. That has long since become inappropriate in our relationship, which has developed into so close a friendship.

Your son is not with me. We shall meet in Macedonia—he has orders to take a squadron of cavalry from Ambracia through Thessaly. I have written to him to meet me at

videro, quoniam nobis permittis, communiter constituemus de reditu eius ad petitionem aut commendatione[2] honoris.

Tibi Glycona, medicum Pansae, qui sororem Achilleos nostri in matrimonio habet, diligentissime commendo. audimus eum venisse in suspicionem Torquato de morte Pansae custodirique ut parricidam. nihil minus credendum est. quis enim maiorem calamitatem morte Pansae accepit? praeterea est modestus homo et frugi, quem ne utilitas quidem videatur impulsura fuisse ad facinus. rogo te, et quidem valde rogo (nam Achilleus noster non minus quam aequum est laborat) eripias eum ex custodia conservesque. hoc ego ad meum officium privatarum rerum aeque atque ullam aliam rem pertinere arbitror.

3 Cum has ad te scriberem litteras, a Satrio, legato C. Treboni, reddita est epistula mihi a Tillio et Deiotaro Dolabellam caesum fugatumque esse. Graecam epistulam tibi misi Cicerei cuiusdam ad Satrium missam.

4 Flavius noster de controversia quam habet cum Dyrrachinis hereditariam sumpsit te iudicem; rogo te, Cicero, et Flavius rogat rem conficias. quin ei qui Flavium fecit heredem pecuniam debuerit civitas non est dubium; neque Dyrrachini infitiantur, sed sibi donatum aes alienum a Caesare dicunt. noli pati a necessariis tuis necessario meo iniuriam fieri.

XIIII Kal. Iun. ex castris ad imam Candaviam.

[2] commendationem (*SB*)

---

[1] Pansa's Quaestor.

Heraclea. When I see him, since you leave it in our hands, we shall take counsel together about his returning to stand for election or about recommending him for the office.

I very particularly recommend to you Pansa's doctor, Glyco, who is married to my friend Achilleus' sister. We hear that Torquatus[1] suspects him in connection with Pansa's death and that he is being kept in custody as a murderer. That is quite incredible. Pansa's death hit nobody harder. Besides he is a well-conducted, decent fellow, who would not seem likely to have been driven to crime even by self-interest. I beg you, and very earnestly (for my friend Achilleus is no less disturbed about it than he should be), to get him out of custody and keep him safe. I regard this as a matter of private obligation for me, of importance equal to any other.

As I was writing you these lines, a letter was delivered to me from C. Trebonius' Legate Satrius giving the news that Dolabella has been cut to pieces and put to flight by Tillius and Deiotarus. I am sending you a letter in Greek from a certain Cicereius, sent to Satrius.

Our friend Flavius has chosen you as arbiter in the dispute he has about an inheritance with the township of Dyrrachium. I beg you, Cicero, and so does Flavius, to settle the matter. There is no question but that the town owed money to the person who made Flavius his heir. The townspeople don't deny it, but say that Caesar made them a present of the debt. Don't let a wrong be done to my friend by your friends.[2]

19 May from camp on the border of lower Candavia.

2 Regarding Cicero's relations with the town of Dyrrachium cf. *Letters to Friends* 8 (XIV.1).7 and 9 (XIV.3).4.

13 (I.1)

Scr. Romae c. Id. Mai. an. 43

CICERO BRUTO SALUTEM

1 L. Clodius, tribunus pl. designatus, valde me diligit vel, ut ἐμφατικώτερον <dicam>,[1] valde me amat. quod cum mihi ita persuasum sit, non dubito (bene enim me nosti) quin illum quoque iudices a me amari. nihil enim mihi minus hominis videtur quam non respondere in amore iis a quibus provocere.

Is mihi visus est suspicari, nec sine magno quidem dolore, aliquid a tuis vel per suos potius iniquos ad te esse delatum quo tuus animus a se esset alienior. non soleo, mi Brute, quod tibi notum esse arbitror, temere adfirmare de altero (est enim periculosum propter occultas hominum voluntates multiplicisque naturas): Clodi animum perspectum habeo, cognitum, iudicatum. multa eius indicia, sed ad scribendum non necessaria; volo enim testimonium hoc tibi videri potius quam epistulam.

Auctus Antoni beneficio est (eius ipsius benefici magna
2 pars a te est); itaque eum salvis nobis vellet salvum. in eum autem locum rem adductam intellegit (est enim, ut scis, minime stultus) ut utrique salvi esse non possint; itaque nos mavult. de te vero amicissime et loquitur et sentit. qua

[1] (*habet Nonius 682 L*)

---

[1] Not necessarily or even probably identical with Ap. Pulcher's Prefect of Engineers in 51.

13 (I.1)

Rome, May 43

From Cicero to Brutus greetings.

L. Clodius,[1] Tribune-Designate, has a high regard for me, or rather (to put it with more *empressement*) a great affection. Since I am satisfied of that, I don't doubt that you, knowing me as well as you do, conclude that I have an affection for *him*. Nothing to my way of thinking becomes a human being less than not to respond to a challenge of affection.

I think Clodius suspects, and is very sorry to suspect, that something has been passed to you by your people, or rather through ill-wishers of *his*, to set your mind against him. As I think you know, my dear Brutus, it is not my habit to make assertions about another person lightly. That is a dangerous thing to do—people's real sentiments are so often concealed and their dispositions so complex. But Clodius' mind is an open book to me, and my opinion is formed. There are many indications, but they need not be put into writing. For I want this to seem like an attestation rather than a letter.

He was advanced by Antony's favour (in that very favour you had a large share). Accordingly, he would have wished him well, compatibly with *our* welfare. But being, as you know, very far from a fool, he realizes that things have come to the point where both cannot survive, and so he prefers us. As for yourself, he speaks and feels about you in the most friendly way. So if anybody has written or

re si quis secus ad te de eo scripsit aut si coram locutus est, peto a te etiam atque etiam mihi ut potius credas, qui et facilius iudicare possum quam ille nescio quis et te plus diligo. Clodium tibi amicissimum existima civemque talem qualis et prudentissimus et fortuna optima esse debet.

14 (I.2)

Scr. Romae med. vel ex. m. Mai. an. 43

CICERO BRUTO SALUTEM

1 Scripta et obsignata iam epistula litterae mihi redditae sunt a te plenae rerum novarum, maximeque mirabile Dolabellam quinque cohortis misisse in Chersonesum. adeone copiis abundat ut is qui ex Asia fugere dicebatur Europam appetere conetur? quinque autem cohortibus quidnam se facturum arbitratus est, cum tu †eo† quinque legiones, optimum equitatum, maxima auxilia haberes? quas quidem cohortis spero iam tuas esse, quoniam latro ille tam fuit demens.

2 Tuum consilium vehementer laudo quod non prius exercitum Apollonia Dyrrachioque movisti quam de Antoni fuga audisti, Bruti eruptione, populi Romani victoria. itaque quod scribis post ea statuisse te ducere exercitum in Chersonesum nec pati sceleratissimo hosti ludibrio esse imperium populi Romani, facis ex tua dignitate et ex re publica.

3 Quod scribis de seditione quae facta est in legione quarta de‹cima et de fraude›[1] C. Antoni, (sed in bonam

[1] (*coni. Watt, ducibus K. F. Hermann et Madvig*)

talked to you amiss about him, let me beg you again rather to trust me, who am in a better position to judge than that somebody-or-other, and have a greater regard for you. Believe that Clodius is a very good friend of yours and as good a citizen as a man of thorough sound sense and excellent worldly position ought to be.

14 (I.2)

Rome, latter May 43

From Cicero to Brutus greetings.

I had already written and sealed a letter to you when one from you was delivered to me full of news, the most surprising item being that Dolabella has sent five cohorts to the Chersonese. Are his forces so ample that after we were told he was in flight from Asia he is trying to lay hands on Europe? And what did he expect to achieve with five cohorts when you have five legions, excellent cavalry, and large auxiliary forces? I hope those cohorts are now yours, since the bandit has been thus crazy.

I strongly commend your prudence in not moving your army from Apollonia and Dyrrachium before you heard of Antony's rout, Brutus' breakout, and the victory of the Roman People. You say that thereafter you decided to march your army into the Chersonese and not allow the authority of the Roman People to be flouted by a criminal and a public enemy. That is for your own prestige and the national interest.

You further write of a mutiny in the Fourteenth Legion and of C. Antonius' treachery. You will take what I say in

partem accipies) magis mihi probatur militum severitas quam tua * * *[2]

15 (I.8)

Scr. Romae m. Mai. aut Iun. (?) an. 43

CICERO BRUTO SALUTEM

1 Multos tibi commendavi et commendem necesse est. optimus enim quisque vir et civis maxime sequitur tuum iudicium tibique omnes fortes viri navare operam et studium volunt, nec quisquam est quin ita existimet, meam
2 apud te et auctoritatem et gratiam valere plurimum. sed C. Nasennium, municipem Suessanum, tibi ita commendo ut neminem diligentius. Cretensi bello Metello imperatore octavum principem duxit, postea in re familiari occupatus fuit; hoc tempore cum rei publicae partibus tum tua excellenti dignitate commotus voluit per te aliquid auctoritatis adsumere. fortem virum, Brute, tibi commendo, frugi hominem et, si quid ad rem pertinet, etiam locupletem. pergratum mihi erit si eum ita tractaris ut merito tuo mihi gratias agere possit.

[2] *finem excidisse vidit Gurlitt (vide ep. 6)*

good part: I approve of the severity of the soldiers more than of your * * *

15 (I.8)

Rome, May or June (?) 43

From Cicero to Brutus greetings.

I have recommended many persons to you, and needs must. For our best men and citizens are most eager for your good opinion and all gallant spirits want to give you enthusiastic service. Nor is there a man who does not believe that my authority and influence counts for a great deal with you. But I recommend to you nobody more earnestly than C. Nasennius, a townsman of Suessa. He was First Centurion of the eighth cohort in the Cretan War[1] under General Metellus. Thereafter he has been busy with his private affairs, but is now moved by loyalty to the patriotic side and your outstanding prestige to wish to take some position of authority by your appointment. I commend him to you, Brutus, as a brave gentleman, a man of worth and (if that is at all relevant) of wealth too. You will greatly oblige me if you handle him so that he can thank me on account of what you do for his benefit.

[1] In 68–67.

16 (I.11)

Scr. in castris m. Iun. an. 43

BRUTUS CICERONI SALUTEM

1 Veteris Antisti talis animus est in rem publicam ut non dubitem quin et in Caesare et Antonio se praestaturus fuerit acerrimum propugnatorem communis libertatis, si occasioni potuisset occurrere. nam qui in Achaia congressus cum[1] Dolabella milites atque equites habente quodvis adire periculum ex insidiis paratissimi ad omnia latronis maluerit quam videri aut coactus esse pecuniam dare aut libenter dedisse homini nequissimo atque improbissimo, is nobis ultro et pollicitus est et dedit HS ⌈XX⌉ ex sua pecunia et, quod multo carius est, se ipsum obtulit et coniunxit.

2 Huic persuadere cupi<i>mus[2] ut imperator in castris remaneret remque publicam defenderet. statuit id sibi <non faciendum>,[3] quoniam exercitum dimisisset. statim vero rediturum ad nos confirmavit legatione suscepta, nisi praetorum comitia habituri essent consules. nam illi ita sentienti de re publica magno opere auctor fui ne differret tempus petitionis suae. cuius factum omnibus gratum esse debet qui modo iudicant hunc exercitum esse rei publicae, tibi tanto gratius quanto maiore et animo gloriaque libertatem nostram defendis et dignitate, si contigerit nostris consiliis exitus quem optamus, perfuncturus es.

Ego etiam <atque etiam>,[4] mi Cicero, proprie familiari-

[1] P. (*Gurlitt*)
[2] (*Vict.*)
[3] (*SB*)
[4] (*Weiske*)

16 (I.11)

Camp, June 43

From Brutus to Cicero greetings.

Vetus Antistius' patriotic spirit is such that I do not doubt he would have shown himself a most ardent champion of our common liberties both in Caesar's case and in Antony's had he been able to meet the occasion. When he encountered Dolabella, who had soldiers and horse, in Greece, he preferred to face any danger from the plots of a totally unscrupulous bandit rather than let it be thought that he had been forced to give money to such an arrant scoundrel or had given it willingly. To me, on the other hand, he voluntarily promised and gave HS 2,000,000 out of his own funds and, what is worth much more, put himself in my way and joined me.

I wished to persuade him to remain in his camp as commander[1] and defend the commonwealth. He decided that he should not do that since he had dismissed his army. But he gave an assurance that he would take a commission as Legate and return to us if the Consuls were not going to hold praetorian elections. I strongly urged him, being the loyal citizen that he is, not to put off his candidature to a later date. His conduct should have won the gratitude of all who regard this army as in the service of the commonwealth and of yourself above all, who are defending our freedom with so much spirit and glory and will enjoy so great a prestige if our plans are crowned with the success we hope for.

Also, my dear Cicero, I ask you personally as a friend to

[1] Imperator.

terque te rogo ut Veterem ames velisque esse quam amplissimum. qui etsi nulla re deterreri a proposito potest, tamen excitari tuis laudibus indulgentiaque poterit quo magis amplexetur ac tueatur iudicium suum. id mihi gratissimum erit.

17 (I.10)

Scr. Romae mid. m. Iun. an. 43

CICERO BRUTO SALUTEM

1 Nullas adhuc a te litteras habebamus, ne famam quidem quae declararet te cognita senatus auctoritate in Italiam adducere exercitum; quod ut faceres idque maturares magno opere desiderabat res publica. ingravescit enim in dies intestinum malum nec externis hostibus magis quam domesticis laboramus, qui erant omnino ab initio belli sed facilius frangebantur. erectior senatus erat non sententiis solum nostris sed etiam cohortationibus excitatus. erat in senatu satis vehemens et acer Pansa cum in ceteros huius generis tum maxime in socerum; cui consuli non animus ab
2 initio, non fides ad extremum defuit. bellum ad Mutinam gerebatur nihil ut in Caesare reprehenderes, non nulla in Hirtio.

Huius belli fortuna 'ut in secundis fluxa, ut in adversis bona.' erat victrix res publica caesis Antoni copiis, ipso expulso. <a> Bruto deinde ita multa peccata ut quodam

[1] Q. Fufius Calenus, Antony's leading supporter in the Senate.

[2] The nature of the criticism is uncertain.

[3] Cf. *Letters to Atticus* 73 (IV.1).8. The line is from an unknown Latin play. Shuckburgh rendered from Milton 'For happy though but ill, for ill not worst.'

be fond of Vetus and to desire his advancement. Although nothing can deter him from his purpose, your praise and indulgence can stimulate him to cling more closely and steadfastly to his intention. You will be obliging me greatly.

17 (I.10)

Rome, mid June 43

From Cicero to Brutus greetings.

We have heard nothing from you as yet, not even a rumour to tell us that you have been apprised of the Senate's resolution and are bringing your army to Italy. The public interest urgently demands that you do this, and quickly. For our internal malady grows worse every day, and the enemies within the gates give us as much trouble as those outside. They existed, it is true, from the beginning of the war, but they used to be more easily put down. The Senate was more resolute, animated by my proposals and also my exhortations. Pansa was there to take a sufficiently strong and stern line with these gentry, his father-in-law[1] especially. As Consul he did not lack spirit from the outset nor loyalty at the end. In the fighting at Mutina Caesar's conduct gave no room for criticism, Hirtius' gave some.[2]

You might say of the fortune of this war

'Unsettled,' when our luck is in;
When out, we call it 'fair.'[3]

The national cause was victorious. Antony's forces were cut to pieces and himself driven out. Then Brutus made so many mistakes that the victory somehow slipped through

modo victoria excideret e manibus; perterritos, inermis, saucios non sunt nostri duces persecuti, datumque Lepido tempus est in quo levitatem eius saepe perspectam maioribus in malis experiremur.

Sunt exercitus boni sed rudes Bruti et Planci, sunt fide-
3 lissima et maxima auxilia Gallorum. sed Caesarem meis consiliis adhuc gubernatum, praeclara ipsum indole admirabilique constantia, improbissimis litteris quidam fallacibusque interpretibus ac nuntiis impulerunt in spem certissimam consulatus. quod simul atque sensi, neque ego illum absentem litteris monere destiti nec accusare praesentis eius necessarios qui eius cupiditati suffragari videbantur nec in senatu sceleratissimorum consiliorum fontis aperire dubitavi. nec vero ulla in re memini aut senatum meliorem aut magistratus. numquam enim in honore extraordinario potentis hominis vel potentissimi potius, quando quidem potentia iam in vi posita est et armis, accidit ut nemo tribunus pl., nemo alio ‹in›[1] magistratu, nemo privatus auctor exsisteret. sed in hac constantia atque virtute erat tamen sollicita civitas. illudimur enim, Brute, tum militum deliciis, tum imperatorum insolentia. tantum quisque se in re publica posse postulat quantum habet virium. non ratio, non modus, non lex, non mos, non officium valet, non iudicium, non existimatio civium, non posteritatis verecundia.

4 Haec ego multo ante prospiciens fugiebam ex Italia tum cum me vestrorum edictorum fama revocavit. incitavisti vero tu me, Brute, Veliae. quamquam enim dolebam in eam me urbem ire quam tu fugeres qui eam liberavisses,

[1] (*T.–P.*)

our fingers. Our generals failed to pursue the demoralized, unarmed, wounded enemy, and Lepidus was given time to let us experience in a graver crisis the irresponsibility he has so often demonstrated.

Brutus' and Plancus' armies are good but raw, and they have large, very loyal contingents of Gaulish auxiliaries. But Caesar, who has so far been guided by my counsels and is a fine young man in himself, remarkably steady, has been prodded by certain persons with rascally letters and shifty go-betweens and messages into a very confident expectation of the Consulship. As soon as I had an inkling of that, I wrote him letter after letter of warning and accused to their faces those friends of his who seemed to be backing his ambition, and I did not scruple to expose the origins of these criminal designs in open Senate. The Senate and magistrates behaved as well as I can remember in any context. In the case of an extraordinary office for a powerful individual—or let us say a *very* powerful individual, since power now resides in armed force—it is unheard of that *nobody*, no Tribune nor other magistrate nor private person, should appear as sponsor. But with all this steadiness and courage, the community is anxious. The fact is, Brutus, we are made a mockery by the caprices of the soldiers and the insolence of generals. Everybody demands as much political power as he has force behind him. Reason, moderation, law, tradition, duty count for nothing—likewise the judgement and views of the citizen body and respect for the opinion of those who come after us.

Foreseeing this long beforehand I was making my escape from Italy when the report of your manifestoes recalled me. But it was you, Brutus, at Velia, who urged me forward. Grieved though I was to be returning to the city

quod mihi quoque quondam acciderat periculo simili, casu tristiore, perrexi tamen Romamque perveni nulloque praesidio quatefeci Antonium contraque eius arma nefanda praesidia quae oblata sunt Caesaris consilio et auctoritate firmavi. qui si steterit ‹f›ide[2] mihique paruerit, satis videmur habituri praesidi; sin autem impiorum consilia plus valuerint quam nostra aut imbecillitas aetatis non potuerit gravitatem rerum sustinere, spes omnis est in te.

Quam ob rem advola, obsecro, atque eam rem publicam, quam virtute atque animi magnitudine magis quam eventis rerum liberavisti, exitu[3] libera. omnis omnium concursus ad te futurus est. hortare idem per litteras Cas-
5 sium. spes libertatis nusquam nisi in vestrorum castrorum
principiis est. firmos omnino et duces habemus ab occidente et exercitus. hoc adulescentis praesidium equidem adhuc firmum esse confido, sed ita multi labefactant ut ne moveatur interdum extimescam.

Habes totum rei publicae statum, qui quidem tum erat cum has litteras dabam. velim deinceps meliora sint; sin aliter fuerit (quod di omen avertant!), rei publicae vicem dolebo, quae immortalis esse debe‹b›at;[4] mihi quidem quantulum reliqui est!

2 (*Buecheler*)
3 exercitu *Studemund*
4 (*Lamb.*)

from which you, her liberator, were taking flight—something which had happened to me too in the days gone by in circumstances of similar peril and sadder fortune—I proceeded none the less and returned to Rome. There, quite unsupported, I shook Antony's position and strengthened the defence against his nefarious arms which Caesar's judgement and prestige had put in our way. If he remains loyal and obeys me, I think we shall have means enough to defend ourselves. But if the advice of miscreants carries more weight with him than mine, or if the frailty of his years proves unequal to the heavy burden of affairs, all hope lies in you.

Therefore, I beg you, hurry here and free in the final issue[4] the commonwealth of which you are the liberator in virtue of your courage and self-devotion rather than in the actual event. Everyone will rally like one man to your side. Write to Cassius and urge him to do the same. Hope of liberty lies nowhere but in your and his headquarters. To be sure, we have strong armies and generals in the west. For my part, I still think that we can rely on this young man, but so many folk are pushing him the wrong way that I am sometimes afraid of his changing his position.

I have given you a complete picture of the state of the commonwealth, such as it is at the time of dispatching this letter. I hope for better things in the future. If it turns out otherwise (which heaven forfend!), I shall grieve for the commonwealth, which ought to be everlasting. For myself, how little time remains!

4 Or 'with your army'; *exercitu* for *exitu* may be right, but see my Commentary.

18 (I.9)

Scr. Romae ex. m. Iun., ut vid., an. 43

CICERO BRUTO SALUTEM

1 Fun<ger>er eo officio quo tu functus es in meo luctu teque per litteras consolarer, nisi scirem iis remediis quibus meum dolorem tum levasses te in tuo non egere; ac velim facilius quam mihi nunc tibi tute medeare. est autem alienum tanto viro quantus es tu, quod alteri praeceperit, id ipsum facere non posse. me quidem cum rationes quas collegeras tum auctoritas tua a nimio maerore deterruit. cum enim mollius tibi ferre viderer quam deceret virum, praesertim eum qui alios consolari soleret, accusasti me per litteras gravioribus verbis quam tua consuetudo fere-
2 bat. itaque iudicium tuum magni aestimans idque veritus me ipse collegi et ea quae didiceram, legeram, acceperam graviora duxi tua auctoritate addita.

Ac mihi tum, Brute, officio solum erat et naturae, tibi nunc populo et scaenae, ut dicitur, serviendum est. nam cum in te non solum exercitus tui sed omnium civium ac paene gentium coniecti oculi sint, minime decet propter quem fortiores ceteri sumus eum ipsum animo debilitatum videri. quam ob rem accepisti tu quidem dolorem (id enim amisisti cui simile in terris nihil fuit), et est dolendum in tam gravi vulnere, ne id ipsum, carere omni sensu doloris, sit miserius quam dolere; sed ut modice, ceteris utile est, tibi necesse est.

3 Scriberem plura nisi ad te haec ipsa nimis multa essent.

---

[1] Brutus' wife Porcia (Cato's daughter) had died by her own hand. For his letter of condolence after Tullia's death, see *Letters to Atticus* 251 (XII.14).4 and 310 (XIII.6).3.

18 (I.9)

Rome, end of June (?) 43

From Cicero to Brutus greetings.

I should do you the same office as you did for me in my bereavement and write you a letter of consolation if I did not know that you have no need in your grief of the remedies with which you alleviated mine.[1] And I hope you find healing now in your own case easier than you found it in mine. It is not like so great a man as you to be unable to do the very thing he recommended to another. The arguments which you assembled and my respect for yourself held me back from undue sorrowing. For when you thought I was taking the blow less bravely than a man should, especially one who was in the habit of consoling others, you wrote and taxed me in terms more severe than you are accustomed to use. And so, esteeming your judgement highly and in awe of it, I pulled myself together and felt that all I had learned and read and been taught gained added weight from your authority.

At that time I owed nothing except to duty and nature, but now *you* have your obligations to the public and the limelight, as they say. Not only your army but all Romans, one might almost say all nations, have their eyes upon you. It would not be seemly if the man who makes us all braver were himself seen to be broken in spirit. You have indeed suffered a blow (the like of what you have lost was nowhere on earth) and you must grieve in so heavy a calamity. To lack all sense of grief might be more pitiable than grief itself. But moderation in grief, which is expedient for other men, is for you a necessity.

I should write more but that as written to *you* this is al-

nos te tuumque exercitum exspectamus, sine quo, ut reliqua ex sententia succedant, vix satis liberi videmur fore. de tota re publica plura scribam et fortasse iam certiora iis litteris quas Veteri nostro cogitabam dare.

19 (I.7)

Scr. in castris m. Mai. aut Iun. an. 43

BRUTUS CICERONI SALUTEM

1 L. Bibulus quam carus mihi esse debeat nemo melius iudicare potest quam tu, cuius tantae pro re publica contentiones sollicitudinesque fuerunt. itaque vel ipsius virtus vel nostra necessitudo debet conciliare te illi. quo minus multa mihi scribenda esse arbitror. voluntas enim te movere debet nostra, si modo iusta est aut pro officio necessario suscipitur. in Pansae locum petere constituit. eam nominationem a te petimus. neque coniunctiori dare beneficium quam nos tibi sumus neque digniorem nominare potes quam Bibulus.[1]

2 De Domitio et Appuleio quid attinet me scribere, cum ipsi per se tibi commendatissimi sint? Appuleium vero tu tua auctoritate sustinere debes. sed Appuleius in sua epistula celebrabitur. Bibulum noli dimittere e sinu tuo, tantum iam virum ex quanto, crede mihi, potest evadere qui nostris fautorum[2] respondeat laudibus.

[1] Bibulum ς: -lus est *coni. Watt*
[2] vestris paucorum (*SB*)

---

[1] In the College of Augurs.

ready too much. We are waiting for you and your army. Without that it looks as though we shall hardly be sufficiently free, even though everything else goes as we wish. I shall be writing more on the whole situation in the letter which I intend to give to our friend Vetus and shall then perhaps have more solid news.

19 (I.7)

Camp, May or June 43

From Brutus to Cicero greetings.

How dear L. Bibulus should be to me nobody can judge better than you, who have been through so much struggle and care for our country's sake. His own qualities and our connection ought to make you his friend. So I do not think I need write at length. My wish ought to weigh with you, provided it be legitimate and in pursuance of a necessary obligation. He has decided to stand for Pansa's vacancy.[1] You cannot do a favour to anyone closer to you than I am, nor can you nominate a worthier candidate than Bibulus.

As for Domitius and Appuleius,[2] it is superfluous for me to write when they are so strongly commended to you by their own persons. But you do have a duty to put your prestige behind Appuleius. However, he shall have a letter to himself to sing his praises. As for Bibulus, don't let him out of your care. He is already a fine fellow and, believe me, he can develop into one on whom the praises of us his backers will be fitly bestowed.

[2] Also presumably interested in Augurates. On the vacant priesthoods see my Commentary.

20 (I.13)

Scr. in castris Kal. Quint. an. 43

BRUTUS CICERONI SALUTEM

1 De M. Lepido vereri me cogit reliquorum timor. qui si eripuerit se nobis, quod velim temere atque iniuriose de illo suspicati sint homines, oro atque obsecro te, Cicero, necessitudinem nostram tuamque in me benevolentiam obtestans, sororis meae liberos obliviscaris esse Lepidi filios meque iis in patris locum successisse existimes. hoc si a te impetro, nihil profecto dubitabis pro iis suscipere. aliter alii cum suis vivunt: nihil ego possum in sororis meae liberis facere quo possit expleri voluntas mea aut officium. quid vero aut mihi tribuere boni possunt, si modo digni sumus quibus aliquid tribuatur, aut ego matri ac sorori puerisque illis praestaturus sum, si nihil valuerit apud te reliquumque senatum contra patrem Lepidum Brutus avunculus?

2 Scribere multa ad te neque possum prae sollicitudine ac stomacho neque debeo. nam si in tanta re tamque necessaria verbis mihi opus est ad te excitandum et confirmandum, nulla spes est facturum te quod volo et quod oportet. qua re noli exspectare longas preces; intuere me ipsum, qui hoc a te, vel a Cicerone, coniunctissimo homine, privatim vel a consulari, tali viro, remota necessitudine privata, debeo impetrare. quid sis facturus velim mihi quam primum rescribas.

Kal. Quint. ex castris.

20 (I.13)

Camp, 1 July 43

From Brutus to Cicero greetings.

The fears of the rest of the world make me apprehensive about M. Lepidus. If he tears himself away from us (I hope the general suspicion that he will is hasty and unjust), I beg and implore you, Cicero, in the name of our friendship and your good will towards me, to forget that my sister's children are Lepidus' sons and to regard me as having replaced him as their father. If you grant so much, I am sure there is nothing you will hesitate to do on their behalf. Others may stand on different terms with their kith and kin, but nothing I can do for my sister's children can satisfy my feelings or my duty. And what mark of favour can honest men confer upon me (that is, if I am worthy of any such), or how am I going to help my mother and my sister and those children, if you and the rest of the Senate will not let their uncle Brutus count against their father Lepidus?

Anxiety and vexation make it impossible for me to write to you at length, nor do I have to. After all, if I need words to rouse and strengthen you in a matter so important and close to my heart, there is no hope of your doing what I ask and what is right. So don't expect a lengthy appeal. Just look at *me*. You ought to grant me this both as a private individual, my very close friend Cicero, and as the great Consular you are, private connections apart. Please write back as soon as you can and let me know your intention.

Kalends of July, from camp.

21 (I.12)

Scr. Romae parte priore m. Quint. an. 43

CICERO BRUTO SALUTEM

1 Etsi daturus eram Messallae Corvino continuo litteras, tamen Veterem nostrum ad te sine litteris meis venire nolui.

Maximo in discrimine res publica, Brute, versatur victoresque rursus decertare cogimur; id accidit M. Lepidi scelere et amentia. quo tempore cum multa propter eam curam quam pro re publica suscepi graviter ferrem, tum nihil tuli gravius quam me non posse matris tuae precibus cedere, non sororis; nam tibi, quod mihi plurimi est, facile me satis facturum arbitrabar.

Nullo enim modo poterat causa Lepidi distingui ab Antoni[1] omniumque iudicio etiam durior erat quod, cum honoribus amplissimis a senatu esset Lepidus ornatus tum etiam paucis ante diebus praeclaras litteras ad senatum misisset, repente non solum recepit reliquias hostium sed bellum acerrime terra marique gerit, cuius exitus qui futurus sit incertum est. ita cum rogamur ut misericordiam liberis eius impertiamus, nihil adfertur quo minus summa supplicia, si (quod Iuppiter omen avertat!) pater puerorum vicerit, subeunda nobis sint.

2 Nec vero me fugit quam sit acerbum parentum scelera filiorum poenis lui. sed hoc praeclare legibus comparatum est, ut caritas liberorum amiciores parentis rei publicae

[1] antonio (*Lamb.** (-nii))

21 (I.12)

Rome, July (first half) 43

From Cicero to Brutus greetings.

Although I shall be giving a letter to Messalla Corvinus presently, I did not want our friend Vetus to join you without a letter from me.

The commonwealth is in the gravest peril, Brutus, and after our victory we are forced to join battle once more. That has happened because of the criminal folly of M. Lepidus. Many things distress me at this time by reason of the care for the commonwealth which I have taken upon myself, but nothing has distressed me more than my inability to comply with your mother's and your sister's entreaties. As for yourself (which is what matters to me most), I believe I shall have no difficulty in justifying my conduct.

Lepidus' case can in no way be distinguished from Antony's, and is universally judged to be even less defensible than his, in that after the Senate had honoured him with the highest distinctions and only a few days after sending a splendid dispatch to that body, Lepidus suddenly let in the remnants of the enemy and, not content with that, is waging war energetically by land and sea. What will be its outcome who can say? So when we are asked to extend compassion to his children, not a word is said to suggest that *we* shall not be punished to extremity if the children's father is victorious, which Jupiter forfend!

Not that I do not recognize the harshness of visiting the sins of the fathers upon the children. But the laws have very wisely ordained this in order that parental affection may better dispose fathers to the commonwealth. There-

redderet. itaque Lepidus crudelis in liberos, non is qui Lepidum hostem iudicat. atque ille si armis positis de vi damnatus esset, quo in iudicio certe defensionem non haberet, eandem calamitatem subirent liberi bonis publicatis. quamquam, quod tua mater et soror deprecatur pro pueris, id ipsum et multa alia crudeliora nobis omnibus Lepidus, Antonius, reliqui hostes denuntiant.

Itaque maximam spem hoc tempore habemus in te atque exercitu tuo. cum ad rem publicam summam tum ad gloriam et dignitatem tuam vehementer pertinet te, ut ante scripsi, in Italiam venire quam primum. eget enim vehementer cum viribus tuis tum etiam consilio res publica.

3 Veterem pro eius erga te benevolentia singularique officio libenter ex tuis litteris complexus sum eumque cum tui tum rei publicae studiosissimum amantissimumque cognovi. Ciceronem meum propediem, ut spero, videbo. tecum enim illum et te in Italiam celeriter esse venturum confido.

22 (I.14)

Scr. Romae prid. (?) Id. Quint. an. 43

CICERO BRUTO SALUTEM

1 Breves litterae tuae—breves dico? immo nullae. tribusne versiculis his temporibus Brutus ad me? nihil scripsisses potius. et requiris meas! quis umquam ad te tuorum sine meis venit? quae autem epistula non pondus habuit?

fore it is Lepidus who is cruel to his children, not he that declares Lepidus a public enemy. If he laid down his arms and was found guilty on charges of breaking the peace, against which he would certainly have no defence, his children would suffer the same penalty—his property being forfeit. Not but what Lepidus, Antony, and the other public enemies are threatening all of us with this very reprisal against which your mother and sister are pleading on behalf of the children, and with many others more cruel.

Accordingly, we pin our best hope at this time on you and your army. It is of great moment to the national cause and to your own glory and prestige that, as I have written before, you return to Italy as soon as possible. The commonwealth sorely needs your strength and your counsel too.

Following your letter I have gladly made a friend of Vetus in view of his good will and outstanding services to you; and I have found him most zealous and loyal to you and to the commonwealth. I hope to see my son Marcus shortly, since I trust that you will quickly come to Italy and he will be with you.

22 (I.14)

Rome, 14 July 43

From Cicero to Brutus greetings.

Your short letter—I say 'short,' but it was not really a letter at all. Does Brutus write me only three lines in times like these? Better nothing at all. And you think *I* should have written more! Which of your friends ever joined you without a letter from me? And which of my letters lacked

quae si ad te perlatae non sunt, ne domesticas quidem tuas perlatas arbitror. Ciceroni scribis te longiorem daturum epistulam, recte id quidem; sed haec quoque debuit esse plenior. ego autem, cum ad me de Ciceronis abs te discessu scripsisses, statim extrusi tabellarios litterasque ad Ciceronem ut, etiam si in Italiam venisset, ad te rediret; nihil enim mihi iucundius, nihil illi honestius. quamquam aliquotiens ei scripseram sacerdotum comitia mea summa contentione in alterum annum esse reiecta, quod ego cum Ciceronis causa elaboravi tum Domiti, Catonis, Lentuli, Bibulorum; quod ad te etiam scripseram, sed videlicet, cum illam pusillam epistulam tuam ad me dabas, nondum erat tibi id notum.

2 Qua re omni studio a te, mi Brute, contendo ut Ciceronem meum ne dimittas tecumque deducas; quod ipsum, si rem publicam, cui susceptus es, respicis, tibi iam iamque faciendum est. renatum enim bellum est, idque non parvum,[1] scelere Lepidi. exercitus autem Caesaris, qui erat optimus, non modo nihil prodest sed etiam cogit exercitum tuum flagitari; qui si Italiam attigerit, erit civis nemo, quem quidem civem appellari fas sit, qui se non in tua castra conferat. etsi Brutum praeclare cum Planco coniunctum habemus; sed non ignoras quam sint incerti et animi hominum[2] infecti partibus et exitus proeliorum. quin etiam si, ut spero, vicerimus, tamen magnam guberna-

[1] parvo (*Gul.*)
[2] animi hominum et (*Lamb.*)

---

[1] Syme showed that, contrary to earlier belief, two sons of M. Calpurnius Bibulus, Consul in 59, were living at this time. See my *Onomasticon to Cicero's Letters*, p. 29.

weight? If they have not been delivered to you, I think your letters from home have not been reaching you either. You say you will give Marcus a longer letter. Right, but this one too should have been fuller. Now when you wrote to me about Marcus' leaving you I immediately pushed out couriers and a letter to Marcus telling him to rejoin you even if he had already returned to Italy. No other course is more agreeable to me or more honourable to him. To be sure, I had written to him more than once that by dint of a great effort on my part, the elections to priesthoods were put off till next year. I exerted myself to bring that about both for Marcus' sake and for that of Domitius, Cato, Lentulus, the Bibuli,[1] and others. I wrote the same to you, but apparently you had not yet heard of it when you dispatched that tiny letter to me.

So I ask you with all urgency, my dear Brutus, not to send my son Marcus away but to bring him back with you. And this latter you should do any day now if you have any thought for the commonwealth which you were bred to serve. For the war is reborn through Lepidus' criminal behaviour, and no small war either. Caesar's army, which used to be excellent, is not only no help but forces us to ask urgently for *your* army. Once the latter touches Italian soil, every Roman who can in conscience be so called will betake himself to your camp. True, we have Brutus in fine combination with Plancus. But you well know how uncertain are the minds of men, tainted with party spirit, and the results of battles. Even if we win, as I hope we shall, the guidance of your counsel and prestige will be greatly

tionem tui consili tuaeque auctoritatis res[3] desiderabit. subveni igitur, per deos, idque quam primum, tibique persuade non te Idibus Martiis, quibus servitutem a tuis civibus depulisti, plus profuisse patriae quam, si mature veneris, profuturum.

II Id. Quint.

23 (I.15)

Scr. Romae m. Quint. an. 43

CICERO BRUTO SALUTEM

1 Messallam habes. quibus igitur litteris tam accurate scriptis adsequi possum subtilius ut explicem quae gerantur quaeque sint in re publica quam tibi is exponet qui et optime omnia novit et elegantissime expedire et deferre ad te potest? cave enim existimes, Brute (quamquam non necesse est ea me ad te quae tibi nota sunt scribere; sed tamen tantam omnium laudum excellentiam non queo silentio praeterire), cave putes probitate, constantia, cura, studio rei publicae quicquam illi esse simile, ut eloquentia, qua mirabiliter excellit, vix in eo locum ad laudandum habere videatur. quamquam in hac ipsa sapientiae[1] plus apparet; ita gravi iudicio multaque arte se exercuit in ‹se›verissimo[2] genere dicendi. tanta autem industria est tantumque evigilat in studio ut non maxima ingenio, quod in eo summum est, gratia habenda videatur.

2 Sed provehor amore. non enim id propositum est huic epistulae Messallam ut laudem, praesertim ad Brutum, cui

[3] res ‹p(ublica)› *coni. SB*

[1] sapientia (*Faërnus*) [2] (*Clark*)

needed. So come to our assistance, in heaven's name, and do so as soon as you can. Be sure that you did your country no greater service on the Ides of March, when you lifted the yoke of servitude from the backs of your fellow countrymen, than you will do her if you come quickly.

14 July.

23 (I.15)

Rome, July 43

From Cicero to Brutus greetings.

Messalla is with you. However carefully I write, I cannot hope to explain the current proceedings and situation more precisely in a letter than he will expound them with his excellent and comprehensive knowledge, and his ability to present you with all the facts in lucid and well chosen terms. For I do assure you, Brutus (not that there is any need for me to tell you what you already know, but I cannot pass over such all-round excellence in silence)—I assure you that in uprightness, resolution, concern, and patriotic zeal the like of Messalla does not exist. In him the gift of eloquence, which he possesses in a quite astonishing degree, hardly seems worth commending. And yet his good sense is specially conspicuous in that very sphere, for he has trained himself in the strictest school of oratory with serious judgement and a great deal of technical skill. He is so industrious and indefatigably studious that his preeminent natural ability seems a secondary qualification.

But my affection carries me too far. It is not my purpose in this letter to praise Messalla, especially to you, my

et virtus illius non minus quam mihi nota est et haec ipsa studia quae laudo notiora. quem cum a me dimittens graviter ferrem, hoc levabar uno, quod ad te tamquam ad alterum me proficiscens et officio fungebatur et laudem maximam sequebatur. sed haec hactenus.

3 Venio nunc longo sane intervallo ad quandam epistulam qua mihi multa tribuens unum reprehendebas quod in honoribus decernendis essem nimius et tamquam prodigus. tu hoc, alius fortasse quod in animadversione poenaque durior, nisi forte[3] utrumque tu. quod si ita est, utriusque rei meum iudicium studeo tibi esse notissimum, neque solum ut Solonis dictum usurpem, qui et sapiens unus fuit ex septem et legum scriptor solus ex septem: is rem publicam contineri duabus rebus dixit, praemio et poena. est scilicet utriusque rei modus, sicut reliquarum,
4 et quaedam in utroque genere mediocritas. sed non tanta de re propositum est hoc loco disputare; quid ego autem secutus hoc bello sim in sententiis dicendis aperire non alienum puto.

Post interitum Caesaris et vestras memorabilis Idus Martias, Brute, quid ego praetermissum a vobis quantamque impendere rei publicae tempestatem dixerim non es oblitus. magna pestis erat depulsa per vos, magna populi Romani macula deleta, vobis vero parta divina gloria, sed instrumentum regni delatum ad Lepidum et Antonium, quorum alter inconstantior, alter impurior, uterque pacem metuens, inimicus otio. his ardentibus perturbandae rei

[3] fortasse (*Crat.*)

friend, who know his worth as well as I and who know those very pursuits which I am eulogizing better than I do. My one consolation in the distress I feel at parting with him is that in going to join you, my alter ego, he is doing his duty and seeking no mean laurels. But enough of this.

Now I come rather belatedly to a letter of yours in which, while paying me a number of compliments, you find one fault, namely that I am excessive and, so to speak, prodigal in voting honours. This you criticize; someone else perhaps might tax me with undue harshness in the infliction of punishments—or perhaps you would charge me with both. If so, I am anxious that you should be thoroughly acquainted with my judgement on either point. I will not just quote the saying of Solon, one of the Seven Wise Men and the only one of them to write a code of law. He said that a state depends on two things, reward and punishment. There is, of course, a due limit in both, as in all other things, a sort of balance in each of the two categories. But it is not my purpose to discuss so wide a theme here. I do, however, think it appropriate to reveal the principle which I have followed in the proposals I have made to the Senate during this war.

You will not have forgotten, Brutus, that after Caesar's death and your memorable Ides of March I said that you and your associates had left one thing undone and that a mighty storm was brewing over the commonwealth. You had driven away a great plague, wiped a great blot from the honour of the Roman people, and won immortal glory for yourselves; but the apparatus of monarchy descended to Lepidus and Antony, one more of a weathercock, the other more of a blackguard, both afraid of peace and hostile to domestic tranquillity. We had no force to pit against their

publicae cupiditate quod opponi posset praesidium non
habebamus. erexerat enim se civitas in retinenda libertate
5 consentiens; <sed>[4] nos tum nimis acres <visi>,[5] vos fortasse sapientius excessistis urbe ea quam liberaratis, Italiae
sua vobis studia profitenti remisistis. itaque cum teneri
urbem a parricidis viderem nec te in ea nec Cassium tuto
esse posse eamque armis oppressam ab Antonio, mihi
quoque ipsi esse excedendum putavi. taetrum enim spec-
taculum oppressa ab impiis civitas opitulandi potestate
praecisa. sed animus idem qui semper infixus in patriae ca-
ritate discessum ab eius periculis ferre non potuit. itaque
in medio Achaico cursu cum etesiarum diebus Auster me
in Italiam quasi dissuasor mei consili rettulisset, te vidi
Veliae, doluique vehementer. cedebas enim, Brute, ce-
6 debas, quoniam Stoici nostri negant fugere sapientis.
Romam ut veni, statim me obtuli Antoni sceleri atque
dementiae. quem cum in me incitavissem, consilia inire
coepi Brutina plane (vestri enim haec sunt propria sanguinis) rei publicae liberandae.

Longa sunt quae restant, <mihi>[6] praetereunda; sunt
enim de me. tantum dico, Caesarem hunc adulescentem,
per quem adhuc sumus, si verum fateri volumus, fluxisse
7 ex fonte consiliorum meorum. huic habiti a me honores
nulli quidem, Brute, nisi debiti, nulli nisi necessarii. ut
enim primum libertatem revocare coepimus, cum se nondum ne Decimi quidem Bruti divina virtus ita commovis-
set ut iam id scire possemus atque omne praesidium esset

[4] (*SB*) [5] (*SB*) [6] (*SB*)

---

[1] With reference to L. Brutus, the first Consul, and Servilius Ahala (cf. *Letters to Atticus* 343 (XIII.40).1.

passionate desire for a political upheaval. The community had risen unanimously in defence of freedom, but we appeared too bold, and you and your friends may perhaps have shown greater wisdom in leaving the city you had liberated and in asking nothing of Italy when she proffered you her enthusiastic support. And so, seeing that Rome was in the hands of traitors, that neither you nor Cassius could live there in safety, and that the city was crushed by Antony's armed force, I thought that I too had better go elsewhere. A community crushed by ruffians, with all hope of rendering help cut off, is a hideous spectacle. But my spirit, anchored as ever upon the love of country, could not endure separation from her perils. Halfway to Greece, when the Etesians should have been blowing, the South Wind carried me back to Italy, as though dissuading me from my plan. I saw you at Velia, and was deeply distressed. For you were retiring, Brutus—retiring, since our friends the Stoics say that the Wise Man never flees. On returning to Rome I immediately set myself in opposition to Antony's wickedness and folly. Having stirred him up against me, I embarked upon a policy to free the commonwealth—a truly Brutine[1] policy, since such aspirations run in your family.

The sequel is long and not to be recounted here, since it is about myself. All I will say is that this young man Caesar, thanks to whom (if we choose to admit the truth) we are still alive, drew his inspiration from my counsels. I have given him no honours, Brutus, but what were due, none but what were necessary. When we first began to call freedom back, before even D. Brutus' superlative valour had visibly come into action, our only protection was this lad,

in puero qui a cervicibus nostris avertisset Antonium, quis honos ei non fuit decernendus? quamquam ego illi tum verborum laudem tribui eamque modicam, decrevi etiam imperium. quod quamquam videbatur illi aetati honorificum, tamen erat exercitum habenti necessarium. quid enim est sine imperio exercitus? statuam Philippus decrevit, celeritatem petitionis primo Servius, post maiorem etiam Servilius. nihil tum nimium videbatur.

8 Sed nescio quo modo facilius in timore benigni quam in victoria grati reperiuntur. ego enim D. Bruto liberato, cum laetissimus ille civitati dies illuxisset idemque casu Bruti natalis esset, decrevi ut in fastis ad eum diem Bruti nomen adscriberetur, in eoque sum maiorum exemplum secutus, qui hunc honorem mulieri Larentiae tribuerunt, cuius[7] vos pontifices ad aram in Velabro sacrificium facere soletis. quod ego cum dabam Bruto, notam esse in fastis gratissimae victoriae sempiternam volebam. atque illo die cognovi <haud>[8] paulo pluris in senatu malevolos esse quam gratos. eos per ipsos dies effudi, si ita vis, honores in mortuos, Hirtium et Pansam, Aquilam etiam. quod quis reprehendet, nisi qui deposito metu praeteriti periculi fuerit
9 oblitus? accedebat ad benefici memoriam gratam ratio illa quae etiam posteris esset salutaris: exstare enim volebam in crudelissimos hostis monumenta odi publici sempiterna. suspicor illud tibi minus probari, quod a tuis familiaribus, optimis illis quidem viris sed in re publica rudibus, non probabatur, quod ut ovanti introire Caesari liceret de-

[7] vos cuius (*Pius**: cui vos *Man.*) [8] (*Man.**)

[2] Acca Larentia, a figure of Roman legend. Various stories are told about her.

who had thrust Antony off our necks. What honour ought we *not* to have voted him? However, I at that time paid him a verbal tribute, and that in moderation, and voted him military authority. That no doubt seemed an honour at his age, but it was necessary since he had an army; for what is an army without military authority? Philippus voted him a statue, Servius the right to stand for office in advance of the legal age, a privilege which was later extended by Servilius. Nothing seemed too much at the time.

But somehow or other it is easier to find good will in the hour of danger than gratitude in victory. There came that most joyful day of D. Brutus' liberation, which happened also to be his birthday. I proposed that Brutus' name be entered in the Calendar beside that day, following the precedent of our ancestors who paid that compliment to a woman, Larentia,[2] at whose altar in Velabrum you Pontiffs offer sacrifice. In trying to confer that on Brutus I wished the Calendar to contain a permanent record of a most welcome victory. That day I realized that gratitude has considerably fewer votes in the Senate than spite. During these same days I showered honours (if you like to put it that way) on the dead, Hirtius and Pansa, even Aquila. Who shall blame me, unless he forgets the bygone danger once the fear is laid aside? Besides the grateful memory of benefit I had another reason, one of advantage to posterity: I wanted memorials of the public hatred for those bloodthirsty rebels to stand for all time. I suspect that another proposal of mine is less to your liking—your friends, excellent persons but lacking political experience, did not like it either—namely that Caesar be granted leave to enter

creverim. ego autem (sed erro fortasse, nec tamen is sum ut mea me maxime delectent) nihil mihi videor hoc bello sensisse prudentius. cur autem ita sit aperiendum non est, ne magis videar providus fuisse quam gratus. hoc ipsum nimium. qua re alia videamus.

D. Bruto decrevi honores, decrevi L. Planco. praeclara illa quidem ingenia quae gloria invitantur; sed senatus etiam sapiens qui, qua quemque re putat, modo honesta, ad rem publicam iuvandam posse adduci, hac utitur. at in Lepido reprehendimur, cui cum statuam in rostris statuissemus, idem illam evertimus. nos illum honore studuimus a furore revocare: vicit amentia levissimi hominis nostram prudentiam. nec tamen tantum in statuenda Lepidi statua factum est mali quantum in evertenda boni.

10 Satis multa de honoribus. nunc de poena pauca dicenda sunt. intellexi enim ex tuis saepe litteris te in iis quos bello devicisti clementiam tuam velle laudari. existimo equidem nihil a te nisi sapienter. sed sceleris poenam praetermittere (id enim est quod vocatur ignoscere), etiam si in ceteris rebus tolerabile est, in hoc bello perniciosum puto. nullum enim bellum civile fuit in nostra re publica omnium quae memoria mea fuerunt, in quo bello non, utracumque pars vicisset, tamen aliqua forma esset futura rei publicae: hoc bello victores quam rem publicam simus habituri non facile adfirmarim, victis certe nulla umquam erit. dixi igitur sententias in Antonium, dixi in Lepidum severas, neque tam ulciscendi causa quam ut et in praesens

Rome in ovation. For my part (but perhaps I am mistaken, though it is not my way to be particularly pleased with my own performances), I do not think I have made a wiser proposal in the course of this war. Why that is so I had better not reveal, or I might seem more farsighted than grateful. I have said too much as it is; so let us pass on.

I voted honours to D. Brutus and to L. Plancus. It is a noble mind that is attracted by glory; but the Senate too has shown good sense in using every means, provided it be honourable, to draw this man and that to the aid of the commonwealth. But there is Lepidus. Oh yes, we are blamed there—we set up a statue for him in the Rostra and then pulled it down. We tried to bring him back from treason by honouring him, but our wisdom was defeated by the folly of a thoroughly irresponsible individual. Not but what the setting up of Lepidus' statue did less harm than the pulling down did good.

That's enough about honours. Let me now say a little about punishment. Your letters have often let me understand that you would like to earn praise by your clemency towards those you have defeated in war. For my part, I look upon anything that comes from you as wise. But to waive the punishment of crime (for that is what is called 'pardoning'), even if it is tolerable in other contexts, I consider to be pernicious in this war. Of all the civil wars in our commonwealth that I remember there has not been one in which the prospect of some form of constitution did not exist whichever side won. In this war I should not like to be positive about what constitution we shall have if we win, but there will certainly be none ever again if we lose. Accordingly I proposed stern measures against Antony and against Lepidus too, not so much for vengeance's sake as to

sceleratos civis timore ab impugnanda patria deterrerem et in posterum documentum statuerem ne quis talem
11 amentiam vellet imitari. quamquam haec quidem sententia non magis mea fuit quam omnium. in qua videtur illud esse crudele, quod ad liberos, qui nihil meruerunt, poena pervenit. sed id et antiquum est et omnium civitatum, si quidem etiam Themistocli liberi eguerunt. et si iudicio damnatos eadem poena sequitur civis, qui potuimus leniores esse in hostis? quid autem queri quisquam potest de me qui si vicisset acerbiorem se in me futurum fuisse confiteatur necesse est?

Habes rationem mearum sententiarum de hoc genere dumtaxat honoris et poenae. nam de ceteris rebus quid senserim quidque censuerim audisse te arbitror.

12 Sed haec quidem non ita necessaria, illud valde necessarium, Brute, te in Italiam cum exercitu venire quam primum. summa est exspectatio tui; quod si Italiam attigeris, ad te concursus fiet omnium. sive enim vicerimus, qui quidem pulcherrime viceramus nisi Lepidus perdere omnia et perire ipse cum suis concupivisset, tua nobis auctoritate opus est ad collocandum aliquem civitatis statum; sive etiam nunc certamen reliquum est, maxima spes est cum in auctoritate tua tum in exercitus tui viribus. sed propera, per deos! scis quantum sit in temporibus, quantum in celeritate.

13 Sororis tuae filiis quam diligenter consulam spero te ex matris et ex sororis litteris cogniturum. qua in causa maiorem habeo rationem tuae voluntatis, quae mihi carissima

deter the criminals among us by terror from attacking our country in the present and to leave an object lesson for the future, so that none shall be minded to imitate such madness. To be sure this proposal was no more mine than everybody's. One feature seems cruel, the extension of the penalty to innocent children. But that is an ancient rule, found in all communities. Even Themistocles' children lived in poverty. If the same penalty applies to citizens judicially condemned, how could we take a more lenient line with public enemies? And what complaint can anyone have of me who must needs admit that he would have treated me more harshly had he won?

There you have the rationale of my proposals so far as this category of honours and punishments is concerned. Of my speeches and votes on other matters I think you have heard.

But all this is not particularly crucial; what *is* extremely crucial, Brutus, is that you come back to Italy with your army as soon as possible. You are most eagerly awaited. As soon as you touch Italian soil there will be a universal rally to your side. If we win the day, as won it we had most gloriously if Lepidus had not had a craving to destroy everything, including himself and his family, we need your prestige to establish some sort of civic settlement. Whereas if a contest is still to come, our best hope lies in your prestige and the strength of your army. But for heaven's sake hurry! You know how much depends on timing and on speed.

I expect you will hear from your mother and sister about the pains I am taking on behalf of your sister's children. In this I am making more account of your wishes, which mean a great deal to me, than of my own consis-

est, quam, ut quibusdam videor, constantiae meae. sed ego nulla in re malo quam in te amando constans et esse et videri.

24 (I.18)

Scr. Romae VI *Kal. Sext. an. 43*

CICERO BRUTO SALUTEM

1 Cum saepe te litteris hortatus essem ut quam primum rei publicae subvenires in Italiamque exercitum adduceres, neque id arbitrarer dubitare tuos necessarios, rogatus sum a prudentissima et diligentissima femina, matre tua, cuius omnes curae ad te referuntur et in te consumuntur, ut venirem ad se a. d. VIII Kal. Sext.; quod ego, ut debui, sine mora feci. cum autem venissem, Casca aderat et Labeo et Scaptius. at illa rettulit quaesivitque quidnam mihi videretur, accerseremusne te atque id tibi conducere puta-
2 remus an tardare et commorari te melius esset. respondi id quod sentiebam, et dignitati et existimationi tuae maxime conducere te primo quoque tempore ferre praesidium labenti et inclinatae paene rei publicae.

Quid enim abesse censes mali in eo bello in quo victores exercitus fugientem hostem persequi noluerint et in quo incolumis imperator honoribus amplissimis fortunisque maximis, coniuge, liberis, vobis adfinibus ornatus bellum rei publicae indixerit? quid dicam 'in tanto senatus populique consensu,' cum tantum resideat intra muros
3 mali? maximo autem, cum haec scribebam, adficiebar do-

tency, as some people see it. But I want to be and seem consistent in my affection for you more than in anything else.

24 (I.18)

Rome, 27 July 43

From Cicero to Brutus greetings.

I have often urged you by letter to come to the aid of the commonwealth and bring your army over to Italy as soon as possible, and I was under the impression that those close to you were in no doubt on this point. On 25 July that very wise and watchful lady your mother, whose every care begins and ends with you, requested me to visit her. Naturally I did so without delay. On my arrival I found Casca, Labeo, and Scaptius already there. Your mother put the question: What did I think? Should we send for you and did we consider this to be in your best interests, or was it better that you should take your time and hold back? I said in answer what I thought, that it was in the highest degree advantageous to your prestige and reputation that you should lend support to our tottering and almost collapsing commonwealth at the earliest possible moment.

Every imaginable evil chance has dogged us in this war. Victorious armies have refused to pursue a fleeing enemy. An army commander in good standing, eminent in public distinction and private fortune, with a wife and children, related by marriage to you and your brother-in-law, has declared war on the commonwealth. I might add 'in the face of a unanimous Senate and People,' were it not that the mischief within the gates remains so strong. As I write I am

lore quod, cum me pro adulescentulo ac paene puero res publica accepisset vadem, vix videbar quod promiseram praestare posse. est autem gravior et difficilior animi et sententiae, maximis praesertim in rebus, pro altero quam pecuniae obligatio. haec enim solvi potest et est rei familiaris iactura tolerabilis: rei publicae quod spoponderis quem ad modum solvas, si is dependi facile patitur pro quo spoponderis? quamquam et hunc, ut spero, tenebo multis repugnantibus. videtur enim esse indoles, sed flexibilis aetas multique ad depravandum parati, qui splendore falsi honoris obiecto aciem boni ingeni praestringi posse confidunt. itaque ad reliquos hic quoque labor mihi accessit, ut omnis adhibeam machinas ad tenendum adulescentem,
4 ne famam subeam temeritatis. quamquam quae temeritas est? magis enim illum pro quo spopondi quam me ipsum obligavi; nec vero paenitere potest rem publicam me pro eo spopondisse qui fuit in rebus gerendis cum suo ingenio <praeclarus>[1] tum mea promissione constantior.

5 Maximus autem, nisi me forte fallit, in re publica nodus est inopia rei pecuniariae. obdurescunt enim magis cottidie boni viri ad vocem tributi. quod ex centesima collatum impudenti censu locupletum in duarum legionum praemiis omne consumitur. impendent autem infiniti sumptus cum in hos exercitus quibus nunc defendimur tum vero in tuum. nam Cassius noster videtur posse satis orna-

1 (*SB*)

1 Income tax imposed by the Senate.

in the greatest distress because it hardly looks as though I can make good my promises in respect of the young man, boy almost, for whom I went bail to the commonwealth. Responsibility for someone else's mind and sentiment, especially in matters of great importance, is more burdensome and difficult than the pecuniary kind. That can be discharged and the loss of money can be borne. But how is one to discharge a pledge to the commonwealth if the person for whom one has made it is quite happy to leave his backer to pay? However, I hope I shall still hold him, though many people are pulling the other way. The natural quality seems to be there, but it is an impressionable age and there are plenty of would-be agents of corruption. They are confident of dazzling his good disposition by dangling in front of him the glitter of a false distinction. So this care is added to my load. I must move every engine at my disposal to hold the young man, or else be judged guilty of indiscretion. And yet, where is the indiscretion? I bound the one on whose behalf I gave the pledge rather than myself. The commonwealth has no reason to find fault with that pledge. Its subject shone in public action from natural disposition and was the steadier because of my promise.

However, unless I am perhaps mistaken, our knottiest political problem is shortage of money. The honest men become more obdurate every day at the mention of a special levy. The proceeds of the 1%,[1] thanks to the scandalously low returns put in by the wealthy folk, are entirely absorbed in the bounties of the two legions. Yet limitless expenses hang over us both for the armies which are now defending us and for yours. As for our friend Cassius, it looks as though he will be able to arrive tolerably well

tus venire. sed et haec et multa alia coram cupio idque quam primum.

6 De sororis tuae filiis non exspectavi, Brute, dum scriberes. omnino ipsa tempora (bellum enim ducetur) integram tibi causam reservant; sed ego a principio, cum divinare de belli diuturnitate ‹non›[2] possem, ita causam egi puerorum in senatu ut te arbitror e matris litteris potuisse cognoscere. nec vero ulla res erit umquam in qua ego non vel vitae periculo ea dicam eaque faciam quae te velle quaeque ad te pertinere arbitrer.

vi Kal. Sext.

[25 (I.16)

BRUTUS CICERONI SALUTEM

1 Particulam litterarum tuarum, quas misisti Octavio, legi missam ab Attico mihi. studium tuum curaque de salute mea nulla me nova voluptate adfecit. non solum enim usitatum sed etiam cottidianum est aliquid audire de te quod pro nostra dignitate fideliter atque honorifice dixeris aut feceris. at dolore quantum maximum capere animo possum eadem illa pars epistulae scripta ad Octavium de nobis adfecit. sic enim illi gratias agis de re publica, tam suppliciter ac demisse—quid scribam? pudet condicionis ac Fortunae, sed tamen scribendum est—commendas nostram salutem illi (quae morte qua non perniciosior?) ut prorsus prae te feras non sublatam dominationem sed do-

[2] (*Man.*)

[1] Letters 25 and 26 cannot be by Brutus; see Introduction.

heeled. But these and many other matters I want to discuss with you in person, and that soon.

About your sister's children, my friend, I did not wait for you to write. To be sure the progress of time is leaving the case uncompromised for you to handle, for the war will be protracted. But from the outset, when I could not prophesy the length of the war, I pleaded the children's cause in the Senate, as I think you will have been able to learn from your mother's letters. There shall never be any matter on which I shall not speak and act in accordance with what I take to be your wish and concern, even at the hazard of my life.

27 July.

[25 (I.16)

From Brutus to Cicero greetings.[1]

I have read a small part of your letter to Octavius, sent to me by Atticus. Your devoted concern for my welfare gave me no novel pleasure, accustomed as I am (indeed it happens every day) to hear of some loyal and complimentary action or words of yours in support of our public standing. But that same extract from your letter to Octavius in which you write about us gave me all the distress of which my mind is capable. You thank him on public grounds in such a fashion, so imploringly and humbly—I hardly know what to write; I am ashamed of the situation, of what Fortune has done to us, but write I must. You commend our welfare to him. Better any death than such welfare! It is a downright declaration that there has been no

minum commutatum esse. verba tua recognosce et aude negare servientis adversus regem istas esse preces. unum ais esse quod ab eo postuletur et exspectetur, ut eos civis de quibus viri boni populusque Romanus bene existimet salvos velit. quid si nolit? non erimus? atqui non esse quam
2 esse per illum praestat. ego me dius fidius non existimo tam omnis deos aversos esse a salute populi Romani ut Octavius orandus sit pro salute cuiusquam civis, non dicam pro liberatoribus orbis terrarum. iuvat enim magnifice loqui et certe decet adversus ignorantis quid pro quoque timendum aut a quoque petendum sit.

Hoc tu, Cicero, posse fateris Octavium et illi amicus es? aut, si me carum habes, vis Romae videri, cum ut ibi esse possem commendandus puero illi fuerim? cui quid agis gratias, si ut nos salvos esse velit et patiatur rogandum putas? an hoc pro beneficio habendum est quod se quam Antonium esse maluerit a quo ista petenda essent? vindici quidem alienae dominationis, non vicario, ecquis supplicat
3 ut optime meritis de re publica liceat esse salvis? ista vero imbecillitas et desperatio, cuius culpa non magis in te residet quam in omnibus aliis, et Caesarem in cupiditatem regni impulit et Antonio post interitum illius persuasit ut interfecti locum occupare conaretur et nunc puerum istum extulit, ut tu iudicares precibus esse impetrandam

abolition of despotism, only a change of despot. Read over your words again and then dare to deny that these are the pleadings of a subject to his king. You say that the one thing asked and expected of him is his good wishes for the welfare of those citizens of whom the honest men and the Roman People think well. What if he should refuse? Shall we cease to exist? And indeed it would be better not to exist than to exist on his sufferance. I really do not believe that all the gods have so turned their faces away from the welfare of the Roman People that Octavius has to be begged on behalf of the welfare of any citizen, let alone on behalf of the liberators of the world—it pleases me to be grandiloquent, nor is that out of place in addressing people who do not know in each particular case what fears it is right to entertain and what favours it is right to ask.

Do you admit, Cicero, that Octavius has such power and are you his friend? If you care for me, do you want me to be seen in Rome when in order to make that possible I have to be recommended to the good graces of this boy? Why do you thank him if you think you have to ask him to wish or to suffer us to survive? Are we to consider him as having done us a kindness in preferring that he himself rather than Antony should be the person to whom such requests must be addressed? Is he our champion against the despotism of another or that other's substitute? If the former, does anybody petition him to let the benefactors of our country survive? It is this weakness and despair, for which the blame rests no more with you than with everybody else, that brought Caesar to dream of monarchy, that persuaded Antony after Caesar's death to try to step into the shoes of the man we killed, and that now has raised this boy so high that *you* think the survival of men like

salutem talibus viris misericordiaque unius vix etiam nunc viri tutos fore nos aut nulla alia re. quod si Romanos nos esse meminissemus, non audacius dominari cuperent postremi homines quam id nos prohiberemus, neque magis irritatus esset Antonius regno Caesaris quam ob eiusdem mortem deterritus.

4 Tu quidem, consularis et tantorum scelerum vindex, quibus oppressis vereor ne in breve tempus dilata sit abs te pernicies, qui potes intueri quae gesseris, simul et ista vel probare vel ita demisse ac facile pati ut probantis speciem habeas? quod autem tibi cum Antonio privatim odium? nempe quia postulabat haec, salutem ab se peti, precariam nos incolumitatem habere a quibus ipse libertatem accepisset, esse arbitrium suum de re publica, quaerenda esse arma putasti quibus dominari prohiberetur, scilicet ut illo prohibito rogaremus alterum qui se in eius locum reponi pateretur, non[1] ut esset sui iuris ac mancipi res publica; nisi forte non de servitute sed de condicione serviendi recusatum est a nobis. atqui non solum bono domino potuimus Antonio tolerare nostram fortunam sed etiam beneficiis atque honoribus ut participes frui quantis vellemus. quid enim negaret iis[2] quorum patientiam videret maximum dominationis suae praesidium esse? sed nihil tanti fuit quo

5 venderemus fidem nostram et libertatem. hic ipse puer,

[1] an (*SB*)

[2] negotiis *vel sim.* (*Crat.*)

ourselves has to be gained by pleading and that we shall be safe through the compassion of an individual (and he scarcely yet a grown man) or not at all. If we remembered that we are Romans, miscreants would not be bolder to become our masters than we to stop them, and Antony would not have been incited by Caesar's monarchy rather than deterred by his death.

As a Consular, one who has put down such atrocious crimes (though I fear that in suppressing them you have only delayed the disaster for a short time), how can you look at what you have achieved and at the same time give your approval to *this*, or if not approval, a tolerance so submissive and ready as to present the appearance of approval? What private quarrel did you have with Antony? It was surely because he demanded that men's safety should be begged from himself, that we to whom he owed his own liberties should hold civic status by his grace and favour, that he should dispose of the commonwealth as he chose—that was why you thought we should look for weapons with which to prevent his despotism, only, as it seems, in order that after stopping him we should ask someone else to let himself be put in Antony's place. Or was it that rights of ownership over the commonwealth should belong to the commonwealth itself? Perhaps, though, it was not servitude but a particular servile situation that we rejected. And yet we could have had a good master in Antony under whom to put up with our condition. Not only that, we could have enjoyed all the favours and honours we wanted as his partners. What would he have refused to men in whose tolerance he would have seen the best guarantee of his regime? But nothing was worth the surrender of our loyalties and liberties. This very boy, who is apparently

quem Caesaris nomen incitare videtur in Caesaris interfectores, quanti aestimet, si sit commercio locus, posse nobis auctoribus tantum quantum profecto poterit, quoniam vivere et pecunias habere et dici consulares volumus! ceterum nequiquam perierit ille (cuius interitu quid gavisi sumus si mortuo ‹eo›[3] nihilo minus servituri eramus?), ‹si›[4] nulla cura adhibetur.

Sed mihi prius omnia di deaeque eripuerint quam illud iudicium quo non modo heredi eius quem occidi non concesserim quod in illo non tuli sed ne patri quidem meo, si reviviscat, ut patiente me plus legibus ac senatu possit. an hoc tibi persuasum est, fore ceteros ab eo liberos quo invito nobis in ista civitate locus non sit? qui porro id quod petis fieri potest ut impetres? rogas enim velit nos salvos esse: videmur ergo tibi salutem accepturi cum vitam acceperimus? quam, si prius dimittimus dignitatem et liber-
6 tatem, qui possumus accipere? an tu Romae habitare, id putas incolumem esse? res, non locus, oportet praestet istuc mihi; neque incolumis Caesare vivo fui, nisi postea quam illud conscivi facinus, neque usquam exsul esse possum, dum servire et pati contumelias peius odero malis omnibus aliis. nonne hoc est in easdem tenebras recidisse, ‹si›[5] ab eo qui tyranni nomen adscivit sibi, cum in Graecis civitatibus liberi tyrannorum oppressis illis eodem supplicio adficiantur, petitur ut vindices atque oppressores dominationis salvi sint? hanc ego civitatem videre velim aut putem ullam quae ne traditam quidem atque inculcatam libertatem recipere possit, plusque timeat in puero nomen

[3] (*Cobet*)
[4] (*P. Meyer*)
[5] (*Baiter, quod noluerat Gron.*)

incited by Caesar's name against Caesar's killers—what would he not give, if there were room for bargaining, in return for our support for the power which I suppose will indeed be his, since we want to keep our lives and our money and be called Consulars? Caesar will have perished for nothing (why did we rejoice at his death if we were going to be slaves just the same after he was dead and gone?), if no care is taken.

But may the gods and goddesses take away everything I have sooner than my determination that nobody shall have more power than the Senate and the laws with my consent. What I did not tolerate in the case of the man I killed, I shall not concede to his heir, I should not concede it to my own father if he came back to life. Do you believe that a personage without whose permission we can have no place in your community is going to leave the rest their liberties? And how is it possible for your petition to be granted? You ask his good wishes for our welfare. Do you think we are getting welfare if we get our lives? How can we get welfare if we let status and liberty go? Or do you think that to live in Rome is to be a citizen? That is a matter of condition, not of place. I had no citizenship in Caesar's lifetime until after I resolved upon that deed, nor can I be in exile anywhere so long as I hate to be a slave and suffer indignities more than all other evils. In Greece when tyrants are suppressed their children suffer the same penalty. Here is one who has taken the tyrant's name, and he is being asked to agree to the survival of the avengers and suppressors of despotism. Is not that a relapse into the same old darkness? Should I wish to see a community, or think it worthy of the name, that cannot take freedom when handed on a platter and rammed down its throat, and has more fear of the name of

sublati regis quam confidat sibi, cum illum ipsum qui maximas opes habuerit paucorum virtute sublatum videat?

Me vero posthac ne commendaveris Caesari tuo, ne te quidem ipsum, si me audies. valde care aestimas tot annos quot ista aetas recipit si propter eam causam puero isti supplicaturus es.

7 Deinde, quod pulcherrime fecisti ac facis in Antonio, vide ne convertatur a laude maximi animi ad opinionem formidinis. nam si Octavius tibi placet a quo de nostra salute petendum sit, non dominum fugisse sed amiciorem dominum quaesisse videberis. quem quod laudas ob ea quae adhuc fecit plane probo. sunt enim laudanda, si modo contra alienam potentiam, non pro sua, suscepit eas actiones. cum vero iudicas tantum illi non modo licere sed etiam a te ipso tribuendum esse ut rogandus sit ne nolit esse nos salvos, nimium magnam mercedem statuis (id enim ipsum illi largiris quod per illum habere videbatur res publica), neque hoc tibi in mentem venit, si Octavius illis dignus sit honoribus quia cum Antonio bellum gerat, iis qui illud malum exciderint cuius istae reliquiae sunt nihil quo expleri possit eorum meritum triburum umquam populum Romanum, si omnia simul congesserit.

8 Ac vide quanto diligentius homines metuant quam meminerint: quia Antonius vivat atque in armis sit, de Caesare vero quod fieri potuit ac debuit transactum est neque

a liquidated monarch borne by a boy than confidence in itself, though it sees the possessor of unlimited power liquidated by the courage of a few individuals?

No, do not in future commend me to your Caesar, nor yourself either, if you will listen to me. You must set great store by the years that can remain to a man of your age if you are going to humble yourself before that boy on their account.

Have a care, furthermore, lest the admirable line you have taken and are taking against Antony, in which your courage is so highly praised, come to look like fear. For if you see in Octavius one whom you can suitably petition for our welfare, you will appear to have acted not in avoidance of a master but in search of a more friendly one. I fully approve of your praise of his conduct so far. It is praiseworthy, provided he entered on it in opposition to someone else's irregular power and not in furtherance of his own. But when you judge that he has the right to be begged not to refuse his good wishes for our welfare, and that even you should accord it to him, you are setting too high a price on his services. You are making him a present of what (thanks to him, as it seemed) belongs to the commonwealth. Nor has it occurred to you that if Octavius merits those honours because he is making war on Antony, those who have cut out the evil growth of which you are now left with the remnants can never be recompensed by the Roman People as richly as they deserve, even if every imaginable reward be heaped upon them at once.

How much more attention people pay to their fears than to their memories! Antony is alive and fighting, whereas what could and had to be done about Caesar is finished and no one can put back the pieces. And so it is

iam revocari in integrum potest, Octavius is est qui quid de nobis iudicaturus sit exspectet populus Romanus, nos ii sumus de quorum salute unus homo rogandus videatur.

Ego vero, ut istuc revertar, is sum qui non modo non supplicem sed etiam coerceam postulantis ut sibi supplicetur; aut longe a servientibus abero mihique esse iudicabo Romam ubicumque liberum esse licebit, ac vestri miserebor quibus nec aetas neque honores nec virtus aliena dul-
9 cedinem vivendi minuere potuerit. mihi quidem ita beatus esse videbor, si modo constanter ac perpetuo placebit hoc consilium, ut relatam putem gratiam pietati meae. quid enim est melius quam memoria recte factorum et libertate contentum neglegere humana? sed certe non succumbam succumbentibus nec vincar ab iis qui se vinci volunt, experiarque et temptabo omnia neque desistam abstrahere a servitio civitatem nostram. si secuta fuerit quae debet fortuna, gaudebimus omnes; si minus, ego tamen gaudebo. quibus enim potius haec vita factis aut cogitationibus traducatur quam iis quae pertinuerint ad liberandos civis meos?

10 Te, Cicero, rogo atque hortor ne defatigere neu diffidas, semper in praesentibus malis prohibendis futura quoque, nisi ante sit occursum, explores ne se insinuent. fortem et liberum animum, quo et consul et nunc consularis rem publicam vindicasti, sine constantia et aequabilitate nullum esse putaris. fateor enim duriorem esse condicionem spectatae virtutis quam incognitae. bene facta pro debitis exigimus; quae aliter eveniunt, ut decepti ab

Octavius whose decision about ourselves is awaited by the Roman People, and it is we whose welfare must apparently be asked of a single individual.

For my part, to return to the point I have already made, I am not one to make petitions. I would rather trim to size those who claim the right to receive them. Or else I shall stay far away from a society of serfs, and wherever I can live as a free man there for me shall be Rome. And I shall pity all of you for whom life has a sweetness from which neither years nor honours nor the courage of other men can take away. I shall think myself so happy, if only I always cling steadfastly to this intention, that I shall regard my patriotism as well rewarded. For what is better than to be indifferent to the vicissitudes of life, content with freedom and the memory of deeds well done? But assuredly I shall not submit to the submissive or be defeated by defeatists. I shall try every expedient and never abandon my efforts to draw our society away from thraldom. If deserved good fortune follow the enterprise, we shall all be glad. If not, *I* shall still be glad. My life cannot be better spent than in such actions and thoughts as conduce to the liberation of my fellow countrymen.

As for yourself, Cicero, I ask and urge you not to grow weary or discouraged, and in forestalling present evils always to be alert for those which, unless measures are taken beforehand, may insinuate themselves into the future. Do not imagine that the free and gallant spirit with which you have championed the commonwealth both as Consul and Consular has any value without steadiness and consistency. I must acknowledge that proven merit makes harder demands than merit still unrecognized. Previous good performances are required as due, and if it turns out

iis, infesto animo reprehendimus. itaque resistere Antonio Ciceronem, etsi maxima laude dignum est, tamen, quia ille consul hunc consularem merito praestare videtur, nemo
11 admiratur; idem Cicero, si flexerit adversus alios iudicium suum, quod tanta firmitate ac magnitudine <animi> derexit in exturbando Antonio, non modo reliqui temporis gloriam eripuerit sibi sed etiam praeterita evanescere coget; nihil enim per se amplum est nisi in quo iudici ratio exstat. * * *,[6] quia neminem magis decet rem publicam amare libertatisque defensorem esse vel ingenio vel rebus gestis vel studio atque efflagitatione omnium.

Qua re non Octavius est rogandus ut velit nos salvos esse. magis tute te exsuscita, ut eam civitatem in qua maxima gessisti liberam atque honestam fore putes, si modo sint populo duces ad resistendum improborum consiliis.]

[26 (I.17)

BRUTUS ATTICO SALUTEM

1 Scribis mihi mirari Ciceronem quod nihil significem umquam de suis actis; quoniam me flagitas, coactu tuo scribam quae sentio.

Omnia fecisse Ciceronem optimo animo scio. quid enim mihi exploratius esse potest quam illius animus in rem publicam? sed quaedam mihi videtur—quid dicam? imperite vir omnium prudentissimus an ambitiose fecisse, qui valentissimum Antonium suscipere pro re publica non dubitarit inimicum? nescio quid scribam tibi nisi unum:

[6] *lac. statuit SB*

otherwise we become indignant critics, as though those performances had deceived us. That Cicero should resist Antony is most creditable; but because the Consul that was is felt to guarantee the Consular that is, no one is surprised. But if the same Cicero changes in relation to others the policy he has applied so firmly and nobly in expelling Antony, he will not only rob himself of future laurels but will make his past lose its lustre. No act is great in itself, unless inspired by reasoned judgement * * *, because on nobody does the role of patriot and defender of freedom sit more fittingly in virtue of your spirit, your record, and the eager demand of all.

Therefore Octavius is not to be asked to wish us well. Instead, rouse yourself! Believe that the community in which you achieved so much will be free and respected if only the people have leaders to resist the designs of wicked men.]

[26 (I.17)

From Brutus to Atticus greetings.

You tell me that Cicero is surprised that I never comment on his proceedings. Since you press me, I will tell you what I think at your insistence.

I know that Cicero has always acted with the best intentions. I am as sure of his patriotism as of anything in the world. But in certain respects he has acted—shall I say 'naively,' of the most worldly-wise of men? Or shall I say 'with a desire to ingratiate' of one who for his country's sake did not hesitate to incur the enmity of Antony in the fulness of his power? I don't know how to put it to you, ex-

pueri et cupiditatem et licentiam potius esse irritatam quam repressam a Cicerone, tantumque eum tribuere huic indulgentiae ut se maledictis non abstineat iis quidem quae in ipsum dupliciter recidunt, quod et pluris occidit uno seque prius oportet fateatur sicarium quam obiciat Cascae quod obicit et imitetur[1] in Casca Bestiam. an quia non omnibus horis iactamus Idus Martias similiter atque ille Nonas Decembris suas in ore habet, eo meliore condicione Cicero pulcherrimum factum vituperabit quam Bestia et Clodius reprehendere illius consulatum soliti sunt?

2 Sustinuisse mihi[2] gloriatur bellum Antoni togatus Cicero noster. quid hoc mihi prodest, si merces Antoni oppressi poscitur in Antoni locum successio et si vindex illius mali auctor exstitit alterius fundamentum et radices habituri altiores, si patiamur, ut iam ‹dubium sit utrum›[3] ista quae facit dominationem an dominum [an] Antonium timentis sint? ego autem gratiam non habeo si quis, dum ne irato serviat, rem ipsam non deprecatur. immo triumphus et stipendium et omnibus decretis hortatio ne eius[4] pudeat concupiscere fortunam cuius nomen susceperit, consularis aut Ciceronis est?

3 Quoniam mihi tacere non licuit, leges quae tibi necesse

1 imitatur (*Middleton, fort. errore, SB*)
2 ‹se› mihi *Lamb.* 3 (*coni. Watt*)
4 hortationis (*Madvig*)

---

1 Octavian's. 2 L. Calpurnius Bestia, Tribune in 62, viciously attacked Cicero for having executed the five Catilinarian conspirators in December 63. Cicero is here said to have attacked Casca for his part in Caesar's assassination—a preposterous notion to anyone acquainted with Cicero's real sentiments.

cept simply to say that the boy's[1] ambition and lawlessness have been stimulated rather than checked by Cicero; and that he goes so far in this indulgence as not to refrain from offensive expressions which recoil upon himself in two ways. For he took more than one life, and he must confess himself an assassin before he says what he says against Casca (in Casca's case imitating Bestia in his own).[2] Because we are not bragging every hour about the Ides of March like Cicero with his everlasting Nones of December,[3] is he in any better position to revile a splendid action than Bestia and Clodius when they used to attack his Consulship?

Our friend Cicero in his gown boasts to me that he has taken the brunt of Antony's war. What good is that to me if the price claimed for crushing Antony is to be succession to Antony's place, and if our champion against that evil has emerged in support of another evil, which is likely to be more firmly based and deeply rooted—if we allow it? His present activities make one begin to wonder whether it is despotism he is afraid of or a particular despot, Antony. For my part I don't feel grateful to anybody who does not object to slavery as long as his master is not angry with him. Triumph, pay for his troops, encouragement in every decree not to let modesty deter him from coveting the position of the man whose name he has assumed—is that worthy of a Consular, of Cicero?

Since I have not been permitted to hold my tongue, you

[3] The Catilinarian conspirators were executed on 5 December 63.

est molesta esse. etenim ipse sentio quanto cum dolore haec ad te scripserim nec ignoro quid sentias in re publica et quam desper‹es neque liber›atam[5] quoque sanari putes posse. nec mehercule te, Attice, reprehendo; aetas enim, mores, liberi segnem efficiunt, quod quidem etiam ex Flavio nostro perspexi.

4 Sed redeo ad Ciceronem. quid inter Salvid‹i›enum et eum interest? quid autem amplius ille decerneret? 'timet' inquies 'etiam nunc reliquias belli civilis.' quisquam ergo ita timet profligatum ut neque potentiam eius qui exercitum victorem habeat neque temeritatem pueri putet extimescendam esse? an hoc ipsum ea re facit quod illi propter amplitudinem omnia iam ultroque deferenda putat? o magnam stultitiam timoris, id ipsum quod verearis ita cavere ut, cum vitare fortasse potueris, ultro accersas et attrahas! nimium timemus mortem et exsilium et paupertatem. haec mihi videntur Ciceroni ultima esse in malis; et, dum habeat a quibus impetret quae velit et a quibus colatur ac laudetur, servitutem, honorificam modo, non aspernatur, si quicquam in extrema ac miserrima contumelia potest honorificum esse.

5 Licet ergo patrem appellet Octavius Ciceronem, referat omnia, laudet, gratias agat, tamen illud apparebit, verba rebus esse contraria. quid enim tam alienum ab humanis sensibus est quam eum patris habere loco qui ne

[5] (*SB*)

---

[4] Atticus' daughter was his only child; but the plural is often so used.

[5] According to Cornelius Nepos (*Life of Atticus*, 8.3f.) C. Flavius asked Atticus to take the lead in raising a fund for Caesar's

will have to read what cannot but be disagreeable to you. I myself know how much pain it has cost me to write these lines to you. I am not unaware of your political views and how little hope you have of healing the commonwealth even if its freedom is established. I am not criticizing you, Atticus, upon my word. Your age and habits and children[4] make you loth to move, as I saw from the episode of our friend Flavius[5] among other things.

But to get back to Cicero. What difference is there between him and Salvidienus? What more would Salvidienus propose? You may say that he is afraid even now of the remnants of the civil war. So afraid of a war that is as good as over that he sees no cause for alarm in the power of a leader of a victorious army and the rashness of a boy? Or does he do it just because he thinks that the boy's greatness makes it advisable to lay everything at his feet now without waiting to be asked? What a foolish thing is fear! When precaution consists in summoning and inviting the very thing you are afraid of, when you might have been able to avoid it! We dread death and banishment and poverty too much. For Cicero I think they are the ultimate evils. So long as he has people from whom he can get what he wants and who give him attention and flattery he does not object to servitude if only it be flattering—if there is any flattery in the sorriest depth of humiliation.

Octavius may call Cicero his father, ask his opinion on everything, flatter him, thank him, but it will be plain to see that the words contradict the realities. It is an outrage to human feeling to regard as a father one who does not

assassins by subscription from the Knights. Atticus refused, though he said that his own fortune was at Brutus' disposal.

liberi quidem hominis numero sit? atqui eo tendit, id agit, ad eum exitum properat vir optimus ut sit illi Octavius propitius. ego vero iam iis artibus nihil tribuo quibus Ciceronem scio instructissimum esse. quid enim illi prosunt quae pro libertate patriae, de dignitate, quae de morte, exsilio, paupertate scripsit copiosissime? quanto autem magis illa callere videtur Philippus, qui privigno minus tribuerit quam Cicero, qui alieno tribuat! desinat igitur gloriando etiam insectari dolores nostros. quid enim nostra victum
6 esse Antonium, si victus est ut alii vacaret quod ille obtinuit? tametsi tuae litterae dubia etiam nunc significant.

Vivat hercule Cicero, qui potest, supplex et obnoxius, si neque aetatis neque honorum neque rerum gestarum pudet. ego certe quin cum ipsa re bellum geram, hoc est cum regno et imperiis extraordinariis et dominatione et potentia quae supra leges se esse velit, nulla erit tam bona condicio serviendi qua deterrear, quamvis sit vir bonus, ut scribit,[6] Octavius,[7] quod ego numquam existimavi; sed dominum ne parentem quidem maiores nostri voluerunt esse.

Te nisi tantum amarem quantum Ciceroni persuasum est diligi ab Octavio, haec ad te non scripsissem. dolet mihi quod tu nunc stomacharis amantissimus cum tuorum om-

[6] scribis (*SB*)
[7] antonius (*Tunstall*: iste *coni. Watt*)

---

[6] Philosophy. The real Brutus could never have written this; see my Cambridge edition, p. 13.

[7] L. Marcius Philippus married Octavian's mother Atia (Caesar's niece) after the death of her first husband. The Pseudo-Brutus will have known of his earlier mistrust of his stepson (my

even count as a free man. And yet that is the goal and purpose, that is the result which our excellent friend impatiently pursues—for Octavius to be gracious to him! For myself, I no longer allow any value to those arts[6] in which I know Cicero is so well versed. What do they do for him, all his copious writings in defence of national freedom, on dignity, on death, banishment, and poverty? Philippus seems to have a much better grasp of these subjects. He has been less ready to make concessions to his stepson[7] than Cicero who makes them to a stranger. So let him stop his boasting which is an aggravation of our distresses. For what is it to us that Antony has been defeated, if he was defeated for somebody else to step into his shoes?—though your letter suggests some uncertainty even now.

By all means let Cicero live, since he can live so, as a helpless petitioner, if his age and honours and past achievements don't put him to shame! No slavery will be so comfortable that *I* shall be turned away from waging war against the thing itself, that is to say against monarchy, and extraordinary commands, and despotism, and power which sets itself above the laws however good a man, as he writes, Octavius[8] may be, though I have never thought so. But our forebears were not willing that even a parent should be a master.

If my affection for you were not as great as Cicero believes Octavius' regard for himself I should not have written to you in this strain. I am sorry that you are now vexed,

Cambridge edition, p. 14. n.2), but overlooked the information in Letter 23 (I.15).7.

[8] Despite the manuscripts, 'Brutus' must be referring to Octavian.

nium tum Ciceronis; sed persuade tibi de voluntate propria mea nihil esse remissum, de iudicio largiter. neque enim impetrari potest quin, quale quidque videatur ei, talem quisque de illo opinionem habeat.

7 Vellem mihi scripsisses quae condiciones essent Atticae nostrae. potuissem aliquid tibi de meo sensu perscribere. valetudinem Porciae meae tibi curae esse non miror. denique quod petis faciam libenter; nam etiam sorores me rogant. et hominem noro et quid sibi voluerit.]

fond as you are of all your friends and especially of Cicero. But you may be sure that there has been no falling off in my personal feelings, though my judgement has changed considerably. After all, we cannot be expected not to think of things the way we see them.

I wish you had told me what matches are in view for our dear Attica. I could have put down for you something of my own views. Your concern for my Porcia's health is only what I should have expected. Finally, I shall be glad to do as you ask. My sisters make the same request. I shall get to know the man and find out his intentions.]

FRAGMENTS

INTRODUCTORY NOTE

The traditional arrangement of fragments of Cicero's Letters is followed here as in my Teubner edition of 1987. This selection is confined (almost) to actual quotations, omitting some items as insignificant and/or unintelligible. Appreciation is due to Christine Weissenhoff's edition of 1970 (referred to as W. throughout the notes) with Latin commentary, a valuable contribution despite some inadequacies (see F. D. R. Goodyear's review in *Gnomon* 1974, 367–69 = his *Papers on Latin Literature* (1992), 190–92). The fragments of letters to Octavian in Nonius Marcellus are included in Beaujeu's posthumous vol. xi of the Budé edition (1996), 190–92.

Nonius Marcellus, an ancient grammarian of uncertain date, quotes from authors to illustrate observations on grammar and usage. His lemmata are usually omitted in my translation. 'L.' = Lindsay's edition.

The text is that of my Teubner edition with a few departures indicated by asterisks in the critical notes.

I. AD M.TITINIUM

L. Plotius Gallus. de hoc Cicero in epistula ad M. Titinium sic refert: equidem memoria teneo pueris nobis primum Latine docere coepisse Plotium quendam. ad quem cum fieret concursus et studiosissimus quisque apud eum exerceretur, dolebam mihi idem non licere; continebar autem doctissimorum hominum auctoritate, qui existimabant Graecis exercitationibus ali melius ingenia posse. (Suet. *Gram*. 26)

II. AD CORNELIUM NEPOTEM

1. *Iocos enim hoc genus veteres nostri 'dicta' dicebant. testis idem Cicero, qui in libro epistularum ad Cornelium Nepotem secundo sic ait*: itaque nostri, cum omnia quae dixissemus 'dicta' essent, quae facete et breviter et acute locuti essemus, ea proprio nomine appellari 'dicta' voluerunt. (Macrob. *Sat*. 2.1.14)

2–3. *Cicero ad Nepotem*: hoc restiterat etiam, ut a te fictis aggrederer donis; *'aggrederer' passive dixit, ἐνεδρευθῶ. in eodem*: qui habet ultro appetitur, qui est pauper aspernatur; *passive, ἐξουθενεῖται.* (Prisc. *GLK* II.383.1)

4. *Cicero . . . ad Cornelium Nepotem de eodem* [sc. *Caesare*] *ita scripsit*: quid? oratorem quem huic antepones eorum qui nihil aliud egerunt? quis sententiis aut acutior

---

[1] Possibly Pontius Titinianus of *Letters to Atticus* 189 (IX.19).2, son of Cicero's and Atticus' friend Q. Titinius, a wealthy Senator.

[2] *Adgredi* is never found passive in classical Latin. Perhaps *a*

I. TO M. TITINIUS

L. Plotius Gallus. Concerning him Cicero in a letter to M. Titinius[1] *has the following*: For my part I remember that when I was a boy a certain Plotius for the first time began teaching in Latin. People flocked to him and everyone anxious to learn trained with him. It distressed me that I was not free to do the same, but I was held back by the authority of very learned men who held that minds could better be nourished by Greek exercises.

II. TO CORNELIUS NEPOS

1. *The Romans of old called jokes of this sort* dicta. *The same Cicero is witness, who in his second Book of letters to Cornelius Nepos says as follows*: And so our countrymen chose that things we said wittily and tersely and pointedly be given specially the name of *dicta*, though all sayings were *dicta* (things said).

2–3. *Cicero to Nepos*: It only remained for me to be attacked by you with false gifts. *He used* adgrederer *as passive, 'be ambushed.' In the same*: He that has is courted, he that is poor is despised. Passive, 'is made naught of.'[2]

4. *Cicero . . . to Cornelius Nepos concerning the same [Caesar] wrote as follows*: Which orator among those who did nothing else will you put ahead of him? As to content, who is more acute or more pregnant? As to expression,

should be omitted, making *te* object of *adgrederer*. *Aspernatur* too is suspicious, the passive being unciceronian, though found in the stylistically underprivileged *Bellum Africanum*.

aut crebrior? quis verbis aut ornatior aut elegantior? (Suet. *Iul.* 55.1)

5. *Ut Tullius quoque docet, crudelitatis increpans Caesarem in quadam ad Nepotem epistula*: neque enim quicquam aliud est felicitas, *inquit*, nisi honestarum rerum prosperitas; vel, ut alio modo definiam, felicitas est Fortuna adiutrix consiliorum bonorum, quibus qui non utitur felix esse nullo pacto potest. ergo in perditis impiisque consiliis quibus Caesar usus est nulla potuit esse felicitas; feliciorque meo iudicio Camillus exsulans quam temporibus isdem Manlius, etiam si, id quod cupierat, regnare potuisset. (Amm. Marc. 21.16.13)

IIA. EP. CORNELII NEPOTIS AD CICERONEM

Nepos quoque Cornelius ad eundem Ciceronem ita scribit: tantum abest ut ego magistram putem esse vitae philosophiam beataeque vitae perfectricem ut nullis magis existimem opus esse magistros vivendi quam plerisque qui in ea disputanda versantur. video enim magnam partem eorum qui in schola de pudore ‹et› continentia praecipiant argutissime eosdem in omnium libidinum cupiditatibus vivere. (Lactant. *Div. inst.* 3.5.10)

III. AD CAESAREM

1. *'Consequi', adipisci. M. Tullius*[1] epistula ad Caesarem lib. I: tunc cum ea quae es ab senatu summo cum honore tuo consecutus (Non. 413 Lindsay). *'honor' est dignitas. M. Tullius in epistula ad Caesarem lib. I*: tu cum . . . consecutus. (idem 501 L.)

2. *'Dicare,' tradere. M. Tullius in epistula ad Caesarem*

[1] -ci tusculanorum vel-narum (*Mercerus*)

who better furnished or more elegant?

5. *As Tullius too tells us, rebuking Caesar for cruelty in a letter to Nepos*: For good luck, *he says*, is nothing but success in good enterprises; or, to define it in another way, good luck is Fortune helping good policies. He who doesn't pursue these cannot possibly be fortunate. With depraved and wicked policies, such as Caesar's were, there could be no good fortune. In my judgement, Camillus in exile was more fortunate than Manlius[3] at the same period, even if the latter had succeeded in making himself king, as was his ambition.

II A. CORNELIUS NEPOS TO CICERO

Nepos Cornelius too writes to the same Cicero as follows:[4] I am so far from looking on philosophy as life's teacher and the perfector of happy life that I believe none to be more in need of teachers of living than most of those who engage in philosophical disputation. For I perceive that a great many of those who talk most eloquently in the classroom about decency and self-restraint, the same live in pursuit of every sort of lust.

III. TO CAESAR[5]

1. *M. Tullius in a letter to Caesar, Book I*: At the time when those items which you obtained from the Senate in a manner most complimentary to yourself . . .

2. *M. Tullius in a letter to Caesar, Book I*: How high a re-

[3] Capitolinus.

[4] Probably in a letter referred to in *Letters to Atticus* 410 (XVI.5).5 of July 44.

[5] Some items in this and the following collection evidently confuse the two Caesars.

lib. I: Balbum quanti faciam quamque ei me totum dicaverim, ex ipso scies. (Non. 444 L.)

3. *'Improbum' est . . . minime probum. M. Tullius epistula ad Caesarem lib. I*: debes odisse improbitatem eius qui[2] impudentissime[3] nomen deleg<av>erit[4] (Non. 513 L.)

5. *'Ferox' . . . arrogans . . . M. Tullius epistula ad Caesarem lib. I*: itaque vereor ne ferociorem faciant tu<a> tam praeclara iudicia de eo.[5] (Non. 474 L.)

7. *'Monumenti' proprietatem a monendo M. Tullius exprimendam putavit ad Caesarem epistula II*: sed ego quae monumenti ratio sit nomine ipso admoneor; ad memoriam magis spectare debet posteritatis quam ad praesentis temporis gratiam. (Non. 47 L.)

8. *'Locandi' significatio manifesta est, ut aut operis locandi aut fundi. M. Tullius epistula ad Caesarem lib. II*: vel quod locatio ipsa pretiosa. (Non. 537 L.)

9. *'Dimittere' est derelinquere. M. Tullius ad Caesarem lib. III*: quae si videres, non te exercitu retinendo tuer<er>is[6] sed eo tradito aut dimisso. (Non. 441 L.)

10. *'Contemnere' et 'despicere' eo distant quod est despicere gravius quam contemnere. M. Tullius . . . ad Caesa-*

[2] quia (*Laetus*)
[3] imprudentissimum (*SB* (impud- *iam Aldus*))
[4] (W.) [5] telo (*Patricius*) [6] (*Madvig*)

---

[6] Clearly written to Octavian: cf. *Letters to Atticus* 364 (XIV.10).3. The elder Caesar would not have needed to be told about Cicero's relations with Balbus.

[7] *Nomen delegare* = make over to a third party a debt owed to oneself.

[8] W.'s suggestion that this relates to Caesar's flattering treat-

gard I have for Balbus, how entirely devoted I am to him, he himself will tell you.[6]

3. *M. Tullius in a letter to Caesar, Book I*: You ought to be disgusted at his effrontery in reassigning the debt[7]—most impudent!

5. So I am afraid that your dazzling appreciations of him may make him rather uppish.[8]

7. *M. Tullius thought that the meaning of* monumentum *is to be derived from* monendo *('reminding'); Letter to Caesar, Book II:* But what a *monument* is about, I am admonished by the word itself. It should pay regard to the memory of posterity rather than the approval of the present day.[9]

8. *M. Tullius in a letter to Caesar, Book II*: The letting itself is expensive.[10]

9. *M. Tullius to Caesar, Book III*: If you saw this, you would protect yourself not by keeping your army but by handing it over or letting it go.[11]

10. *M. Tullius to Caesar, Book III*: Some of your friends

ment of Q. Cicero in Gaul has much to commend it (cf. *Letters to Atticus* 93 (IV.19).2), but if so, Cicero is playful.

[9] Probably from a letter to Caesar in Gaul in 54 relating to the Forum Iulium in Rome which Cicero and Oppius were building as Caesar's agents; cf. *Letters to Atticus* 89 (IV.16).8, where the building is called a *monumentum*. So W. A 'monument,' says Cicero, is a reminder of the past. But *ad . . . gratiam* is his comment, not an explanation of the word. Taken impersonally as *oportet, debet* with active infinitive would be unclassical Latin.

[10] Perhaps from the same letter.

[11] Seemingly to Caesar in 50, though something to sugar the pill seems needed. Perhaps *quae* ('all this') had supplied it: e.g. Caesar should rely on his great achievements and the admiration of the people.

rem lib. III: amici non nulli <a> te contemni et despici et pro nihilo haberi senatum volunt. (Non. 702 L.)

12. *'Levare' . . . relevare . . . M. Tullius epistularum ad Caesarem*: iam amplitudinem gloriamque tuam magno mihi ornamento esse <e>t fore existimo. quid <quaeris>[7]? me levas cura. (Non. 530 L.)

IIIA. EPP. CAESARIS AD CICERONEM

3. *Itaque Caesar epistularum ad Ciceronem* neque, *inquit*, pro cauto ac diligente se castris continuit. (Iulius Romanus ap. Charis. *GLK* I.126.9)

IV. AD CAESAREM IUNIOREM

2. *'Accipere', tractare, increpare. M. Tullius . . . ad Caesarem iuniorem lib. I*: roga ipsum quem ad modum eum ego Arpini[8] acceperim. (Non. 358 L.) *'rogare,' quaerere, scitari. M. Tullius ad Caesarem iuniorem lib. I*: roga . . . ego eum . . . acceperim. (idem 611 L.)

4. *'Comparare,' adaequare. M. Tullius ad Caesarem iuniorem lib. I*: neminem tibi profecto hominem ex omnibus aut anteposuissem umquam aut etiam comparassem. (Non. 388 L.)

5. *'Conficere,' colligere . . . M. Tullius ad Caesarem iuniorem lib. I*: in singulas tegulas impositis sestertiis <III>[9] sescenties confici posse. (Non. 411 L.)

7 (*SB*) 8 arimini *vel* arini (*W.*) 9 (*W.*)

---

12 Surely to Octavian, on whose evil counselors cf. *Letters to Friends* 428 (X.4).6 and *to M. Brutus* 17.3, 4; 24.3.

13 Obviously to Octavian, the fledgling with a great future, Cicero's protégé. Addressed to the elder Caesar, the patronage would be insufferable.

want the Senate contemned and despised and set at naught by you.[12]

12. Already I think your greatness and glory is and will be a great feather in my cap. In short, you relieve me of anxiety.[13]

III A. CAESAR TO CICERO

3. *So Caesar in Book * of Letters to Cicero:* Nor did he, like a cautious and careful commander, keep to his camp.[14]

IV. TO CAESAR THE YOUNGER

2. *M. Tullius . . . to Caesar the younger, Book I*: Ask himself how I received him at Arpinum.[15]

4. *M. Tullius to Caesar the younger, Book I*: Naturally I should never have put any man in the world ahead of you or even made a comparison.[16]

5. *M. Tullius to Caesar the younger, Book I*: That sixty million sesterces can be made up if three sesterces be placed on each tile.[17]

14 The commander thus criticized is likely to be Titurius Sabinus, who lost his life and army in 54 (Caesar, *Gallic War* 5.28–37). W. favours Q. Cicero, but Cicero's feelings might have been hurt.

15 The same fragment is cited in Nonius 611 L. In the first citation the place name appears as *arini*, in the second as *arimini*, read by editors prior to W. If that is right, the letter will have been written by Octavian, but W.'s conjecture *Arpini* is most attractive, as a reference to Oppius' mission in late 44 (*Letters to Atticus* 426 (XVI.15).3).

16 Surely to the elder Caesar, not his fledgling great-nephew (so W.).

17 Each tile of every house in Rome. The letter belongs to February 43; cf. Dio 46.31.3.

6. *'Conficere,' consumere, finire . . . M. Tullius ad Caesarem iuniorem lib. I*: bellum, ut opinio mea fert, consensu civitatis confectum iam haberemus. (Non. 412 L.)

7. *'Ducere,' trahere, differre. M. Tullius ad Caesarem iuniorem lib. I*: ne res duceretur, fecimus ut Hercules Ant<on>ianus[10] in alium locum transferretur. (Non. 437 L.)

8. *'Expedire,' colligere. M. Tullius ad Caesarem iuniorem lib. I*: ex ceteris autem generibus tunc pecunia expedietur cum legionibus victricibus erunt quae spopondimus persolvenda. (Non. 460 L.)

9. *'Involvere,' implicare. M. Tullius ad Caesarem iuniorem lib. I*: sed quod viderem nomine pacis bellum involutum fore. (Non. 516 L.)

10. *'Opinio' est fama. M. Tullius ad Caesarem iuniorem lib. I*: erat opinio bona de Planco, bona de Lepido. (Non. 565 L.)

11. *'Praestare,' exhibere. M. Tullius ad Caesarem iuniorem lib. I*: tu si meam fidem praestiteris, quod confido te esse facturum. (Non. 590 L.)

12. *'Relatum' dicitur perlatum, dictum a M. Tullio ad Caesarem iuniorem lib. I*: sed haec videbimus cum legati responsa rettulerint. (Non. 607 L.)

14. *'Vindicare,' revocare. M. Tullius ad Caesarem iuniorem lib. I*: qui si nihil ad id beneficium adderes quo per te me una cum re publica in libertatem vindicassem. (Non. 676 L.)

[10] (*Hirschfeld*)

---

[18] Datable to about February 43; see *Phil.* 3.2 and other passages in W.'s note.

6. *M. Tullius to Caesar the younger, Book I*: In my opinion we should now have the war wrapped up, by consent of the community.[18]

7. *M. Tullius to Caesar the younger, Book I*: Not to let the matter drag on, we had Antonian Hercules[19] transferred elsewhere.

8. *M. Tullius to Caesar the younger, Book I*: The money will be raised from the other sources when our pledges to the victorious legions have to be discharged.[20]

9. *M. Tullius to Caesar the younger, Book I*: But because I saw that war would be cocooned in the name of peace.[21]

10. *M. Tullius to Caesar the younger, Book I*: Plancus was well thought of, so was Lepidus.[22]

11. *M. Tullius to Caesar the younger, Book I*: If you make good my pledge, as I am confident you will.[23]

12. *So M. Tullius to Caesar the younger, Book I*: But we shall see about all this when the envoys[24] bring back an answer.

14. *M. Tullius to Caesar the younger, Book I*: If you had added nothing to that benefaction whereby, thanks to you, I had claimed freedom for myself along with the commonwealth.[25]

[19] Perhaps a statue of Hercules with Antony's head substituted for the original (W.). He claimed descent from Anton, son of Hercules. [20] Perhaps from the same letter as frag. 5 (see W.).

[21] Reporting *Phil.* 7, delivered in the Senate in mid January 43 (*Phil.* 7.19; cf. 12.7). [22] Probably written after *Phil.* 13 (20 March 43) (W.). [23] Probably in early January 43 (W.).

[24] The three Consulars sent to Antony by the Senate. They left on 5 January 43 and returned (minus Ser. Sulpicius) on 1 or 2 February. [25] Date uncertain.

16. *'Sagum,' vestimentum militare . . . M. Tullius ad Caesarem iuniorem lib. I*: prid. Non. Febr., cum ad te litteras mane dedissem, descendi ad forum sagatus,[11] cum reliqui consulares togati vellent descendere. (Non. 863 L.)

17. *'Insulsum,' proprie fatuum, quasi sine sale. M. Tullius ad Caesarem iuniorem epistula II*: sed ita locutus insulse est ut mirum senatus convicium exceperit. (Non. 48 L.)

18. *'Segne' est ignavum, torpidum, feriatum, et sine igni . . . M. Tullius ad Caesarem iuniorem lib. II*: in quo tua me provocavit oratio, mea consecuta est segnis. (Non. 48 L.)

19. *'Constat,' convenit, manifestum est. M. Tullius ad Caesarem iuniorem lib. II*: cum const<ar>et[12] Caesarem Lupercis id vectigal dedisse; qui autem poterat id constare? (Non. 418 L.)

20. *'Deicere,' elidere. M. Tullius ad Caesarem iuniorem lib. II*: at statuam[13] nescio cuius Clodi, quam tu<m> restitui iussisset Antonius, cum hero<o>[14] deiectam esse ex senatus consulto. (Non. 445 L.)

11 togatus (*Abeken*) 12 (*Halm*)
13 ad est atba *vel sim.* (*Hirschfeld*) 14 (*Gurlitt*)

---

26 Immediately after the return of the envoys the Senate decreed that military cloaks (*saga*) be worn in public, thus signifying a state of war. Consulars were by custom exempt from the order (*Phil.* 8.32).

27 W. suggests that the letter was to the elder Caesar (in Gaul) describing Gabinius' reception in the Senate in October 54 (cf. *Letters to Quintus* 22.2).

16. *M. Tullius to Caesar the younger, Book I*: On 4 February, after dispatching a letter to you early in the morning, I went down to the Forum wearing a military cloak,[26] though the other consulars chose to go in gowns.

17. *M. Tullius to Caesar the younger, Book II*: But he spoke so tamely that he collected a marvellous booing from the Senate.[27]

18. *M. Tullius to Caesar the younger, Book II*: In which your speech challenged me, mine followed, a languid effort.[28]

19. *M. Tullius to Caesar the younger, Book II*: 'Since it was agreed that Caesar had given that revenue to the Luperci.' But how could that be agreed?[29]

20. *M. Tullius to Caesar the younger, Book II*: But that the statue of one Clodius, which Antony had ordered restored at that time, be thrown down along with the hero's shrine in accordance with the Senate's decree.[30]

[28] The context cannot be determined.

[29] Cf. *Phil.* 13 of 20 March 43, in which Cicero read out in the Senate a letter of Antony's addressed to Hirtius and Octavian and answered it sentence by sentence. W. plausibly ties the fragment to the reference to the Luperci in §31, as quoting the letter ('since . . . Luperci') and answering ('But . . . agreed?').

[30] W. reads *Cloeli*, i.e. P. Clodius' lieutenant Sex. Cloelius, whose name is often so corrupted. But Cicero would not have referred to so notorious a character as *nescio quis*. The statue is likely to be that of P. Clodius mentioned in *Letters to Atticus* 232 (XI.23).3. L. Müller's *Antonius* for *ancone* is probably right, as also Gurlitt's *cum heroo*, ironically (?) of a monument that went with the statue. *Nescio cuius* remains puzzling. I cannot take it with Beaujeu simply as irony. Perhaps *nescio quam*?

21. *'Insolens' impudens et audax dicitur consuetudine. M. Tullius ad Caesarem iuniorem lib. II*: insolens, adrogans, iactans. (Non. 505 L.)

22. *'Meret,' meretur . . . M. Tullius ad Caesarem iuniorem lib. II*: quem perisse ita de re publica merentem consulem doleo. (Non. 544 L.)

23. *'Secundum,' prosperum . . . M. Tullius ad Caesarem iuniorem lib. II*: scriptum erat equestre proelium valde secundum, †in his† autem potius adversum. (Non. 623 L.)

23A. [13]: *'Spurcum,' vehemens, asperum. M. Tullius ad Caesarem iuniorem lib. II*: cum iter facerem ad Aquinum[15] cum lacerna[16] tempestate spurcissima. (Non. 632 L.)

23B. [15]: *'Ignoscere' et 'concedere' quem ad modum inter se distent aperit M. Tullius ad Caesarem iuniorem lib. II*: quod[17] mihi et Philippo vacationem das, bis gaudeo; nam et praeteritis ignoscis et concedis futura. (Non. 702 L.)

25. *'Paludamentum' est vestis quae nunc chlamys dicitur . . . M. Tullius ad Caesarem iuniorem lib. II*: Antonius demens ante lucem paludatus. (Non. 864 L.)

26. *'Invehi,' aggredi, increpare. M. Tullius ad Caesarem iuniorem lib. III*: itaque in eam[18] Pansa vehementer est invectus. (Non. 518 L.)

15 ad (*vel* at) qui iam (W.) 16 claterna (*W*)
17 qui 18 eum *Sigonius*

---

31 Antony, as W. surmises, citing passages from the *Philippics* impugning his *insolentia* and *adrogantia*.

32 Hirtius or Pansa.

33 Dio 46.37.1–3 mentions cavalry engagements between

21. *M. Tullius to Caesar the younger, Book II*: Insolent, arrogant, boastful.[31]

22. *M. Tullius to Caesar the younger, Book II*: I grieve for his death, a Consul deserving so well of the commonwealth.[32]

23. *M. Tullius to Caesar the younger, Book II*: It was written that the cavalry battle was very successful * * * but adverse rather.[33]

23A. *M. Tullius to Caesar the younger, Book II*: When I was on the road to Aquinum wearing a soldier's cloak in the foulest weather.[34]

23B. *M. Tullius to Caesar the younger, Book I*: The leave you give to Philippus and myself rejoices me doubly; for you both pardon the past and concede the future.[35]

25. *M. Tullius to Caesar the younger, Book II*: Antony left before dawn beside himself, in general's cloak.[36]

26. *M. Tullius to Caesar the younger, Book III*: So Pansa inveighed against it vehemently.[37]

Antonians and republicans prior to the main fighting around Mutina.

[34] With W.'s conjecture this refers to Cicero's journey from Sinuessa to Aquinum on 9 November 44 (*Letters to Atticus* 423 (XVI.13).2). *The lacerna*, originally for soldiers, was a thick cloak with hood.

[35] The last extant words of Cicero, written after 19 August 43, the date of Octavian's election as Consul.

[36] Antony left Rome for Cisalpine Gaul on 28/29 November 44 (*Phil.* 3.24 *al.*).

[37] Written at the end of February or beginning of March 43 with reference to Cicero's proposal (*sententia*) that Cassius be declared governor of Syria and charged with the war against Dolabella (*Phil.* 11: cf. *Letters to M. Brutus* 4.2).

27. *'Anticus' et 'antiquior,' ut gradu, ita et intellectu distant. nam 'anticum' significat vetus . . . 'antiquior' melior . . . M. Tullius ad Caesarem iuniorem lib. III*: ego autem antiquissimum, oriundum Scythis, quibus antiquior iustitia[19] est quam lucrum. (Non. 688 L.)

28. *'Opinio,' spes, opinatio. M. Tullius ad Caesarem iuniorem*: posthac quod voles a me fieri scribito;[20] vincam opinionem tuam. (Non. 565 L.)

29. *'Promittere,' est polliceri . . . M. Tullius ad Caesarem iuniorem*: promissa tua memoria teneas. (Non. 575 L.)

V. AD C. PANSAM

1. *'Humaniter.' M. Tullius ad Pansam lib. I*: de Ampio[21] fecisti humaniter; quem quidem ego semper dilexi meque ab eo diligi sensi. (Non. 819 L. et Prisc. *GLK* III.70.13 (de . . . humaniter))

2. *'Inaudire', audire. M. Tullius ad Pansam lib. I*: quorum erupit illa vox de qua ego ex te primum quiddam inaudieram. (Non. 183 L.)

3. *'Concalfacere,' exercitare vel incendere vel hortari. Cicero . . . ad Pansam lib. III*: nos Ventidianis rumoribus <con>calfacimur.[22] (Non. 131 L.)

4. *barones dicendum, sicut Cicero ad Pansam.* (incerti de dub.nom., *GLK* V.572.17)

[19] laetitiae (*L. Mueller*)

[20] scripto (*Sigonius*)

[21] antio *codd. Nonii*: antiocho *codd. Prisciani* (*W.*)

[22] (*L. Mueller*)

27. *M. Tullius to Caesar the younger, Book III*: I, however, * a very ancient personage, born among the Scythians, a people that put justice ahead of gain.[38]

28. *M. Tullius to Caesar the younger*: In future just write what you want me to do. I shall better your expectation.

29. *M. Tullius to Caesar the younger*: Keep your promises in mind.

V. TO C. PANSA

1. *M. Tullius to Pansa, Book I*: About Ampius, that was kind of you. I always had a regard for him and felt that he had a regard for me.[39]

2. *M. Tullius to Pansa, Book I*: There burst out the words of which I had first heard something from yourself.

3. *Cicero . . . to Pansa, Book III*: We are much exercised[40] by the rumours about Ventidius.[41]

4. *One should say* barones,[42] *as Cicero to Pansa*.

[38] Date unknown. The personage will be the Scythian sage Anacharsis (cf. *Tusc*. 5.90). Nonius' citation does not include the verb governing *antiquissimum*.

[39] Written not long after *Letters to Friends* 226 (VI.12) of early October (?) 46.

[40] Lit. 'warmed up.' Probably written in July 44: cf. *Letters to Atticus* 409 (XVI.1).4.

[41] Probably written in July 44: cf. *Letters to Atticus* 409 (XVI.1).4.

[42] 'Blockheads,' a term used for Epicureans in *Letters to Atticus* 104 (V.11).6; cf. *Fin*. 2.76. Pansa was an Epicurean.

VI. AD A. HIRTIUM

1. *'Error' masculini est generis . . . neutri: M. Tullius ad Hirtium lib. II*: qua in re si mediocriter lapsus sum, defendes meum tolerabile erratum. (Non. 300 L.)

2. *'Impertire' est participare et partem dare . . . M. Tullius . . . ad Hirtium lib. V*: et quoniam, ut hoc tempus est, nihil habeo patriae quod impertiam. (Non. 54 L.)

3. *'Vetustiscere' et 'veterascere.' quid intersit, Nigidius . . . deplanavit: 'dicemus quae vetustate deteriora fiunt "vetustiscere"; "inveterascere," quae meliora.' M. <Tullius> ad Hirtium lib. VII*: cum enim nobilitas nihil aliud sit quam cognita virtus, quis in eo quem veterascentem[23] videat ad gloriam generis antiquitatem desideret? (Non. 704 L.)

VII. AD M. BRUTUM

1. *'Ex alto,' argumentatione longe repetita* (Serv. *Aen*. 8. 395).*—est autem de usu dictum. Cicero primo libro ad Brutum*: si Pompeius non ex alto peteret et multis verbis me iam hortaretur. (Scholia Danielis ibid.)

3. *'Vel' pro 'etiam' est. M. Tullius epistula ad Brutum lib. VIII*: et quod te tantum amat ut <vel> me audeat provocare. (Non. 847 L.)

6. *Poterat me liberare Cicero, qui ita scribit ad Brutum praepositis plurimis quae honeste suaderi Caesari possint*: simne bonus vir, si haec suadeam? minime; suasoris enim finis est utilitas eius cui quisque suadet. at recta sunt. quis

[23] invet- *Halm*

VI. TO A. HIRTIUS

1. *M. Tullius to Hirtius, Book II*: If I made something of a slip in that matter, you will defend my venial error.[43]

2. *M. Tullius to Hirtius, Book V*: And since, as things are now, I have nothing to share with my country . . .[44]

3. *M. Tullius to Hirtius, Book VII*: For since nobility is nothing but worth recognized, who would feel antiquity of race to be lacking in one whom he saw aging as to glory?[45]

VII. TO M. BRUTUS

1. *Cicero in the first Book to Brutus*: If Pompey were not asking, going a long way back and urging me with plenty of words . . .[46]

3. *M. Tullius in a letter to Brutus, Book VIII*: And because he[47] loves you so much that he dares challenge even me.

6. *Cicero could be my quittance, who writes as follows to Brutus, after suggesting many items that could decently serve as advice to Caesar*: Should I be an honest man if I so advised him? Far from it, for an adviser's aim should be the interest of the person he is advising. But the advice, you

[43] March 43? The error may well have been Cicero's initial support for the Senate's mission to Antony; cf. my introductory note to *Phil.* 12 (*Cicero's Philippics* (1986), p. 299).

[44] The sentence might continue: 'except my advice and vigilance' or the like. Perhaps written after Hirtius' departure in mid January 43.

[45] Hirtius was not *nobilis*.

[46] On behalf of Ap. Claudius; cf. *Letters to Atticus* 116 (VI.2).10 and *to Friends* 73 (III.10).10. Probably written in April 50 from Cilicia.

[47] M. Cicero junior, serving under Brutus in Greece (43).

negat? sed non est semper rectis in suadendo locus. (Quint. 3.8.41)

7. *'Argumentum' quoque plura significat . . . et ipse Cicero ad Brutum ita scribit*: veritus fortasse ne nos in *Catonem* nostrum transferremus illim aliquid, etsi argumentum simile non erat. (Quint. 5.10.9)

8. *Recteque Cicero his ipsis ad Brutum verbis quadam in epistula scribit*: nam eloquentiam quae admirationem non habet nullam iudico. (Quint. 8.3.6)

10. *Cicero ad Brutum* populo, *inquit*, imposuimus et oratores visi sumus, *cum de se tantum loqueretur.* (Quint. 8.6.20 et rursus ibid. 55 (oratores visi sumus et populo imposuimus)).

11. *Hanc frequentiorem repetitionem πλοκὴν vocant, quae fit ex permixtis figuris, ut supra dixi, utque se habet epistula ad Brutum*: ego cum in gratiam redierim cum Appio Claudio et redierim per Cn. Pompeium; *et* ego ergo cum[24] redierim. (Quint. 9.3.41)

12. . . . *cum subtractum verbum aliquod satis ex ceteris intellegitur, ut . . . Cicero ad Brutum*: sermo nullus scilicet nisi ‹de› te; quid enim potius? tum Flavius 'cras,' inquit, 'tabellarii'; et ego ibidem has inter cenam exaravi. (Quint. 9.3.58)

[24] quam

---

[48] I.e. for the general good, which is not necessarily in the interest of the person advised. The items in question will have had to do with restoring a constitutional system. On Cicero's letter of advice to Caesar, composed but never sent to its addressee, see *Letters to Atticus* 281 (XII.40).2 (9 May 45) etc.

say, is right. Who disputes it? But in giving advice there is not always a place for what is right.[48]

7. *Cicero himself writes to Brutus as follows*: Afraid perhaps that I might transfer something from there[49] to my *Cato*, though the theme was quite different.

8 For *Cicero rightly writes in a letter to Brutus in these very words*: Eloquence which does not startle I don't consider eloquence.[50]

10 *Cicero writes to Brutus*: I have duped the public and am regarded as an orator.

11 *Cicero writes to Brutus*: Since I have been reconciled to Appius Claudius and reconciled with Cn. Pompeius as intermediary—since therefore I have been reconciled . . .[51]

12. *Cicero to Brutus*: Our talk was naturally all about you. What better subject? Then Flavius said 'the couriers leave tomorrow,' and I scribbled this on the spot at dinner.[52]

[49] From *Orator*, not *Brutus* (as W. following O. E. Schmidt). The latter had appeared in the winter of 47–46 (*Parad. Stoic*. 5), the former was begun immediately after the completion of *Cato*, which was composed in June–July 46 (*Or*. 35; cf. *Letters to Friends* 185 (XVI.22).1). Evidently it had not yet been circulated, so that transfers from *Orator* (in process of composition) to *Cato* would be possible.

[50] From a correspondence concerning oratory in September 48–September 47; see W.

[51] See frag. 1 above.

[52] Probably of date February 43.

VIII. AD MARCUM FILIUM

5. *Cicero per epistulam culpat filium, dicens male eum dixisse 'direxi litteras duas,' cum 'litterae,' quotiens epistulam significant, numeri tantum pluralis sint.* (Serv. *Aen.* 8, 168)

9. *Quid? illam vocem nonne de visceribus cunctorum patrum Cicero emisit ad filium, ad quem scribens ait*: solus es omnium a quo me in omnibus vinci velim? (Augustin. c. *Iul. op. imperf.* 6.22 (P.L. 45, col. 1551))

X. AD Q. AXIUM

4. *'Humaniter.' M. Tullius . . . ad Axium lib. II*: invitus litteras tuas scinderem: ita sunt humaniter scriptae. (Non. 819 L.)

5. *De hac* [sc. *coniuratione*] *significare videtur et Cicero in quadam ad Axium*[25] epistula, referens Caesarem in consulatu confirmasse regnum de quo aedilis cogitarat. (Suet. *Iul.* 9.2)

6. *Quam flebiles voces exprimit* [sc. *Cicero*] *in quadam ad Axium epistula iam victo patre Pompeio, adhuc filio in Hispania fracta arma refovente*: quid agam, *inquit*, hic quaeris. moror in Tusculano meo semiliber. *alia deinceps adicit quibus et priorem aetatem complorat et de praesenti queritur et de futura desperat*. (Sen. *De brev. vit.* 5,2)

XI. AD CATONEM

'Plus' a 'multo' vetustas voluit discrepare . . . 'multum' a plurimo minus ac non supra modum . . . 'plus' . . . maioris modi est quam necessarium est . . . atque ideo M. Tullius [maius] discrevit epistula ad Catonem: nec idcirco mihi

[25] atticum *vel* actium (*Lipsius*)

VIII. TO HIS SON MARCUS

5. *Cicero answers his son in a letter, saying he should not have written* direxi litteras duas *('I sent two letters'), since* litterae *meaning 'a letter' can only be used in the plural.*[53]

9. *Did not Cicero send these words to his son from every father's heart when he wrote to him*: Of all persons in the world you are the only one whom I should wish to excel me in all things?

X. TO Q. AXIUS

4. *M. Tullius . . . To Axius, Book II*: I should have been sorry to tear up your letter; it was such a kind letter.

5. *Cicero too seems to allude to this [conspiracy] in a letter to Q. Axius, remarking that in his Consulship Caesar had established the despotism which he had in mind when he was Aedile.*[54]

6. *How lugubriously does he write in a letter to Q. Axius after Pompey the elder had already been defeated and his son was still refurbishing the shattered arms in Spain*: You ask what I am doing here. I am staying on in my place at Tusculum, semi-free. *He goes on to lament his past life, complain of his present one, and despair of the future.*

XI. TO CATO

And so M. Tullius distinguished [between multum *and* plus] *in a letter to Cato*: Nor did I think I should abnegate

[53] He should have written *binas*. *Dirigere litteras* too is not good classical Latin, as Cicero may have pointed out.

[54] In 65.

deserendam[26] esse dignitatem meam quod eam multi[27] impugnarint, sed eo magis recolendam quod plures desiderarint. (Non. 705 L.)

XII. AD CAERELLIAM

Etiam illud [sc. *potest inter ridicula numerari*] *quod Cicero Caerelliae scripsit reddens rationem cur illa Caesaris tempora tam patienter toleraret*: haec aut animo Catonis ferenda sunt aut Ciceronis stomacho. (Quint. 6.3.112)

XVII. EX EPISTULIS INCERTIS

5. *Cicero vero, non contentus in quibusdam epistulis scripsisse a satellitibus eum* [sc. *Caesarem*] *in cubiculum regium eductum in aureo lecto veste purpurea decubuisse floremque aetatis a Venere orti in Bithynia contaminatum, quondam etiam in senatu sqq*. (Suet. *Iul*. 49.3)

[26] desiderandam (*Madvig*)
[27] multum (*Patricius*)

my standing because many impugned it but cultivate it afresh because more wished it back.[55]

XII. TO CAERELLIA

Also what Cicero wrote to Caerellia explaining why he put up with the Caesarian period so patiently: All this must be borne with Cato's courage or else with Cicero's digestion.[56]

XVII. TO CORRESPONDENTS UNKNOWN

5. *Not content with writing in certain letters that he [Caesar] was brought into the royal bedroom*[57] *by attendants and lay down on a golden bed with purple covering and that the virginity of Venus' descendant was polluted in Bithynia, Cicero also once in the Senate* etc.

[55] Perhaps from a letter of the same period (end of 51 through summer of 50) as *Letters to Friends* 110 and 112 (XV.4 and 6) bearing on Cicero's hopes of a triumph.

[56] *Stomachus* in such a context normally means a weak stomach, i.e. irritability ('spleen'). Here it has to mean the lack of such an organ (Cicero had grown a thick skin); cf. *Letters to Atticus* 92 (IV.18).2, *to Friends* 177 (IX.2).3.

[57] Of Nicomedes III, king of Bithynia (died 75 or 74).

PSEUDO-CICERO
LETTER TO OCTAVIAN

INTRODUCTORY NOTE

The composition of letters ostensibly written by some well-known figure of legend or history was a standard exercise in the rhetorical schools of the Augustan period and onwards, essentially parallel to the *suasoriae* of which the elder Seneca has left us examples; e.g. Cicero deliberates whether to beg Antony's pardon, Agamemnon deliberates whether to sacrifice Iphigenia. Other specimens are the two spurious letters of Brutus to Cicero and Atticus (*Letters to Brutus* 25 and 26), the pseudo-Sallustian letters to Caesar, and, except in form, the spurious speeches of Cicero against Sallust and Sallust against Cicero (*Invectivae*). Whatever the intentions of the 'forgers,' contemporaries and posterity were sometimes deceived.

The pseudo-Ciceronian *Letter to Octavian* is in this sorry genre. The actual date of composition is uncertain, but the third or fourth century A.D. is probable.[1] The purported date falls within the last few weeks of Cicero's life, between the end of October 43 (allusion to the lex Pedia in §. 8) and the arrival of the Triumvirs in Rome on 27 November. The writer draws largely on Cicero's phraseology, mainly in the *Philippics*, but style and content rule out any question of Cicero's authorship.

[1] See Lamacchia (1), 18ff.

Most of the manuscripts of Cicero's letters with their separate traditions contain this item, so that the textual situation, expounded by Watt (1 and 2) and Lamacchia (1) is highly complex. There are two main groups, the 'Italian' (Ω, containing the letters to Atticus, Quintus, and Brutus) and χ (*Letters to Friends* IX–XVI; but the most important manuscript, the Mediceus, lacks the Letter), both subdivided. Readings in the margins of two sixteenth-century editions, Cratander's and Lambinus', belong to χ. Sjogren contended for the superiority of χ to Ω, though his practice hardly conformed to his theory. Watt (1 and 2) convincingly asserts the contrary.[2]

This edition and translation is new; the Letter was not included in my Teubner edition of the Correspondence.

Works Cited

Lamacchia (1): *Pseudo-Ciceronis epistula ad Octavianum*, ed. Rosa Lamacchia 1967 (Mondadori series). With bibliography of works cited and list of manuscripts and editions.

Lamacchia (2): *M. Tulli Ciceronis epistola ad Octavianum*

[2] A reservation is in order. The readings in Cratander's margin according to Watt derive from an extant fifteenth-century manuscript or a sibling thereof. It has however been shown that their source in the Atticus letters is the eleventh- to twelfth-century Würzburgensis (or a sibling) of which fragments survive (see my Cambridge edition, vol. I, 86–88). If their source is here the same, χ's authority is significantly enhanced where they support it; see Lamacchia (1), 18ff. As for the readings in Lambinus' margin, their provenance, also controverted, is of hardly any relevance in the present context.

with introduction, text, and commentary by Rosa Lamacchia, Florence 1968 (both items reviewed in *Gnomon* 1970, 197f.).
Watt, W. S. (1): *Classical Quarterly* NS 8 (1958).27ff.
Watt, W. S. (2): M. T. Ciceronis, *Epistulae* III (1958, Oxford Classical Text).
Watt, W. S. (3): *Hermes* 93 (1965).244–49.

EPISTULA AD OCTAVIANUM

CICERO OCTAVIANO SALUTEM

1 Si per tuas legiones mihi licitum fuisset, quae nomini meo populique Romani sunt inimicissimae, venire in senatum coramque de re publica disputare, fecissem, neque tam libenter quam necessario; nulla enim remedia quae vulneribus adhibentur tam faciunt dolorem, quam quae sunt salutaria. sed quoniam cohortibus circumsaeptus senatus nihil aliud libere[1] potest [decernere][2] nisi timere—in Capitolio signa sunt, in urbe milites vagantur, in Campo castra ponuntur, Italia tota legionibus ad libertatem nostram conscriptis ad servitutem adductis equitatuque exterarum nationum distinetur—cedam tibi in praesentia foro et[3] curia et sanctissimis deorum immortalium templis, in quibus reviviscente iam libertate rursus oppressa senatus nihil consulitur, timet multa, assentatur[4] omnia.

2 Post etiam paulo temporibus ita postulantibus cedam urbe, quam per me conservatam ut esset libera in servitute

[1] vere *Wes.* [2] (*SB*)
[3] et χ: *om.* Ω [4] adsentatur χ: -titur Ω

[1] I.e. debating with you would have been unpleasant, as effective treatments of a wound usually are, but I would have done it all the same.

LETTER TO OCTAVIAN

From Cicero to Octavian greetings.

Had not your legions, bitterly hostile as they are to me personally and to the Roman People, debarred me from coming to the Senate and debating on public affairs face to face, I should have done so, not so much of will as of necessity—no treatments applied to wounds are so painful as those that heal.[1] But the Senate surrounded by armed cohorts, can do nothing freely except tremble. There are standards on the Capitol, soldiers roaming the streets, a camp in Mars' Field, all Italy in her different parts[2] is held down by legions enrolled to free us but brought along to enslave us and by horsemen of foreign nations.[3] So for the present I shall leave you in possession of the Forum and the Senate House and the most hallowed temples of the immortal gods,[4] in which with renascent freedom crushed anew the Senate is consulted about nothing, fears many things, and assents to everything.

A little later on I shall leave Rome as well if conditions call for it; saved by me[5] to be free, I shall not have the heart

[2] *Distinetur* combines the ideas of parcelling out and holding down. [3] Antony had Gaulish and Moorish cavalry.

[4] The Senate House (curia Hostilia) adjoined the Forum, but the Senate often met in a temple. [5] From Catiline in 63.

videre non potero; cedam vita, quae quamquam sollicita est, tamen si profutura est rei publicae, spe[5] posteritatis me consolatur, qua sublata non dubitanter occidam; atque ita cedam ut Fortuna iudicio meo, non animus mihi defuisse videatur. illud vero quod et praesentis doloris habet indicium et praeteritae iniuriae testimonium et absentium sensus significationem non praetermittam quin, quoniam coram id facere prohibeor, absens pro me reque publica expostulem tecum. atque ita dico 'pro me' si quidem mea salus aut utilis rei publicae est aut coniuncta certe publicae saluti. nam per deum immortalium fidem, nisi forte frustra eos appello quorum aures atque animus a nobis abhorret, perque Fortunam populi Romani, quae, quamquam nobis infesta est, fuit aliquando propitia et, ut spero, futura est, quis tam expers humanitatis, quis huius urbis nomini ac sedibus usque eo est inimicus ut ista aut dissimulare possit aut non dolere aut, si nulla ratione publicis incommodis mederi queat, non morte proprium[6] malum[7] vitet?

3 Nam ut ordiar ab initio et perducam ad extremum et novissima conferam primis, quae non posterior dies acerbior priore et quae non insequens hora antecedente calamitosior populo Romano illuxit? M. Antonius, vir animi maximi—quod[8] utinam etiam sapientis consili fuisset!—C. Caesare fortissime sed parum feliciter a rei publi-

[5] spe χ: bona spe Ω [6] proprium Ω: -ria χ
[7] malum χ: periculum Ω [8] quod χ: *om.* Ω

[6] Authority favours *periculum* (Ω) over *malum* (χ), but sense makes the other way. The suicide would be avoiding foreseeable misery rather than danger (to life?), *proprium malum* as opposed

to see her in bondage. I shall leave life, a troubled life, but if it is to be of benefit to the commonwealth, it consoles me with hope for the future; that hope taken away, I shall die without a qualm. And my leaving shall be such that Fortune shall be seen as having failed my policy, not my courage as failing me. But in token of present indignation and in attestation of past injury, and as indication of how the absent feel, I shall not fail to remonstrate with you in absence, since I am forbidden to do so in person, on my own behalf and on that of the commonwealth. And I say 'on my own behalf' if indeed my welfare is useful to the commonwealth or at any rate linked to the public welfare. For by the faith of the immortal gods, unless perchance I call upon them in vain and their ears and mind are averse from us, and by the Fortune of the Roman People, which though hostile to us now was once propitious and, as I hope, will be again: who is so devoid of human feeling and so inimical to the name and dwellings of our city that he can either pretend unawareness of what goes on or be indifferent to it or, if he cannot by any means bring healing to the public ills, would not avoid personal suffering[b] by death?

Let me begin from the beginning and pursue to the end and compare latest with first: what day after has not dawned for the Roman People more bitter than the day before, what following hour has not been more disastrous than the hour preceding? When C. Caesar had been removed from his domination of the commonwealth (act of exalted courage on which Fortune did not smile), M.

to *publica incommoda* (with *propriā* the same applies). Admittedly, poor sense in this production is not a total bar.

cae dominatione semoto concupierat magis regium quam libera civitas pati poterat principatum: publicam dilapidabat pecuniam, aerarium exhauriebat, minuebat vectigalia, donabat civitates immunitate, nationes ‹civitate›,[9] ex commentario; dictaturam gerebat, leges imponebat, prohibebat dictatorem creari, legibus senatusconsultis ipse repugnabat in senatu, provincias unus omnes concupiebat, cui sordebat Macedonia provincia, quam victor sibi sumpserat Caesar. Quid de hoc sperare aut expectare nos oportebat?

4 Exstitisti tu vindex nostrae libertatis, ut tunc quidem optimus—quod utinam neque nostra nos opinio neque tua fides fefellisset!—et veteranis in unum conductis et duabus legionibus a pernicie patriae ad salutem avocatis subito prope iam afflictam et prostratam rem publicam tuis opibus extulisti. quae tibi non antequam postulares, maiora quam velles, plura quam sperares, detulit senatus? dedit fasces, ut cum auctoritate defensorem haberet, non ut imperio se adversum armaret; appellavit imperatorem hostium exercitu pulso tribuens honorem, non ut tua[10] caede

9 (*Lamacchia*) 10 sua (*Wes.*)

---

7 Lit. 'had formed a desire.' For *concupiscere* thus cf. Horace *Epodes* 3.19 *si quid umquam tale concupiveris*, Valerius Maximus 7.1.2 *adstimulatorem vanae opinionis deum habere concupiscit* et al. 8 Caesar's private memoranda. As surviving Consul after Caesar's death Antony took these over and used them to claim authority for his measures. According to Cicero, Caesar's secretary Faberius forged whatever was required.

9 Shortly after Caesar's death Antony abolished this office in perpetuity as a sop to anti-Caesarians.

Antonius, a man of highest spirit (would that he had been of wise counsel as well!), conceived an ambition[7] for primacy of more monarchical a character than a free community could tolerate. He proceeded to dissipate public funds, empty the treasury, reduce revenues, grant tax exemptions to communities and citizenship to peoples—out of a notebook.[8] He exercised Dictatorship, imposed laws, forbade the appointment of a Dictator,[9] personally resisted laws and senatorial decrees in the Senate, wanted all provinces for himself alone,[10] while scorning the province of Macedonia, which victorious Caesar had chosen for himself.[11] What were we to hope for or expect from him?

You stood forth as champion of our freedom, in the best of dispositions as it seemed at the time—would that we had not been deceived in our opinion and your good faith! You brought the veterans together and diverted two legions from the destruction of the Fatherland to its rescue, thus suddenly raising up the well-nigh beaten down and prostrate commonwealth by your own resources. What did the Senate not bestow upon you—before you asked, more than you would have wished, more than you would have hoped? It gave you the rods[12] in order to have a champion with authority, not to arm you with power against itself. It gave you the title of *imperator* when the enemy army had been vanquished, paying you honour, not for that fleeing

[10] This seems to refer to Antony's high-handed disposal of provincial governorships at a meeting of the Senate on 28 November 44 (*Phil.* 3.24ff.). [11] Antony had exchanged Macedonia for Cisalpine Gaul by plebiscite in June 44. The reference to Caesar is obscure. [12] The fasces, symbolizing military authority (*imperium*) as Propraetor.

caesus[11] ille fugiens exercitus te nominaret imperatorem; decrevit in foro statuam, locum in senatu, summum honorem ante tempus. si quid aliud est quod dari possit, addet.

5 quid aliud est, ‹quid›[12] maius quod velis sumere? sin autem supra aetatem, supra consuetudinem, supra etiam mortalitatem [tuam][13] tibi sunt omnia tributa, cur aut ut ingratum crudeliter aut ut memorem[14] beneficii tui scelerate circumscibis senatum? quo te misimus? a quibus reverteris? contra quos armavimus? quibus arma cogitas inferre? a quibus exercitum abducis? [et][15] quos adversus aciem instruis? cur hostis relinquitur, civis hostis loco ponitur?[16] cur castra medio itinere longius ‹ab› adversariorum castris et propius urbem moventur? cogit illorum spes aliquid nos timere.

6 O me numquam sapientem sed[17] aliquando, id quod non eram, frustra existimatum! quantum te, popule Ro-

11 rursus *vel* ausus (ς) 12 (*SB*) 13 (*SB*)
14 memorem *cod. Paris. Lat. 16248, SB*: immemor *vel* -orem (*hoc vulg.*) *codd. cett.* 15 (ς)
16 ponitur Ω: petitur χ 17 sed χ: et Ω

13 The reading follows Lamacchia, though *caesus* has virtually no manuscript authority. After Antony's defeat at Mutina in April 43, which the writer credits to Octavian, ignoring the Consuls to whom the credit really belonged, Antony took what was left of his army across the Alps, joined up with Caesarian armies in Gaul, and returned to Italy to make an accord with Octavian, forming with him and Lepidus the Triumvirate for the Constitution of the Republic. Then as the writer would have it, his army, which Octavian had defeated, saluted Octavian as Imperator. It remained of course under Antony's command.

14 Octavian was given license to hold the Consulship ten years

army, defeated by the defeat you inflicted,[13] to call you by the same. It decreed you a statue in the Forum, a place in the Senate, the highest office before its time.[14] If there is anything else to give, it will give you that too. What else is there, what greater gift that you would wish to take? But if everything has been vouchsafed you beyond the limits of age and custom and even mortality,[15] why do you violate the Senate's rights, cruelly if it has been ungrateful, or criminally if mindful of what it owes you?[16] Where did we send you? Who are they from whom you return? Against whom did we arm you? Whom do you intend to attack? From whom are you leading your army away? Against whom are you drawing up your line of battle? Why is the enemy left behind and the citizen put in the enemy's place? Halfway on your route, why is your force moved away from the opposing force and towards Rome?[17] *Their* hope obliges *us* to fear.

Never wise, alas, was I, and sometimes vainly supposed to be what I was not. People of Rome, how mistaken was

before the minimum legal age of 43, a mere gesture, since he was only nineteen.

[15] The Senate's generosity had gone beyond normal human limitations.

[16] Suppose (for argument's sake) the Senate had been ungrateful, Octavian's treatment of it was still cruel; suppose the contrary, it was criminal.

[17] Instead of marching against Antony, Octavian had marched on Rome (19 August 43) to demand and get the Consulship along with his kinsman Pedius. But that was some three months prior to the putative date of the Letter. Are the present tenses 'historic' or is the writer's imprecise chronology at fault? See however Lamacchia (2), 16.

mane, de me fefellit opinio! o meam calamitosam ac praecipitem senectutem! o turpem exacta dementique aetate canitiem! ego patres conscriptos ad parricidium induxi, ego rem publicam fefelli, ego ipsum senatum sibi manus adferre coegi, cum te Iunonium puerum et matris tuae partum aureum esse dixi. at te fata patriae Paridem futurum praedicebant,[18] qui vastares urbem incendio, Italiam bello, qui castra in templis deorum immortalium, senatum
7 in castris habiturus esses. o miseram et in brevi tam celerem et tam variam rei publicae commutationem! quisnam tali futurus ingenio est, qui possit haec ita mandare litteris ut facta, non ficta videantur [esse][19]? quis erit tanta animi facilitate qui quae verissime memoria propagata fuerint non fabulae similia sit existimaturus? cogita enim Antoniuam hostem iudicatum, ab eo circumsessum consulem designatum eundemque rei publica parentem, te profectum ad consulem liberandum et hostem opprimendum hostemque a te fugatum et consulem obsidione liberatum, deinde paulo post fugatum illum hostem arcessitum tamquam coheredem mortua re publica ad bona populi Romani partienda, consulem designatum rursus inclusum eo ubi

[18] praedicabant (*Lamb.*)
[19] (*Lamacchia*)

---

[18] Following Cicero's advice the Senate had cosseted Octavian and so destroyed the Fatherland.

[19] I.e. Romulus, son of Juno's son Mars; so Lamacchia (2). These phrases may be loosely based on something in Cicero's poem on his Consulship, of which only fragments survive.

your opinion of me! How disastrous my old age, how rash! Alas for my white hairs dishonoured now that my life is spent and turned foolish! I led the Conscript Fathers into parricide,[18] I deceived the commonwealth, I made the Senate turn its hand against itself, calling you 'Juno's boy'[19] and your mother's birth-giving 'golden.' But the Fates foretold that you would be your country's Paris,[20] to lay waste Rome by fire and Italy by war, destined to pitch camp in the temples of the immortal gods and to have the Senate inside your camp. Ah, what a sad revolution of the commonwealth, so rapid and various, in so short a time! Who shall have the genius so to write these events into history that they seem fact and not fiction? Who shall possess the flexibility of mind not to think them quasi-fabulous, quite truthfully propagated by memory though they be? Call it all to mind: Antony declared a public enemy; a Consul-Designate, the same the father of the commonwealth,[21] by him besieged; you setting out to free the Consul and crush the enemy and the enemy routed by you and the Consul[22] freed from blockade; then a little later that routed enemy called in like a co-heir after the death of the commonwealth to divide up the estate of the Roman People, the Consul-Designate shut in once again and defend-

[20] I.e. destroyer, as Paris of Troy. The 'prophecy' was only fulfilled to a very limited extent by Octavian's war against L. Antonius in 41–40 (Perusine War).

[21] D. Brutus, besieged by Antony in Mutina and extravagantly praised by Cicero in the *Philippics*, as in 4.8 *conservator rei publicae Brutus*.

[22] I.e. Consul-Designate.

se non moenibus sed fluminibus et montibus tueretur: haec quis conabitur[20] exponere?

8 Liceat semel impune peccare, sit errantis medicina confessio. verum enim dicam: utinam te potius, Antoni, dominum non expulissemus quam hunc reciperemus! non quo ulla sit optanda servitus, sed quia dignitate domini minus turpis est fortuna servi. in duobus autem malis, cum fugiendum maius sit, levius est eligendum. ille ea tamen exorabat quae volebat auferre, tu extorques; ille consul provinciam petebat, tu privatus ‹consulatum›[21] concupisti;[22] ille ad malorum salutem iudicia constituebat et leges ferebat, tu ad perniciem optimorum; ille a sanguine et incendio servorum Capitolium tuebatur, tu cruore et flamma cuncta delere vis. si qui dabat provincias Cassio et Brutis et illis custodibus nominis nostri regnabat, quid faciet qui vitam adimit? si qui ex urbe eiciebat tyrannus erat, quem

[20] conabitur Ω: poterit χ [21] (*SB*)
[22] concupisti Ω: -piscis χ

---

[23] Deserted by his army in Gaul, D. Brutus fled, but was eventually hunted down and killed by Antony's orders. The notion of a second siege is the writer's embroidery.

[24] Antony had hastily left Rome for north Italy on 29 November 44 on the news that two legions had gone over to Octavian.

[25] On *concupisti* see n. 7. It has better authority than *concupis* and is needed with the supplement *consulatum*. Octavian became Consul in August and had not wanted a province either before or afterwards.

[26] As Consul Antony passed a law permitting appeal by persons convicted of violence (*vis*) or lese majesty (*maiestas*). Another law added a new jury panel of soldiers to the existing two of Senators and Knights.

ing himself not by walls but by rivers and mountains.[23] Who shall attempt to set forth all this? Who shall dare believe it?

Let one blunder go unpunished, let confession medicine the error. For I will be frank: would that we had not driven out our master Antony[24] rather than take in this one instead! Not that slavery is ever desirable; but the master's high station makes the slave's condition less humiliating, and of two evils the milder is to be chosen since the greater is to be avoided. After all, Antony used to beg for what he wanted to take, whereas you snatch it. He was a Consul and asked for a province; you were a private citizen and set your mind on the Consulship.[25] He established courts and passed laws for the good of the wicked,[26] you for the destruction of the best.[27] He protected the Capitol from bloodshed and fire by slaves,[28] you want to destroy everything in gore and flame. If a man who was giving provinces to Cassius and the Bruti[29] and those guardians of our name[30] was a despot, what will one who is taking their lives do? If he that drove them from Rome was a tyrant, what

[27] Allusion to the lex Pedia providing for the prosecution and outlawry of Caesar's assassins. [28] Allusion to disturbances in Rome following Caesar's murder.

[29] Some time in the summer of 44 Cassius and M. Brutus (Praetors) had been assigned Cyrene and Crete as provinces.

[30] I.e. others of the assassins (read *aliis* for *illis*?). In fact D. Brutus, Trebonius, and Tillius Cimber had been assigned their provinces by Caesar not Antony, who on the contrary transferred Cisalpine Gaul from D. Brutus to himself. But Plutarch (*Brutus* 19.3) makes the same mistake; see however Lamacchia (2), 15. Antony did offer a province to another conspirator, L. Cinna, who refused it (*Phil.* 3.25f.).

hunc vocemus qui ne locum quidem relinquit exsilio?

9 Itaque si quid illae maiorum nostrorum sepultae reliquiae sapiunt, si non una cum corpore sensus omnis uno atque eodem consumptus est igni, quid illis interrogantibus quid agat nunc populus Romanus respondebit aliquis nostrum qui proximus[23] illam aeternam domum discesserit? aut quem accipient de suis posteris nuntium illi veteres Africani, Maximi, Pauli[24]? quid de sua patria audient quam spoliis triumphisque decorarunt? an esse quendam annos XVIII‹I›[25] natum cuius avus fuerit argentarius, adstipulator pater, uterque vero precarium quaestum fecerit, sed alter usque ad senectutem ut non negaret, alter a pueritia ut non posset non confiteri; eum agere rapere rem publicam, cui nulla virtus, nullae bello subactae et ad imperium adiunctae provinciae, nulla dignitas maiorum conciliasset eam potentiam, sed forma per dedecus pecuniam et nomen nobile consceleratum impudicitia dedisset; veteres vulneribus et aetate confectos Iulianos gladiatores, egentes reliquias Caesaris ludi, ad rudem compulisset, quibus

[23] proximus Ω: -me χ
[24] pauli χ: -li scipiones Ω
[25] XIII *vel* XVI (*Wes.*: XVIII *vulg. ante Lamacchia*)

---

[31] The elder and younger Scipio Africanus, Fabius Maximus (Cunctator), and L. Aemilius Paullus, conqueror of Macedonia.

[32] The meaning of *adstipulator* here is doubtful.

[33] I.e. he started at it as a boy and thenceforward could not deny it. Octavian's grandfather lived to over seventy, whereas his father died at forty-three after becoming a highly respected Praetor.

[34] The writer may have found in Suetonius (*Aug.* 68) the alle-

shall we call him that does not even leave them a place of exile?

And so, if the buried remains of our ancestors have consciousness, if all sensation has not been consumed along with their bodies by one and the same fire, and they ask how the Roman People is faring at this time, what answer will one of us make, the latest to depart for that eternal dwelling? Or those men of old, the Africani, Maximi, Pauli,[31] what will they hear about the country they adorned with spoils and triumphs? What news will they get about their descendants? That there is a young man of nineteen, whose grandfather was a money-changer and his father a subcontractor[32] (both made a precarious living, but whereas the one down to old age did not deny it, the other from boyhood upward could not but admit it[33]); that he is harrying and plundering the commonwealth, not owing that power to any achievement, any provinces added to the empire, any ancestral prestige: no, good looks gave money through shame and unchastity a noble name stained with crime.[34] They will hear that he forced old Julian gladiators,[35] the starveling remnants of Caesar's troupe, worn

gations that Octavian in youth made money by self-prostitution and gained his adoption by Caesar (his great-uncle) through a sexual relationship.

[35] Caesar did own gladiators, but the writer seems to be travestying Octavian's mustering of Caesar's veterans in 44. In his desire to say something denigratory it does not seem to have occurred to him that decrepit seniors would not make the best intimidators.

ille saeptus omnia misceret, nulli parceret: qui tamquam in dotali matrimonio rem publicam testamento legatam sibi obtineret? audient duo Decii servire eos cives, qui ut hostibus imperarent, victoriae se devoverunt, audiet C. Marius impudico domino parere nos, qui ne militem quidem habere voluit nisi pudicum; audiet Brutus eum populum, quem ipse primo, post progenies eius a regibus liberavit, pro turpi stupro datum in servitutem. quae quidem, si nullo alio, me tamen internuntio celeriter ad illos deferentur; nam si vivus ista subterfugere non potero, una cum istis vitam simul fugere decrevi.

---

36 Lit. 'forced them to the wooden sword' (i.e. to retire as gladiators in order to take on a new role). A wooden sword (*rudis*) was presented to gladiators on retirement; cf. Juvenal 7.171 of a professor of rhetoric giving up his school to plead in a real law court *sibi dabit ipse rudem . . . et vitae diversum iter ingredietur.* Otherwise, but erroneously, M. I. Henderson.

out with age and wounds, into retirement,[36] so that surrounded by them he could throw everything into turmoil, spare none, live only for himself, and possess the commonwealth as though bequeathed to him by testament in dotal matrimony.[37] The two Decii, who devoted themselves to victory[38] so that their countrymen should have mastery over their enemies, will hear that these same are slaves. C. Marius, who would not have a pervert even as a private soldier, will hear that we obey one as a master.[39] Brutus[40] will hear that the people which he first and his descendant after him liberated from kings has been given into bondage in exchange for filthy sex. All this shall be conveyed to them speedily and, if nobody else, I shall be their informant. For I have made up my mind that if I cannot evade these things alive, I shall escape them and life together.

37 Caesar's will made Octavian his adopted son and heir to his estate. *In dotali matrimonio* alludes to the alleged sexual relationship, but *dotalis*, which could refer either to dowry or bridegroom's gift to bride, is probably used quite loosely. If pressed, it could mean that Caesar gave his power (i.e. the reversion of it) to his 'bride' at their marriage.

38 The father in 340, the son in 295, vowing their lives in return for victory in battle.

39 The *miles Marianus* who killed the officer who tried to seduce him and was exonerated by the general was a stock rhetorical theme; cf. *Pro Milone* 9.

40 The first Consul.

PSEUDO-SALLUST
INVECTIVE AGAINST CICERO

PSEUDO-CICERO
INVECTIVE AGAINST SALLUST

INTRODUCTORY NOTE

These two pieces, purporting to be speeches delivered in the Senate, are spurious beyond any reasonable doubt, probably school exercises of uncertain date, even though the first is quoted by Quintilian (*Inst.* 4.1.68, 9.3.89) apparently without misgiving. Its dramatic date appears to be 54 B.C., whereas the second, ostensibly a reply to the first, ranges over Sallust's entire career. They are preserved in over two hundred manuscripts, mostly in conjunction with genuine works of Sallust or Cicero. The standard edition is now L. D. Reynolds' Oxford Classical Text of Sallust (1991), to whose preface I am content to refer for further diplomatic information; apart from that, A. Ernout's Budé edition of 1974 may be consulted. This text and translation are new; the *Invectivae* are not in my Teubner edition of Cicero's Correspondence.

ς in my critical notes stands for corrections or conjectures in manuscripts of no authority. Departures from Reynolds' text are indicated by asterisks.

IN CICERONEM

1 Graviter et iniquo animo maledicta tua paterer, M. Tulli, si te scirem iudicio magis quam morbo animi petulantia ista uti. Sed cum in te neque modum neque modestiam ullam animadverto, respondebo tibi ut si quam male dicendo voluptatem cepisti, eam male audiendo[1] amittas.

Ubi querar, quos implorem, patres conscripti, diripi rem publicam atque audacissimo cuique esse praedae?[2] apud populum Romanum? qui ita largitionibus corruptus est, ut se ipse ac fortunas suas venales habeat. an apud vos, patres conscripti? quorum auctoritas turpissimo cuique et sceleratissimo ludibrio est; ubi[3] M. Tullius leges, iudicia, rem publicam defendit atque in hoc ordine ita moderatur quasi unus reliquus e familia viri clarissimi, Scipionis Africani, ac non reperticius, accitus,[4] ac paulo ante insitus huic urbi civis.

2 An vero, M. Tulli, facta tua ac dicta obscura sunt? an non ita a pueritia vixisti ut nihil flagitiosum corpori tuo putares quod alicui collibuisset? aut scilicet istam immodera-

[1] dicendo

[2] perfidiae (*Eussner*)

[3] ubiubi (*cod. Harleianus* 2682* *saec.XI*)

[4] *anne* a(d)scitus ?

INVECTIVE AGAINST CICERO

I should find your insults hard to bear, Marcus Tullius, and they would make me angry if I knew that this insolence of yours came from judgment rather than from a mind diseased. But since I find neither moderation nor modesty in you, I shall answer you in the hope that you may lose any pleasure you get from abusing another when you become the target.

Where shall I make my protest, to whom shall I appeal, Conscript Fathers, for that the commonwealth is being torn to pieces, a prey to every out and out ruffian? To the Roman People, that is so corrupted by largesses that they have themselves and their own fortunes for sale? Or to you, Conscript Fathers? Your authority is a laughingstock to every foul villain, when M. Tullius defends the laws and the courts of justice and the commonwealth and acts chairman in this House as if he were the sole survivor of the family of the illustrious Scipio Africanus, not a foundling citizen, called in, recently grafted upon this city.

Really, M. Tullius, are your actions and your words not well-known? Have you not lived from boyhood in the persuasion that nothing anyone liked to do to your body could outrage it? I suppose you did not master this unbridled

tam eloquentiam apud M. Pisonem non pudicitiae iactura perdidicisti! itaque minime mirandum est quod eam flagitiose venditas quam turpissime parasti.

Verum, ut opinor, splendor domesticus tibi animos tollit, uxor sacrilega ac periuriis delibuta, filia matris paelex, tibi iucundior atque obsequentior quam parenti par est. domum ipsam tuam vi et rapinis funestam tibi ac tuis comparasti, videlicet ut nos commonefacias quam conversa res sit, cum in ea domo habites, homo flagitiosissime, quae P.
3 Crassi, viri clarissimi, fuit. atque haec cum ita sint, tamen se Cicero dicit in concilio deorum immortalium fuisse, inde missum huic urbi civibusque custodem * * *[5] absque carnificis nomine, qui civitatis incommodum in gloriam suam ponit. quasi vero non illius coniurationis causa fuerit consulatus tuus et idcirco res publica disiecta eo tempore quo[6] te custodem habebat.

Sed, ut opinor, illa te magis extollunt quae post consulatum cum Terentia uxore de re publica consuluisti, cum

[5] *lac. susp. Reitzenstein*
[6] quod *Baiter*

---

[1] M. Pupius Piso Frugi, Consul in 61. According to Asconius (Clark 15), Cicero in his youth was introduced by his father to Piso, perhaps some seven years his senior, because of the latter's old-style way of life and literary attainments. In later life Cicero's opinion of him varied widely at different periods. The aspersion here is a commonplace in this kind of writing, not to be taken seriously.

[2] Terentia's half-sister Fabia was a Vestal Virgin. In 73 she was accused of having sexual relations with Catiline and acquitted

eloquence of yours with M. Piso[1] by sacrificing your chastity? Far from surprising then that you sell it as outrageously as you gained it shamefully!

But I imagine the distinction of your domestic scenario makes you proud! A wife smeared with sacrilege and perjuries,[2] a daughter, her mother's rival, more pleasing and submissive to you than a daughter should be to a parent. You acquired your house itself, a disaster for you and yours, with violence and plunderings, presumably to impress upon us how greatly things have changed, seeing that you, disreputable as you are, live in the house that belonged to the illustrious P. Crassus.[3] And all this notwithstanding, Cicero says that he was in the assembly of the immortal gods and from there despatched to guard this city and its citizens[4] * * * executioner apart from the name (?), who credits the misfortune of the community to his own glory; as though your Consulship were not the cause of that conspiracy and for that reason the commonwealth was torn apart at the time when it had you for its guardian.

But I imagine your political decisions subsequent to your Consulship in consultation with your wife Terentia make you prouder, when you two proceeded to set up trials

(Asconius (Clark) 91). 'Sallust' seems to have transferred the item to Terentia.

[3] Cicero's house on the Palatine had belonged to P. Licinius Crassus, Consul in 97, and was purchased from his son, M. Crassus the 'Triumvir.' In 58 Clodius destroyed it but it was rebuilt with a public subsidy after Cicero's return.

[4] In his speech *On his House* (141) Cicero calls himself the guardian and protector of the temples of the gods. The assembly of the gods will refer to something in his poem *On his Consulship*.

legis Plautiae iudicia domo faciebatis, cum alios ‹exilio,
alios›[7] pecunia condemnabas, cum tibi alius Tusculanam,
alius Pompeianam villam exaedificabat, alius domum eme-
bat: qui vero nihil poterat, is erat Catilinae[8] proximus, is
aut domum tuam oppugnatum venerat aut insidias senatui
4 fecerat, denique de eo tibi compertum erat. quae si tibi
falsa obicio, redde rationem quantum patrimonii acceperis, quid tibi litibus accreverit, qua ex pecunia domum
paraveris, Tusculanum et Pompeianum infinito sumptu
aedificaveris; aut si retices, cui dubium potest esse quin
opulentiam istam ex sanguine et miseriis civium pararis?[9]

Verum, ut opinor, homo novus Arpinas, ex C. Marii[10]
familia, illius virtutem imitatur, contemnit simultatem hominum nobilium, rem publicam caram habet, neque terrore neque gratia removetur a vero,[11] †amicitia†[12] tantum
5 ac virtus est animi. immo vero homo levissimus,[13] supplex
inimicis, amicis contumeliosus, modo harum, modo illa-
rum partium, fidus nemini, levissimus senator, mercenna-

7 (*Halm*) 8 calumniae (*Wirz*)
9 parasti (*Jordan**: paraveris *ed. princ.*)
10 M. crassi (*Glareanus**): L. Crassi (*Rawson*)
11 aliud vero (*Reitzenstein*) 12 *anne* iustitia*?
13 vilissimus *Petzold*

---

5 A law penalizing acts of violence against public order. 'Sallust' is probably hallucinating here. Apart from the execution of the five Catilinarians in December 63 under the Senate's authority Cicero is not known to have had anyone put to death or exiled or fined.

6 See *Letters to Friends* 5 (V.5).2.

under the lex Plautia[5] in your house, sentencing some of the conspirators to exile, others to fines. One of them would build you your villa at Tusculum, another one at Pompeii, another bought your house. But anyone who could do nothing for you was Catiline's closest associate; he either had come to assault your house or had plotted against the Senate, in fact you had 'informed yourself'[6] about him. If these charges that I bring against you are false, give us an account of how much you inherited from your father, what you gained in law suits, where you got the money to buy your house[7] and build your Tusculan and Pompeian properties at infinite expense; or if you say nothing, who can doubt that you acquired your affluence from the blood and miseries of your fellow countrymen?

But, I suppose, as a new man from Arpinum, from the family of C Marius,[8] he imitates his qualities, despises the enmity of noblemen, holds the commonwealth dear, lets neither fear nor favour part him from the truth, loves (?) only justice (?) and virtue. On the contrary, he is the most irresponsible of mankind, suppliant to his enemies, insolent to his friends, in one party one day, in another the next, loyal to none, an irresponsible Senator, a mercenary advo-

[7] Actually the purchase was financed by borrowing from former clients; cf. *Letters to Atticus*, 13 (I.3).6.

[8] Reynolds adopts Rawson's conjecture *L. Crassi* for *M. Crassi* in the manuscripts. L. Crassus, the famous orator, was indeed Cicero's mentor in youth, but they were not related. Moreover, he did not come from Arpinum and did not despise nobles. Marius was and did, and the Ciceros and the Marii were related by marriage. Whatever the origin of the mistake, there can be no doubt about who is meant.

rius patronus, cuius nulla pars corporis a turpitudine vacat: lingua vana, manus rapacissimae, gula immensa, pedes fugaces, quae honeste nominari non possunt inhonestissima. atque is cum eius modi sit, tamen audet dicere: 'o fortunatam natam me consule Romam'! ⟨Romam⟩[14] te consule fortunatam, Cicero? immo vero infelicem et miseram, quae crudelissimam proscriptionem eam[15] perpessa est, cum tu perturbata re publica metu perculsos omnis bonos parere crudelitati tuae cogebas, cum omnia iudicia, omnes leges in tua libidine erant, cum tu, sublata lege Porcia, erepta libertate omnium nostrum, vitae necisque potesta-
6 tem ad te unum revocaveras. atque parum[16] quod impune fecisti, verum etiam commemorando exprobras, neque licet oblivisci [iis] servitutis suae. egeris, oro te, Cicero, profeceris quidlibet, satis est perpessos esse: etiamne aures nostras odio tuo onerabis, etiamne molestissimis verbis insectabere? 'cedant arma togae, concedat laurea linguae.' quasi vero togatus et non armatus ea quae gloriaris confeceris, atque inter te Sullamque dictatorem praeter nomen imperii quicquam interfu⟨er⟩it.

7 Sed quid ego plura de tua insolentia commemorem? quem Minerva omnis artis edocuit, Iuppiter Optimus Maximus in concilio deorum admisit, Italia exulem suis

[14] (*Winterbottom*)
[15] *om. cod. Edinburgensis saec. XI–XII*
[16] parum est ς

[9] From Cicero's poem *On his Consulship*, 'a famous mark for the banter of ancient critics' (J. D. Duff on Juvenal 10.122) with its disagreeable assonance.

[10] Forbidding the execution of Roman citizens without the People's authority.

cate, with no part of his body clear of turpitude: false tongue, grasping hands, immense gullet, runaway feet, most indecent the parts that cannot decently be named. And being what he is, he yet dares to say 'Fortunate Rome, born when I was Consul'![9] Rome fortunate when you were Consul, Cicero? On the contrary, hapless and miserable. She suffered an atrocious proscription when you forced all honest men, stricken as they were by fear in a troubled commonwealth, to obey your cruelty; when all the law courts, all the laws were at the mercy of your whim when, with the lex Porcia[10] abolished and freedom snatched away, you had brought the power of life and death over us all into your single hands. That you *did* this with impunity is not enough; you continually threw it in our faces, and Rome is not allowed to forget her bondage. I beg of you, Cicero: allow that you have done and accomplished whatever you please, it is enough that we have borne it. Will you also burden our ears with your offensiveness, will you still pursue us with your disgusting phrases? 'Let arms yield to the gown, let the laurel bow to the tongue.'[11] As though you achieved your boasts in gown and not in arms, and anything but the *name* of military authority distinguished you from Dictator Sulla!

But why dwell further on your presumption? Minerva taught you all arts,[12] Jupiter Best and Greatest admitted you to the council of the gods,[13] Italy brought you back

[11] Another 'target for Cicero's detractors' (A. R. Dyck on *Off.* 77) from the same source.

[12] Cf. *Dom.* 144.

[13] See n. 4 above.

umeris reportavit. Oro te, Romule Arpinas, qui egregia tua virtute omnis Paulos, Fabios, Scipiones superasti, quem tandem locum in hac civitate obtines? quae tibi partes rei publicae placent? quem amicum, quem inimicum habes? cui in civitate insidias fecisti, <ei>[17] ancillaris. quo auctore[18] de exsilio tuo Dyrrachio redisti, eum <in>sequeris. quos tyrannos appellabas, eorum potentiae faves; qui tibi ante optimates videbantur, eosdem dementes ac furiosos vocas. Vatini causam agis, de Sestio male existimas. Bibulum petulantissimis verbis laedis, laudas Caesarem. quem maxime odisti, ei maxime obsequeris. aliud stans, aliud sedens sentis de re publica. his male dicis, illos odisti, levissime transfuga, neque in hac neque in illa parte fidem habens.

17 (*Wirz*)
18 iure cum (*Wirz*)

---

14 Cicero's own phrase (*Post red. in sen.* 39).

15 Caesar. History knows nothing of such a plot, but I suspect it is a travesty of Sallust, *Catiline* 49.1.

16 Pompey, though Cicero did nothing of the kind.

17 The 'First Triumvirate.'

18 On Cicero's grievances against the 'optimates' who had supported his recall see *Letters to Friends* 20 (I.9).

from exile on her shoulders![14] I beg you, Romulus of Arpinum, you that by your splendid achievements have surpassed all the Pauli and Fabii and Scipios, what place do you occupy in the community? What political party do you favour? What friend do you have, what enemy? The man in the community against whom you plotted,[15] you are his lackey; the man at whose instance you came back from Dyrrachium, from your exile, him you harass.[16] Those whom you used to call tyrants,[17] their power you support; those you formerly thought optimates,[18] the same you call fools and madmen. You appear in court for Vatinius,[19] and you have a poor opinion of Sestius.[20] You insult Bibulus in the most offensive terms,[21] and you laud Caesar. You are most obsequious to the man you hate the most. You stand with one set of political views, you sit with another. One lot you insult, you hate another. Neither here nor there do you keep faith.

19 Cicero defended this former enemy in 54 at the behest of Pompey and Caesar, after which they were good friends.

20 Though Cicero was mindful of his heavy obligations to Sestius and defended him successfully in an extant speech, there was some temporary ill-feeling in 56 (*Letters to Quintus* 8 (II.4).1). But his public references are always eulogistic, notwithstanding Ernout's phantasy in his edition (p. 82) that Sestius was attacked by Cicero for having joined Caesar.

21 False again. Cicero's public references are always complimentary, though privately there was no love lost on either side; cf. *Letters to Friends* 117 (II.17).6–8.

IN SALLUSTIUM

1 Ea demum magna voluptas est, C. Sallusti, aequalem ac parem verbis vitam agere neque quicquam tam obscaenum dicere cui non ab initio pueritiae omni genere facinoris aetas sua[1] respondeat, ut omnis ‹o›ratio moribus consonet. Neque enim qui ita vivit ut tu aliter ac tu loqui potest, neque qui tam illoto sermone utitur vita honestior est.

Quo me praevertam, patres conscripti, unde initium sumam? maius enim mihi dicendi onus imponitur quo notior est uterque nostrum; ‹quid›[2] quod aut, si de mea vita atque actibus huic conviciatori respondero, invidia gloriam consequetur, aut, si huius facta, mores, omnem aetatem nudavero, in idem vitium incidam procacitatis quod huic obicio? id vos si forte offendimini, iustius huic quam
2 mihi suscensere debetis, qui initium introduxit. ego dabo operam ut pro me minimo cum fastidio respondeam et in hunc minime mentitum esse videatur. scio me, patres conscripti, in respondendo non habere magnam exspectationem, quod nullum vos sciatis[3] novum crimen in Sallus-

[1] tua (*SB**) [2] (*SB**) [3] scio ς*

[1] The Senate could not *know* this, though they might suspect that Sallust's known offences were too many and grave to leave

INVECTIVE AGAINST SALLUST

It is indeed a great pleasure, Gaius Sallustius, to live a life in parity and conformity with one's words, to say nothing so obscene that one's career from earliest boyhood does not correspond in every kind of malefaction, so that all one's speech is consonant with one's morals. For anyone who lives as you live cannot but speak as you speak, and anyone who practices such filthy speech lives no less indecently.

Where am I to turn first, Conscript Fathers, what shall I take as my starting point? The better known each of us is, the heavier burden of speech is laid upon me. Add that if I reply to this reviler in terms of *my* life and actions, malice will follow self-praise; or if I lay bare *his* doings and morals and entire career, I shall full into licence—the same fault of which I accuse him. If that perchance offends you, in fairness you ought to blame him, the one who started it, rather than me. I shall be careful to reply on my own behalf with the minimum of assumption and so that what I say against him shall be seen as the minimum of mendacity. I know, Conscript Fathers, that my response awakens no great expectancy, for you know[1] that you will hear no new

room for anything new. But *scio*, read by Reynolds, is no more logical, and for the same reason: the speaker's knowledge that he had nothing new to say did not extend to his audience.

tium audituros, sed omnia vetera recognituros, quis et meae et vestrae iam et ipsius aures calent. verum eo magis odisse debetis hominem, qui ne incipiens quidem peccare ‹in›[4] minimis rebus posuit rudimentum, sed ita ingressus est ut neque ab alio vinci possit neque ipse se omni[5] reliqua aetate praeterire.

3 Itaque nihil aliud studet nisi ut lutulentus sus cum quovis volutari. longe vero fallitur opinione; non enim procacitate linguae vitae sordes eluuntur, sed est quaedam calumnia quam unusquisque nostrum testante animo suo fert de eo quod[6] falsum crimen bonis obiectat.[7] quod si vita istius memoriam vicerit, illam,[8] patres conscripti, non ex oratione sed ex moribus suis spectare debebitis. iam dabo operam, quam maxime potuero, breve ut faciam. neque haec altercatio nostra vobis inutilis erit, patres conscripti;
4 plerumque enim res publica privatis crescit inimicitiis, ubi nemo civis qualis sit vir potest latere.

Primum igitur, quoniam omnium maiores C. Sallustius ad unum exemplum et regulam quaerit, velim mihi respondeat num quid his[9] quos protulit Scipiones et Metellos ante fuerit[10] aut opinionis aut gloriae quam eos res

[4] (*SB**) [5] omnino (*cod. Vaticanus saec.* XIII*)
[6] qui *vel* quia *codd. nonnulli*
[7] de eo . . . obiectat *del. Jordan**
[8] aliam (*Cortius*) [9] hos *vel* hi(i) *vel om.* (*F. Schmidt*)
[10] fuerint (*F. Schmidt*)

---

[2] *Calumniam ferre* is 'to be convicted of (making a) false charge'; see my Commentary on *Letters to Friends* 84 (VIII.8).1 *calumniam . . . tulisse*. Reynolds secludes *de eo . . . obiectat*; but each one of us does *not* know himself guilty of falsely accusing

charge against Sallustius but recognize all the old items with which my ears and yours and his own are already buzzing. But you ought to be all the more disgusted with him; he did not make even his debut as a wrongdoer in trifling concerns but launched out in such a style that for all the rest of his life he could neither be outdone by someone else nor surpass himself.

So his one endeavour is to wallow like a muddy pig with somebody, no matter whom. But he is much mistaken. Stains of life are not washed away by an impudent tongue. But there is a verdict of false accusation which each one of us incurs on the testimony of his own conscience with reference to a false charge that he has brought against good men.[2] But if this man's life overtaxes memory, it will be for you to look at it not from words but from his general conduct.[3] I shall take care to be as brief as I can. And this exchange of ours will not be without advantage to you, Conscript Fathers. The public generally finds its account in private feuds, in which no citizen can hide from revealing what sort of man he is.

First of all then, since C. Sallustius seeks everybody's ancestors according to one pattern and standard, I should like his answer to a question: did those Scipios and Metelli whom he has brought up have any reputation or glory

good men. *De eo* could be deleted, with *qui* instead of *quod*. But in this writer crabbed is not necessarily corrupt. The sense implied is: 'if any of us brings a false charge against the innocent, his own conscience will convict him.'

[3] If his career is too full of misdeeds for you to remember them all, you should judge of it from his character; no need for me to spell them out.

gestae suae et vita innocentissime acta commendavit. quod si hoc fuit illis initium nominis et dignitatis, cur non aeque <de> nobis existimetur, cuius et res gestae illustres et vita integerrime acta? quasi vero tu sis ab illis, Sallusti, ortus! quod si esses, non nullos iam tuae turpitudinis pige-
5 ret.[11] ego meis maioribus virtute mea praeluxi, ut, si prius noti non fuerunt, a me accipiant initium memoriae suae: tu tuis vita quam turpiter egisti magnas offudisti tenebras, ut, etiamsi fuerint egregii cives, per te[12] venerint in oblivionem. quare noli mihi antiquos viros obiectare; satius est enim me meis rebus gestis florere quam maiorum opinione niti et ita vivere ut ego sim posteris meis nobilitatis initium et virtutis exemplum. neque me cum iis conferri decet, patres conscripti, qui iam decesserunt omnique odio carent et invidia, sed cum iis qui mecum una in re
6 publica versati sunt. sed [se][13] fuerim [aut][14] in honoribus petendis nimis ambitiosus—non hanc dico popularem ambitionem, cuius me principem confiteor, sed illam perniciosam contra leges, cuius primos ordines Sallustius duxit—<quis fuit>[15] aut in gerundis magistratibus <tam diligens>[16] aut in vindicandis maleficiis tam severus aut in tuenda re publica tam vigilans? quam tu proscriptionem vocas, credo quod non omnes tui similes incolumes in urbe vixissent: at quanto meliore loco res publica staret, si tu par

11 *anne* nullos . . . non pigeret?
12 certe (*van der Hoeven*)
13 (*Cortius*) 14 (*SB**)
15 (*SB**) 16 (*SB**)

---

4 Of course they did, coming from great noble families. But the writer's addled head confuses them with the Scipio or Metel-

before their own performances and blameless lives commended them?[4] But if this was the beginning of their name and prestige, why should the same standard not be applied to myself, seeing that my performances are celebrated and my life passed without reproach? As though you, Sallustius, were a descendant of theirs! If you had been, some would now be sorry for your turpitude. As for me, I have outshone my forebears by my achievement, so that if previously unknown they begin to be remembered owing to me. You, on the other hand, have cast deep shadows on yours by your disgraceful life, so that even if they were outstanding citizens they have passed into oblivion because of you. So don't throw men of old in my face. Better that I win distinction through my own performances than rely on the reputation of my forebears, and live so as to start nobility for those who come after me and be a shining example. Furthermore, it is not fitting, Conscript Fathers, that I be compared with men who have passed away and are now beyond all hate and envy; the comparison should be with my fellow actors on the political stage. But suppose I was too competitive in seeking office—and I don't mean competition for popular approval, in which I admit I have taken the lead, but the deleterious, law-breaking kind in which Sallustius led the front ranks: who has been so diligent in the conduct of magistracies, or so strict in punishing wrongdoings, or so vigilant in protecting the commonwealth? You call it a proscription, because, I suppose, not everybody of your ilk lived on in our city unscathed; but in how much better shape the commonwealth would stand if

lus who originally brought distinction into his family by his own merits—a familiar point; cf. e.g. *Letters to Friends* 71 (III.7).5.

ac similis scelestorum civium una cum illis adnumeratus
7 esses! an ego tunc falso scripsi 'cedant arma togae'? qui togatus armatos et pace bellum oppressi? an illud mentitus sum 'fortunatam me consule Romam'? qui tantum intestinum bellum ac domesticum urbis incendium exstinxi? neque te tui piget, homo levissime, cum ea culpas quae <in> historiis mihi gloriae ducis? an turpius est scribentem mentiri quam [illum][17] palam <in>[18] hoc ordine dicentem? nam quod in aetatem increpuisti, tantum me abesse puto ab impudicitia quantum tu pudicitia.

8 Sed quid ego de te plura querar? quid enim mentiri turpe ducis, qui mihi ausus sis eloquentiam ut vitium obicere, cuius semper nocens eguisti patrocinio? an ullum existimas posse fieri civem egregium qui non his artibus et disciplinis sit eruditus? an ulla alia putas esse rudimenta et incunabula virtutis quibus animi ad gloriae cupiditatem aluntur? sed minime mirum est, patres conscripti, si homo qui desidiae et luxuriae plenus sit haec ut nova atque inusi-
9 tata miratur. nam quod ista inusitata rabie in uxorem et in filiam meam invasisti, quae facilius mulieres se a viris abstinuerunt quam tu vir [a viris],[19] satis docte ac perite fecisti. non enim me sperasti mutuam tibi gratiam relaturum, ut vicissim tuos compellarem; unus enim satis es materiae [habens],[20] neque quicquam domi tuae turpius est quam

17 (*Heraeus*) 18 (*SB**)
19 (*Holford-Strevens*)
20 (*SB**)

---

5 Sallust's *Histories*, covering the years 78–67, could hardly have dealt with Cicero's Consulship, but Cicero gets some praise in his *Catiline*.

you, the equal and counterpart of the criminals, had been counted in along with them! When at that time I wrote: 'let arms yield to the gown,' was it not true? Did I not in my gown crush men in arms and in peace did I not crush war? Or did I lie when I wrote 'Rome, fortunate in my Consulship,' after extinguishing so formidable an intestine war and domestic conflagration of the city? Are you not disgusted with yourself, fribble that you are, when you find fault with actions which in your *Histories*[5] you set down to my glory? Or is it more disgraceful to lie in writing than in open speech, in this order?[6] As for your attacks on my early life, I fancy I am as far off from unchastity as you from chastity.

But why complain about you further? For what lie can you be ashamed of after daring to throw eloquence in my face, as though it were a fault, when your guilty self has ever needed its advocacy? Or do you suppose that anyone not versed in these arts and disciplines could become an outstanding citizen? Or that there are any other rudiments and cradles of excellence by which minds are nurtured in desire for glory? But it is not at all surprising, Conscript Fathers, that a fellow full of sloth and luxury is surprised at such, to him, strange novelties. As for your vicious attacks upon my wife and daughter in your unseemly rage, ladies who have found it easier to keep clear of men than your masculine self—quite a cultured,[7] skilful performance! You did not expect me to retaliate in kind by calling *your* household names in turn, for you are material enough and nothing in your home is more shameful than you. But I

[6] The Senate.

[7] Or 'clever' (*docte*).

tu. multum vero te, opinor, fallit, qui mihi parare putasti invidiam ex mea re familiari, quae mihi multo minor est quam habere dignus sum. atque utinam ne tanta quidem esset quanta est, ut potius amici mei viverent quam ego testamentis eorum locupletior essem!

10 Ego fugax, C. Sallusti? furori tribuni plebis cessi: utilius duxi quamvis fortunam unus experiri quam universo populo Romano civilis essem dissensionis causa. qui postea quam suum annum in re publica perbacchatus est omniaque quae commoverat pace et otio resederunt, hoc ordine revocante atque ipsa re publica manu retrahente me reverti. qui mihi dies, si cum omni reliqua vita conferatur, animo quidem meo superet, cum universi vos populusque Romanus frequens adventu meo gratulatus est: tanti me fugacem, mercennarium patronum, hi aestimaverunt!
11 neque hercules mirum est, si ego semper iustas omnium amicitias aestimavi: non enim uni privatim ancillatus sum neque me addixi, sed quantum quisque rei publicae studuit <aut inimicus fuit>,[21] tantum mihi fuit aut amicus aut adversarius. ego nihil plus volui valere quam pacem: multi privatorum audacias nutriverunt. ego nihil timui nisi leges: multi arma sua timeri voluerunt. ego numquam volui quicquam posse nisi pro vobis: multi ex vobis potentia freti in vos suis viribus abusi sunt. itaque non est mirum, si nullius amicitia usus sum qui non perpetuo rei publicae amicus
12 fuit. neque me paenitet, si aut petenti Vatinio reo patroci-

[21] (*SB**)

---

[8] Clodius.

[9] So indeed Cicero claims in his public speeches. His letters tell a very different story.

think you were far off the mark when you thought to create ill will against me by talking about my means, which are far less than I deserve. And I only wish they were not as large as they are, with my friends alive rather than me richer by their wills.

A runaway? I, Gaius Sallustius? I gave way before the frenzy of a Tribune.[8] I deemed it more expedient to take whatever fortune came to me individually than to be the cause of civil strife to the People of Rome universally.[9] After he had whirled through his year in public life and everything he had stirred up settled down in peace and tranquillity, this order recalled me and the hand of the commonwealth itself drew me back: I returned. If that day were compared to all the rest of my life, it would turn the scale, at least in my mind: the day when all of you and the Roman People in large numbers hailed my arrival. That was how highly they thought of me, the runaway, the mercenary advocate! Nor is it surprising, upon my word, if I always valued all friendships aright. I did not become any individual's private lackey or bind myself over, but in so far as each man was loyal or hostile to the commonwealth, to that extent I was his friend or his adversary. I wanted nothing to count for more than peace; many others encouraged the audacity of private individuals. I feared nothing but the law; many others wanted their own arms to be feared. I never wanted any power except in your interests; many others in reliance on the power they had from you abused their strength against you. So it is not surprising if I had friendship with nobody who was not consistently a friend to the commonwealth. And I don't regret that I promised to defend Vatinius when he was under prosecu-

nium pollicitus sum aut Sesti insolentiam repressi aut Bibuli patientiam culpavi aut virtutibus Caesaris favi. hae enim laudes egregii civis et unicae sunt; quae si tu mihi ut vitia obicis, temeritas tua reprehendetur, non mea vitia culpabuntur. plura dicerem, si apud alios mihi esset disserendum, patres conscripti, non apud vos, quos ego habui omnium mearum actionum monitores. sed ubi rerum testimonia adsunt, quid opus est verbis?

13 Nunc ut ad te revertar, Sallusti, patrem tuum praeteream, qui si numquam in vita sua peccavit, tamen maiorem iniuriam rei publicae facere non potuit quam quod te talem filium genuit. Neque tu si qua in pueritia peccasti, exsequar, ne parentem tuum videar accusare, qui eo tempore summam tui potestatem habuit, sed qualem adolescentiam egeris; hac enim demonstrata facile intellegetur quam petulanti pueritia tam impudicus et procax adoleveris. postea quam immensae gulae impudicissimus corporis quaestus sufficere non potuit et aetas tua iam ad ea patienda quae alteri facere collibuisset exoleverat, cupiditatibus infinitis efferebaris, ut quae ipse corpori tuo turpia non
14 duxisses in aliis experireris. ita non est facile exputare, patres conscripti, utrum inhonestioribus corporis partibus rem quaesierit an amiserit. domum paternam vivo patre turpissime venalem habuit [vendidit]; et cuiquam dubium potest esse quin mori coegerit eum quo hic nondum mortuo pro herede gesserit omnia? neque pudet eum a me quaerere quis in P. Crassi domo habitet, cum ipse respon-

---

[10] See 'Sallust's' piece § 7. [11] For this sense of *patientia* cf. Cicero, *Brutus* 95 *is qui . . . fregit Ti. Gracchum patientia . . . M. Octavius.* [12] In his speech *On the Consular Provinces*.

[13] As a pathic.

tion and asked me, or that I checked Sestius' insolence,[10] or blamed Bibulus' doggedness,[11] or backed Caesar's achievements —I praised an outstanding citizen, and once only.[12] If you bring that against me as a fault, your rashness will be blamed, not my shortcomings. I should say more if I had to hold forth before others, Conscript Fathers, and not before you, who have been the monitors of my every course of action. But where the facts are my witnesses, what need of words?

To turn now to yourself, Sallustius, let me pass over your father. If he never did anything wrong in his life, all the same he could have done no greater harm to the commonwealth than by begetting a son like you. And I shall not pursue any wrongdoings in your boyhood since I don't want to seem to accuse your father, who had complete power over you at that time. I shall speak of your early manhood, for when I have made that clear it will be easily understood how wayward was the boyhood which developed so immoral and outrageous a young man. After the earnings of your shameless body could no longer satisfy your limitless appetite and you had passed the age for submitting to whatever it pleased the other party to do, you were carried away by unbounded lusts in your desire to try upon others things that you yourself had not felt as degrading to your own person. So it is difficult to compute, Conscript Fathers, which of his bodily parts were the more indecent, those by which he made money[13] or those by which he lost it. He put his father's house up for sale while his father was still alive, a shocking act; and can anybody doubt that he brought about his death, seeing that before his father died he behaved in all respects as an inheritor? And he is not ashamed to ask who lives in P. Crassus' house

dere non queat quis in ipsius habitet paterna domo. 'at hercules lapsus aetatis tirocinio postea se correxit.' non ita est,
sed abiit in sodalicium sacrilegi Nigidiani; bis iudicis ad
subsellia attractus extrema fortuna stetit et ita discessit
ut non hic innocens esse sed iudices peierasse existimaren-
15 tur. primum honorem in quaestura adeptus hunc locum
et hunc ordinem despectui <habuit>,[22] cuius aditus sibi
quoque sordidissimo homini patuisset. itaque timens ne
facinora eius clam vos essent, cum omnibus matrum fami-
liarium viris opprobrio esset, confessus est vobis audientibus adulterium neque erubuit ora vestra. vixeris ut libet,
Sallusti, egeris quae volueris: satis sit unum te tuorum scelerum esse conscium. noli nobis languorem et soporem nimium exprobrare: sumus diligentes in tuenda pudicitia
uxorum nostrarum, sed ita experrecti non sumus ut a te ca-
16 vere possimus; audacia tua vincit studia nostra. ecquod
hunc movere possit, patres conscripti, factum aut dictum
turpe, quem non puduerit palam nobis audientibus adulterium confiteri? quod si tibi per me nihil respondere vo-
luissem, sed illum censorium eloquium Appii Claudii et L.
Pisonis, integerrimorum virorum, quo usus est quisque

[22] despectus (*Norden*)

---

[14] The learned P. Nigidius Figulus was well known as a student of the occult and leader of a group of self-styled Pythagoreans. He was also a friend and political ally of Cicero—who did not accuse him of necromancy and ritual murder in *Vatin*. 14, as stated by Ernout (p. 65).

[15] Irony, of course. On Sallust's widely reported affair with Milo's wife Fausta, which allegedly earned him a beating at the

though he himself cannot answer when asked who lives in his own paternal home. Ah, but I shall be told that these were the slips of inexperienced youth, and that he later reformed. Not so; he fell into Nigidius' sacrilege club.[14] Twice brought before a judge's bench, he was in the direst straits and came off leaving the impression, not that he was innocent, but that the jury had perjured themselves. Beginning his official career as Quaestor, he held this place and this order in contempt seeing that it had given admittance to despicable a creature as himself. Fearing therefore that his misdeeds might not come to your knowledge,[15] scandal though he was to all respectably married men, he confessed to adultery in your hearing and your faces did not bring a blush to his. Never mind how you have lived, Sallustius, or what you have done: all we ask is that only yourself be privy to your crimes. Don't tax us too much with our slackness and lethargy. We are careful to protect our wives, but not wide awake enough to guard against you; your boldness is too much for our endeavours. Could any shaming act or speech disturb him, Conscript Fathers, a man who was not embarrassed to confess to adultery in your hearing? Suppose I had not chosen to answer you myself but recited that censorial pronouncement of Appius Claudius and Lucius Piso,[16] gentlemen of the highest character, openly and to all citizens, a pronounce-

hands of the injured husband, see Funaioli in Pauly–Wissowa, *Real-Encyclopädie* IA, 1916f. The confession in the Senate is not mentioned anywhere else.

16 Caesoninus (Consul in 58), not Frugi (as Ernout). As Censors the two expelled Sallust from the Senate in 51. But their own characters were not above reproach.

eorum pro lege,[23] palam universis recitarem, nonne tibi viderer aeternas inurere maculas, quas reliqua vita tua eluere non posset?

Neque post illum dilectum senatus umquam te vidimus; nisi forte in ea te castra coniecisti quo omnis sentina
17 rei publicae confluxerat. at idem Sallustius, qui in pace ne senator quidem manserat, postea quam res publica armis oppressa est, [et] idem a victore[24] qui exsules reduxit in senatum per[25] quaesturam est reductus. quem honorem ita gessit ut nihil in eo non venale habuerit cuius aliquis emptor fuerit, ita egit ut nihil non aequum ac verum duxerit quod ipsi facere collibuisset, neque aliter vexavit ac debuit
18 si quis praedae loco magistratum accepisset. peracta quaestura, postea quam magna pignora eis dederat cum quibus similitudine vitae se coniunxerat, unus iam ex illo grege videbatur. eius enim partis erat Sallustius quo tamquam in unam voraginem coetus omnium vitiorum excesserat: quicquid impudicorum, c<h>ilonum,[26] parricidarum, sacrilegorum, debitorum fuit in urbe, municipiis, coloniis, Italia tota, sicut in fretis subsederant, homines[27] perditi ac notissimi, nulla in parte castris apti nisi licentia vitiorum et cupiditate rerum novarum.

19 'At postea quam praetor est factus, modeste se gessit et abstinenter.' non<ne> ita provinciam vastavit ut nihil

[23] *dist. SB** [24] et idem victores (*Jordan*)
[25] post (*Mommsen*) [26] (*Maurenbrecher*)
[27] nominis (*Gul.*)

[17] There was no 'perhaps.' Sallust fought on Caesar's side in the Civil War.

ment which each one of them has treated as a law, don't you think I would have branded you for all time with marks that the remainder of your life could not wash away?

After that selection of the Senate we saw no more of you—unless perhaps[17] you flung yourself into that army into which all the bilge water of the commonwealth had flowed. But that same Sallustius who in peacetime had not even kept his place as a Senator, that same was brought back into the Senate by way of a Quaestorship[18] after the commonwealth had been crushed by arms, by a conqueror who restored exiles. He so functioned in that office that there was nothing for which there was a buyer that he did not have for sale. He exploited it on the principle that nothing he wanted to do was other than fair and right. He abused it as anyone receiving a magistracy as a kind of plunder might be expected to do. Having got through his Quaestorship, he now seemed one of that crew with whom he had associated himself by similarity of life; he had given them no small pledges. For Sallustius belonged to that party into which a conflux of all vices had overflowed as into a single quagmire. Every rake, every pervert, every murderer, every sacrilege-monger, every debtor in Rome and the municipalities and the colonies and all Italy had sunk as it were to the bottom of the sea, desperate and notorious men,[19] in no way fitted for soldiering except in the license of their vices and their eagerness for revolution.

Ah, but after he was elected Praetor he behaved with temperance and self-restraint. Did he not lay his province

18 A second Quaestorship, probably in 48.

19 Sallust *Catiline* 14 may be in mind; cf. also *Letters to Atticus* 187 (IX.18).2.

neque passi sint neque exspectaverint gravius in bello socii nostri quam experti sunt in pace hoc Africam interiorem obtinente? unde tantum hic exhausit quantum potuit aut fide nominum traici aut in naves contrudi: tantum, inquam, exhausit, patres conscripti, quantum voluit. Ne causam diceret sestertio duodecies cum Caesare paciscitur. quod si quippiam eorum falsum est, his palam refelle: ‹dic›[28] unde, qui modo ne paternam quidem domum reluere[29] potueris, repente tamquam somnio beatus hortos pretiosissimos, villam Tiburtem[30] C. Caesaris, reliquas pos-
20 sessiones paraveris. neque piguit quarere cur ego P. Crassi domum emissem, cum tu eius[31] villae dominus sis cuius paulo ante fuerat Caesar. modo, inquam, patrimonio non comesto sed devorato quibus rationibus repente factus es tam adfluens et tam beatus? nam quis te faceret heredem, quem ne amicum quidem suum satis honestum quisquam sibi ducit nisi similis ac par tui? at hercules egregia facta maiorum tuorum te extollunt, quorum sive tu similis es sive illi tui nihil ad omnium scelus ac nequitiam addi potest.
21 verum, ut opinor, honores tui te faciunt insolentem. tu, C. Sallusti, idem[32] putas esse bis senatorem et bis quaestorem fieri quod bis consularem et bis triumphalem? carere decet omni vitio qui in alterum dicere parat; is[33] demum male dicit qui non potest verum ab altero ‹male›[34] audire. sed tu, omnium mensarum assecula, omnium cubiculo-

[28] (*SB**) [29] relinire
[30] tiburti (*Cortius*)
[31] vetus (*Baiter*)
[32] totidem (*Jordan*: tantundem *vel* tantum *codd. nonnulli*)
[33] paratus *vel* p- est *vel* parat (*Jordan*)
[34] (*SB* coll. Ter. Hec. 600*)

waste? Did our allies ever suffer or expect in war anything worse than they experienced in peace when this man was governor of Inner Africa? He drained the province of all that could be transferred in bonds or thrust aboard ships. Yes, Conscript Fathers, he scooped up as much as he wanted. To avoid prosecution he struck a bargain with Caesar: 1,200,000 sesterces. If any of this is false, refute it in front of these gentlemen: state the source from which you, who could not even pay off the mortgage on your father's house, suddenly rich as in a dream acquired a very valuable suburban estate,[20] Caesar's villa at Tibur,[21] and the rest of your properties. And you, owner of a villa that had recently been Caesar's, did not scruple to ask why I bought P. Crassus' house! You had just, I won't say consumed but devoured your patrimony; by what means did you suddenly become so affluent, so rich? Nobody would have left you his money, for nobody thinks you respectable enough to be his friend, except someone of the same breed as yourself. Oh, but the splendid deeds of your forebears raise you high! Whether you resemble them or they resembled you, all of them were criminals or good-for-nothings of the very worst description. But I suppose it's your offices that make you insolent! Gaius Sallustius, do you think that being twice a Senator and twice a Quaestor is the same as having two Consulships and two Triumphs? Anyone who sets about to denounce another person should be beyond reproach. Only someone who cannot be reviled truthfully reviles. But you! A hanger-on at every dinner table, a fancy

20 The *horti Sallustiani* of Tacitus *Annals* 13.47.

21 Not attested otherwise.

rum in aetate paelex et idem postea adulter, omnis ordinis
22 turpitudo es et civilis belli memoria. quid enim hoc gravius pati potuimus quam quod te incolumem in hoc ordine videmus? desine bonos petulantissime consectari, desine morbo procacitatis isto uti, desine unumquemque moribus tuis aestimare. his moribus amicum tibi efficere non potes: videris velle inimicum habere.

Finem dicendi faciam, patres conscripti; saepe enim vidi gravius offendere animos auditorum eos qui aliena flagitia aperte dixerunt quam eos qui commiserunt. mihi quidem ratio habenda est, non quae Sallustius merito debeat audire, sed ut ea dicam, si qua ego honeste effari possim.

boy in every bedroom when you were young and an adulterer later on, you are a disgrace to every order and a reminder of the Civil War. What worse could we undergo than to see you as a citizen in this order? Give it up: the truculent attacks on good men, the indulgence in your pathological insolence, the judging of others by your own character—give it up! You can't make a friend by such behaviour. You seem to want to have an enemy.

I shall bring my words to a close, Conscript Fathers. For I have often seen that those who speak candidly of the enormities of others offend the ears of their audience more gravely than those who perpetrate the same. I have to put my mind not to what Sallustius deserves to hear but to saying what can properly be said by me.

HANDBOOK OF ELECTIONEERING

EDITED BY D. R. SHACKLETON BAILEY

TRANSLATION AND INTRODUCTION BY

MARY ISOBEL HENDERSON

PREFATORY NOTE

An edition of the *Commentariolum* appeared in the Loeb series (Cicero XXVIII) in 1972 with translation, notes, and introduction by M. I. Henderson, who died before completing it. Her work was revised by E. H. Warmington, then Editor of the series, who added a text and critical notes along with the supplementary matter at the end of the Introduction.

I have kept most of this valuable legacy. But the text, with three changes, is that of my Teubner edition of 1998, and the critical notes are in line with the others in this volume. A few changes have been made in Henderson's translation. Some of her notes have been retained, others replaced, and further notes have been added. And the index is new.

To the bibliography Warmington gives in his addendum to the Introduction should now be added: D. Nardo, *Il Commentariolum Petitionis* (Padua 1970) 1–37, and the bibliographical survey by J.-M. Davies et al. in *Aufstieg und Niedergang der römischen Welt* 1.3(1973). 239–77.

There still appears to be no consensus on the question of authorship. If the treatise is indeed apocryphal, it is on a very different level from the other 'forgeries' in this volume.

D.R.S.B.

INTRODUCTION

From mid-65 to mid-64 B.C. Marcus Tullius Cicero was campaigning for election to a consulship of 63. Of his six competitors two were formidable. Both were "nobles" (i.e., of consular ancestry). C. Antonius, who ca. 77 had evaded trial for plundering Greece, was desperate for office and money, and talked of raising a slave rebellion if he failed.[1] L. Sergius Catilina, who had bribed a court to acquit him of misgovernment in Africa, did not launch his rebellion until 63, after a second defeat, but he was known to be capable of violence.[2] A notorious killer in Sulla's proscriptions, he was suspected of some part in an abortive plot in 66 which had by now leaked out; Cicero, attacking his rivals in the pre-election speech *In toga candida*, hinted darkly at these current rumours.[3] In alarm the leading nobles turned to Cicero, a "new man" or commoner, who had at first expected little help from them.[4] Against their authority he had carried the appointment of Pompey to the command which still kept him away in the east. In

[1] *In toga cand.*, Asconius p. 78 Kiessling-Schoell.

[2] *In toga cand.*, Asconius 76; Sallust, *Cat.* 18, 23 (unreasonably doubted because the speech of *Cat.* 20 is fictitious).

[3] *In toga cand.*, Asconius 82.

[4] Cic. *Ad Att.* I. 2. 2.

general repute he was reckoned "Popular," as opposed to the aristocratic "Optimates." But these were rhetorical labels, and implied no rigid political alignments. Cicero was favoured by the class of his origin, the wealthy Knights, including the big contractors of public revenue; his connections with the Italian bourgeoisie were wide; his influence could unite the stable elements of society in the election itself and in any danger to come; and the Roman nobility were intelligent enough to recognize the mental power and fire that matched him with Catiline's versatile energy. Their judgement was endorsed. Cicero headed the poll; Antonius narrowly beat Catiline for the other consulship.

The "Handbook of Electioneering" (as it calls itself) or Canvassing either is, or pretends to be, addressed to Marcus Cicero by his younger brother Quintus during this canvass. The question of its authenticity starts from the transmission of the text.[5] It is preserved with Letters *ad Familiares*, but is not contained in our oldest and best manuscript, the Codex Mediceus 49.9. In other manuscripts it occurs after the spurious "Letter of Cicero to Octavian." These facts do not prove that it is spurious, but they place burden of proof equally upon those who accept the authorship of Quintus and those who ascribe it to some later ancient writer. There is no presumption in favour of either.

Although it has the usual epistolary superscription, the document is not a letter but a treatise. At the end Marcus is asked to improve it, as if for publication. Its flat-footed

[5] For the stemmatology see W. S. Watt, *Ciceronis Epistulae* III (Oxford Classical Texts), pp. 180ff.

pedagogic style, broken by one ineptly rhetorical patch, is disappointing in the brother whose diction Marcus praised for simple elegance, and whose four extant letters are at least lively.[6] Letters, however, cannot provide a proper stylistic criterion for a treatise; and we have no other prose of Quintus to compare.

More specific arguments have been based on verbal reminiscence. Several passages in the handbook correspond so closely to extant passages of Marcus' lost invective *In toga candida* that one of the two indubitably lifted them from the other.[7] Nearly all these correspondences fall in the rhetorical patch, *Comm.* 8–12; and the abrupt stylistic switch would be easier to explain if the handbook were a later work drawing on Marcus' invective. The alternative is to suppose that Quintus capriciously garnished his treatise with some few rhetorical flourishes which, by a lucky chance, came in useful for the impromptu invective of Marcus. This hypothesis seems the less probable of the two; yet it is not to be rigorously excluded.

Such factual items as the handbook contains might be common knowledge both to Quintus and to a later student

[6] Cic. *De or.* 2.10; *Ad fam.* XVI.8, 16, 26, 27.

[7] § 2: consulatu putari: *In toga cand.*, Asconius 76–77. § 8: certare non posse: *In toga* cand., Asconius 74. § 9: Tanusiorum: compare Asconius 75, summarizing *In toga cand.* (but the list of names has a variant). § 10: dextra secuerit: *In toga cand.*, Asconius 78. § 10: manu tulerit: *In toga cand.*, Asconius 80. § 10: suspicionem relinqueret: *In toga cand.*, Asconius 82. § 12: sicas destringere: *In toga cand.*, Asconius 83. Further coincidences with speeches may or may not be accidental—§ 9: Quam ob rem?: *Pro Murena* 73. § 9: in caede civium: *De har. resp.* 42. § 34: facultatis habiturus: *Pro Mur.* 44. § 35: pluris veniunt: *Pro Mur.* 44.

of Marcus' speeches.[8] It has been argued that no later writer would have omitted the abortive plot of 66, as the handbook does—whereas Quintus might, theoretically, have written before the story leaked.[9] But in fact, most imperial writers do omit this dim affair; and an imperial reader of *In toga candida* would be little impressed by the brief and oblique allusion to a plot which never matured.[10] The plot is indispensable only in modern books; for antiquity, the argument from silence is negative.

Positive errors have not been demonstrated; nor have doubts been dispelled. Almost certainly (for instance) the handbook dates Marcus' defence of Q. Gallius before the election, against the weighty authority of Asconius.[11] It appears unaware of the distinction between the genuine Sodalities—religious or social clubs—and the gangs for electoral bribery which usurped the name of Sodality, probably not before 58.[12] It implies that Marcus had defended ex-consuls, which he is not known to have done before 63.[13] It denounces Catiline for the same misdeeds, including incest with a sister, for which Marcus denounced

[8] The few details not known to ourselves (mostly in *Comm.* 8–10) might come from *In toga candida* or other lost works.

[9] Something, however, was rumoured by July/August, 65 (Cic. *Pro Sulla* 81).

[10] *In toga cand.*, Asconius 82, beginning "praetereo" ("I pass over"); Asconius supplies the omitted data. See further *Journ. Rom. Stud.*, 1950, pp. 13f.

[11] *Comm.* 19; Asconius 78. [But see on this J. P. V. D. Balsdon, in *Classical Quarterly* N.S. 13 (1963), p. 249.—*E.H.W.*]

[12] *Comm.* 19. See further *Journ. Rom. Stud.*, 1950, p. 12.

[13] *Comm.* 2. See R. G. M. Nisbet, *Journ. Rom. Stud.*, 1961, pp. 84–87 (also arguing derivation from *In toga candida* 76–77).

Clodius in similar words.[14] The reply that incest was a commonplace of invective would be more relevant if the *commentariolum* were a speech; it does nothing to allay suspicion of the manual's invective repertory. None of these points, indeed, can be carried to the length of formal proof, but their cumulative effect is disquieting in a document of dubious transmission.

The question remains: why was the handbook written? Manuals addressed as letters were common in Greek, and two Latin works of Ciceronian date are cited as parallels. About Varro's *commentarius* of 71, instructing Pompey in senatorial procedure, no details are known;[15] but Marcus Cicero's letter of 59 to Quintus, on the duties of a provincial governor, has some general likeness to the *commentariolum*. In particular, both confess that the recipient has nothing to learn from them;[16] and therefore the triteness of the handbook's information is no argument against its authenticity. Yet Marcus wrote his letter with a practical purpose: to console Quintus for being kept in Asia, and exhort him to improve his ways as a governor. More simply, he wrote because Quintus was abroad. But in 65/64 Quintus was in Italy, and presumably with his brother canvassing.[17] At this time, a plausible reason for pestering Marcus with platitudes on electioneering is hard to con-

[14] *Comm.* 9; cf. Cic. *De har. resp.* 42.

[15] Gellius 14.7 describes a more general treatment written thirty or forty years later, after the *commentarius* was lost.

[16] *Comm.* 1 and 58; Cic. *Ad Q.F.* I.1.18. (*Cf. Ad Q.F.* I.2 for Marcus' more outspoken criticism of Quintus).

[17] Aedile 65, private senator 64. Had he been prevented from his canvassing duty, he must surely have referred to the fact.

ceive. The handbook itself seems uncertain of its own purpose; it hints at publication, yet includes some items which could not be published without damage to both brothers.[18]

Alternatively, the *commentariolum* may have been suggested to a later writer by the letter of 59. That the subject should occur to a forger or an essayist would not be surprising. The election of 64 was among the chosen topics of Ciceronian fakes; bogus replies to *In toga candida* from Antonius and Catiline were circulating more than a century later.[19] Exercises impersonating historical characters on set occasions were taught and practised keenly in higher education.[20] A favourite type was the letter of advice to a great man from a counsellor; and the picture of Quintus as his brother's counsellor had been painted for posterity by Marcus himself.[21] The theme and the literary interest were ready to hand at any time down to (say) Trajan's reign. What some scholars doubt is whether an imitator could have avoided transparent blunders. Others would attribute higher standards of accomplishment to the ancient art of literary impersonation (*prosopopoeia*).[22]

In the present division of opinion, simple observation may be more useful than argument. Whether Quintus wrote it or not, the *commentariolum* is, as it claims to

[18] e.g., *Comm.* 5, 19, 35, 42, 45–47, 52.

[19] Asconius 84.

[20] Quintilian III. 8. 48–70, and see Letter to Octavian. On supposititious letters of instruction, see Sykutris, P.-W. Suppl. V, 202–203 (in art. "Epistolographie").

[21] Cic. *Post red. in sen.* 37; *De or.* 1.4; *Ad Q.F.* I.1.43.

[22] Compare R. Syme, *Sallust*, p. 324 (discussing the parallel dispute over the *Suasoriae* ascribed to Sallust).

be, an academic composition, undertaken "for the sake of bringing into one focus, by logical classification, matters which in real life seem disconnected and indeterminate."[23] Its practical advice is superfluous, as it admits, and often inept or naïve: for instance, Marcus is to tell the "Optimate" nobles (who detested Pompey) that he had posed as "Popular" only to get Pompey's support.[24] As it also implies, it is written in leisured circumstances.[25] Its comments and aphorisms, though sometimes vivacious, lack the sense of urgency. Marcus, in two letters of 65, reveals the personal pressures and shifting odds within the electorate, which he later compared to the deep sea surge;[26] the handbook presents a blueprint of the perfect canvass in which every good citizen will vote for Marcus. Whatever its date, the attempt to reduce a Roman election to terms of an armchair exercise is deliberate and successful.

[The author in § 58 refers to his work as *commentariolum petitionis*. This title or designation appears as *Commentarium Consulatus Petitionis* in the better manuscripts, as *De Petitione Consulatus* in inferior manuscripts, which also say that the work is Quintus Cicero's addressed to his brother Marcus.

That the author was not Quintus Cicero was argued long ago by A. Eussner, *Comment. Pet. examinatum atque*

[23] *Comm.* 1.

[24] *Comm.* 5. For Marcus' very different view of the absent Pompey's standpoint see Cic. *Ad Att.* I.1.2, with D. R. Shackleton Bailey's comment.

[25] *Comm.* 58.

[26] Cic. *Ad Att.* I.1 and 2; *Pro Planc.* 15.

emendatum, Würzburg, 1872, and by G. L. Hendrickson, in *Amer. Journ. of Philol.* 13 (1892), pp. 200–212, and *The Comm. Pet. attributed to Q. Cicero*, Univ. of Chicago, 1904; and the attribution was defended by others (see, *e.g.*, R. Y. Tyrrell and L. C. Purser, *The Correspondence of Cicero*, I, ed. 3, 1904, pp. 116–132). More recently it was defended vigorously by E. H. Clift, *Latin Pseudepigrapha*, Baltimore, 1945, and supported by R. Till in *Historia*, 11 (1962), pp. 315–338. But Mrs. Henderson (of whose arguments Till does not take account), in *Journ. of Roman Studies*, 40 (1950), pp. 8–21, presented a cogent case against it (cf. R. G. M. Nisbet, "*The Comm. Pet.*: Some arguments against authenticity," in *Journ. of Roman Studies*, 51 (1961), pp. 84–87; W. S. Watt, *M. Tull. Cic. Epp.* Vol. III, 1958, p. 179). Her arguments were criticized by J. P. V. D. Balsdon in *Classical Quarterly*, 56 = N.S. 13 (1963), pp. 242–250. When she wrote this introduction to the *Comm. Pet.* for the Loeb Classical Library, she had modified her attitude. In any case the matter must be left undecided. –E.H.W.]

COMMENTARIOLUM PETITIONIS

Scr., si modo Q. Ciceronis est, priore parte an. 64

QUINTUS MARCO FRATRI S.D.

1 Etsi tibi omnia suppetunt ea quae consequi ingenio aut usu homines aut diligentia possunt, tamen amore nostro non sum alienum arbitratus ad te perscribere ea quae mihi veniebant in mentem dies ac noctes de petitione tua cogitanti, non ut aliquid ex his novi addisceres,[1] sed ut ea quae in re dispersa atque infinita viderentur esse ratione et distributione sub uno aspectu ponerentur. [quamquam plurimum natura[2] valet, tamen videtur in paucorum mensum negotio posse simulatio naturam vincere.][3]

2 Civitas quae sit cogita, quid petas, qui sis. prope cottidie tibi hoc ad forum descendenti meditandum est:[4] 'novus sum, consulatum peto, Roma est.'

Nominis novitatem dicendi gloria maxime sublevabis. semper ea res plurimum dignitatis habuit; non potest qui dignus habetur patronus consularium indignus consulatu

[1] addiscerem (*Lamb.*)

[2] naturarum

[3] quamquam . . . vincere (*SB: post 42* videare *Puteanus, bene*)

[4] sit (*Tydeman*)

HANDBOOK OF ELECTIONEERING

QUINTUS TO HIS BROTHER MARCUS

Although you are furnished with all that men can acquire by ability, experience, or application, I thought it in keeping with our affection to write in full to you what has been coming into my mind as I think day and night about your canvass—not that you would learn anything new from it, but for the sake of bringing into one focus, by logical classification, matters which in real life seem disconnected and indeterminate. Though nature is strong indeed, yet an assumed personality can, it seems, overcome the natural self for an affair of a few months.[1]

Consider what city this is, what is it you seek, who you are. Every day or so, as you go down to the Forum, you must repeat to yourself: "I am 'new'; I seek the consulship; this is Rome."

For your status as a "new man" you will compensate chiefly by your fame as a speaker. Great prestige has always attached to this; an advocate deemed worthy to defend ex-consuls cannot be thought unworthy of the consulship.

[1] [I bracketed the text. The sentence is irrelevant here, but could well follow 'natural act' in § 42, as suggested by Puteanus. – SB.]

putari. quam ob rem quoniam ab hac laude proficisceris et quicquid es ex hoc es, ita paratus ad dicendum venito quasi in singulis causis iudicium de omni ingenio futurum sit.
3 eius facultatis adiumenta, quae tibi scio esse seposita, ut parata ac prompta sint cura, et saepe quae <de>[5] Demosthenis studio et exercitatione scripsit Demetrius recordare. deinde <fac>[6] ut amicorum et multitudo et genera appareant; habes enim ea quae <non multi homines>[7] novi habuerunt: omnis publicanos, totum fere equestrem ordinem, multa propria municipia, multos abs te defensos homines cuiusque ordinis, aliquot collegia, praeterea studio dicendi conciliatos plurimos adulescentulos, cottidianam
4 amicorum adsiduitatem et frequentiam. haec cura ut teneas comm<on>endo[8] et rogando et omni ratione efficiendo ut intellegant qui debent tua causa, referendae gratiae, qui volunt, obligandi tui tempus sibi aliud nullum fore. etiam hoc multum videtur adiuvare posse novum hominem, hominum nobilium voluntas et maxime consularium; prodest, quorum in locum ac numerum pervenire velis, ab
5 iis ipsis illo loco ac numero dignum putari. ii rogandi omnes sunt diligenter et ad eos adlegandum est persuadendumque est iis nos semper cum optimatibus de re publica sensisse, minime popularis fuisse; si quid locuti populariter videamur, id nos eo consilio fecisse ut nobis Cn. Pompeium adiungeremus, ut eum qui plurimum posset aut amicum in nostra petitione haberemus aut certe non ad-

5 (*Squarzaficus*) 6 (*Buecheler*)
7 (*Baiter*) 8 (*Koch*)

2 See Cic. *De div*. 2.96: by practising, Demosthenes learned to pronounce R.

Therefore—since you start with this repute, and are what you are because of it—present yourself as well prepared for your speeches as if all your intellectual powers were to be judged on each single case. Take care that the aids to eloquence, which I know you have in reserve, are ready to hand; and often remind yourself what Demetrius wrote of Demosthenes' efforts and exercises.[2] Then, see to it that you show off both the number and the variety of your friends, for not many "new men" have had as many as *you* have—all the contractors of public revenues, virtually all the Order of Knights, many boroughs in your pocket, many men of all ranks whom you have defended at law, several Colleges; also, large numbers of young men drawn to you by the pursuit of oratory, and a crowd of friends in daily and constant attendance. See that you hold on by admonitions, requests, or any other means of making it clear that there will never be another chance for those who owe you a debt to thank you, or for the well-disposed to put you under an obligation to themselves. Further, a "new man" can be greatly helped by the good will of nobles, and especially of the ex-consuls; it is an advantage that those whose position and company you wish to attain should think you worthy of that position and company. They must all be diligently canvassed, and you must send friends to persuade them that our political sympathies have always been with the "Optimates"; we have been far from "Popular" in politics;[3] if we ever appear to have spoken in a "Popular" way, we did it with the purpose of attaching Gnaeus Pompey to ourselves, in order to have him, with his very great power, as a friend in our canvass, or at least not an opponent. Take

[3] See Introduction.

6 versarium. praeterea adulescentis nobilis elabora ut habeas, vel ut teneas studiosos quos habes; multum dignitatis adferent. plurimos habes; perfice ut sciant quantum in iis putes esse. si adduxeris ut ii qui non nolunt cupiant, plurimum proderunt.[9]

7 Ac multum etiam novitatem tuam adiuvat quod eius modi nobiles tecum petunt ut nemo sit qui audeat dicere plus illis nobilitatem quam tibi virtutem prodesse oportere. nam P. Galbam et L. Cassium summo loco natos quis est qui petere consulatum putet? vides igitur amplissimis ex familiis homines, quod sine nervis sint, tibi paris non
8 esse. at Antonius et Catilina molesti sunt. immo homini navo,[10] industrio, innocenti, diserto, gratioso apud eos qui res iudicant, optandi competitores, ambo a pueritia sicarii, ambo libidinosi, ambo egentes. eorum alterius bona proscripta vidimus, vocem denique audivimus iurantis se Romae iudicio aequo cum homine Graeco certare non posse, ex senatu eiectum scimus optimorum[11] censorum existimatione, in praetura competitorem habuimus amico Sabidio et Panthera, cum[12] ad tabulam quos poneret non haberet (quo iam[13] in magistratu amicam quam domi palam haberet de machinis emit); in petitione autem consulatus caupones omnis compilare per turpissimam

[9] proderit *Facciolati*
[10] novo (*Puteanus*)
[11] optima vero (*Eussner*)
[12] quam (*Lamb.*)
[13] tamen (*SB*)

---

[4] See Asconius 72; Cic. *Pro Mur.* 17; *Ad Att.* I.1.1.
[5] Antonius (Asconius 75).

pains, besides, to acquire young nobles, or rather to keep the enthusiasm of those whom you have acquired; they will bring you great prestige. You have acquired a large number; make them realize how important you think them. If you can bring those who are not against you to be eager for you, they will be most useful to you.

Another great help for your status as a "new man" is that your noble competitors are persons of whom nobody would venture to say that they should get more from their rank than you from your moral excellence. Who would think that Publius Galba and Lucius Cassius, high-born as they are, are candidates for the consulship?[4] So you see that men of the greatest families are not equal to you, because they lack vigour. Or are Antonius and Catiline supposed to be the trouble? On the contrary, two assassins from boyhood, both libertines, both paupers, are just the competitors to be prayed for by a man of energy, industry, and blameless life, an eloquent speaker, with influence among those who judge in the law courts. Of those two, we have seen the one[5] sold up by legal process; we have heard him declare on oath that he cannot compete in fair trial in Rome against a Greek; we know he was expelled from the Senate by the decision of admirable censors. He was a fellow candidate of ours for the praetorship, when Sabidius and Panthera were his only friends, when he had no slaves left to auction off (already in office he bought from the stands in the slave market a girl friend to keep openly at home).[6] In consular candidature, rather than present himself to solicit the votes of the Roman People, he preferred

[6] [See critical note. Even after his election he had to go to the slave market to get himself a girl. –SB.]

legationem maluit quam adesse et populo Romano sup-
9 plicare. alter vero, di boni! quo splendore est? primum nobilitate eadem [qua Catilina].[14] num maiore? non. sed virtute. quam ob rem? quod Antonius umbram suam metuit, hic ne leges quidem, natus in patris egestate, educatus in sororiis[15] stupris, corroboratus in caede civium, cuius primus ad rem publicam aditus in equitibus Romanis occidendis fuit (nam illis quos meminimus Gallis, qui tum Titiniorum ac Nann‹e›iorum ac Tanusiorum capita deme‹te›bant,[16] Sulla unum Catilinam praefecerat); in quibus ille hominem optimum, Q. Caucilium,[17] sororis suae virum, equitem Romanum, nullarum partium, cum semper
10 natura tum etiam aetate iam quietum, suis manibus occidit. quid ego nunc dicam petere eum tecum consulatum qui hominem carissimum populo Romano, M. Marium, inspectante populo Romano vitibus per totam urbem ceciderit, ad bustum egerit, ibi omni cruciatu lacerarit, ‹vix›[18] vivo ‹et›[19] spiranti[20] collum gladio sua dextera secuerit, cum sinistra capillum eius a vertice teneret, caput sua manu tulerit, cum inter digitos eius rivi sanguinis fluerent; qui postea cum histrionibus et cum gladiatoribus ita vixit ut alteros libidinis, alteros facinoris adiutores haberet; qui

14 (*Muretus*: qua C. Antonius *Man.*)
15 sororis *vel* -ore *vel* -orum (*Watt*)
16 (*Verburgius*)
17 Caecilium *Ascon., vulg., ut coni. Man.*
18 (*SB; cf. Harv. Stud. 96 (1994).197 sq.*) 19 (*SB*)
20 stanti (*Puteanus*)

7 [Or possibly 'sisters'; as in Clodius' case there may have been more than one. –SB.]

a most wicked mission abroad, where he plundered all the innkeepers. As to the other, good heavens! What is his claim to glory? First, he has the same noble birth. Any greater nobility? No. But he has greater manliness. Why? Only because Antonius is afraid of his own shadow, whereas Catiline does not even fear the law. Born in his father's beggary, bred in debauchery with his sister,[7] grown up in civil slaughter, his first entry into public life was a massacre of Roman Knights (for Sulla had put Catiline in sole charge of those Gauls we remember, who kept mowing off the heads of Titinius and Nanneius and Tanusius and all). Among them he killed with his own hands his sister's husband, the excellent Quintus Caucilius,[8] a Roman Knight, a neutral in politics, a man always inoffensive by nature and by that time also through advancing age. Need I go on? *He* to be running for the consulship with you—he who scourged Marcus Marius, the Roman People's darling, all around the town before the Roman People's eyes, drove him to the tomb,[9] mangled him there with every torture, and with a sword in his right hand, holding his head of hair in his left, severed the man's neck as he barely lived and breathed and carried the head in his hand, while rills of blood flowed between his fingers! And then he lived with actors and gladiators as his accomplices, the former in lust, the latter in crime—he who could not enter any place

[8] [From Asconius on, this rare name has been 'banalized' into Caecilius. It was restored in my Teubner edition. –SB.]

[9] M. Marius Gratidianus, a partisan of the great Marius, was killed in 82 by the Sullan Catiline at the tomb of Catulus, who had been forced to suicide by the Marians in 87. The *commentariolum* omits the genitive *Catuli* (*Journ. Rom. Stud.*, 1961, pp. 86f.).

nullum in locum tam sanctum ac tam religiosum accessit in quo non, etiam si in aliis culpa non esset, tamen ex sua nequitia dedecoris suspicionem relinqueret; qui ex curia Curios et Annios, ab atriis Sapalas et Carvilios, ex equestri ordine Pompilios et Vettios sibi amicissimos comparavit;[21] qui tantum habet audaciae, tantum nequitiae, tantum denique in libidine artis et efficacitatis, ut prope in parentum gremiis praetextatos liberos constuprarit? quid ego nunc tibi de Africa, quid de testium dictis scribam? nota sunt, et ea tu saepius legito; sed tamen hoc mihi non praetermittendum videtur, quod primum ex eo iudicio tam egens discessit quam quidam iudices eius ante illud iudicium fuerunt, deinde tam invidiosus ut aliud in eum iudicium cottidie flagitetur. hic se sic habet ut magis contemnam
11 siquid commoverit quam ut timeam etiam si quierit.[22] quanto melior tibi fortuna petitionis data est quam nuper homini novo, C. Coelio! ille cum duobus hominibus ita nobilissimis petebat ut tamen in iis omnia pluris essent quam ipsa nobilitas, summa ingenia, summus pudor, plurima beneficia, summa ratio ac diligentia petendi; ac tamen eorum alterum Coelius, cum multo inferior esset genere,
12 superior nulla re paene, superavit. qua re tibi, si facies ea quae natura et studia quibus semper usus es largiuntur, quae temporis tui ratio desiderat, quae potes, quae debes,

[21] compararit (*Squarzaficus*)

[22] magis timeat (-ant *Tydeman, vulg.*) etiam si quierit quam ut contemnat (-ant *idem*) si quid commoverit (*sero sapiens SB**, *qui etiam* -as . . . -as *conieceram*).

---

[10] [See P. Harvey, *Amer. Journ. Phil.* 109 (1980).116. –SB.]

[11] [Probably the informer of *Letters to Atticus* 44 (II.24). –SB]

[12] Catiline was tried in July/August, 65 for misgovernment in

so sacred and holy that he did not leave it under suspicion of being polluted by his mere wickedness, even if other people were guiltless; who got as his closest friends from the Senate House men like Curius and Annius, from the auctioneers' halls men like Sapala[10] and Carvilius, from the Order of Knights men like Pompilius and Vettius;[11] who has such impudence, such wickedness, and besides such skill and efficiency in his lust that he has raped children in smocks practically at their parents' knees. Need I write now to you of Africa and the statements of the witnesses? All *that* is well known; read it yourself, again and again. Yet this, I think, I should not leave out—that he came out of that trial as impoverished as some of his jury were before that trial, and so hated that there are daily clamours for another prosecution against him.[12] His condition is such that, so far from fearing him even if he is doing nothing, I should despise him if he makes trouble.[13] How much better luck has fallen to you in your canvass than to C. Coelius, another "new man," a while ago![14] He stood against two men of the highest nobility, yet whose nobility was the least of their assets—great intelligence, high conscience, many claims to gratitude, great judgement and perseverance in electioneering; yet Coelius, though much inferior in birth and superior in almost nothing, defeated one of them. So for you, if you do what you are well endowed for doing by nature and by the studies which you have always practised—what the occasion demands, what

Africa and acquitted through bribery.

13 [See critical note. The new reading belatedly restores sense. –SB.].

14 C. Coelius Caldus, consul in 94 with L. Domitius Ahenobarbus (the unsuccessful noble is unknown).

non erit difficile certamen cum iis competitoribus qui nequaquam sunt tam genere insignes quam vitiis nobiles;[23]
quis enim reperiri potest tam improbus civis qui velit uno
suffragio duas in rem publicam sicas destringere?
13 Quoniam quae subsidia novitatis haberes et habere
posses exposui, nunc de magnitudine petitionis dicendum
videtur. consulatum petis, quo honore nemo est quin te dignum arbitretur, sed multi qui invideant; petis enim homo
ex equestri loco summum locum civitatis, atque ita summum ut forti homini, diserto, innocenti multo idem ille honos plus amplitudinis quam ceteris adferat. noli putare eos
qui sunt eo honore usi non videre, tu cum idem sis adeptus, quid dignitatis habiturus sis. eos vero qui consularibus
familiis nati locum maiorum consecuti non sunt suspicor
tibi, nisi si qui admodum te amant, invidere. etiam novos
homines praetorios existimo, nisi qui tuo beneficio vincti
14 sunt, nolle abs te se honore superari. iam in populo quam
multi invidi sint, quam multi consuetudine horum annorum ab honoribus novorum alienati, venire tibi in mentem
certo scio; esse etiam non nullos tibi iratos ex iis causis quas
egisti necesse est. iam illud tute circumspicito, quod ad
Cn. Pompei gloriam augendam tanto studio te dedisti,
num quos tibi putes ob eam causam esse <non>[24] amicos.
15 quam ob rem cum et summum locum civitatis petas et vi-
deas esse studia quae tibi adversentur, adhibeas necesse
est omnem rationem et curam et laborem et diligentiam.
16 Et petitio magistratuum divisa est in duarum rationum

[23] notabiles *coni. Warmington*

[24] (*Lamb.*)

you can and should do—it will not be a hard contest with these competitors who are by no means as eminent in birth as they are notable in vice. Can there be a citizen so vile as to want to unsheathe, with one vote, two daggers against the State?

Having explained what compensations for your status as a "new man" you have or could have, I think I should speak of the importance of this canvass. You seek the consulship, and there is nobody who does not think you worthy of the office, but many who envy you. You, by origin a Knight, seek the highest place in the body politic—the highest, and to a brave, accomplished, and upright man this office brings far more dignity than to any others. Do not think that those who have held the office will fail to see how much prestige will be yours when you have reached it. Men of consular families who have not risen to the position of their ancestors envy you, I suspect, unless they are very fond of you; and I think "new men" of praetorian standing, unless attached to you by your kindnesses, do not want to be surpassed by you in rank. Then, how many among the people are envious, how many, in the fashion of these years, are averse to "new men" in office, is a point which occurs to you, I am quite sure; and a good many must be angry with you in consequence of the cases that you have pleaded. Then, turn your thoughts to this: do you not think that certain people will be less than friendly because of your devoted efforts to glorify Pompey? Therefore, since you seek the highest place in the body politic, and since you see that there are interests opposed to you, it is necessary to apply all your judgement and care and effort and attentiveness.

Canvassing for magistracies is classified as attentive-

diligentiam, quarum altera in amicorum studiis, altera in
populari voluntate ponenda est. amicorum studia beneficiis et officiis et vetustate et facilitate ac iucunditate naturae parta esse oportet. sed hoc nomen amicorum in petitione latius patet quam in cetera vita; quisquis est enim qui
ostendat aliquid in te voluntatis, qui colat, qui domum ven-
titet, is in amicorum numero est habendus. sed tamen qui
sunt amici ex causa iustiore cognationis aut adfinitatis aut
sodalitatis aut alicuius necessitudinis, iis carum et iucun-
17 dum esse maxime prodest. deinde ut quisque est intimus
ac maxime domesticus, ut is amet ‹et› quam[25] amplissimum esse te cupiat valde elaborandum est, tum ut tribu-
les, ut vicini, ut clientes, ut denique liberti, postremo
etiam servi tui; nam fere omnis sermo ad forensem famam
18 a domesticis emanat auctoribus. deinde sunt instituendi
cuiusque generis amici: ad speciem, homines illustres honore ac nomine (qui, etiam si suffragandi studia non na-
vant, tamen adferunt petitori aliquid dignitatis); ad ius
obtinendum, magistratus (ex quibus maxime consules,[26]
deinde tribuni plebi); ad conficiendas centurias, homines
excellenti gratia. qui abs te tribum aut centuriam aut aliquod beneficium aut habeant aut ut habeant sperent, eos
prorsus magno opere et compara et confirma; nam per hos
annos homines ambitiosi vehementer omni studio atque
opera ‹e›laborarunt[27] ut possent a tribulibus suis ea quae
peterent impetrare; hos tu homines, quibuscumque poteris rationibus, ut ex animo atque [ex illa][28] summa volun-

[25] quod [26] consul (*Squarzaficus*) [27] (*Turn.*)
[28] (*Watt** (illa *iam del. Constans*))

---

[15] Here used in its proper sense of a religious or social club.

ness to two objects, the one concerned with securing support of friends, the other with securing favour of the People. The endeavours of friends should be enlisted by kindnesses and observance of duties and old acquaintance and affability and natural charm. But that word "friends" has a wider application in a canvass than in the rest of life, for anybody who shows you some good will, or cultivates your society, or calls upon you regularly, is to be counted as a "friend." Still, it is very useful to be on affectionate and pleasant terms with those who are friends on more genuine grounds—ties of blood or marriage, fellowship in a Sodality,[15] or some other bond. Next, all those who are nearest and most in your family circle must with every effort be brought to feel affection and wish you all possible success; so too must your fellow tribesmen, neighbours, and clients, then your freedmen, and finally even your slaves, for the talk which makes one's public reputation generally emanates from sources in one's own household. Then, you must set up friends of every sort: for show, men of illustrious career and name (who bring a candidate some prestige, even if they do not take an active interest in canvassing); to maintain your legal rights, magistrates (especially the consuls; next the tribunes of the People); for getting the votes of the centuries, persons of exceptional influence. Take special pains to recruit and retain those who have from you, or hope to have, control of a tribe or a century, or some other advantage; for in these days, electioneering experts have worked out, with all their eager will and resources, how to get what they want from their fellow tribesmen. Work by any means you can to make these persons sincere and whole-hearted supporters of your cause.

19 tate tui studiosi sint elaborato. quod si satis grati homines essent, haec tibi omnia parata esse debebant, sicuti parata esse confido. nam hoc biennio quattuor sodalitates hominum ad ambitionem gratiosissimorum tibi obligasti, C. Fundani, Q. Galli, C. Corneli, C. Orchivi; horum in causis ad te deferendis quid tibi eorum sodales receperint et confirmarint scio; nam interfui. qua re hoc tibi faciendum est, hoc tempore ut ab his quod debent exigas saepe commonendo, rogando, confirmando, curando ut intellegant nullum se umquam aliud tempus habituros referendae gratiae; profecto homines et spe reliquorum tuorum officiorum et[iam] recentibus beneficiis ad studium na-
20 vandum excitabuntur. et omnino, quoniam eo genere amicitiarum petitio tua maxime munita est quod ex causarum defensionibus adeptus es, fac ut plane iis omnibus quos devinctos tenes discriptum ac dispositum suum cuique munus sit; et quem ad modum nemini illorum molestus nulla in re umquam fuisti, sic cura ut intellegant omnia te
21 quae ab illis tibi deberi putaris ad hoc tempus reservasse. sed quoniam tribus rebus homines maxime ad benevolentiam atque haec suffragandi studia ducuntur,[29] beneficio, spe, adiunctione animi ac voluntate, animadvertendum est quem ad modum cuique horum generi sit inserviendum. minimis beneficiis homines adducuntur ut satis causae putent esse ad studium suffragationis, nedum ii quibus saluti fuisti, quos tu habes plurimos, non intellegant, si hoc tuo tempore tibi non satis fecerint, se probatos nemini um-

[29] adducuntur *Lamb.*

---

[16] Here "Sodality" is used in its usurped sense of a gang for

However, if people were grateful enough, all this should have been arranged for you, as I am sure it has; for in these last two years you have laid under obligation four Sodalities run by men of great influence in electioneering,[16] C. Fundanius, Q. Gallius, C. Cornelius, and C. Orchivius. I know (for I was present) what the members of the Sodalities undertook and assured for you when they entrusted you with the briefs for these four. So what you have to do is to exact from them on this occasion what they owe you by frequent admonitions, requests, assurances, making it clear that they will never have another chance to thank you. They will surely be spurred to active interest by the hope of your good offices in future and by your recent services. In general, since your campaign is amply supported by the kind of friendship which you have acquired by defending cases, make quite sure that a particular duty is apportioned and assigned to each of all whom you have laid under obligation; and since you have never before troubled any of them for anything, make it clear that you have kept in reserve for this occasion all your claims to what in your opinion they owe you. Now, since men are brought to good will and this interest in electoral support by three things in particular—benefits received, expectations, and spontaneous personal attachment—we must consider how to deal favourably with each of these categories. Very small benefits induce men to think that they have sufficient cause to support a canvass—much more would those (and you have a large number thus in your debt) whom you have saved from ruin understand that if they do not do their

electoral bribery. Cornelius, defended by Marcus in 65, ran a gang of this kind (Cic. *Pro Corn.*, Asconius 67; *Ad Q.F.* II.3.5; *In Vat.* 5).

quam fore; quod cum ita sit, tamen rogandi sunt atque etiam in hanc opinionem adducendi ut, qui adhuc nobis obligati fuerint, iis vicissim nos obligari posse videamur.
22 qui autem spe tenentur, quod genus hominum multo etiam est[30] diligentius atque officiosius, iis fac ut propositum ac paratum auxilium tuum esse videatur, denique ut spectatorem te suorum officiorum esse intellegant diligentem, ut videre te plane atque animadvertere quantum
23 a quoque proficiscatur appareat. tertium illud genus est studiorum voluntarium, quod agendis gratiis, accommodandis sermonibus ad eas rationes propter quas quisque studiosus tui esse videbitur, significanda erga illos pari voluntate, adducenda amicitia in spem familiaritatis et consuetudinis confirmari oportebit. atque in his omnibus generibus iudicato et perpendito quantum quisque possit, ut scias et quem ad modum cuique inservias et quid a
24 quoque exspectes ac postules. sunt enim quidam homines in suis vicinitatibus et municipiis gratiosi, sunt diligentes et copiosi qui, etiam si antea non studuerunt huic gratiae, tamen ex tempore elaborare eius causa cui debent aut volunt facile possunt; his hominum generibus sic inserviendum est ut ipsi intellegant te videre quid a quoque exspectes, sentire quid accipias, meminisse quid acceperis. sunt autem alii qui aut nihil possunt aut etiam odio sunt tribulibus suis nec habent tantum animi ac facultatis ut enitantur ex tempore; hos ut internoscas videto, ne spe in aliquo maiore posita praesidi parum comparetur.

25 Et quamquam partis ac fundatis amicitiis fretum ac munitum esse oportet, tamen in ipsa petitione amicitiae permultae ac perutiles comparantur; nam in ceteris moles-

[30] si (*Gruter*)

duty by you on this special occasion, nobody will ever respect them; but even so, you must solicit them and also bring them to believe that we in our turn may be obliged to those who have hitherto been obliged to us. As to those who are attached to us by their expectations—a far more painstaking and devoted category of persons—make them perceive that your help is ready at hand for them; also let them see that you are watching their services carefully, that you look and notice exactly how much comes of each of them. The third category, of the voluntary helpers, will have to be encouraged by thanks, by adapting what you say to the considerations why each person will appear keen for your interests, by indicating that you return their good will, by carrying the acquaintance to a hope of close intimacy. In all these categories, judge and ponder each man's capacity, in order to know how you should cultivate him and what you should expect or demand of him. For there are men of influence in their own neighbourhoods and towns, persistent and prosperous persons who, even if they have not felt inclined to exercise their influence before, still can easily make efforts at a moment's notice for someone to whom they are indebted or well disposed. In cultivating these kinds of men, let them understand that you know what to expect of each, realize what you get, and remember what you have got. But there are others who count for nothing or who are actually disliked by their fellow tribesmen, and have not the spirit or talent for improvisation. Be sure to distinguish these, lest by placing too great a hope in somebody you may get too little help.

Again, while you should be supported and fortified by friendships already formed and established, many useful friendships are acquired in the canvass itself, since a can-

tiis habet hoc tamen petitio commodi: potes honeste, quod in cetera vita non queas, quoscumque velis adiungere ad amicitiam, quibuscum si alio tempore agas ut te utantur, absurde facere videare, in petitione autem nisi id agas et
26 cum multis et diligenter, nullus petitor esse videare. ego autem tibi hoc confirmo, esse neminem, nisi si aliqua necessitudine competitorum alicui tuorum sit adiunctus, a quo non facile si contenderis impetrare possis ut suo beneficio promereatur se ut ames et sibi ut debeas, modo ut intellegat te magni se aestimare,[31] ex animo agere, bene se ponere, fore ex eo non brevem et suffragatoriam sed
27 firmam et perpetuam amicitiam. nemo erit, mihi crede, in quo modo aliquid sit, qui hoc tempus sibi oblatum amicitiae tecum constituendae praetermittat, praesertim cum tibi hoc casus adferat, ut ii tecum petant quorum amicitia aut contemnenda aut fugienda sit et qui hoc quod ego te hortor non modo adsequi sed ne incipere quidem possint.
28 nam qui[32] incipiat Antonius homines adiungere atque invitare ad amicitiam quos per se suo nomine appellare non possit? mihi quidem nihil stultius videtur quam existimare esse eum studiosum tui quem non noris. eximiam quandam gloriam et dignitatem ac rerum gestarum magnitudinem esse oportet in eo quem homines ignoti nullis suffragantibus honore adficiant; ut quidem homo nequam,[33] iners, sine officio, sine ingenio, cum[34] infamia, nullis amicis, hominem plurimorum studio atque omnium bona existimatione munitum praecurrat, sine magna culpa
29 neglegentiae fieri non potest. Quam ob rem omnis centurias multis et variis amicitiis cura ut confirmatas habeas. et

[31] magnis est- *vel sim.* (*Koch*) [32] quid (*Gesner*)
[33] homine(m) quam (*Gul.*) [34] summa *Schütz*

vass, for all its nuisances, has the convenience that you can make friends of any people you wish without disgrace, which you cannot do in the rest of life. If at some other time you were to exert yourself to court friendship with them, you would seem to act in bad taste; but in a canvass you would be thought a very poor candidate if you did not so act and with vigour too in connection with many such people. But I assure you that there is nobody (unless closely connected with one of your competitors in some way) whom you cannot easily induce, if you try, to earn your affection and obligation to him by doing you a good turn—that is, if he conceives that you value him highly, that you are sincere, that it is a good investment for him, that the result will not be a brief vote-catching friendship but a solid and permanent one. Believe me, there will be nobody, in so far as he is of the least intelligence, who will miss this opportunity offered to him of setting up a friendship with you, especially as chance gives you competitors whose friendship is to be despised or shunned, and who cannot even begin—let alone accomplish—what I am urging you to do. For how should Antonius begin to attach or invite to his friendship people whom he cannot call by their names without a prompter? To my mind, nothing is so silly as to think that a man whom you do not know is your eager supporter. It needs outstanding renown, prestige, and achievements to make strangers, if no one solicits them to do so, confer an honour upon one. A lazy good-for-nothing, with no sense of duty, no brains, a bad name, and no friends, cannot outpace a man supported by the favour of most people and the approbation of all, unless gross negligence is to blame. Therefore, take care to secure all the centuries through many friends of different sorts.

primum, id quod ante oculos est, senatores equitesque Romanos, ceterorum ‹ordinum› omnium[35] navos homines et gratiosos complectere. multi homines urbani industrii, multi libertini in foro gratiosi navique versantur; quos per te, quos per communis amicos poteris, summa cura ut cupidi tui sint elaborato, appetito, adlegato, summo bene-
30 ficio te adfici ostendito. deinde habeto rationem urbis totius, collegiorum, montium,[36] pagorum, vicinitatum; ex his principes ad amicitiam tuam si adiunxeris, per eos reliquam multitudinem facile tenebis. postea totam Italiam fac ut in animo ac memoria tributim discriptam comprehensamque habeas, ne quod municipium, coloniam, praefecturam, locum denique Italiae ne quem esse patiare in
31 quo non habeas firmamenti quod satis esse possit, perquiras et investiges homines ex omni regione, eos cognoscas, appetas, confirmes, cures ut in suis vicinitatibus tibi petant et tua causa quasi candidati sint. volent te amicum si suam a te amicitiam expeti videbunt; id ut intellegant, oratione ea quae ad eam rationem pertinet habenda consequere. homines municipales ac rusticani, si nomine nobis noti sunt, in amicitia se esse arbitrantur; si vero etiam praesidi se aliquid sibi constituere putant, non amittunt occasionem promerendi. hos ceteri et maxime tui competitores ne norunt quidem, tu et nosti et facile cognosces, sine quo
32 amicitia esse non potest. neque id tamen satis est, tametsi magnum est, si non sequitur spes utilitatis atque amicitiae,

[35] hominum (*Buecheler*: ordinum *Petreius*)
[36] omnium (*Mommsen*)

---

[17] Trade guilds; the term was also used as cover for the electoral gangs.

First—and this is obvious—draw to yourself senators, Roman Knights, active and influential men of all other ranks. Many energetic city folk, many influential and active freedmen are about the Forum; as many as possible should be most diligently brought by yourself or by mutual friends to desire your success; pursue them, send agents to them, show them how you esteem the benefaction. Then, reckon up the whole city—all the Colleges,[17] the wards, the hills;[18] if you strike a friendship with the leading men from among their number, you will easily, through them, secure the masses that remain. After that, comprehend in your mind and memory the whole of Italy divided into its tribal divisions, and let there be no town, colony, rural district, or indeed any place in Italy where you have not a sufficiency of support; inquire and seek out men everywhere, get to know them, pursue them, secure them, see that they canvass their localities for you and act like candidates on your behalf. They will want you as a friend if they see that you are anxious for their friendship; pursue the object of making them understand that point by using discourse appropriate to the purpose. Small-town and country folk think themselves our friends if we know them by name; and if indeed they think they are also gaining some protection for themselves, they lose no opportunity of deserving it. To the rest, especially to your competitors, they are total strangers, whereas *you* know them and will easily recognize them—without which there can be no friendship. Yet merely to know them, though important, is not enough unless it is followed by the hope of advantage and friendship,

[18] [Administrative districts; see Mommsen, *Röm. Staatsrecht* III.114, n.5. –SB.]

ne nomenclator solum sed amicus etiam bonus esse videare. ita cum et hos ipsos, propter suam ambitionem qui apud tribulis suos plurimum gratia possunt,[37] studiosos in centuriis habebis et ceteros qui apud aliquam partem tribulium propter municipi aut vicinitatis[38] aut collegi rationem valent cupidos tui constitueris, in optima spe esse
33 debebis. iam equitum centuriae multo facilius mihi diligentia posse teneri videntur: primum cognosci equites <oportet>[39] (pauci enim sunt), deinde appeti (multo enim facilius illa adulescentulorum ad amicitiam aetas adiungitur). deinde habes tecum ex iuventute optimum quemque et studiosissimum humanitatis; tum autem, quod equester ordo tuus est, sequentur illi auctoritatem ordinis, si abs te adhibebitur ea diligentia ut non ordinis solum voluntate sed etiam singulorum amicitiis eas centurias confirmatas habeas. nam studia adulescentulorum in suffragando, in obeundo, in nuntiando, in adsectando mirifice et magna et honesta sunt.

34 Et, quoniam adsectationis mentio facta est, id quoque curandum est ut cottidiana cuiusque generis et ordinis et aetatis utare; nam ex ea ipsa copia coniectura fieri poterit quantum sis in ipso campo virium ac facultatis habiturus. huius autem rei tres partes sunt: una salutatorum [cum domum veniunt],[40] altera deductorum, tertia adsectatorum.
35 in salutatoribus, qui magis vulgares sunt et hac consuetudine quae nunc est <ad>[41] pluris veniunt, hoc efficiendum est ut hoc ipsum minimum officium eorum tibi gratis-

[37] possint (*Palermus*)
[38] civitatis (*Petreius*)
[39] (*Watt, sed post* primum)
[40] (*Or.*)
[41] (*Watt*)

so that you are seen to be a good friend and not only a recollector of names. So, when those whose own electioneering ambition has gained them most influence with their tribesmen are busy for you in the centuries—and when you have established, as persons desirous of your interests, those others who carry weight with some of their tribesmen by reason of their home town, district, or College—then your hopes should be high. And the centuries of Knights[19] can, I think, be secured much more easily, with care. First you should get to know the Knights (there are not many); then, try hard to win them (young men at that age are much more easily attached as friends). Further, you have with you those of the best breeding and highest culture among the young generation; and then, as the Order of Knights is on your side, they will follow the Order's authority, if you take the trouble to secure its centuries not only by the general good will of the Order, but by individual friendships. Young men's enthusiasm in winning support, visiting electors, carrying news, and attending on you is amazingly important, and confers credit on you.

And now that I have mentioned attendance, you must take care to have it daily, from all sorts and ranks and ages, for the very numbers will give an idea of the resources of strength you will have at the poll itself. This subject falls into three parts: the first, callers at your house; the second, escorts from your house; the third, attendants in general. The callers are a more promiscuous crowd, and in the fashion of today visit more than one candidate. You must make even this small service of theirs appear to be very gratify-

19 [These are the 'sex suffragia;' see *Letters to Friends* 50 (II.6).2 n.2. –S.B.]

simum esse videatur; qui domum tuam venient, iis significato te animadvertere (eorum amicis qui illis renuntient ostendito, saepe ipsis dicito); sic homines saepe, cum obeunt pluris competitores et vident unum esse aliquem qui haec officia maxime animadvertat, ei se dedunt, deserunt ceteros, minutatim ex communibus proprii, ex fucosis firmi suffragatores evadunt. iam illud teneto diligenter, si eum qui tibi promiserit audieris fucum, ut dicitur, facere aut senseris, ut te id audisse aut scire dissimules, si qui tibi se purgare volet quod suspectum esse arbitretur, adfirmes te de illius voluntate numquam dubitasse nec debere dubitare; is enim qui se non putat satis facere amicus esse nullo modo potest. scire autem oportet quo quisque animo sit, ut
36 et quantum cuique confidas constituere possis. iam deductorum officium quo maius est quam salutatorum, hoc gratius tibi esse significato atque ostendito, et, quod eius fieri poterit, certis temporibus descendito; magnam adfert opinionem, magnam dignitatem cottidiana in deducendo
37 frequentia. tertia est ex hoc genere adsidua adsectatorum copia. in ea quos voluntarios habebis, curato ut intellegant te sibi in perpetuum summo beneficio obligari; qui autem tibi debent, ab iis plane hoc munus exigito,[42] qui per aetatem ac negotium poterunt, ipsi tecum ut adsidui sint, qui ipsi sectari non poterunt, suos necessarios in hoc munere constituant. valde ego te volo et ad rem pertinere arbitror
38 semper cum multitudine esse. praeterea magnam adferet laudem et summam dignitatem si ii tecum erunt qui a te

[42] exigitur *vel* -git *vel* -ge (*Or.*)

ing to you; indicate that you notice who comes to your house (tell it to friends of theirs who will repeat it to them, and often tell them yourself). So, callers who visit several of the candidates, seeing that one of them takes special notice of this service, often devote themselves to him, desert the rest, and gradually emerge as his own men instead of everybody's, solid supporters instead of double-faced. Now retain this carefully: if anybody has committed himself to you, and you hear or see that he is (as they say) double-crossing you, pretend not to have heard or noticed it; and if anybody, thinking that you suspect him, tries to clear himself, assure him that you have never doubted his good faith nor have any right to doubt it; for nobody can be a friend if he thinks that he does not come up to standard. You should know how each man is disposed towards you, so that you can decide, accordingly, how much confidence to place in each. Now as to the escorts, inasmuch as their services are more important than those of the callers, indicate clearly that they are more gratifying to you, and so far as possible, go down to the Forum at regular hours; a large company of daily escorts makes a great impression and adds great prestige. The third item under this heading is the supply of full-time attendants. To those who are volunteers, make it clear that you are forever in their debt for a very great kindness. To those who owe you this service, insist absolutely that any who are not too old or too busy should regularly attend on you themselves, and that those who cannot themselves do so should appoint their relatives to this duty. I am very anxious that you should always have a crowd about you; I think it important to the occasion. Further, it will bring you great credit and high prestige if you have around you those whom you have defended, who

defensi et qui per te servati ac iudiciis liberati sunt; haec tu plane ab his postulato ut, quoniam nulla impensa per te alii rem, alii honestatem, alii salutem ac fortunas omnis obtinuerint,[43] nec aliud ullum tempus futurum sit ubi tibi referre gratiam possint, hoc te officio remunerentur.

39 Et quoniam in amicorum studiis haec omnis oratio versatur, qui locus in hoc genere cavendus sit praetermittendum non videtur. fraudis atque insidiarum et perfidiae
plena sunt omnia. non est huius temporis perpetua illa de
hoc genere disputatio, quibus rebus benevolus et simula-
tor diiudicari possit; tantum est huius temporis admonere.
summa tua virtus eosdem homines et simulare tibi se esse
amicos et invidere coegit. quam ob rem Ἐπιχάρμειον illud teneto, nervos atque artus esse sapientiae non temere
40 credere, et, cum tuorum amicorum studia constitueris,
tum etiam obtrectatorum atque adversariorum rationes et
genera cognoscito. haec tria sunt: unum quos laesisti, alterum qui sine causa non amant, tertium qui competitorum
valde amici sunt. quos laesisti, cum contra eos pro amico
diceres, iis te plane purgato, necessitudines commemora-
to, in spem adducito te in eorum rebus, si se in amicitiam
contulerint, pari studio atque officio futurum. qui sine
causa non amant, eos aut beneficio aut spe aut significando
tuo erga illos studio dato operam ut de illa animi pravitate
deducas. quorum voluntas erit abs te propter competitorum amicitias alienior, iis quoque eadem inservito ratione

[43] obtinuerunt (*Mueller*)

---

[20] Quoted in Greek by Marcus, *Ad Att.* I.19.8.

have been preserved and saved from condemnation by you. Demand of them plainly that since it is due to your unpaid efforts that they have retained their property, or their reputation, or their life and all their fortunes, and since there will never be another chance for them to thank you, they should repay you by this service.

Now, since all this discourse of mine is concerned with the zealous aid of friends, I think that I should not omit to say what point under this heading requires caution. All things are full of deceit, snares, and treachery. This is not the time for the whole long argument on this heading—how genuine good will can be distinguished from counterfeit; this is the time for a warning only. The excellence of your moral nature has impelled the same persons both to feign friendship for you and to bear you envy. Hold fast, therefore, to the old saying of Epicharmus that the bone and sinew of wisdom is, "Never trust rashly";[20] and as you assemble the zealous aid of your friends, get to know also the methods and types of your detractors and your opponents. The types are three: first, those whom you have hurt; second, those who do not like you, though they have no reason; third, those who are close friends of your competitors. As to those whom you have hurt by defending a friend against them, exculpate yourself in full, reminding them of your personal obligations, and make them hope that, if they become friends of yours, you will do them equally zealous service in their own affairs. Those who do not like you, though they have no reason, you should endeavour to turn away from that perverse frame of mind by doing them a kindness, or promising one, or indicating your own affection for them. Those who are estranged from you by friendship with your competitors should be

qua superioribus et, si probare poteris, te in eos ipsos competitores tuos benevolo esse animo ostendito.

41 Quoniam de amicitiis constituendis satis dictum est, dicendum est de illa altera parte petitionis quae in populari
ratione versatur. ea desiderat nomenclationem, blandi-
tiam, adsiduitatem, benignitatem, rumorem, ‹speciem›,
42 spem[44] in re publica. primum id quod facis, ut homines noris, significa ut appareat, et auge ut cottidie melius fiat; nihil mihi tam populare neque tam gratum videtur. deinde id
quod natura non habes induc in animum ita simulandum
esse ut natura facere videare; nam comitas tibi non deest
ea quae bono ac suavi homine digna est, sed opus est magno opere blanditia, quae, etiam si vitiosa est et turpis in
cetera vita, tamen in petitione necessaria est; etenim[45]
cum deteriorem aliquem adsentando facit, tum improba
est, cum amiciorem, non tam vituperanda, petitori vero
necessaria est, cuius et frons et vultus et sermo ad eorum
quoscumque convenerit sensum et voluntatem commu-
43 tandus et accommodandus est. iam adsiduitatis nullum est
praeceptum, verbum ipsum docet quae res sit; prodest
quidem vehementer nusquam discedere, sed tamen hic
fructus est adsiduitatis, non solum esse Romae atque in
foro sed adsidue petere, saepe eosdem appellare, non
committere ut quisquam possit dicere, quod eius consequi
possis, se abs te non [sit][46] rogatum et valde ac diligenter
44 rogatum. benignitas autem late patet: [et][47] est in re familiari, quae quamquam ad multitudinem pervenire non potest, tamen ab amicis si laudatur, multitudini grata est; est

[44] (*SB**: *Pro* spem *Lamb.*) *vide nunc* §§ 52 (*speciem*) et 53 (*spes*) *rei publicae* [45] te enim (*Petreius*: ea e- *Buecheler*) [46] (*Watt*: esse *Lamb.*) [47] (*Baiter*)

treated by the same methods as the others; and if you can make them believe it, convey that you feel kindly towards your competitors themselves.

Now that enough has been said of instituting friendships, I must now speak of the other part of the canvass, which concerns method in dealing with the People. This requires a memory for names, an ingratiating manner, constant attendance, generosity, publicity, a fine show, political promise. First, show off your habit of *knowing people* so that it is obvious, and increase and improve it daily; nothing, to my mind, is so popular and gratifying. Then, be determined that what you lack by nature should be so well simulated that it seems a natural act. You are not wanting in the pleasant manners proper to a kind and agreeable man, but what you urgently need is *ingratiation*, which may be a base fault in the rest of life, but in a canvass it is indispensable. For it is vile when flattery is used to corrupt a man, but less execrable when used to conciliate friendship, and indispensable for a candidate, whose facial expression and conversation must be modified and adapted to the humour and the inclination of all whom he meets. Now, *attendance* needs no instructions; the word itself explains what it is. Never to leave town is very rewarding; yet the gains from your personal attendance consist not merely in being at Rome and in the Forum, but in canvassing continuously, soliciting the same people many times, and, so far as possible, not letting anybody be in a position to say that that he has not been canvassed by you—and thoroughly and diligently canvassed too. Next, *generosity* has a wide field. It is shown in the use of one's private means, for although this cannot reach the masses, the masses like hearing it praised by your friends; it is shown in banquets, to which

in conviviis, quae fac ut et abs te et ab amicis tuis concelebrentur et passim et tributim; est etiam in opera, quam pervulga et communica, curaque ut aditus ad te diurni nocturnique pateant, neque solum foribus aedium tuarum sed etiam vultu ac fronte, quae est animi ianua; quae si significat voluntatem abditam esse ac retrusam, parvi refert patere ostium. homines enim non modo promitti sibi, praesertim quod a candidato petant, sed etiam large atque
45 honorifice promitti volunt. qua re hoc quidem facile praeceptum est, ut quod facturus sis id significes te studiose ac libenter esse facturum; illud difficilius et magis ad tempus quam ad naturam accommodatum tuam, quod facere non possis, ut id aut iucunde neges <aut etiam non neges>;[48] quorum alterum est tamen boni viri, alterum boni petitoris. nam cum id petitur quod honeste aut sine detrimento nostro promittere non possumus, quo modo si qui roget ut contra amicum aliquem causam recipiamus, belle negandum est, ut ostendas necessitudinem, demonstres quam moleste feras, aliis te id rebus exsarturum[49] esse per-
46 suadeas. audivi hoc dicere quendam de quibusdam oratoribus, ad quos causam suam detulisset, gratiorem sibi orationem <eius>[50] fuisse qui negasset quam illius qui recepisset; sic homines fronte et oratione magis quam ipso beneficio reque capiuntur. verum hoc probabile est, illud alterum subdurum tibi homini Platonico suadere, sed

[48] (*Watt, auct. Purser et Constans*)
[49] exa(u)cturum (*Lamb.*) [50] *om., cod. Canonicianus**

[21] [For 'or, better, don't decline' (Henderson), which is not what the writer meant. Even so, this translation ignores *tamen*, omitted in one unimportant manuscript but probably authentic. I

you and your friends should often convoke the people at large or tribe by tribe; also in rendering services, which you will widely advertise, and seeing that you are approachable day and night, not only through the door of your house but through your facial expression, which is the gate of the mind; if it shows that your feelings are reserved and withdrawn, it hardly matters that your door is open. People want not only promises (especially in their demands from a candidate), but promises made in a lavish and complimentary way. And so—an easy rule—if you are going to do what is asked, show that you will do it willingly and gladly; but the next thing is harder, and accords better with your circumstances than with your character: whatever you cannot perform, decline gracefully or even[21] *don't* decline. A good man will do the former, a good candidate the latter. If asked for something which we cannot decently or with impunity promise—if, for instance, somebody asks you to accept a brief against a friend—you must refuse nicely, explaining your obligation to your friend, declaring how sorry you are, assuring the man that you will patch it all up in other ways. Somebody told me of certain advocates to whom he had referred his case, that he was more gratified by the words of the one who refused than by those of him who accepted; and indeed, people are charmed more by looks and words than by the substantial benefit received. That, however, is fair enough; the alternative course of *not* declining is rather difficult to commend to a Platonist like

take the underlying thought to be: 'both courses are expedient, but whereas the former, while expedient is honourable all the same, the latter is—just expedient.' But this is hard to bring out in translation while remaining faithful to the text. –SB.]

tamen tempori tuo consulam. quibus enim te propter aliquod officium necessitudinis adfuturum negaris, tamen ii
possunt abs te placati aequique discedere; quibus autem
idcirco negaris, quod te impeditum esse dixeris aut amicio-
rum[51] hominum negotiis aut gravioribus causis aut ante
susceptis, inimici discedunt omnesque hoc animo sunt ut
47 sibi te mentiri malint quam negare. C. Cotta, in ambitione
artifex, dicere solebat se operam suam, quod non contra
officium rogaretur, polliceri solere omnibus, impertire iis
apud quos optime poni arbitraretur; ideo se nemini negare, quod saepe accideret causa cur is cui pollicitus esset
non uteretur, saepe ut ipse magis esset vacuus quam putasset; neque posse eius domum compleri qui tantum modo
reciperet quantum videret se obire posse; casu fieri ut
agantur ea quae non putaris, illa quae credideris in manibus esse ut aliqua de causa non agantur; deinde esse
48 extremum ut irascatur is cui mendacium dixeris. id, si pro-
mittas, et incertum est et in diem et in paucioribus; sin
autem [id][52] neges, et certe abalienes et statim et pluris;
plures enim multo sunt qui rogant ut uti liceat opera alterius quam qui utuntur. qua re satius est ex his aliquos
aliquando in foro tibi irasci quam omnis continuo domi,
praesertim cum multo magis irascantur iis qui negent
quam ei quem videant ea ex causa impeditum ut facere
49 quod promisit cupiat si ullo modo possit.

51 amicorum (*Eussner*) 52 (*Puteanus*)

---

22 [A prior commitment would be a valid excuse and could not reasonably be resented, but in practice resentment could be unreasonable, as in Phamea's case (*Letters to Atticus* 347 (XIII.49)). –SB.]

you, but I am going to have regard for your present circumstances. If you tell people that you cannot help them because of some personal duty to others, they may still go away pacified and unruffled; but if you refuse because you are prevented (you say) by affairs of friends or by previous[22] or more important engagements, they go away hating you; they are all in the mood that they had rather you lied to them than refused them. C. Cotta,[23] a past master of electioneering, used to say that (unless duty forbade a request) he used to promise his help to all, but give it to those in whom he expected he was making the best investment; he refused nobody because it often turned out, for some reason, that the man to whom he had promised help did not use it, or that he himself was less busy than he expected; if one undertook only what one could be sure to perform, one's house would be empty; by chance, a case you didn't expect is tried, but one you thought you were busy with is not tried for some reason; and finally, the anger of the man to whom one lied would be the last event in the series—for if you do promise, the anger is uncertain, not immediate and occurs in fewer cases; but if you refuse you are sure to rouse antagonism at once, and in more people; since those who ask that they be allowed to employ the services of a person are many more than those who actually employ them. So it is better that some of these people should sometimes be angry with you in the Forum than all of them all the time in your house—especially as they are much angrier with those who refuse them than with a man who (as they see) has a reason for not fulfilling his promise, although he would want to do so if he possibly could.

[23] Consul 75; admired and often mentioned by Marcus.

Ac ne videar aberrasse a distributione mea, qui haec in hac populari parte petitionis disputem, hoc sequor, haec omnia non tam ad amicorum studia quam ad popularem famam pertinere: etsi inest aliquid ex illo genere, benigne respondere, studiose inservire negotiis ac periculis amicorum, tamen hoc loco ea dico quibus multitudinem capere possis, ut de nocte domus compleatur, ut multi spe tui praesidi teneantur, ut amiciores abs te discedant quam accesserint, ut quam plurimorum aures optimo sermone compleantur.

50 Sequitur enim ut de rumore dicendum sit, cui maxime serviendum est. sed quae dicta sunt omni superiore oratione, eadem ad rumorem concelebrandum valent, dicendi laus, studia publicanorum et equestris ordinis, hominum nobilium voluntas, adulescentulorum frequentia, eorum qui abs te defensi sunt adsiduitas, ex municipiis multitudo eorum quos tua causa venisse appareat, bene <te>[53] ut homines nosse, comiter appellare, adsidue ac diligenter petere, benignum ac liberalem esse loquantur et existiment, domus ut multa nocte[54] compleatur, omnium generum frequentia adsit, satis fiat oratione omnibus, re operaque multis, perficiatur id quod fieri potest labore et arte ac diligentia, non ut ad populum ab his hominibus
51 fama perveniat sed ut in his studiis populus ipse versetur. iam urbanam illam multitudinem et eorum studia qui contiones tenent adeptus es in Pompeio ornando, Manili causa recipienda, Cornelio defendendo; excitanda nobis

[53] (*Schütz*) [54] <de> nocte *Malaespina*

---

[24] Manilius sponsored the bill of 66 for Pompey's eastern command; Cornelius was another Pompeian defended by Marcus.

(And, in case you think I have wandered from my own classification of subject matter by putting this argument into the part of the canvass concerning the People, my view is that all this pertains to Popular Reputation rather than to Zealous Aid of Friends. Although something of this latter category enters in—gracious answers, zealous service in friends' affairs or dangers—I am here speaking of ways to capture the masses, so as to fill your house before dawn, to hold many people in hope of your protection, to send them away better friends than they came, to fill as many ears as possible with excellent reports of you.)

The next required talking point is *publicity*, which you must court to the full. But for widespread publicity the strong points are those of my whole discourse above—your fame as an orator, the favour of the public revenue contractors and the Order of Knights, the good will of the nobles, the crowd of young men about you, the attendance of clients defended by you, the numbers from Italian towns who have obviously come for your sake; so that they say and believe that you know people well, solicit them courteously, canvass continuously and thoroughly, are a gracious and generous person; and so that your house is full long before dawn with crowds of all classes, you give satisfaction to everybody in what you say and to many in what you actually do, you achieve the result (so far as hard work, skill, and application can achieve it) that the People itself, instead of hearing at second hand from these acquaintances of yours, shares their devotion to you. You have already won over those city masses and the favour of their political managers by advancing Pompey, by undertaking the case of Manilius and defending Cornelius;[24] we have to mobilize the sup-

sunt quae adhuc habuit nemo qui[55] idem splendidorum
hominum voluntates haberet. efficiendum etiam illud est
ut sciant omnes Cn. Pompei summam esse erga te volunta-
52 tem et vehementer ad illius rationes te id adsequi quod petis pertinere. postremo tota petitio cura ut pompae plena
sit, ut illustris, ut splendida, ut popularis sit, ut habeat
summam speciem ac dignitatem, ut etiam, si qua[56] possit
‹ratio›ne,[57] competitoribus tuis exsistat aut sceleris aut
53 libidinis aut largitionis accommodata ad eorum mores
infamia. atque etiam in hac petitione maxime videndum
est ut spes rei publicae bona de te sit et honesta opinio; nec
tamen in petendo res publica capessenda est neque in
senatu neque in contione. sed haec tibi sunt retinenda: ut
senatus te existimet ex eo quod ita vixeris defensorem auctoritatis suae fore, equites Romani et viri boni ac locupletes ex vita acta te studiosum oti ac rerum tranquillarum,
multitudo ex eo quod dumtaxat oratione in contionibus ac
iudicio popularis fuisti te a suis commodis non alienum
54 futurum.

Haec mihi veniebant in mentem de duabus illis commentationibus[58] matutinis, quod[59] tibi cottidie ad forum descendenti meditandum esse dixeram: 'novus sum, consulatum peto.' tertium restat: 'Roma est,' civitas ex nationum conventu constituta, in qua multae insidiae, multa fallacia,[60] multa in omni genere vitia versantur, multorum adrogantia, multorum contumacia, multorum malevolentia, multorum superbia, multorum odium ac molestia per-

[55] quin *Man.* [56] qu(a)e (*Palermus*)
[57] (*Watt*) [58] commonitio- *vel* commotio- (*Palermus*)
[59] quo (*Lamb.*: quas *Facciolati*)
[60] multae fallaciae *Lamb.*

port which nobody has ever possessed along with the good graces of the highest personages. You have also to make everybody know that Pompey is a strong supporter of yours and that your success in this candidature would suit his plans extremely well.[25] Lastly, see that your whole canvass is a *fine show*, brilliant, resplendent, and popular, with the utmost display and prestige; and also, if it can be managed at all, that there should be scandalous talk, in character, about the crimes, lusts, and briberies of your competitors. Above all, it must be shown in this canvass that high hopes and good opinions are entertained for your political future. Yet, during your canvass, you must not deal with politics either in the Senate or in political meetings of the People. Instead, you must keep in mind that the Senate should deem you, on your life's record, to be in future an upholder of its authority; the Roman Knights and men of worth and substance, from your past life, to be devoted to peace and quiet times; the masses, to be favourably inclined to their interests, since you have been "Popular" at least in your speeches in political meetings and lawcourts.

This is what occurred to me about those first two morning meditations, when I said that every day as you go down to the Forum you must repeat to yourself: "I am 'new'; I seek the consulship." There remains the third, "This is Rome"—a conglomerate of nations, in which there are many snares, intrigues, and vices of all sorts, many people's insolence, contumacy, malice, haughtiness, animosity, and vexation to be borne. I see that among so many people of such great and various vices, it needs much judgement and

[25] See, however, Introduction, note 24.

ferenda est. video esse magni consili atque artis in tot hominum cuiusque modi vitiis tantisque versantem vitare offensionem, vitare fabulam, vitare insidias, esse unum
55 hominem accommodatum ad tantam morum ac sermonum ac voluntatum varietatem. qua re etiam atque etiam perge tenere istam viam quam institisti.[61] excelle dicendo; hoc et tenentur Romae homines et adliciuntur et ab impediendo ac laedendo repelluntur. et quoniam in hoc vel maxime est vitiosa civitas, quod largitione interposita virtutis ac dignitatis oblivisci solet, in hoc fac ut te bene noris, id est ut intellegas eum esse te qui iudici ac periculi metum maximum competitoribus adferre possis. fac ut se abs te custodiri atque observari sciant; cum diligentiam tuam,
56 cum auctoritatem vimque dicendi, tum profecto equestris ordinis erga te studium pertimescent. atque haec ita te volo illis proponere, <non>[62] ut videare accusationem iam[63] meditari, sed ut hoc terrore facilius hoc ipsum quod agis consequare. et plane sic contende omnibus nervis ac facultatibus ut adipiscamur quod petimus. video nulla esse
57 comitia tam inquinata largitione quibus non gratis aliquae centuriae renuntient suos magno opere necessarios. qua re si advigilamus pro rei dignitate, et si nostros ad summum studium benevolos excitamus, et si hominibus studiosis nostri gratiosisque suum cuique munus discribimus, et si competitoribus iudicium proponimus, sequestribus metum inicimus, divisores ratione aliqua coercemus, perfici
58 potest ut largitio nulla fiat aut nihil valeat.

Haec sunt quae putavi non melius scire me quam te sed

[61] instituisti (*Gruter*)
[62] (*Lamb., sed ante* acc-)
[63] tum (*Lamb.*)

skill to escape resentment, gossip, or treacherous attack, to be a man whose one personality has been adapted to such multifarious ways of behaving, speaking, or feeling. So, go steadily on by the path you have chosen to tread, and be supreme in oratory; this is what holds and attracts men in Rome, and keeps them off from hampering or harming you. Further, as the worst vice of this city is to forget moral worth when bribery enters in, know yourself—I mean, understand that you, of all people, can put the fear of prosecution and its dangers into your competitors. Let them know that they are under your watchful observation; they will be terrified not only by your application, your authority and power as an orator, but also by the favour that you have with the Order of Knights. I want you so to present these advantages to them not so as to give the impression that you are already contemplating a prosecution, but only, through their terror of one, to gain your end more easily.[26] Strive, then, with all your strength and talents to obtain what we are seeking. I see that no election is so polluted with bribery that some centuries do not return, without bribes, the candidates with whom they have a very special bond. So, if we keep as alert as the high occasion demands, and if we stir up our well-wishers to the utmost zeal, and if we assign a particular task to each of our influential supporters, and if we set prosecution before the eyes of our competitors, strike alarm into the agents of bribery and somehow curb the distributors, we can achieve the result that bribery does not occur or has no effect.

Here it is; I thought, not that I knew all this better than

26 [Competitors should be made to understand that the *possibility* of a prosecution existed; cf. *Pro Murena* 43. –SB.]

facilius his tuis occupationibus colligere unum in locum posse et ad te perscripta mittere. quae tametsi scripta ita sunt ut non ad omnis qui honores petant sed ad te proprie et ad hanc petitionem tuam valeant, tamen tu, si quid mutandum esse videbitur aut omnino tollendum, aut si quid erit praeteritum, velim hoc mihi dicas; volo enim hoc commentariolum petitionis haberi omni ratione perfectum.

you, but that, considering how busy you are, I could more easily pull it together into one whole and send it to you in writing. Although it is written in such a way that it applies not to all who are seeking office but to you in particular and to this canvass, still, please tell me if you think that anything should be changed or struck out altogether, or if anything has been left out. For I want this handbook of electioneering to be considered perfect in every way.

APPENDIX

Roman Dates

Until Julius Caesar reformed the calendar the Roman year consisted of 355 days divided into twelve months, all of which bore the Latin forms of their present names except Quintilis (July) and Sextilis (August). Each month had 29 days, except February with 28 and March, May, July, and October with 31. The first, fifth and thirteenth days of each month were called the Kalends *(Kalendae)*, Nones *(Nonae)*, and Ides *(Idus)* respectively, except that in March, May, July, and October the Nones fell on the seventh and the Ides on the fifteenth. I have kept these names in translation.

The calendar was adjusted by means of intercalation. At the discretion of the College of Pontiffs, usually every other year, an intercalary month of 23 or 22 days was inserted after 24 or 23 February. But in the years immediately before the Civil War the College neglected this procedure, so that by 46 the calendar was well over two months in advance of the sun. Julius Caesar rectified the situation by inserting two intercalary months totalling 67 days between November and December of that year in addition to the traditional one in February. He also gave the months their present numbers of days, thus almost obviat-

ing the need for future intercalations, though in 1582 a further discrepancy had to be met by the institution of a leap year.

Roman Money

The normal unit of reckoning was the sesterce (HS), though the denarius, equal to 4 sesterces, was the silver coin most generally in use. Differences of price structure make any transposition into modern currency misleading. Sometimes sums are expressed in Athenian currency. The drachma was about equal to the denarius, the mina (100 drachmae) to HS400, and the talent (60 minae) to HS2,400. The Asiatic cistophorus was worth about 4 drachmae.

Roman Names

A Roman bore the name of his clan *(gens)*, the *nomen* or *nomen gentilicium,* usually ending in *ius,* preceded by a personal name *(praenomen)* and often followed by a *cognomen,* which might distinguish different families in the same *gens*: e.g., Marcus Tullius Cicero. The *nomen* was always, and the *cognomen* usually, hereditary. Sometimes, as when a family split into branches, an additional *cognomen* was taken: e.g., Publius Licinius Crassus Dives. Other additional *cognomina* were honorific, sometimes taken from a conquered country as Africanus or Numidicus, or adoptive (see below). Women generally had only the one clan name (e.g., Tullia), which they retained after marriage.

Only a few personal names were in use and they are

generally abbreviated as follows: A. = Aulus; Ap(p). = Appius; C. = Gaius; Cn. = Gnaeus; D. = Decimus; K. = Kaeso; L. = Lucius; M. = Marcus; M'. = Manius; N. = Numerius; P. = Publius; Q. = Quintus; Ser. = Servius; Sex. = Sextus; Sp. = Spurius; T. = Titus; Ti. = Tiberius (I omit one or two which do not occur in our text). The use of a *praenomen* by itself in address or reference is generally a sign of close intimacy, whether real or affected, but in the case of a rare or distinctive praenomen, as Appius and Servius, this is not so.

The practice of adoption, of males at any rate, was very common in Rome. According to traditional practice the adopted son took his new father's full name and added his old *nomen gentilicium* with the adjectival termination *-ianus* instead of *-ius*: e.g., C. Octavius, adopted by C. Julius Caesar, became C. Julius Caesar Octavianus. But in Cicero's time the practice had become variable. Sometimes the original name remained in use.

A slave had only one name, and since many slaves came from the East, this was often Greek. If freed, he took his master's *praenomen* and *nomen*, adding his slave name as a *cognomen:* e.g., Tiro, when freed by M. Tullius Cicero, became M. Tullius Tiro. Occasionally the *praenomen* might be somebody else's. Atticus' slave Dionysius became M. Pomponius Dionysius in compliment to Cicero (instead of Titus).

Much the same applied to Greek or other provincials on gaining Roman citizenship. Such a man retained his former name as a *cognomen* and acquired the *praenomen* and *nomen* of the person to whom he owed the grant: e.g., the philosopher Cratippus became M. Tullius Cratippus after Cicero had got Caesar to give him the citizenship.

APPENDIX

For further information on names see my *Two Studies in Roman Nomenclature*, pp. 53–54 (Adoptive Nomenclature) and the introductions to my three Onomastica (to Cicero's Speeches, Letters, and Treatises).

CONCORDANCES

AD QUINTUM FRATREM

Vulgate	*This Edition*	*Vulgate*	*This Edition*
I.1	1	II.11	15
I.2	2	II.12	16
I.3	3	II.13	17
I.4	4	II.14	18
II.1	5	II.15	19
II.2	6	II.16	20
II.3	7	III.1	21
II.4	8	III.2	22
II.5	9	III.3	23
II.6	10	III.4	24
II.7	11	III.5	25
II.8	13	III.6	26
II.9	12	III.7	27
II.10	14		

AD M. BRUTUM

Vulgate	*Watt*	*This Edition*	*Vulgate*	*Watt*	*This Edition*
I.1	VI	13	I.11	XIX	16
I.2	VII	14	I.12	XX	21
I.2a	VIII	6	I.13	XXI	20
I.3	IX	7	I.14	XXII	22
I.3a	X	8	I.15	XXIII	23
I.4	XI	10	I.16	XXIV	[25]
I.4a	XII	11	I.17	XXV	[26]
I.5	XIII	9	I.18	XXVI	24
I.6	XIV	12	II.1	I	1
I.7	XV	19	II.2	II	3
I.8	XVI	15	II.3	III	2
I.9	XVII	18	II.4	IV	4
I.10	XVIII	17	II.5	V	5

GLOSSARY

ACADEMY *(Academia)*: A hall *(gymnasium)* and park at Athens sacred to the hero Academus, in which Plato established his philosophical school. Hence Plato's school or system of philosophy, which went through various phases after his time. The terminology became confused, but Cicero recognized the 'Old Academy' of Plato and his immediate successors and the 'New' Academy of Arcesilas and Carneades, which maintained the uncertainty of all dogma and to which he himself professed to belong. In his own times this was modified by his teachers Philo of Larisa and Antiochus of Ascalon, the latter of whom claimed to represent the Old Academy with a system akin to Stoicism. Cicero gave the name 'Academy' to a hall which he built on his estate at Tusculum.

AEDILE *(aedilis)*: Third in rank of the regular Roman magistracies. Four at this time were elected annually, two Curule and two Plebeian. They were responsible for city administration and the holding of certain public Games. The chief magistrates in some municipalities were also so called.

ASSEMBLY: I sometimes so translate *populus* or *comitia*, as describing the Roman people convened for electoral or legislative purposes. There were several different sorts

varying with the convening magistrate and the business to be done.

ATTIC(ISM): One use of the word was in connection with Roman oratory. In Cicero's time a movement principally represented by Calvus and M. Brutus favoured an austere style like that of the Athenian Lysias.

AUGUR: The priestly College of Augurs were official diviners interpreting signs (mostly from the flight and cries of wild birds or the behaviour of the Sacred Chickens) before major acts of public (and sometimes private) business. The College, like that of Pontiffs, was in practice almost a preserve of the nobility, so that for a 'new man' like Cicero membership was a coveted social distinction.

AUSPICES *(auspicia)*: Divination from birds or other signs was officially necessary as a preliminary to major acts by magistrates, who were said to 'have auspices,' i.e. the power of taking them.

BACCHUS' DAY *(Liberalia)*: The festival of Liber Pater, commonly identified with the Greek god Dionysius or Bacchus, and Libera on 17 March. It was the usual day for a coming of age ceremony.

BOARD OF FOUR: Municipalities (not Roman colonies) were commonly governed by four principal magistrates *(quattuorviri)*, divided into two pairs *(duoviri)*, and a senate of *decuriones*.

BONA DEA: See GOOD GODDESS.

BOY *(puer)*: Male slaves of any age were so called, as in later times.

CAMPANIAN LAND (DOMAIN, *ager Campanus*): Fertile land in Campania, originally confiscated by Rome in 211

and leased to small tenants. Caesar as Consul passed a bill (the Campanian Law) to distribute it among Pompey's veterans and the Roman poor.

CAMPUS (MARTIUS): The plain adjoining the Tiber on which assemblies of the Centuries were held, often for elections.

CENSOR: Two magistrates usually elected every five years for a tenure of eighteen months. They revised the roll of citizens, with property assessments, also the rolls of Knights and Senators, removing those deemed guilty of misconduct. They further supervised public contracts, including the lease of revenues to the tax farmers, and issued decrees as guardians of public morals.

CENTURIES, ASSEMBLY OF *(comitia centuriata)*: Form of assembly in which voting took place by 'Centuries,' i.e. groups unequally composed so as to give preponderance to birth and wealth. It elected Consuls and Praetors, and voted on legislation proposed by them. The first Century to vote *(centuria praerogativa)* traditionally had a determining effect on the rest.

CENTURION: See LEGION

COHORT: See LEGION.

COMITIAL DAYS: Days in the Roman calendar on which the popular assemblies *(comitia)* could legally be held. The Senate normally did not meet on these days.

COMITIUM: An area north of the Forum where assemblies were held.

COMMISSION, FREE or VOTIVE: See LEGATE.

COMPITALIA: See CROSSWAYS' DAY.

CONSUL: Highest of the annual Roman magistrates. Two were elected, usually in July, to take office on the following 1 January.

CONSULAR: An ex-Consul. The Consulars made up a corps of elder statesmen to whom the Senate would normally look for leadership.

CROSSWAYS' DAY *(Compitalia)*: Festival in honour of the Lares Compitales (gods of the crossroads) held annually soon after the Saturnalia on a day appointed by the Praetor.

CURIATE LAW *(lex curiata)*: A law passed by the Curies *(curiae)*, the oldest form of Roman assembly. In Cicero's time it survived only in form, each of the thirty Curies being represented by a lictor, but still had certain legislative functions, notably the passage of laws to confirm the executive authority *(imperium)* of individual magistrates; but the precise nature of these laws is much in doubt.

CURULE CHAIR *(sella curulis)*: Ivory chair, or rather stool, of state used by regular 'curule' magistrates, i.e. Consuls, Praetors, Curule Aediles, and certain others.

DICTATOR: A supreme magistrate with quasi-regal powers appointed to deal with emergencies under the early Republic; his second-in-command, the Master of the Horse, was appointed by himself. The office was revived to legitimize the autocratic regimes of Sulla and Julius Caesar.

EDICT: A public announcement or manifesto issued by a magistrate. The name applied to the codes issued by City Praetors and provincial governors at the beginning of their terms setting out the legal rules which they intended to follow.

EPICUREANISM: A materialistic school of philosophy named after its founder Epicurus, much in vogue among the Roman intelligentsia in Cicero's time.

EQUESTRIAN ORDER: See KNIGHTS.
ETESIAN WINDS *(etesiae)*: Northerly winds which blew every year during the dog days.
FASCES: Bundles of rods carried by lictors in front of magistrates as a symbol of authority. Those of victorious generals were wreathed in laurel.
FLAMEN: Priest in charge of the cult of a particular deity. There were fifteen, three (those of Jupiter, Mars, and Quirinus) being superior to the rest.
FORUM: The chief square of Rome, centre of civic life.
FREEDMAN *(libertus)*: A manumitted slave.
GAMES *(ludi)*: Gladiatorial and other shows, some recurring annually and supervised by magistrates, others put on for an occasion by private individuals. Of the former the Roman Games *(ludi Romani)* were held from 5 to 19 September, the Games of Apollo *(ludi Apollinares)* from 5 to 13 July. 'Greek Games' seem to have consisted of performances of Greek plays in the original language.
GOOD GODDESS *(Bona Dea)*: A goddess whose worship was confined to women. Her yearly festival was held in the house of a Consul or Praetor and supervised by his wife.
GOWN *(toga)*: Formal civilian dress of a Roman citizen. The gown of boys and curule magistrates *(toga praetexta)* had a purple hem. At sixteen or seventeen on coming of age a boy was given his White (or Manly) Gown *(toga pura, toga virilis)*.
GREEK GAMES: See GAMES.
GREEKS: In Cicero's time the word was loosely used to include the more or less hellenized inhabitants of Western Asia and Egypt as well as those of Greece proper and the old Greek settlements elsewhere.

HONEST MEN: So I translate Cicero's *boni* (good men, *les gens de bien*), a semipolitical term for people of substance and respectability, supporters of the established order. Their opposites he calls *improbi* (rascals).

IMPERATOR: Commander of a Roman army. But at this period the title was conferred on generals by their soldiers after a victory and retained until they relinquished their imperium.

IMPERIUM: Literally 'command'; the executive authority appertaining to higher magisterial and promagisterial office.

INTERREX, INTERREGNUM: If through death or otherwise the consular office stood vacant and no patrician magistrates holding *imperium* were in office, an Interrex was appointed from among the patrician members of the Senate to exercise consular functions for five days. He was then replaced by another Interrex, and so on until new Consuls could be elected.

KNIGHTS *(equites)*: In effect non-Senators of free birth possessing property over a certain level. They were regarded as forming a class of their own *(ordo equestris)* with special privileges and insignia.

LATIN FESTIVAL *(Feriae Latinae)*: Movable annual festival of the Romano-Latin League held on Mt Alba. Its date was determined from year to year by the Consuls.

LECTURE HALL *(gymnasium)*: The Greek gymnasium was originally a sports ground containing a *palaestra* (which see). But literature, philosophy, and music were also taught in them.

LEGATE *(legatus)*: A provincial governor took several Legates, normally Senators, on his staff as deputies. Caesar in Gaul made them commanders of legions. The duties

might, however, be purely nominal. The Senate could also appoint its members to 'free' or 'votive' (i.e. to discharge a vow) *legationes*, thus enabling them to travel abroad with official status. I sometimes translate with 'commission(er).' The word can also be used for any kind of envoy.

LEGION: Roman army unit with a full complement of 6,000 men divided into ten cohorts. Each legion was officered by six Military Tribunes. Each cohort had six Centurions, the highest in rank being called *primi pili* (Chief Centurion). The ensign of a Legion was an eagle, and each cohort had its standard *(signum)*.

LESE-MAJESTY *(maiestas)*: The term *maiestas* covered acts 'in derogation of the majesty of the Roman People,' as of magistrates or governors exceeding the bounds of their authority.

LEX CORNELIA *(de provinciis)*: Law of Sulla regulating provincial administration.

LEX CURIATA: See CURIATE LAW.

LEX DOMITIA: of 104, introducing popular election to the major priesthoods.

LEX GABINIA: A law of 67 or 58 forbidding or restricting loans from Roman citizens to provincials.

LEX JULIA *(de provinciis)*: Consular law of Caesar's on provincial administration.

LEX JULIA: after 49, restoring popular election to priesthoods (abolished by Sulla)

LEX JUNIA-LICINIA: A law of 62 requiring that copies of proposed legislation be deposited in the Treasury.

LEX PLAUTIA or PLOTIA *(de vi)*; of 89 or 70

LEX POMPEIA: Pompey's law against electoral corruption in 52.

LEX PORCIA: three leges Porciae, protesting Roman citizens from physical punishments, were passed in the second century.

LEX ROSCIA: A law of 67 assigning the first fourteen rows in the theatre to the Knights (the Senate sat below in the Orchestra).

LEX SCANTINIA: A law of uncertain date penalizing homosexual acts committed upon persons of free birth.

LIBERALIA: See BACCHUS' DAY.

LICTOR: Official attendant of persons possessing magisterial authority *(imperium)*, the number varying with the rank.

LUPERCALIA: Fertility festival on 25 February held in a cave below the Palatine Hill by the Luperci. There were two Colleges of these until 45–44, when Caesar added a third called the *Luperci Iulii*.

MANUMISSION: Process of freeing a slave. This could be done either formally or informally ('between friends'), but in the latter case the master could revoke it at will.

MILE *(mille passus)*: The Roman mile was 1,618 yards.

MIME *(mimus)*: Type of entertainment with dancing, music, and dialogue which became highly popular in the first century B.C. It was considered more sophisticated and risqué than the Atellan Farce, which it virtually superseded.

MINERVA'S DAY *(Quinquatrus)*: Festival of Minerva on 19 March.

NOBILITY: Practically, a noble *(nobilis)* at this period meant a direct descendant of a Consul in the male line. In the early Republic the Roman community was divided into patricians and plebeians, the former holding a virtual monopoly of political power. But after the Con-

sulship was thrown open to plebeians in the fourth century many plebeian families became 'noble,' and the remaining patricians were distinguished chiefly by their ineligibility to hold both Consulships in one year and for the plebeian offices of Tribune and Plebeian Aedile. They also wore special insignia.

NOMENCLATOR: A slave whose duty it was to remind his master of the names of clients and acquaintances whom he happened to meet.

OPS: Roman goddess in whose temple on the Capitol Caesar deposited the state treasure.

OPTIMATES: Literally 'those belonging to the best'—the leading conservatives in the Senate and their supporters throughout the community. Sometimes the term is practically equivalent to the 'honest men' *(boni)*, though more purely political in its implications.

OVATION: A lesser form of Triumph.

PALAESTRA: A space surrounded by colonnades, found in all *gymnasia*. Literally 'wrestling school' (Greek).

PATRICIANS: See NOBILITY.

PAYMASTER TRIBUNES *(tribuni aerarii)*: At this time probably a class similar to the Knights but with a lower property qualification. Under the lex Aurelia of 70, juries were composed in equal numbers of Senators, Knights, and Paymaster Tribunes.

PLEBEIANS: See NOBILITY.

PONTIFF *(pontifex)*: These formed a priestly College in general charge of Roman religious institutions (including the Calendar), presided over by the Chief Pontiff *(pontifex maximus)*, who was Julius Caesar from 63 until his death.

PRAETOR: Second in rank of the annual magistracies.

Eight were elected at this period until Caesar increased the number to twenty. The City Praetor *(praetor urbanus)* was in charge of the administration of justice between Roman citizens, others presided over the standing criminal courts. After his year of office a Praetor normally went to govern a province as Propraetor or Proconsul.

PRAETORIAN COHORT *(cohors praetoria)*: A special military unit forming a general's bodyguard.

PREFECT: Officer appointed by a magistrate (usually as provincial governor) for military or civil duties. These might be only nominal, the appointment merely conferring official status and privileges. The Prefect of Engineers *(praefectus fabrum)* acted as adjutant to his chief—no longer any connection with engineers.

PROCONSUL *(pro consule)*: 'Acting Consul,' one who, not holding the office, exercised consular authority outside Rome by senatorial appointment. Similarly Propraetor *(pro praetore)* and Proquaestor *(pro quaestore)*.

PROSCRIPTION *(proscriptio)*: A procedure first employed by Sulla, then by the Triumvirs in 43. Lists of names were published, the persons thus 'proscribed' being declared outlaws and their goods confiscated. Their killers were rewarded, their protectors punished.

QUAESTOR: The first stage in the regular 'course of offices,' election to which carried life membership of the Senate. Since Sulla's time twenty were elected annually. The two City Quaestors *(quaestores urbani)* had charge of the Treasury and the Quaestors assigned to provincial governors (usually by lot) were largely concerned with finance.

QUARTAN: A fever recurring every third day; less grave therefore than a tertian, which recurred every other day.

QUIRINUS' DAY (Quirinalia): Festival in honour of Quirinus (the deified Romulus, founder of Rome) on 17 February.

RESOLUTION *(auctoritas)*: A decree of the Senate vetoed by a Tribune was sometimes recorded under this name.

ROSTRA: The speakers' platform in the comitium, so called from the beaks *(rostra)* of captured warships which decorated it.

SATURNALIA: Festival of Saturn beginning on 17 December, marked by merrymaking reminiscent of modern Christmas, to which it contributed some elements.

SECRETARY: I so translate (with a capital letter) Latin *scriba*. The 'scribes' were a corporation of civil servants working in the Treasury and otherwise. City magistrates and provincial governors might be assigned official Secretaries for their personal assistance. Private clerks were called *librarii*.

SENATE: Governing body of the Roman Republic, numbering about 600 (increased to 900 by Caesar) and composed of magistrates and ex-magistrates.

SHEPHERDS' DAY *(Parilia)*: Festival of the god and goddess Pales, protectors of flocks and herds, on 21 April.

SOPHIST: A professional 'wise man,' making money as a teacher and lecturer, often itinerant.

STOICISM: Philosophical school, named from the portico *(stoa)* in which its founder, Zeno of Citium (ca. 300), taught. Cato was its most prominent Roman adherent in Cicero's time.

SUMPTUARY LAW: A series of laws during the Republic at-

tempted to impose restrictions on luxury spending, especially on food. One was enacted by Julius Caesar in 46.

SUPPLICATION *(supplicatio)*: A thanksgiving ceremony decreed by the Senate in honour of a military success, the number of days varying according to the importance of the victory. It was generally regarded as a preliminary to a Triumph,

TABLETS *(codicilli)*: Wooden tablets coated with wax and fastened together with thread, used for memoranda and short notes.

TAX FARMERS *(publicani)*: Roman taxes, as on grazing land in the provinces or excise, were largely farmed out by the Censors to private companies who bid for the right of collection. The capitalists in Rome as well as their local agents were called *publicani*. In political terms *publicani* and Knights often amount to the same thing.

TELLUS: Earth goddess, whose temple was one of the meeting places of the Senate.

TESTIMONIAL: Renders *laudatio* (eulogy) in one of its senses. It was customary for defendants to ask prominent persons to offer witness to their good character in court either orally or in writing.

TETRARCH: Literally 'ruler over a fourth part.' In Cicero's time many minor eastern princes were called by this title.

TOGA: See GOWN.

TREASURY *(aerarium)*: The Roman state treasury was in the temple of Saturn in the Forum, managed by the City Quaestors with the assistance of Secretaries.

TRIBE *(tribus)*: A division, mainly by locality, of the Roman citizen body. The number had risen over the centuries

from three to thirty-five (four of them 'urban,' the rest 'rustic'). Assemblies voting by tribes *(comitia tributa)* elected magistrates below Praetor and could pass legislation proposed by Tribunes.

TRIBUNE: (1) Of the Plebs. A board of ten, originally appointed to protect plebeians from patrician high-handedness. They had wide constitutional powers, the most important being that any one of them could veto any piece of public business, including laws and senatorial decrees. They could also initiate these. They took office on 10 December. (2) Military: See LEGION. (3) See PAYMASTER TRIBUNES.

TRIUMPH: Victory celebration by a general on his return to Rome. Permission had to be granted by the Senate.

UNIFORM: Magistrates leaving to take command of armies wore the general's red cloak *(paludamentum)* and were said to set out *paludati.*

VALUATION *(aestimatio)*: Process by which a debtor's property could be transferred to his creditor in settlement. Caesar made such transfers compulsory on terms favourable to the debtor.

WEAL: The goddess Salus, who had a temple on the Quirinal Hill near Atticus' house.

INDEX

LETTERS TO QUINTUS

LETTERS TO BRUTUS

FRAGMENTS

INDEX

LETTER TO OCTAVIAN

INVECTIVES

Reference is to I (In Ciceronem) and II (In Sallustium)

HANDBOOK OF ELECTIONEERING

Composed in ZephGreek and ZephText by
Technologies 'N Typography, Merrimac, Massachusetts.
Printed in Great Britain by St Edmundsbury Press Ltd,
Bury St Edmunds, Suffolk, on acid-free paper.
Bound by Hunter & Foulis Ltd, Edinburgh, Scotland.